I0762222

Dressed to Impress

Dressed to Impress

The Anonymous Project

Lee Shulman

PRESTEL
Munich • London • New York

Not Another Fashion Book!

By Lee Shulman

I have vivid memories of my parents getting ready for a special night out—a well-deserved escape from the everyday worries of middle-class suburban life: mortgage payments, extortionate school fees, and, let's face it, just a break from me and my brother. As a father, I get it. The meticulous care and selection process of an evening out was, in itself, a fabulous event. Especially for my mother, whose wardrobe was a color-coded rainbow of flowing gowns and stylish 1970s looks. Color was even bigger and bolder then. Clothes were thrown onto the bed and paired with shoes and accessories, but the selection was refined down to the perfect combination for the evening's theme. I remember observing my father slipping on his cufflinks and asking me to help thread them through—like a surgical operation. It was a spectacle to behold, watching my parents transform into elegant superheroes, ready to head out into the night for an adventure I could only imagine, likely more glamorous than the reality, only to find them again the next morning around the breakfast table—slightly disheveled in pajamas and nightgowns, unkempt hair, leaving no trace of an evening well spent—or maybe not.

Through the framework of *The Anonymous Project*, I am often asked about the main differences between these images and modern-day family photography. I don't think much has changed. We still celebrate and immortalize family moments in exactly the same way as we always have—family celebrations, holidays, and leisure time. This still remains the main preoccupation of most photography… except for one simple reflection: "Well, I guess people dressed better." I guess this is a subjective viewpoint, and maybe a little simplistic as an answer, but it remains true. Fashion is not just a marker of a period of time; it also says a lot about the social and economic values of that society. It is often dissociated from real life in magazines and books, but here we get to see the two together, and these family photos are very telling. They show a postwar society that wanted to celebrate life in all its facets. I am always amazed by the incredible colors and use of patterns and fabrics in what we mistakenly think of as a very monochrome period. Here the clothes shout: "Look at me!" and "Life is fabulous." I agree.

The 1950s and 1960s were periods of seismic change, not just in the world of politics or technology, but in the way people dressed, presented themselves, and viewed their roles in society. For many, the family photo album became a personal archive of social and economic standing, capturing moments that spoke volumes about aspirations, identity, and the influence of the larger cultural landscape—most notably, the world of fashion. Amateur family photography, taken in the comfort of home or during family outings, often acted as a mirror reflecting the postwar shifts in American society.

When you look through those photo albums, you see men in sharply cut suits and women in neatly pressed dresses, with children often decked out in the latest trends. But beyond the fabric and style choices, these images represent so much more—they reveal the ways in which fashion played a role in navigating a newly prosperous, yet rigidly structured, world. The 1950s, in particular, were a time of stability following the tumult of World War II. Families were eager to restore a sense of normality, and fashion became a tool for signaling this newfound order.

Family photography has always been a fascination—if not an obsession—of mine. It seems to present a truth in a medium that has often been manipulated and twisted to create false representations of our history and culture. The privileged relationship between the photographer and subject, whether it be a family member or friend, is often comforting and devoid of any real political intentions, yet it was, without a doubt, a middle-class white privilege to those who could afford it.

One stark and often uncomfortable truth about family photography in the 1950s and 1960s is the glaring absence of African Americans in these portrayals of middle-class life. The rise of consumer culture, coupled with the dominance of white-centric fashion and media, meant that African Americans were largely excluded from the aspirational narratives presented in family photography and advertising. This exclusion reflected broader societal inequalities, with African Americans facing systemic barriers not only in fashion but in every aspect of life—from segregation to limited access to the job market.

In mainstream fashion advertisements and cinema of the time, African Americans were largely invisible. When they were represented, it was often in stereotypical or marginalized roles. This exclusion was particularly painful, given the economic and social strides African American families were beginning to make in the postwar years. In the context of family photography, African Americans often had to create their own visual narratives—sometimes taking pride in their clothing choices and fashion sense in ways that allowed them to assert their identity despite the lack of mainstream representation. Their fashion, though often overlooked by popular culture, was no less significant, blending creativity with resilience. It is, however, cruelly missing from this narrative, highlighting this historical and political void that cannot be ignored.

I by no means pretend to be a fashion historian, and my interest is purely that of an admirer of the extraordinary fashions, creativity, and design of the clothes represented here. The more I leaf through these images, the more I notice the incredible detail and workmanship in the fashions worn. These are not just simple garments; they are genuine works of art. They seem more fantastic and extravagant than most clothes we see today on the streets of many fashion capitals of the world—expressions of carefree freedom and individuality that now seem almost lost in time.

This newfound freedom coincided with the rise of advertising and mass consumerism, especially in the American way of life, where clothes, cars, and even architecture were all about the future and reaching for the stars. They represented a promise of a brave new world, which we now know to be an illusion in the political landscape that followed. But maybe, for a moment, we were living our best lives. These fashions seem to be a celebration of the extraordinary advances in technology, new materials, and techniques that could bring what was once inaccessible into the home. I find the advertising of the time fascinating—not only for its aesthetics and my subjective love for 1950s and 1960s graphic design, but also because it marked the start of what would become an insatiable push to sell an aspirational lifestyle. Though problematic on many social and ethical levels, it also created its own language, with taglines that seem almost more fantastic than the clothes they were trying to sell: "You look better in LEE" and "Hello, Good Looking!"

When editing these images together, I have always made a conscious choice to leave them as they were taken—full framed, uncropped, warts and all—a real testament to the incredible talent of some of these anonymous family photographers. Some of the images, in my eyes, are works of art and surpass the often contrived ideas we have about amateur photography. Today, in this accessible world of smartphone photography and technological advances that make photography child's play and disposable, it's easy to undervalue these images. Yet these photos were taken with enormous care and love.

All these images come from unique Kodachrome slides, stored away for decades in precious boxes, often ordered and edited to be seen by future generations. With *The Anonymous Project*, I have never tried to intellectualize the work, but simply present it as a window for the spectator to make up their own mind. I always go back to that first instinctive moment when I raised the very first slide to my eye and entered into this intimate world of family life, which has become my personal obsession over the past few years. I fall in love daily with these incredible characters from the past, and even though I am not a particularly nostalgic person, I do fantasize about being in the frame to dance the night away, sip cheap alcohol, and share in the conversations. I guess it's a bit of old-school voyeurism—but guilty as charged.

When I started the collection in 2017, I was taken with the emotional content of these family moments captured in glorious Kodachrome color. But on closer observation, the emotional value is elevated by the way people presented and packaged themselves. These are not just simple family moments; they are expressions of styles and looks that seem incredibly modern and familiar. In our daily world of fast fashion and consumables, these images represent something rare and extraordinary. In many ways, these photographs are like little time capsules, preserving not only the styles of the day but also the complex social fabric of an era. The clothes we wore and the way we documented them in family photos tell us much about who we thought we were—and who we still aspire to be. Fashion, in all its glamorous or everyday forms, remains a powerful, ever-evolving part of our collective story.

These clothes are the story of all our lives and the enduring creativity of designers who wanted to challenge the status quo and bring elegance and style into the home—to make fashion accessible and affordable. These designers are the unsung heroes of this book, and this book is dedicated to them.

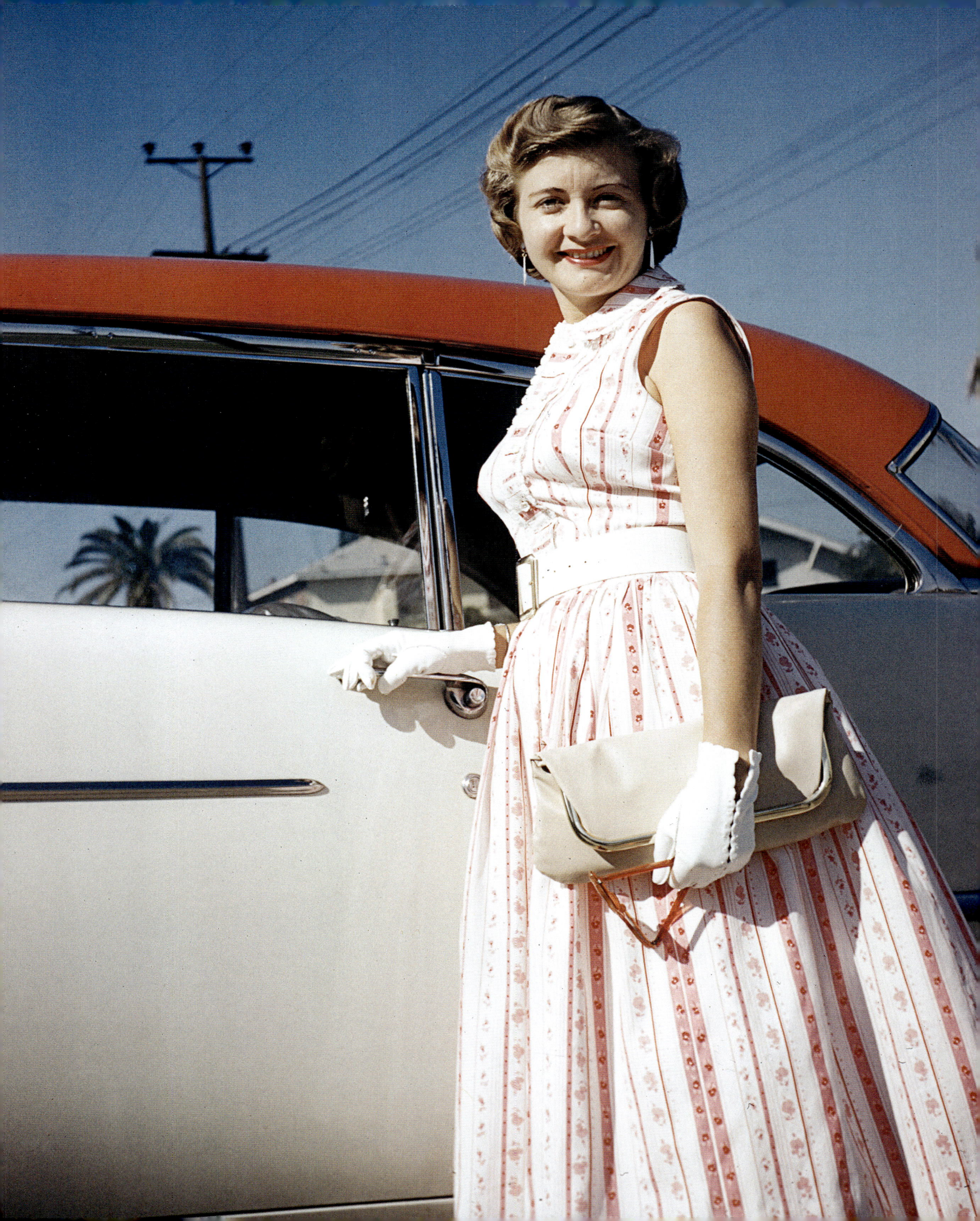

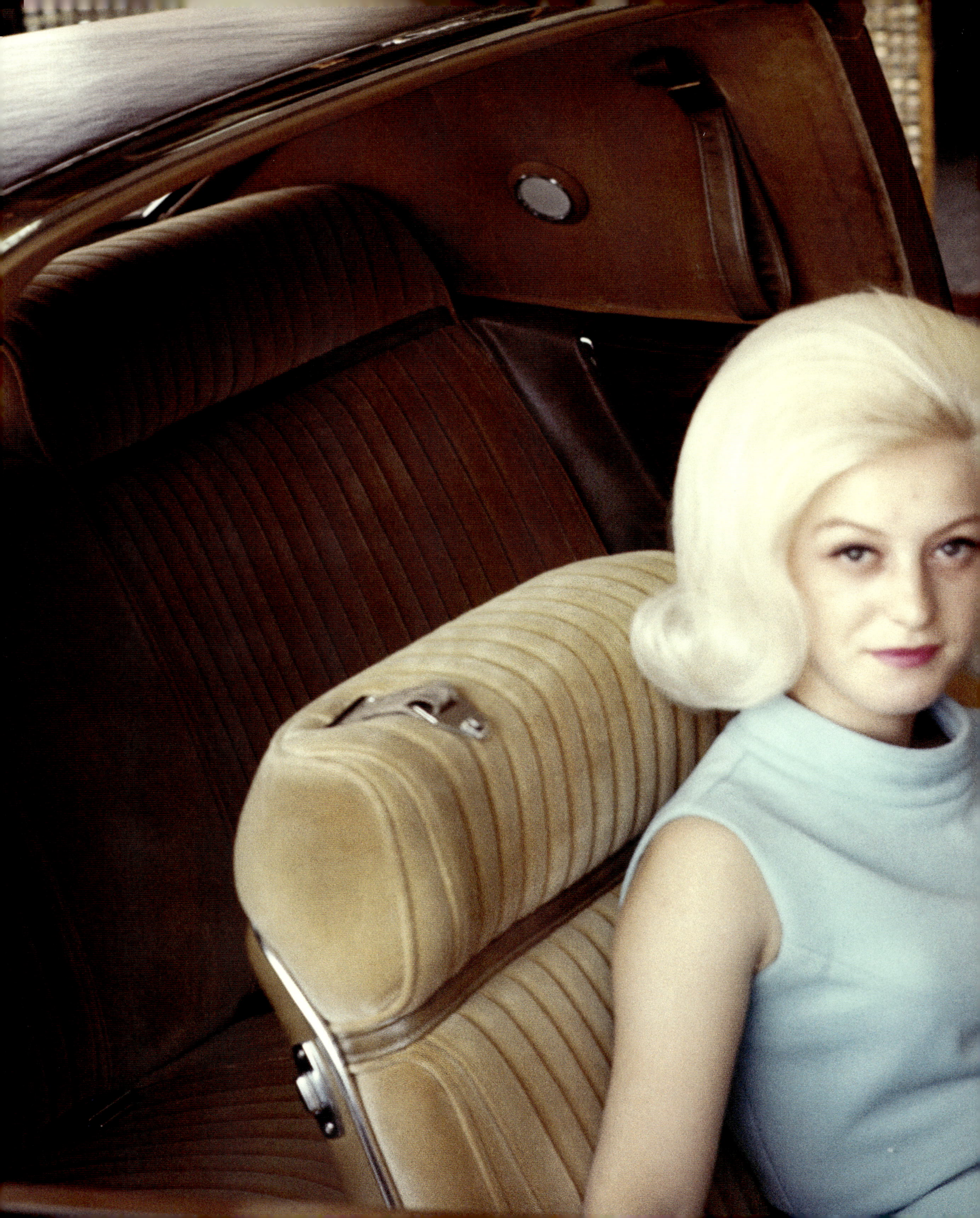

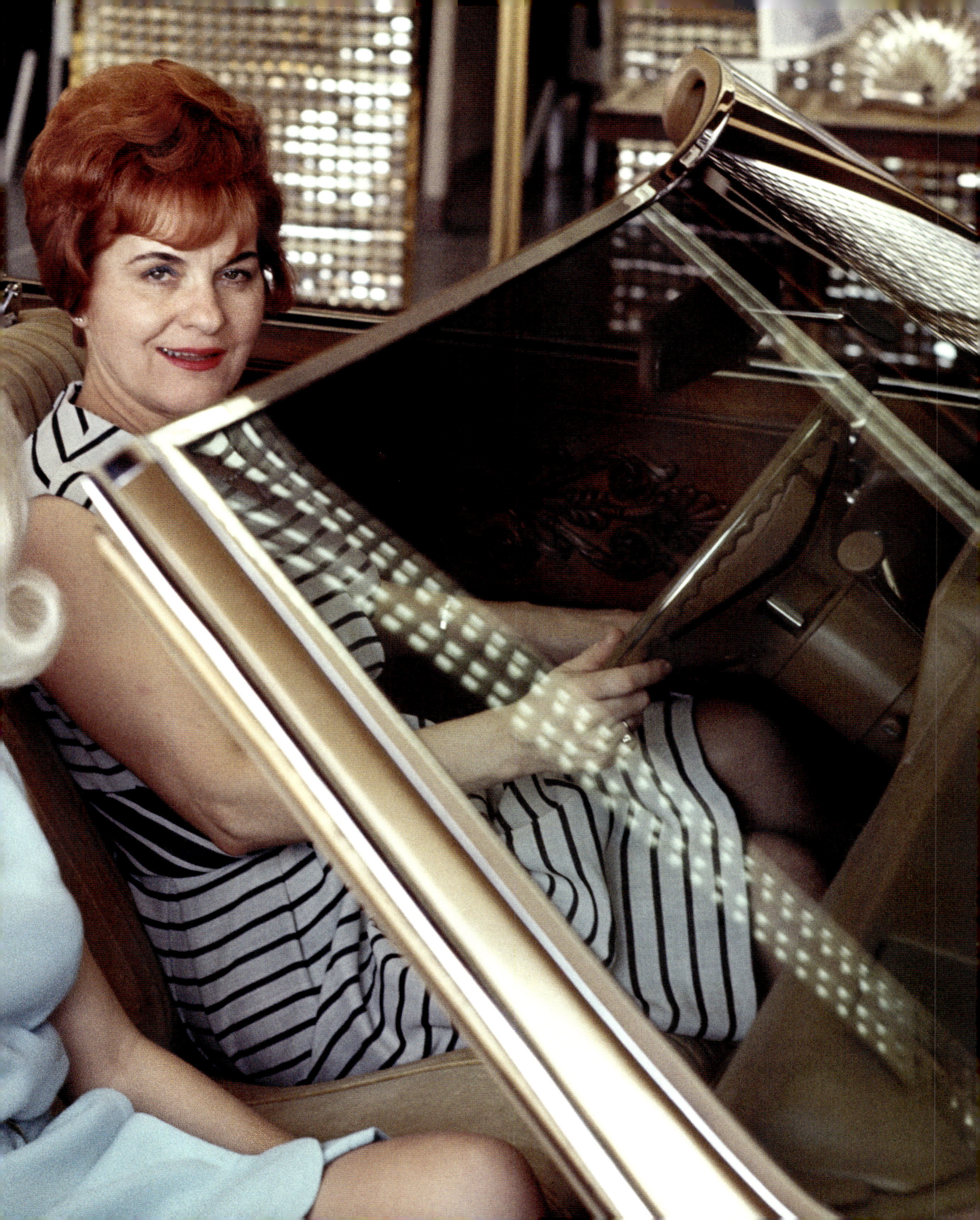

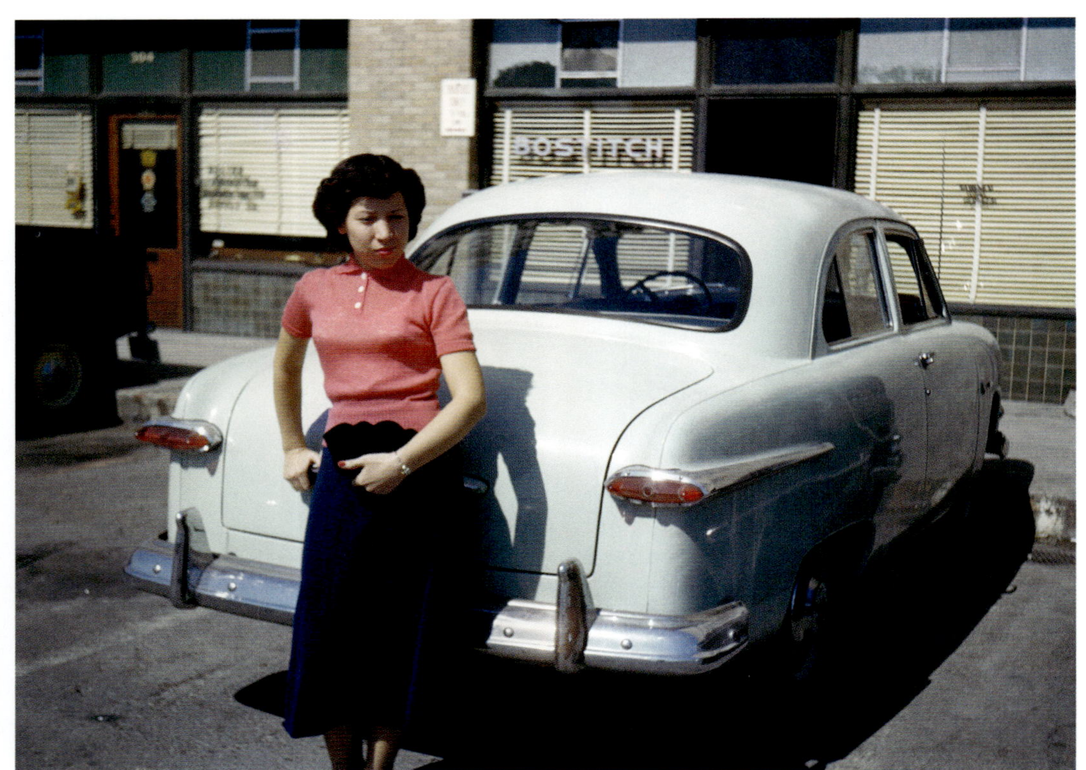
BOSTITCH

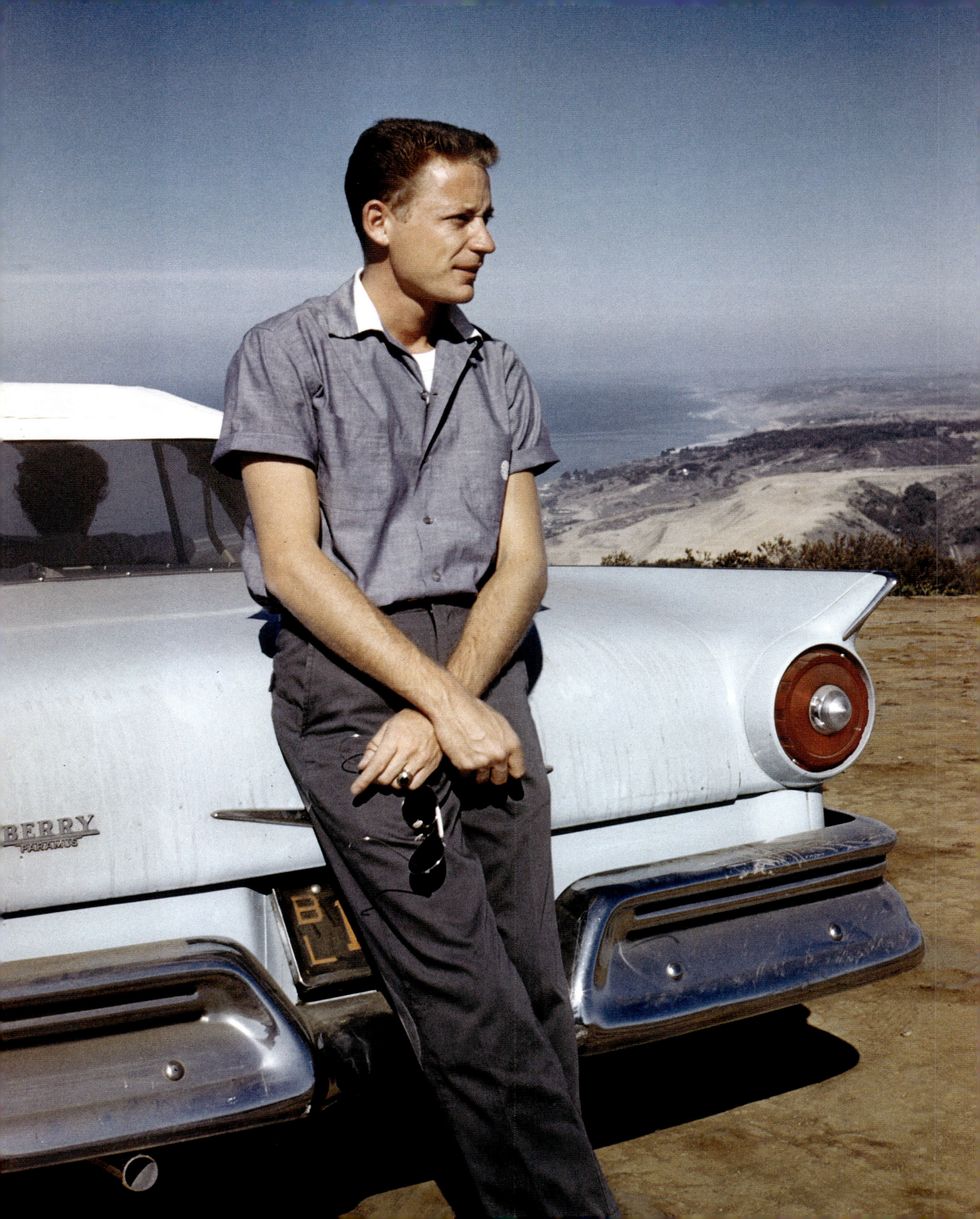
BERRY
PARAMUS

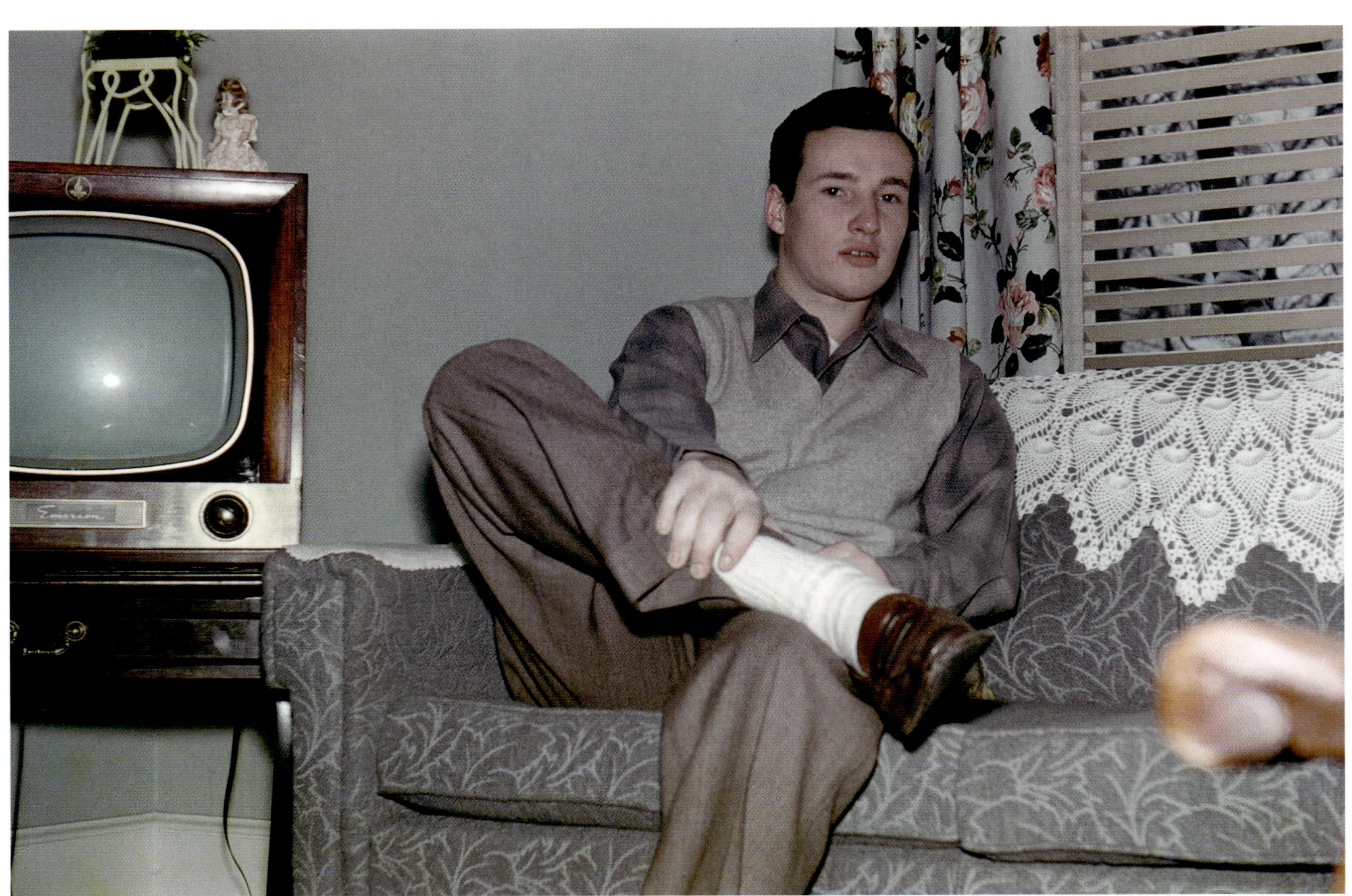
Emerson

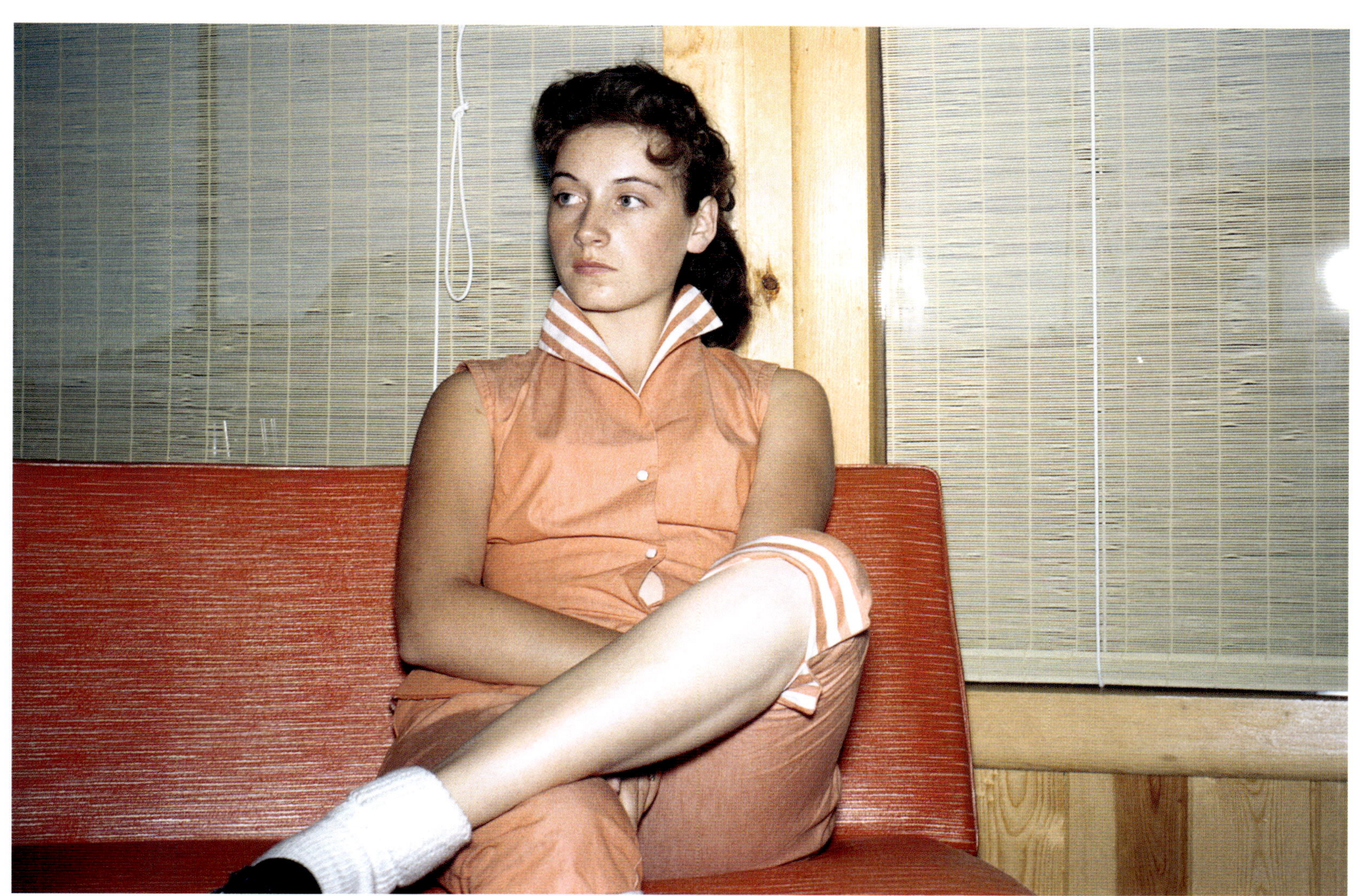

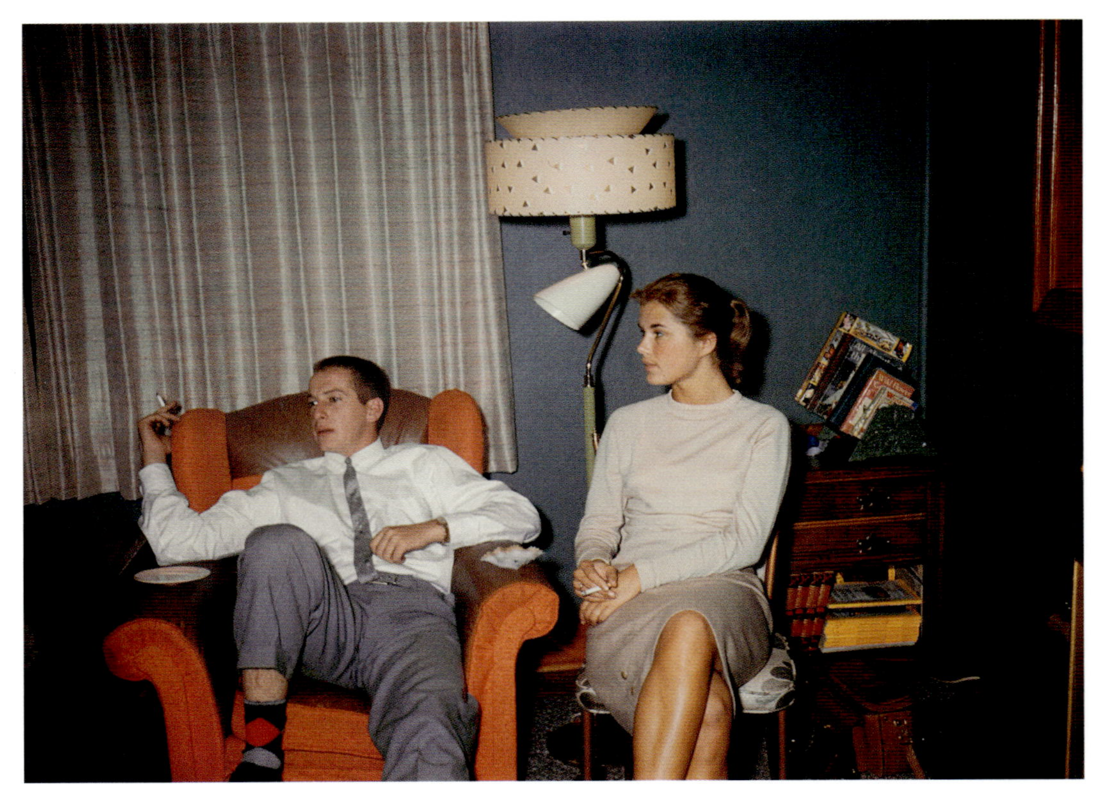

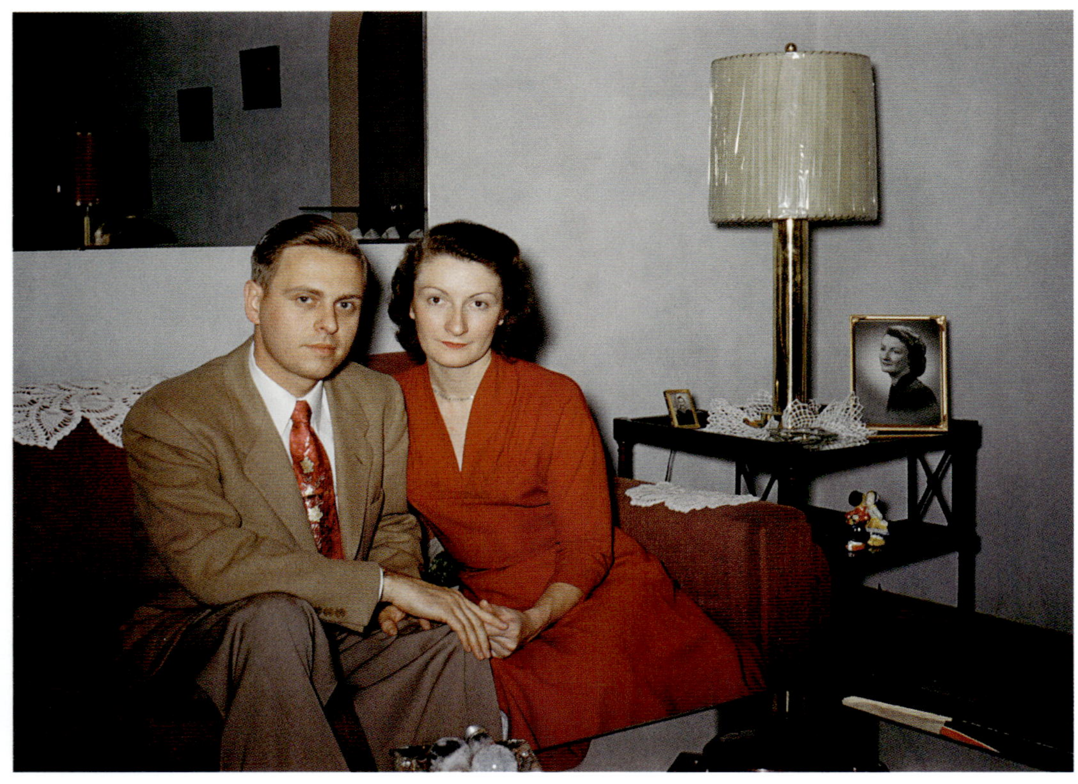

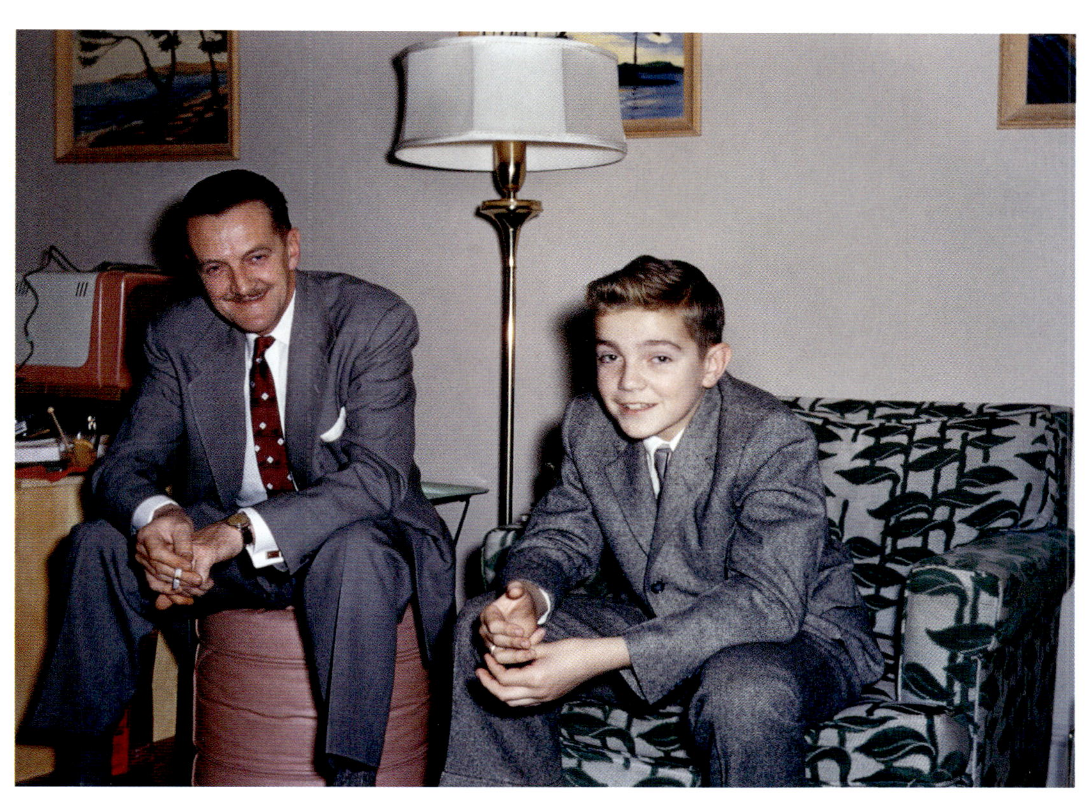

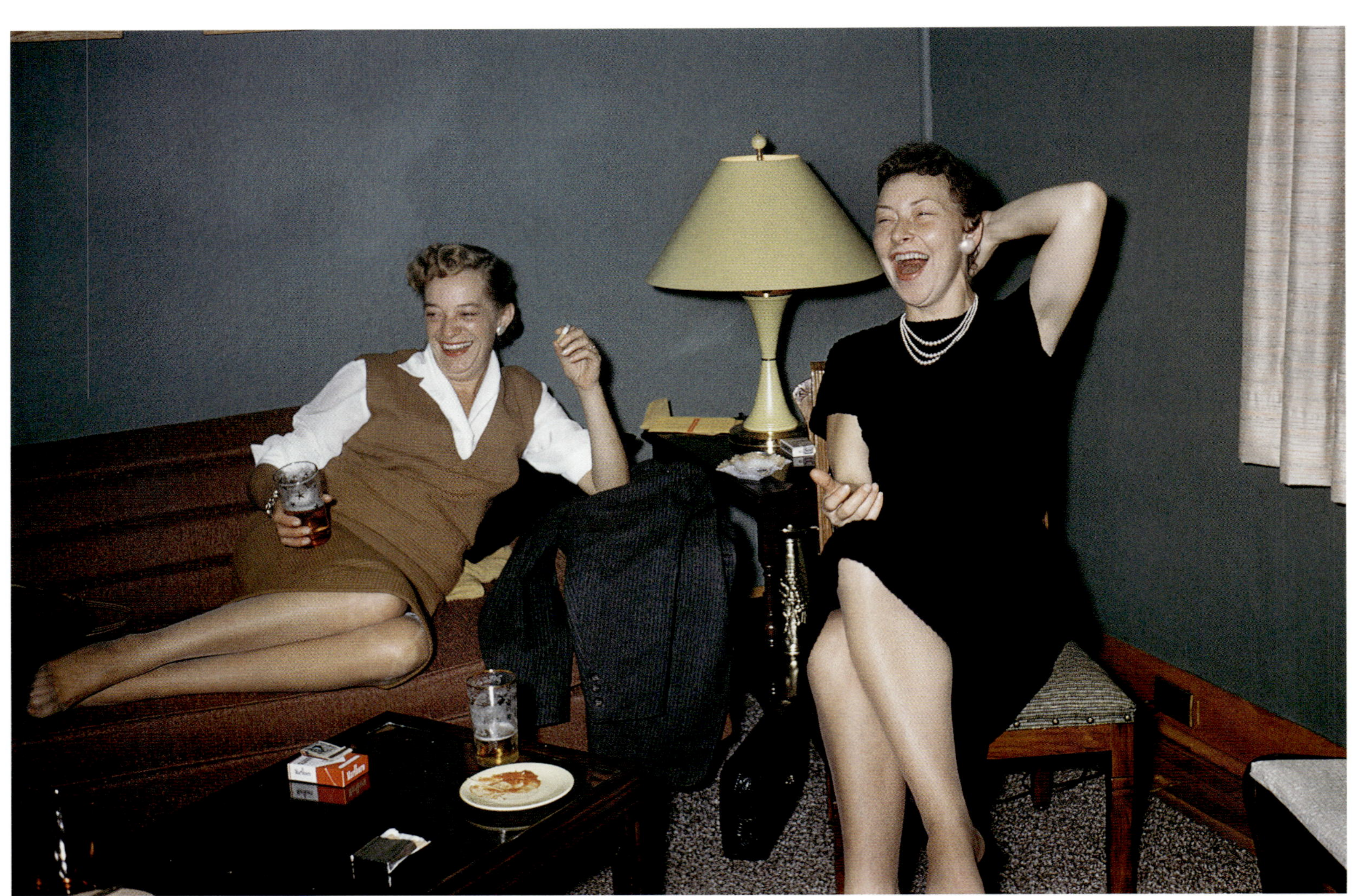

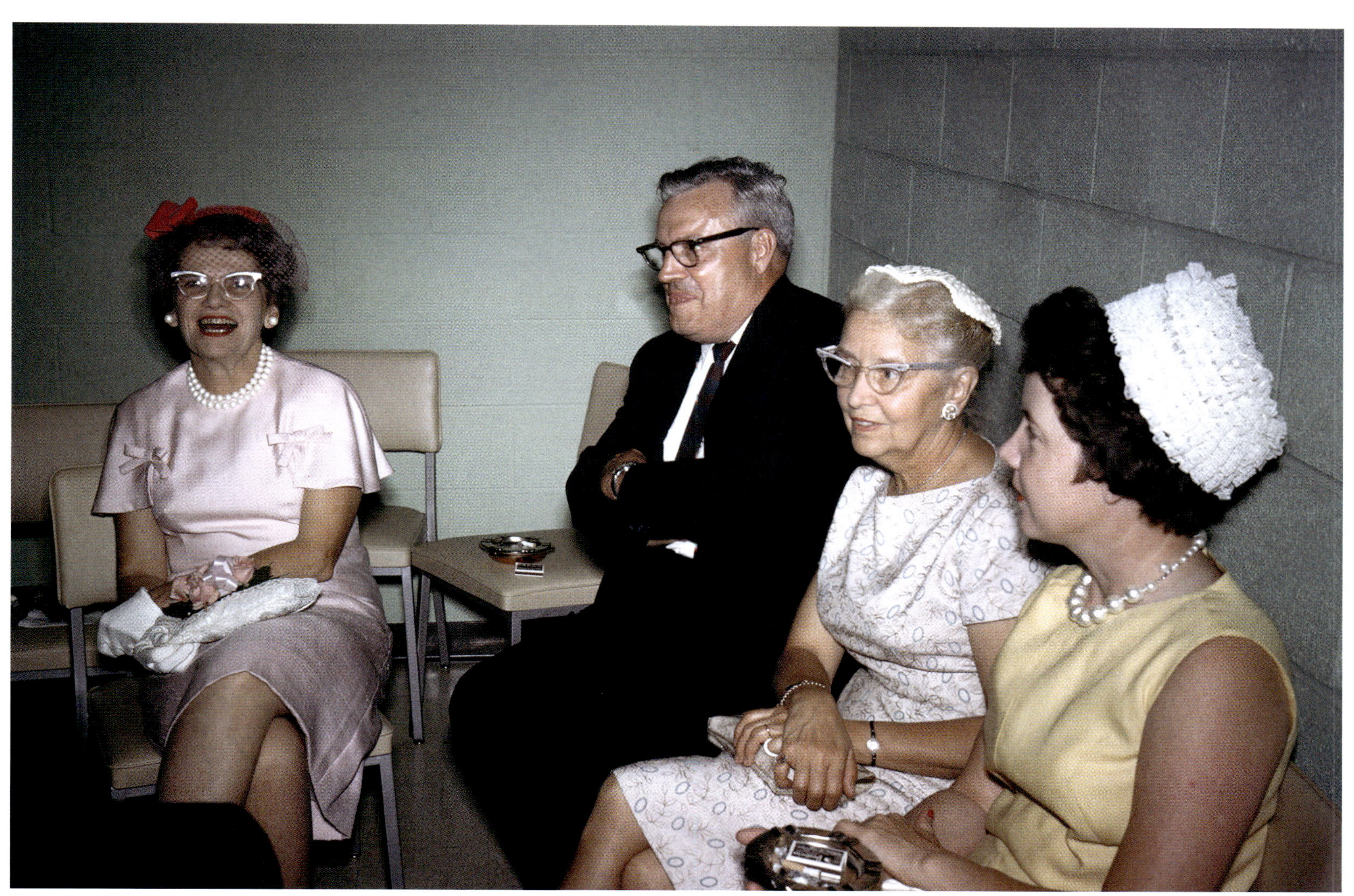

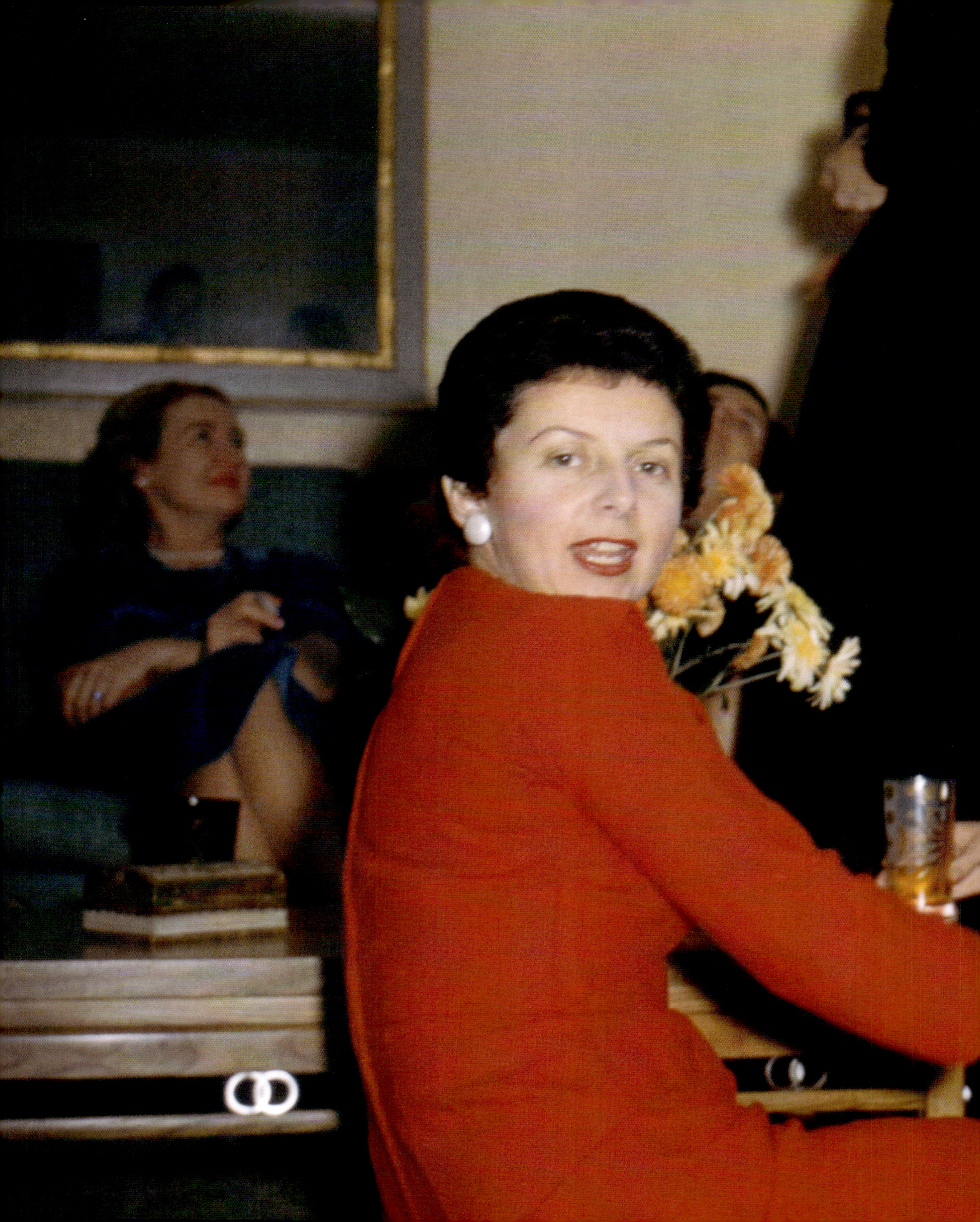

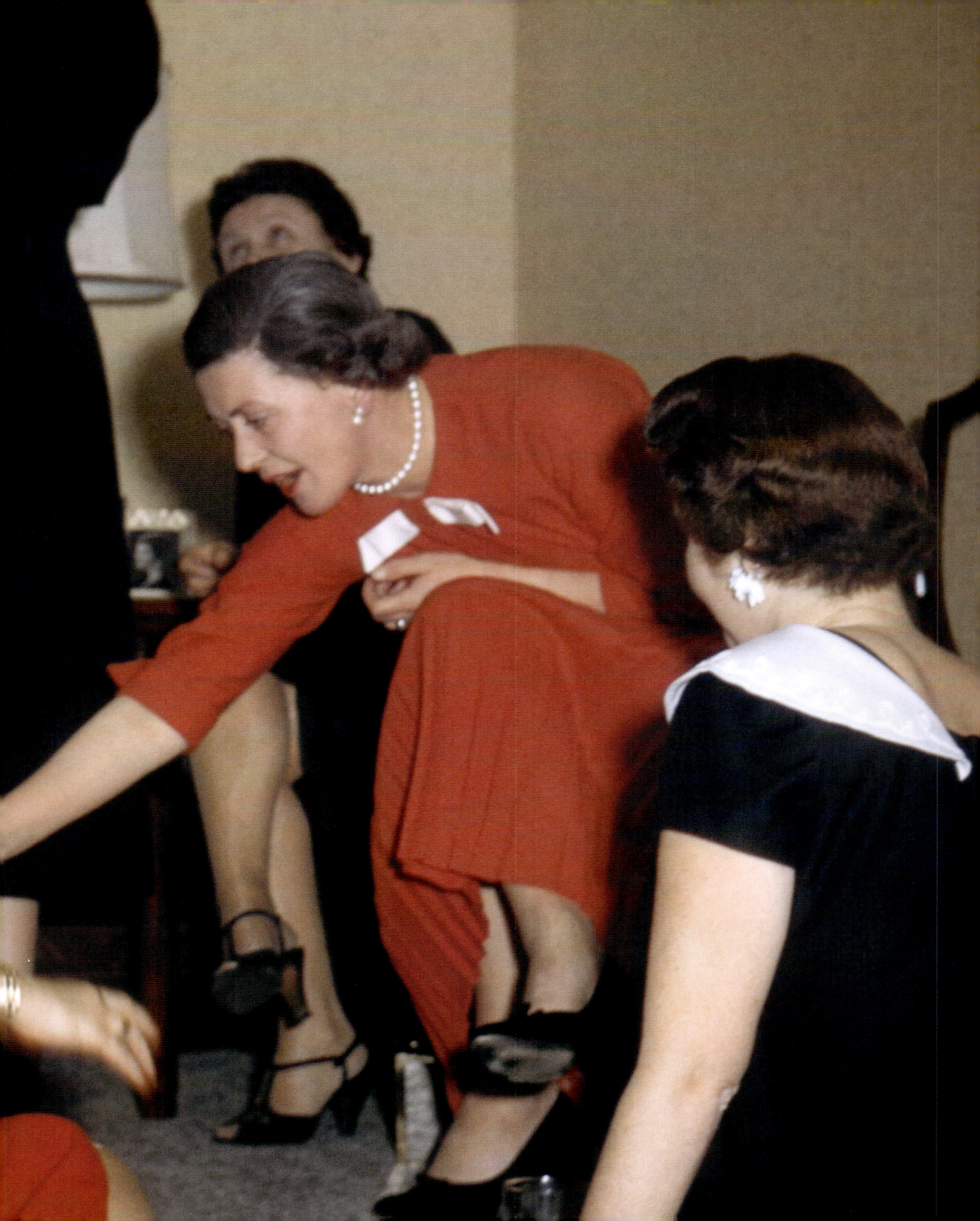

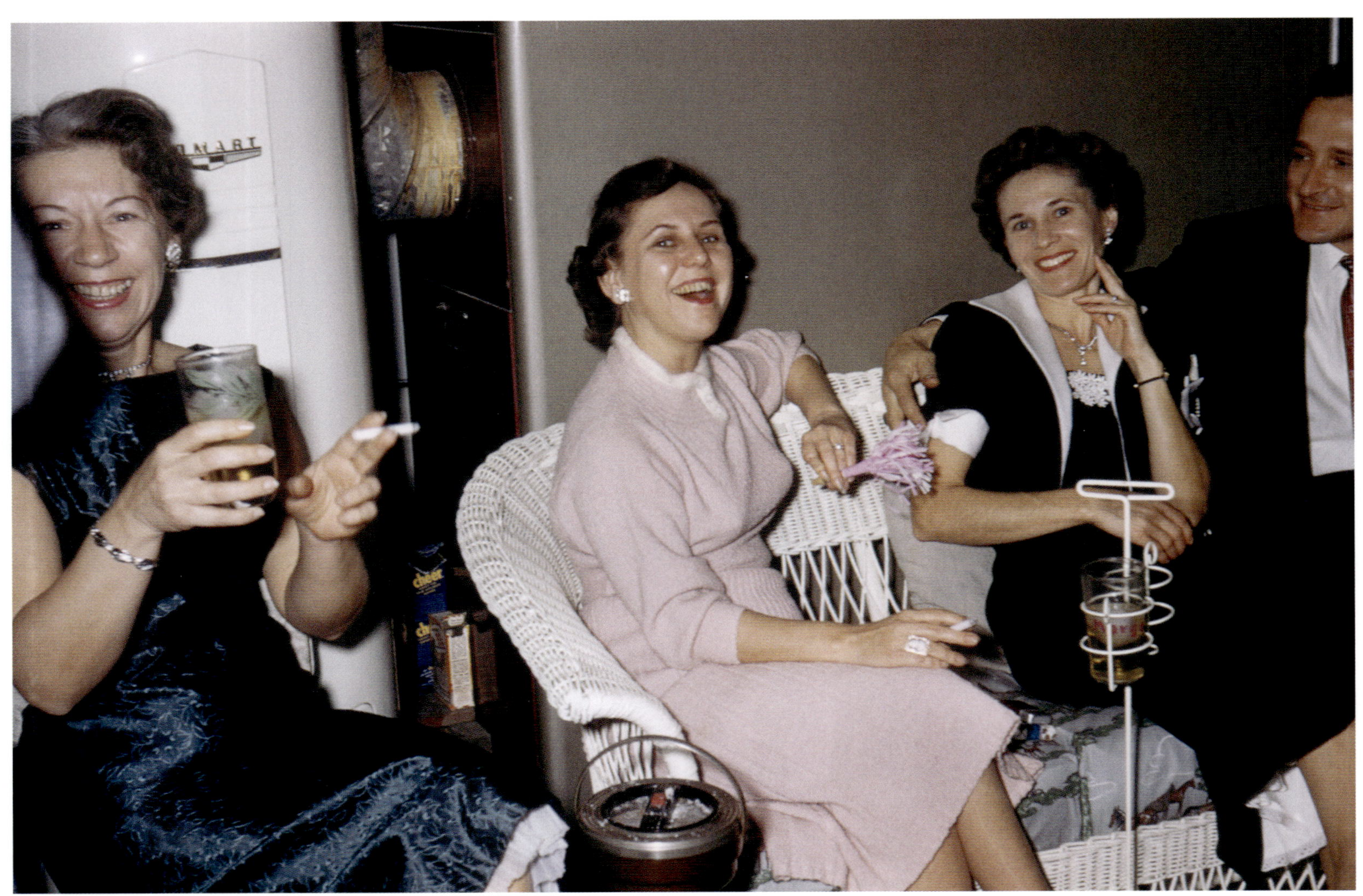

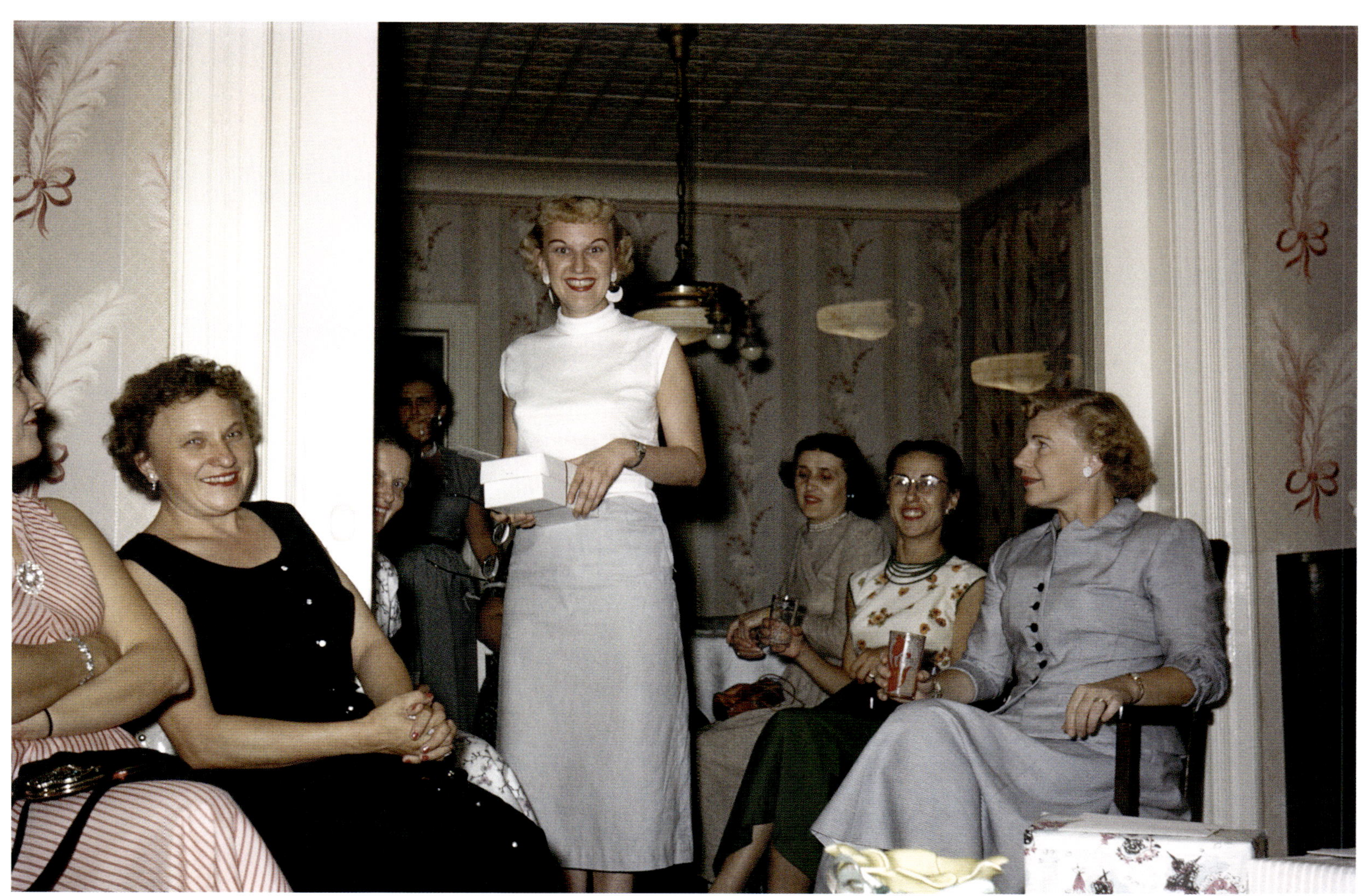

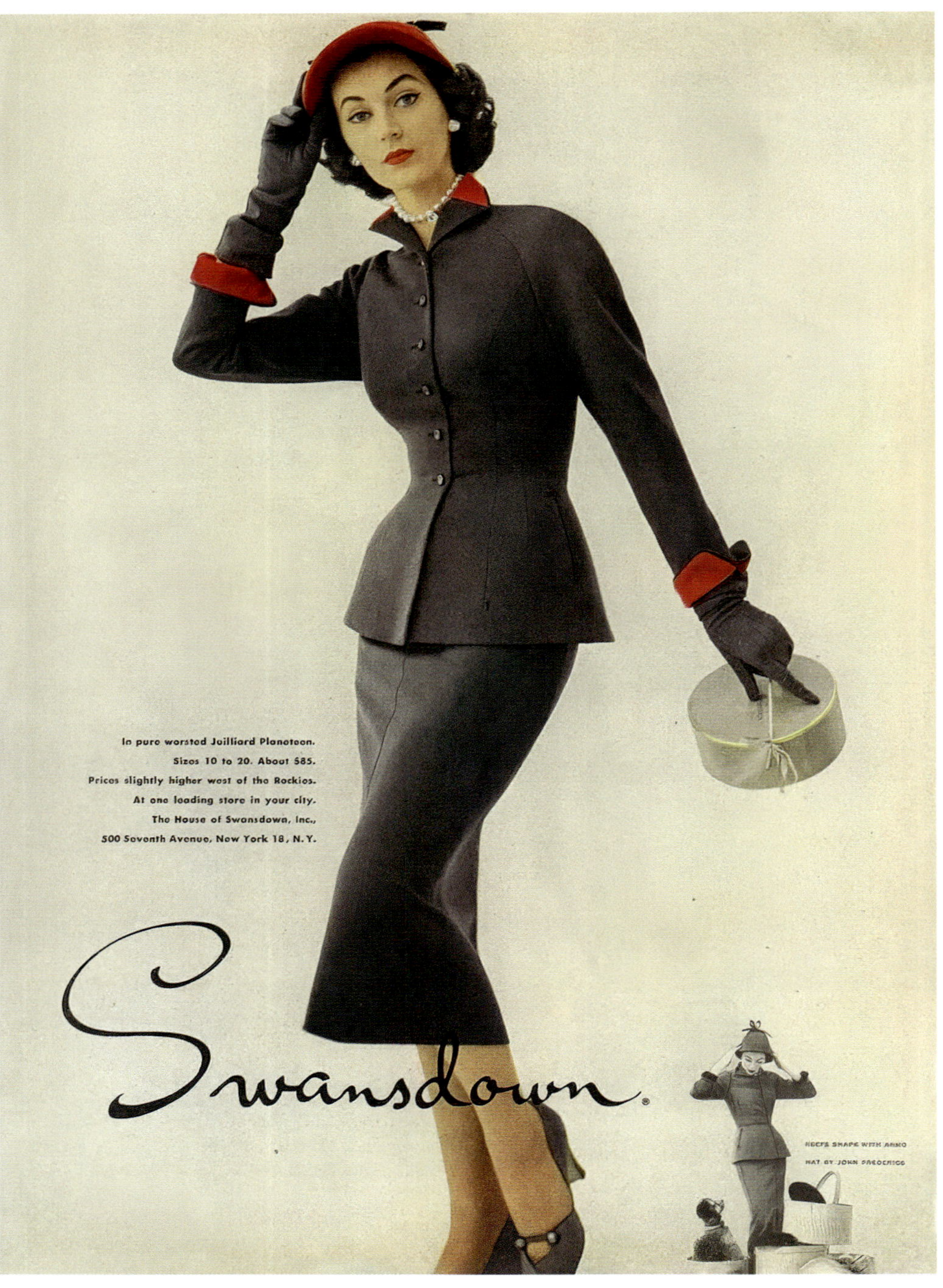
In pure worsted Juilliard Planeteen.
Sizes 10 to 20. About $85.
Prices slightly higher west of the Rockies.
At one leading store in your city.
The House of Swansdown, Inc.,
500 Seventh Avenue, New York 18, N.Y.
Swansdown®

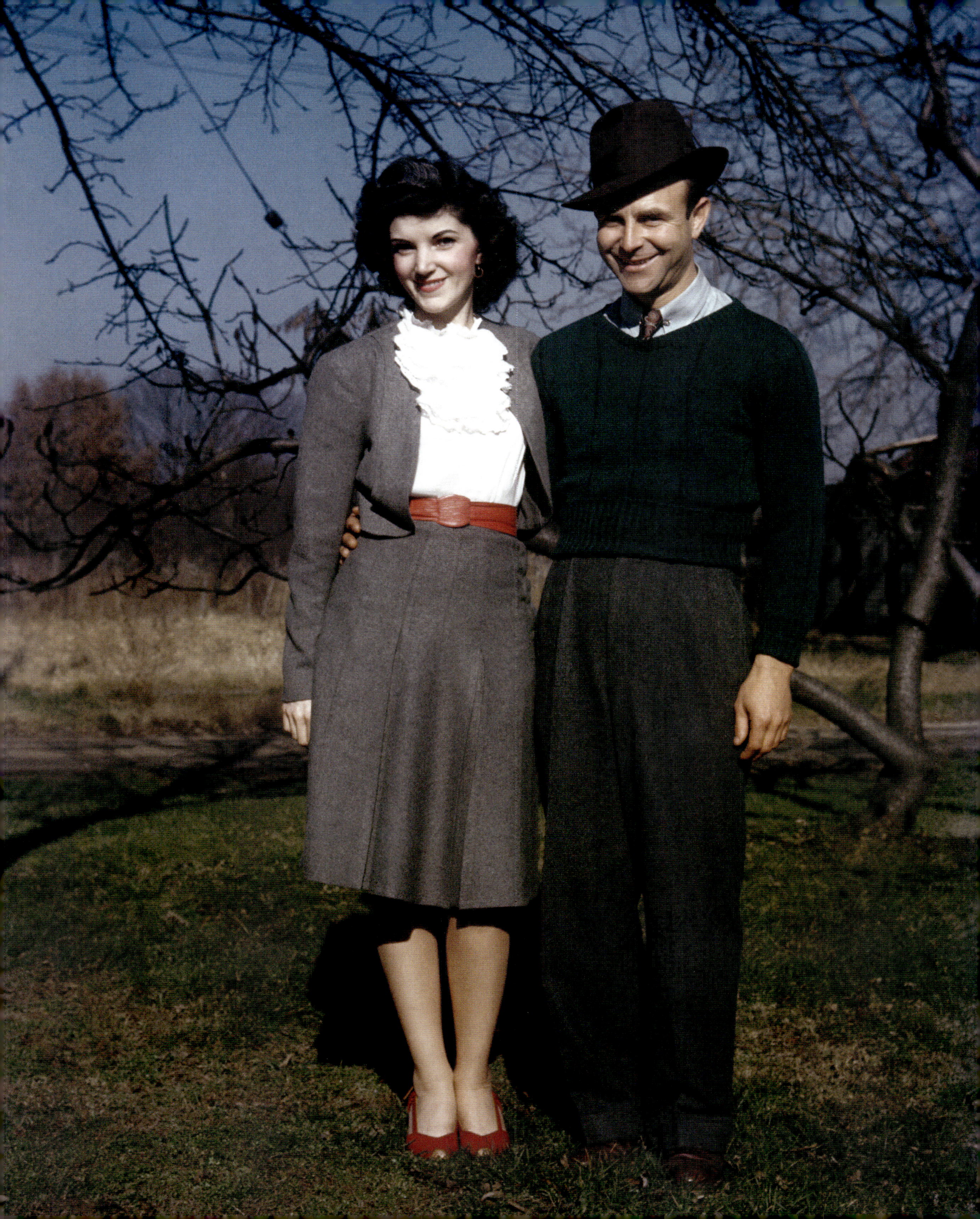

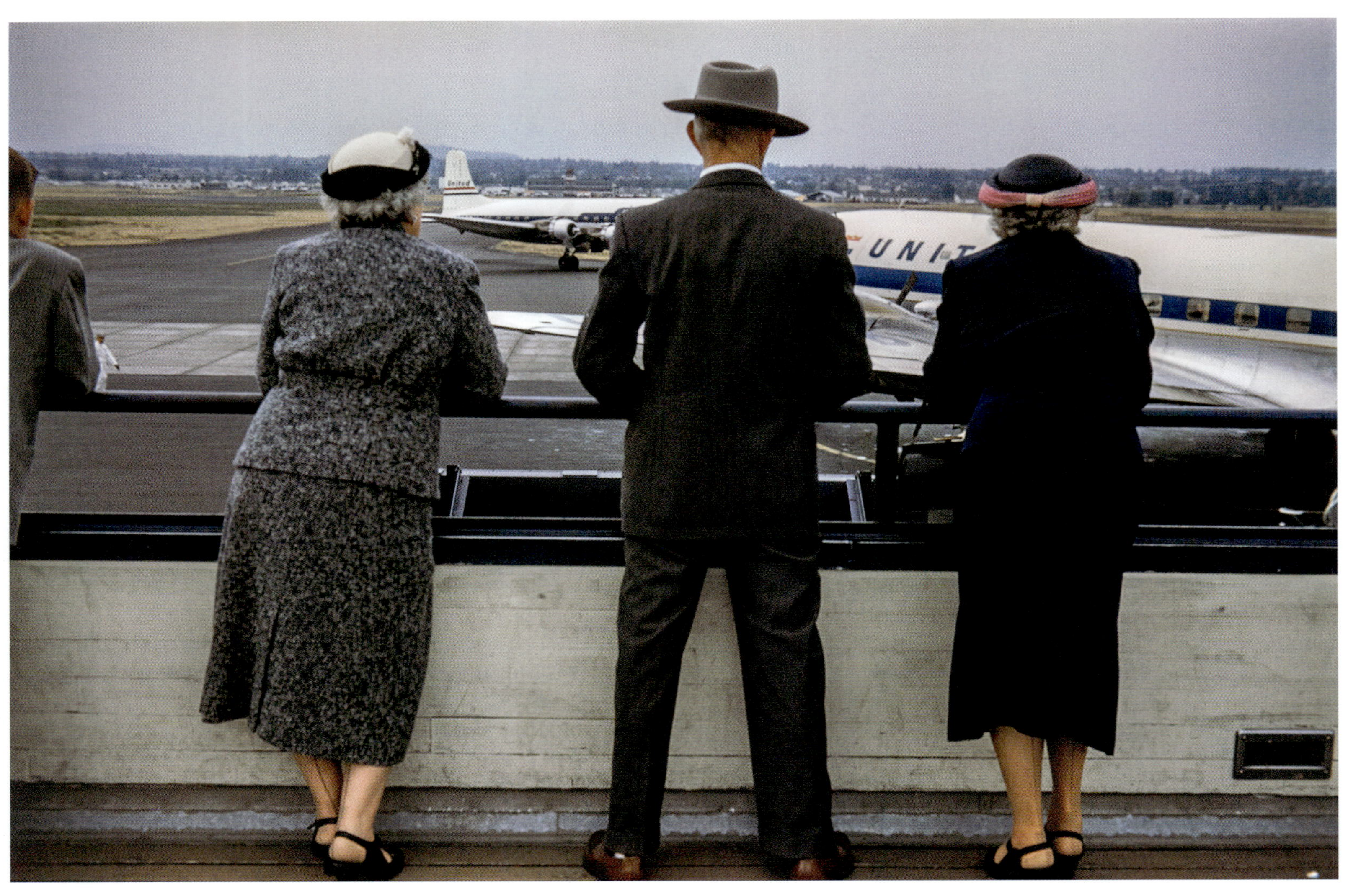

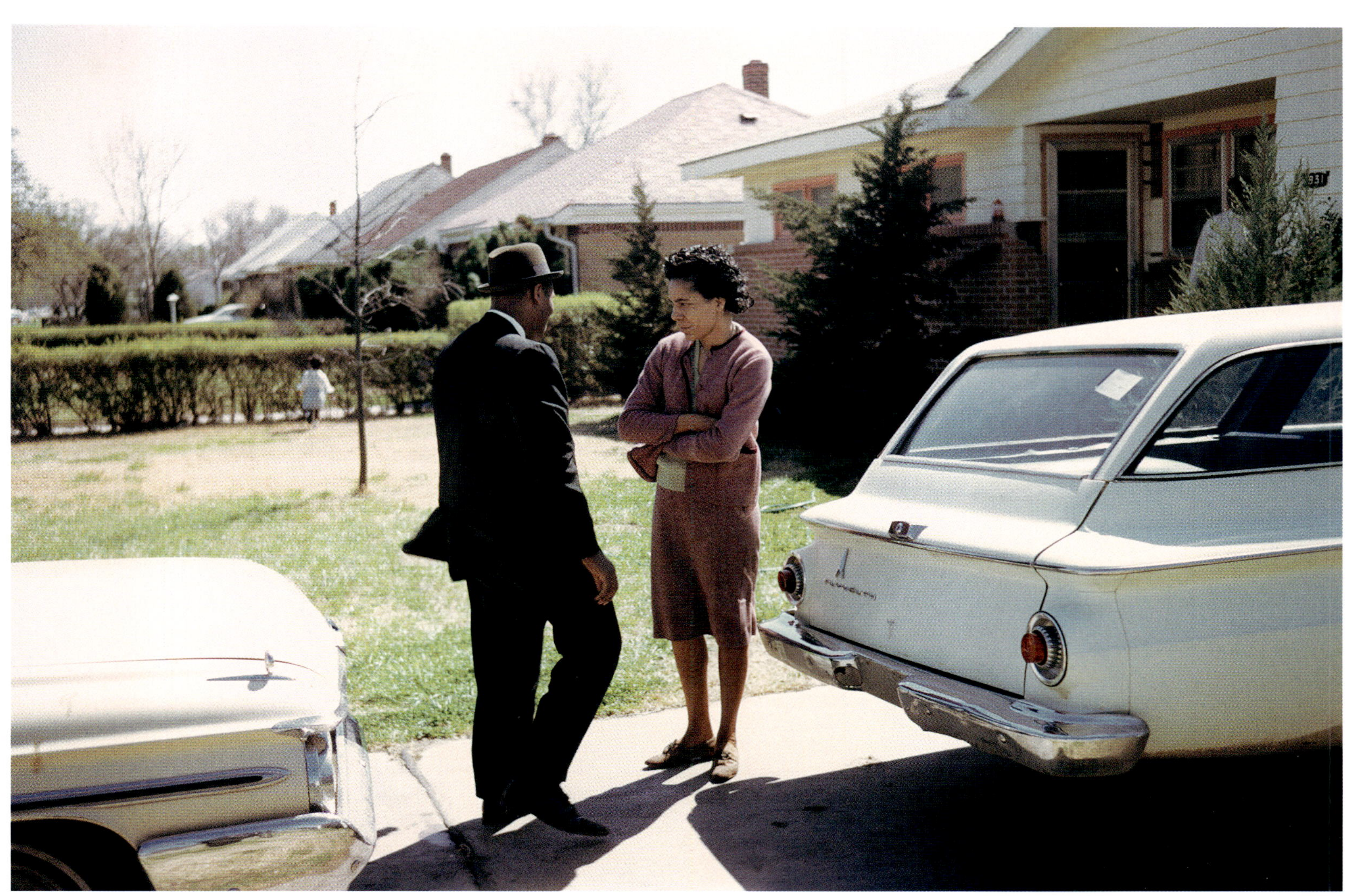

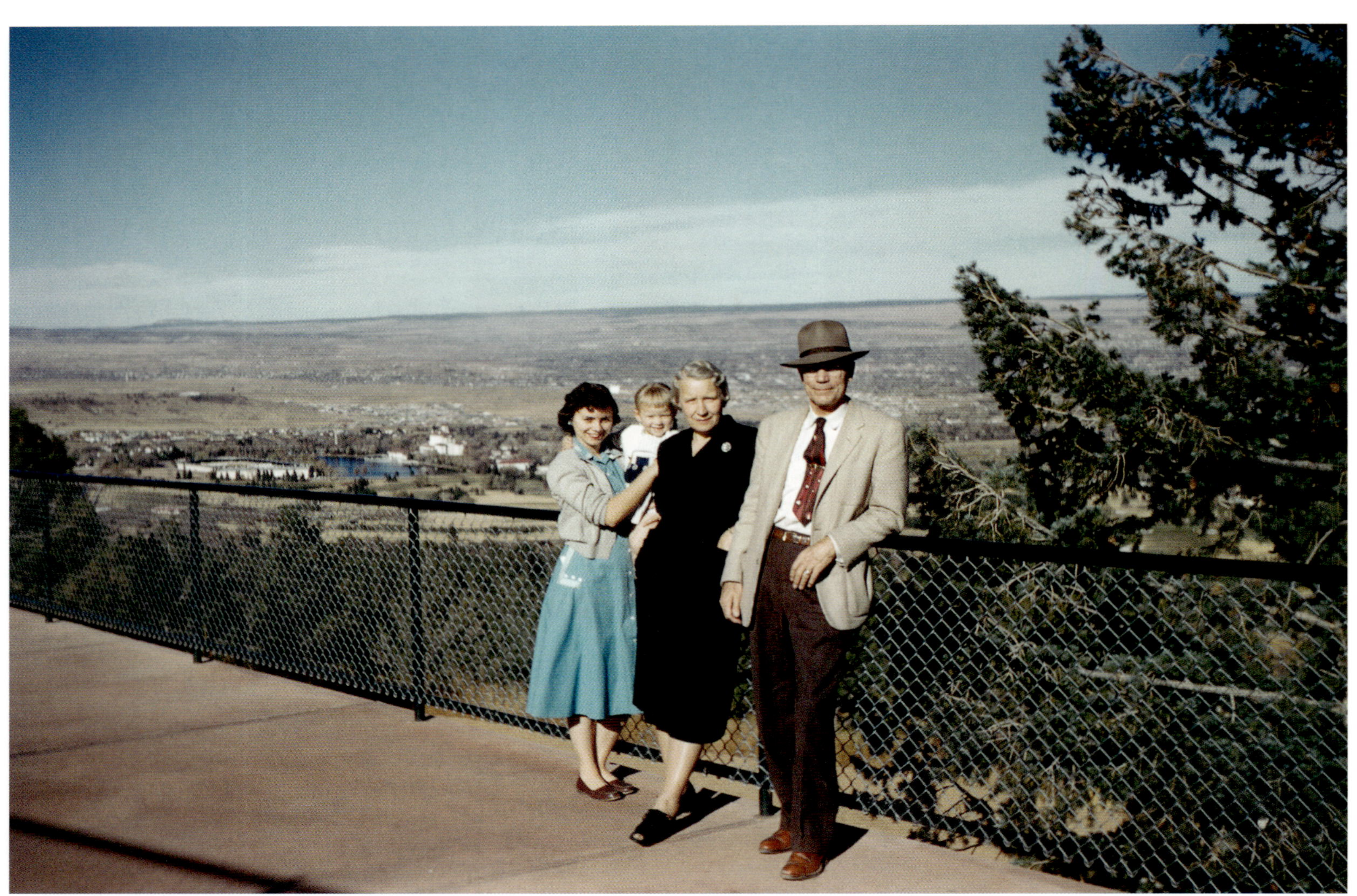

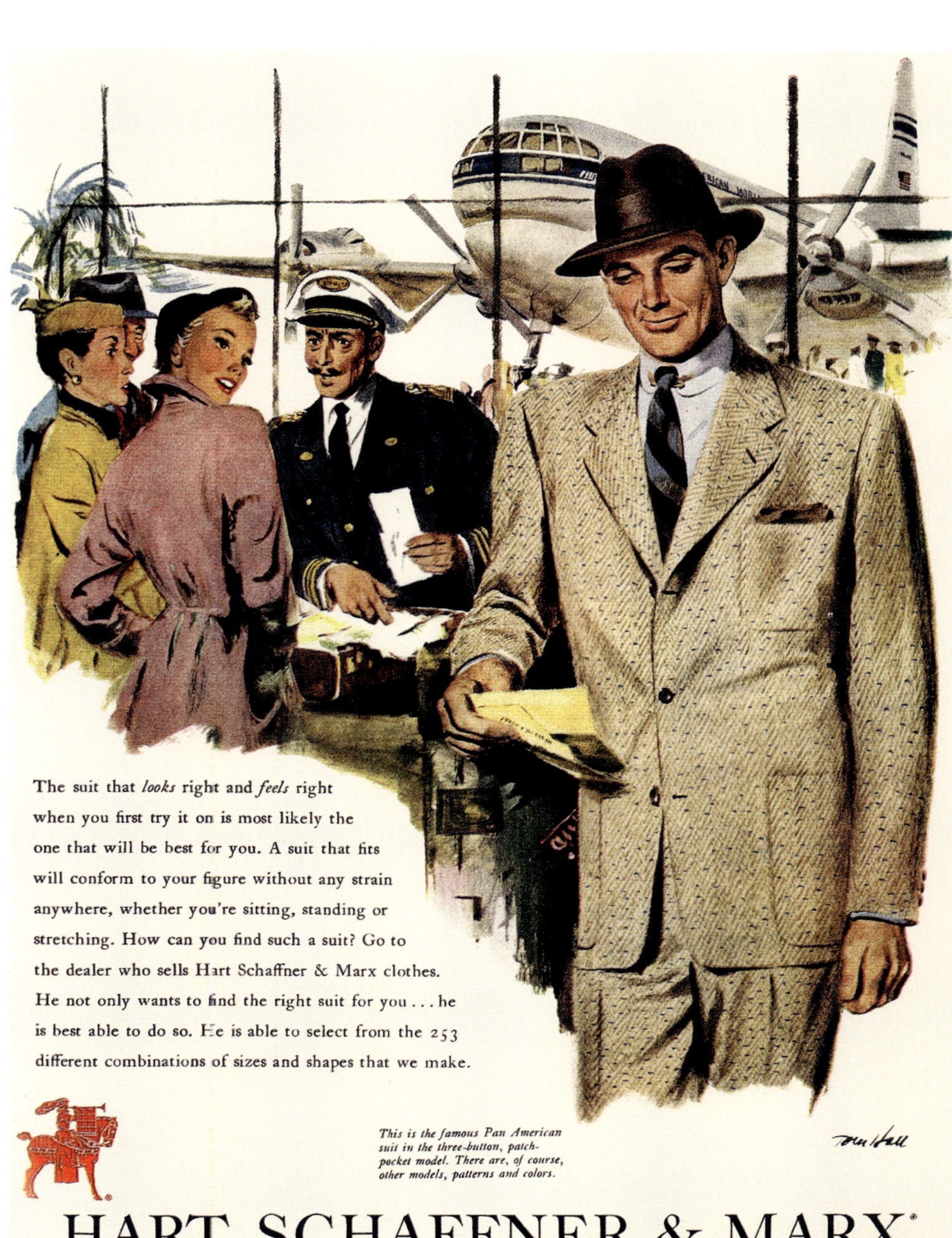
The suit that *looks* right and *feels* right when you first try it on is most likely the one that will be best for you. A suit that fits will conform to your figure without any strain anywhere, whether you're sitting, standing or stretching. How can you find such a suit? Go to the dealer who sells Hart Schaffner & Marx clothes. He not only wants to find the right suit for you . . . he is best able to do so. He is able to select from the 253 different combinations of sizes and shapes that we make.
This is the famous Pan American suit in the three-button, patch-pocket model. There are, of course, other models, patterns and colors.
HART SCHAFFNER & MARX®

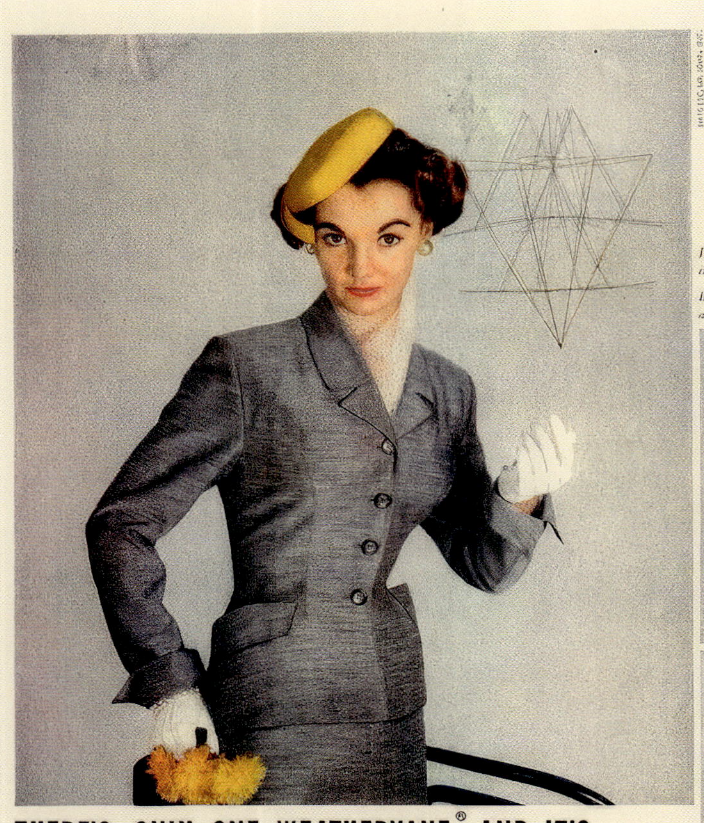

Jutting-pocket suit in Sheen-tex, $30.

Below, winged pocket and collar suit, $30.

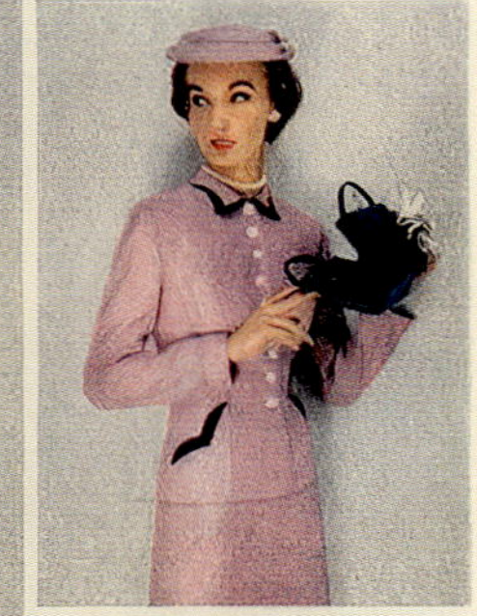

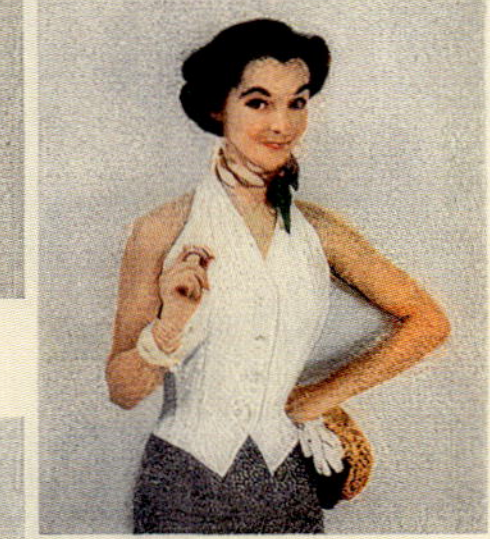

New: Weathervane halter-vest makes a costume of your suit, $8.95.

THERE'S ONLY ONE WEATHERVANE® — AND IT'S TAILORED BY HANDMACHER

If you've worn a Weathervane . . . you know the feel of flawless fit, the assurance of being dressed in great good taste. If you've never owned a Weathervane . . . you owe it to yourself to wear the best loved suit in America. Only then can you enjoy the expensive look that, amazingly, costs you just $25 or $30!

tailored by handmacher

← Belted peplum suit, $25.

Weathervane's stay-crisp Celanese acetate fabric comes in 17 exciting, new colors. Misses, junior or Proportioned Plus sizes, one of which is sure to be your size.

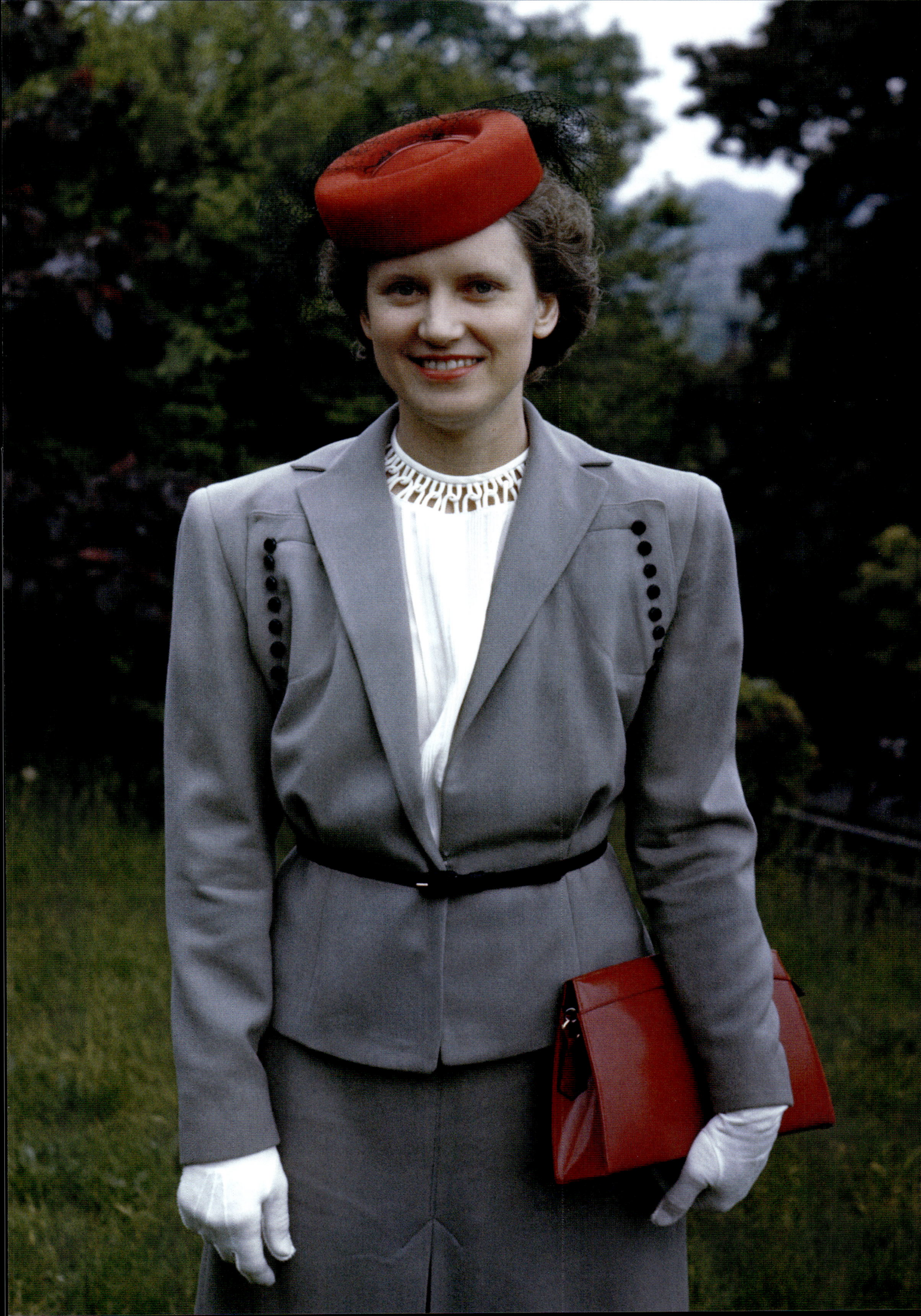

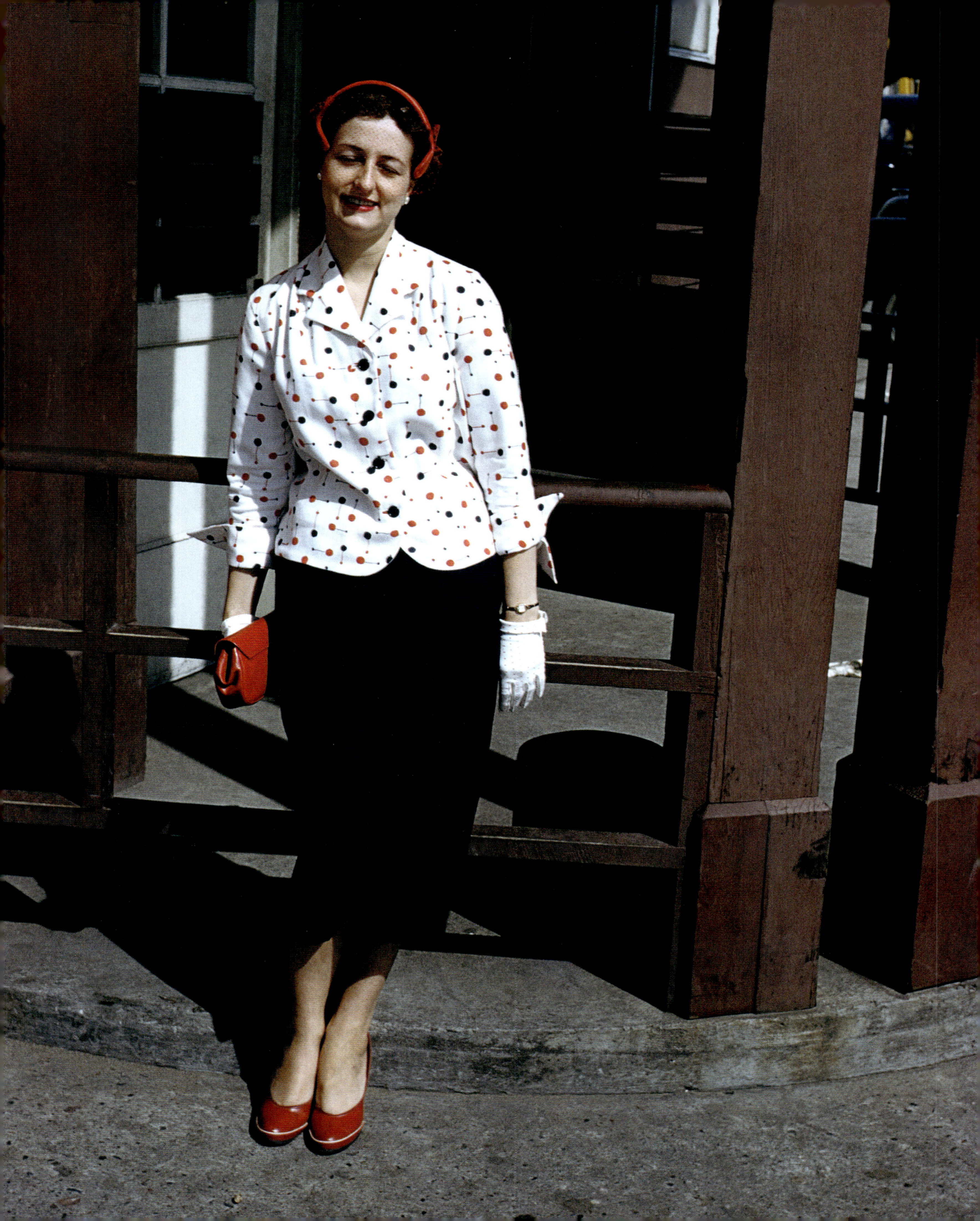

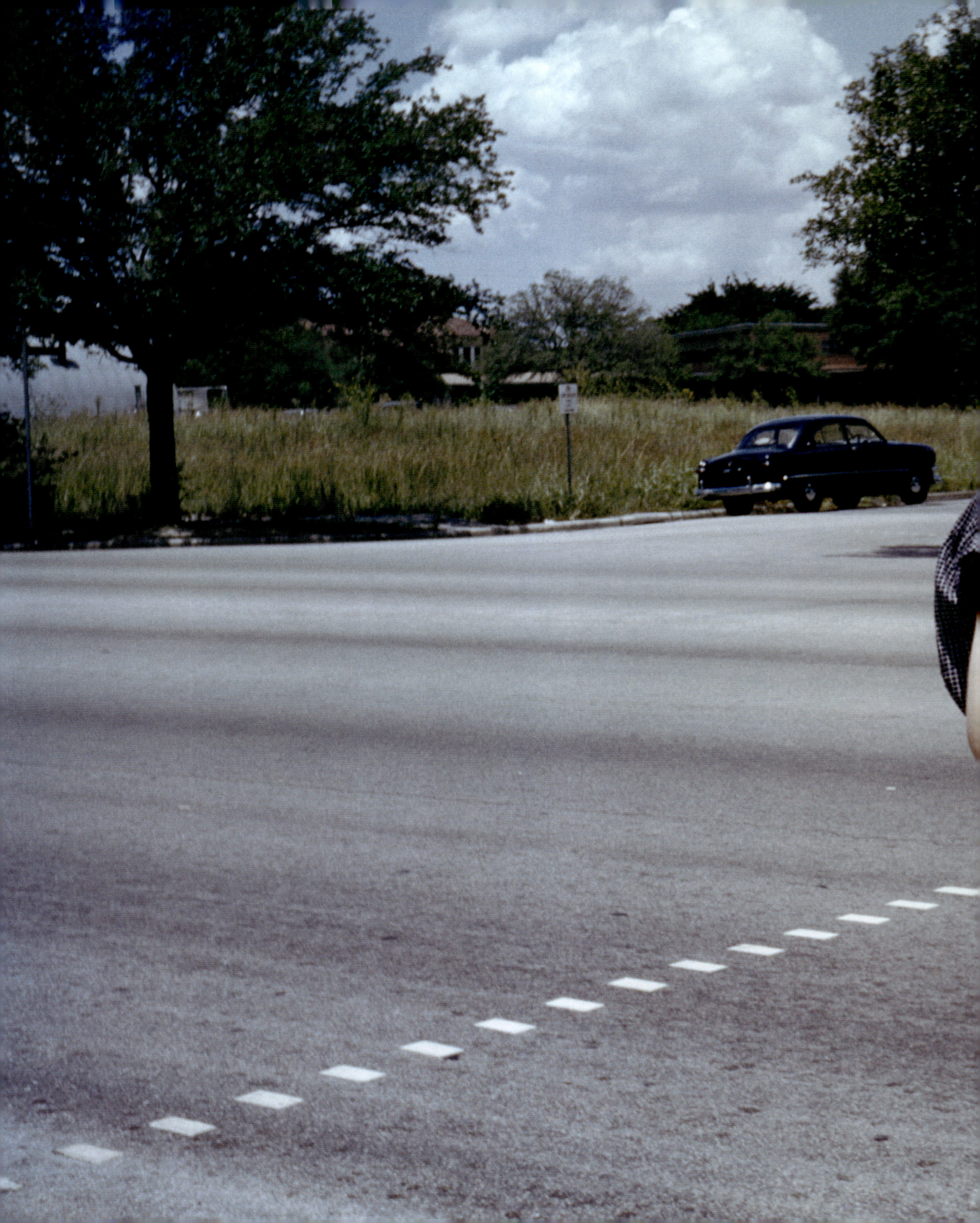

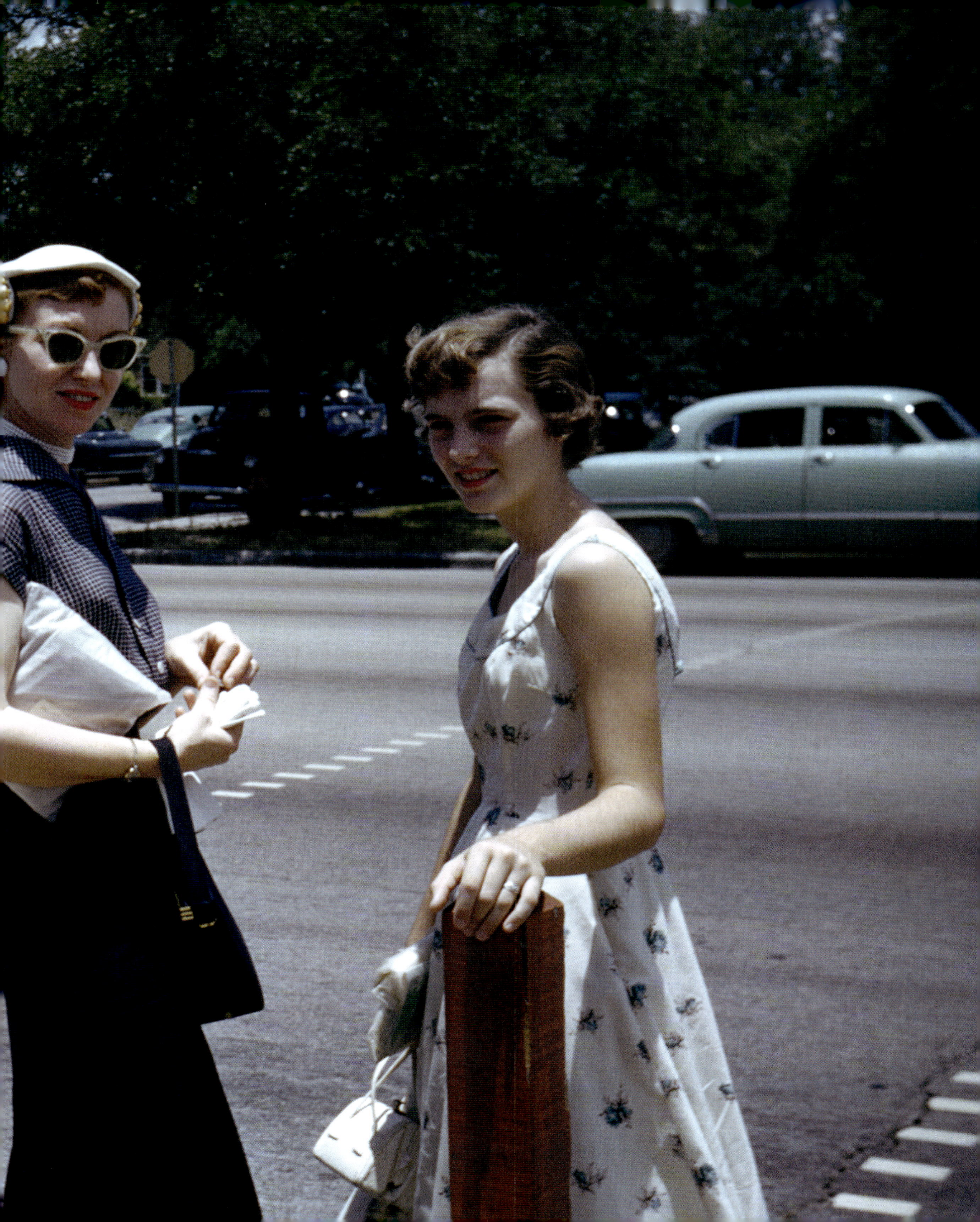

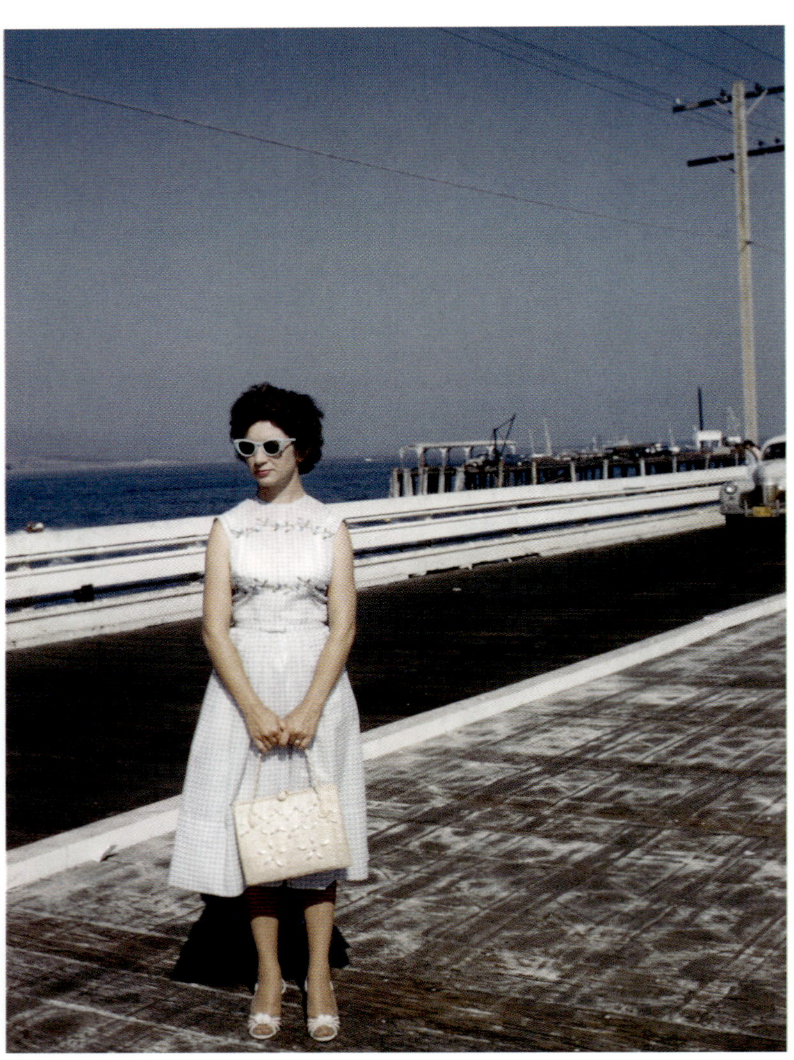

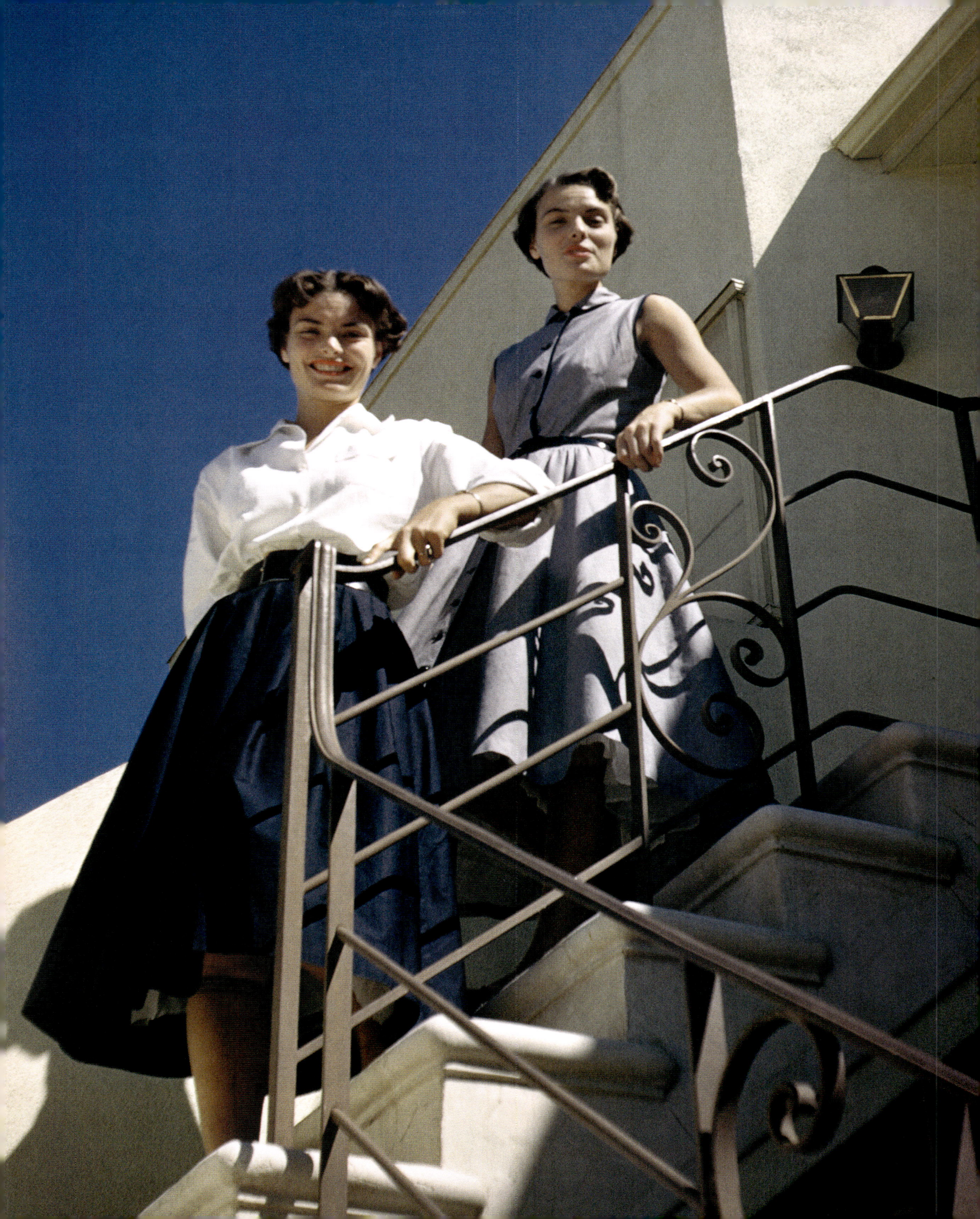

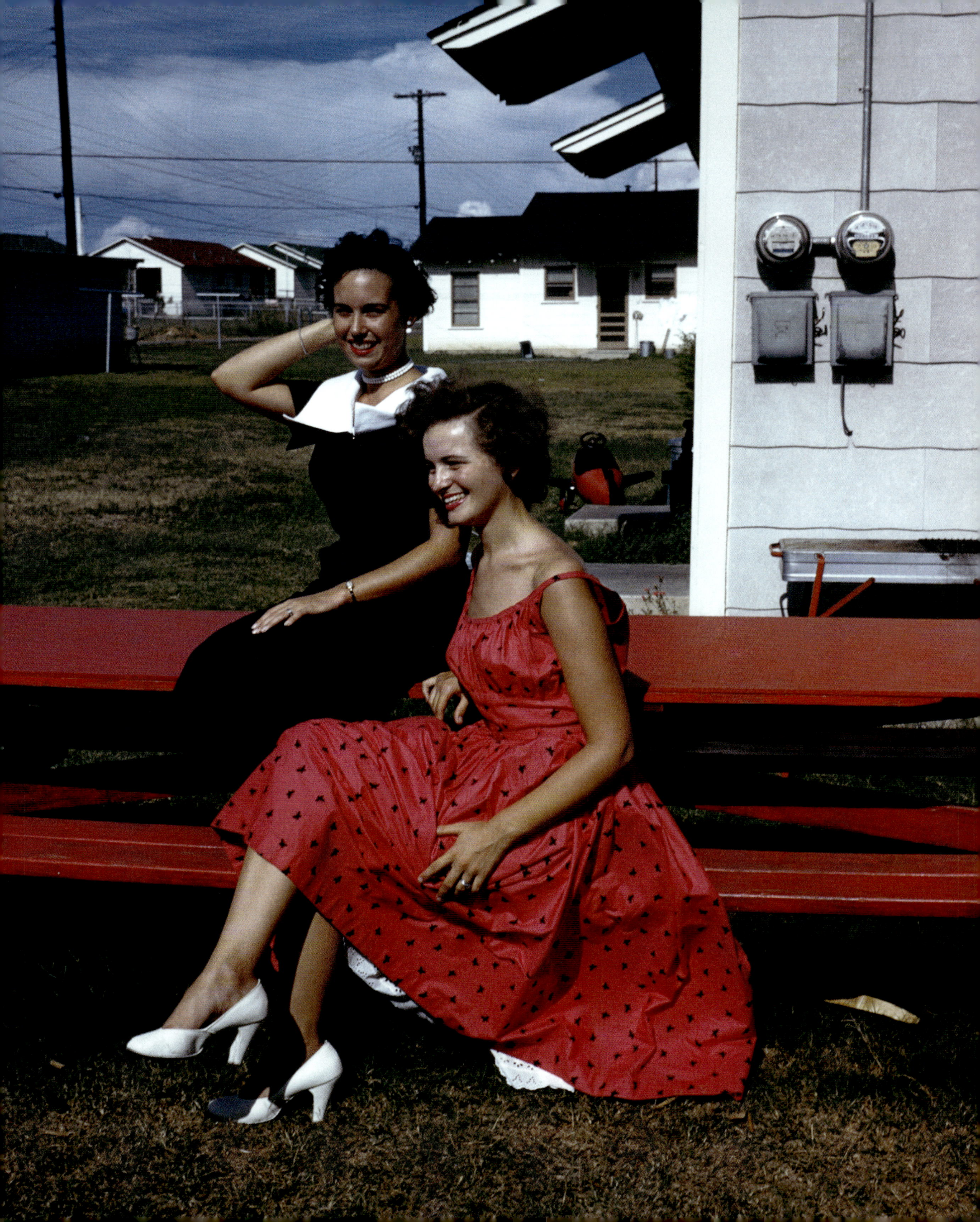

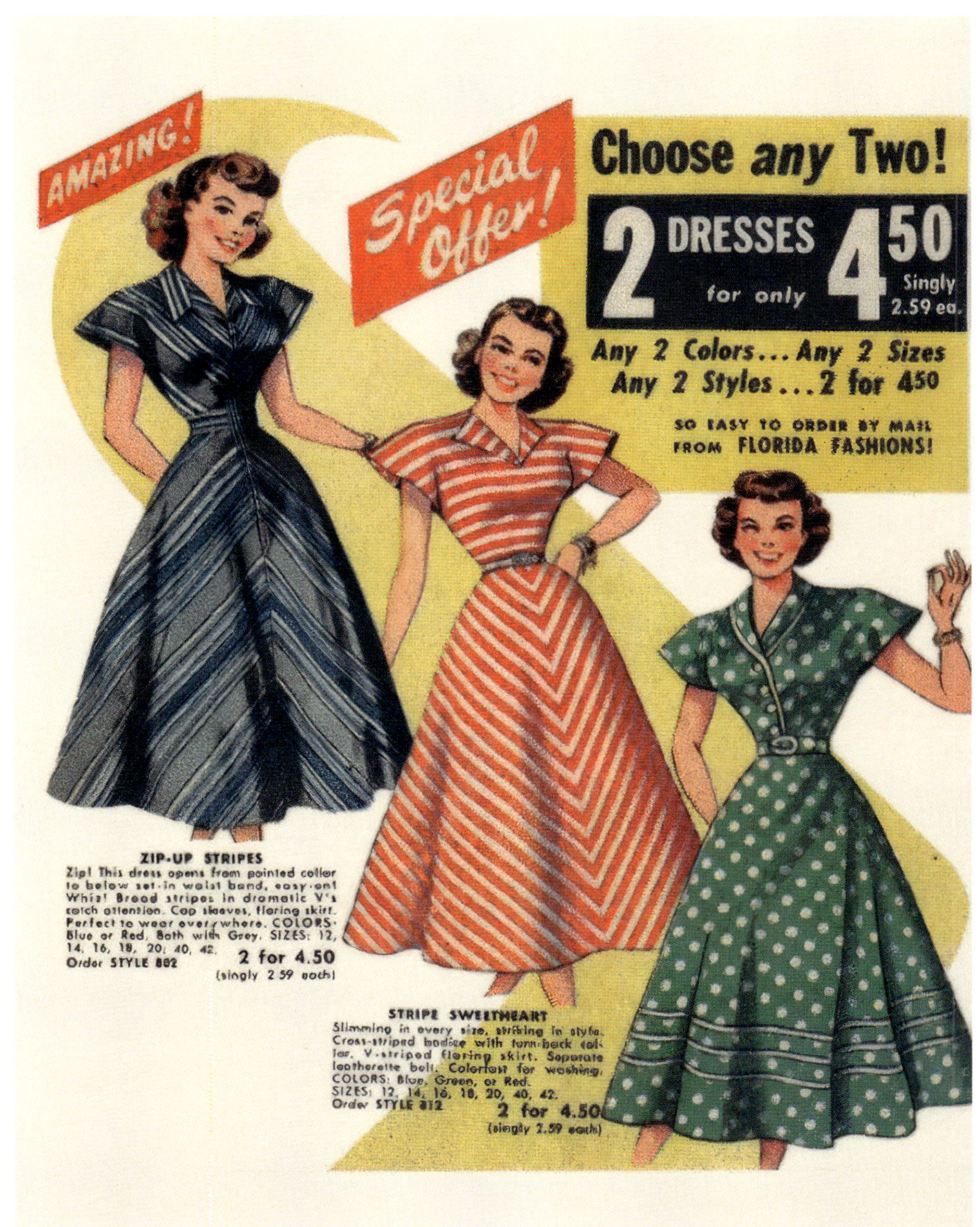

AMAZING!
Special Offer!
Choose any Two!
2 DRESSES for only 4.50
Singly 2.59 ea.
Any 2 Colors... Any 2 Sizes
Any 2 Styles... 2 for 4.50
SO EASY TO ORDER BY MAIL FROM FLORIDA FASHIONS!
ZIP-UP STRIPES
Zip! This dress opens from pointed collar to below set-in waist band, easy-on! Whiz! Broad stripes in dramatic V's catch attention. Cap sleeves, flaring skirt. Perfect to wear everywhere. COLORS: Blue or Red, Both with Grey. SIZES: 12, 14, 16, 18, 20; 40, 42.
Order STYLE 802
2 for 4.50
(singly 2.59 each)
STRIPE SWEETHEART
Slimming in every size, striking in style. Cross-striped bodice with turn-back collar. V-striped flaring skirt. Separate leatherette belt. Colorfast for washing. COLORS: Blue, Green, or Red.
SIZES: 12, 14, 16, 18, 20, 40, 42.
Order STYLE 812
2 for 4.50
(singly 2.59 each)

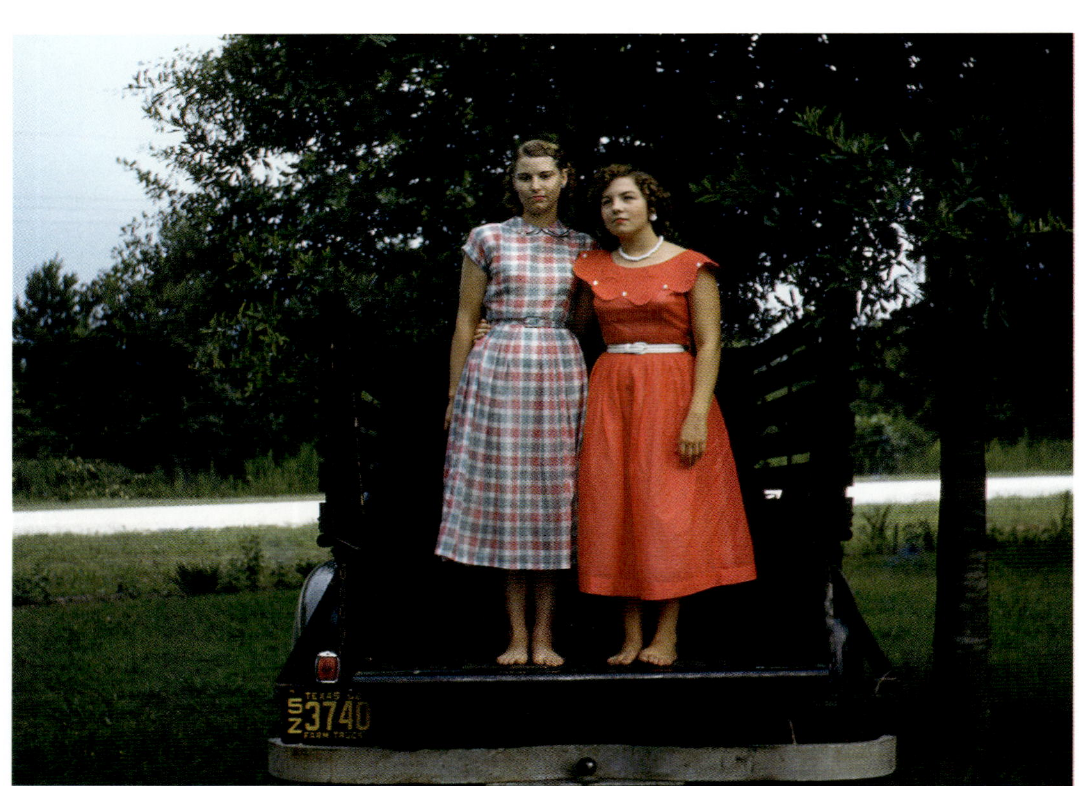
TEXAS
5Z 3740
FARM TRUCK

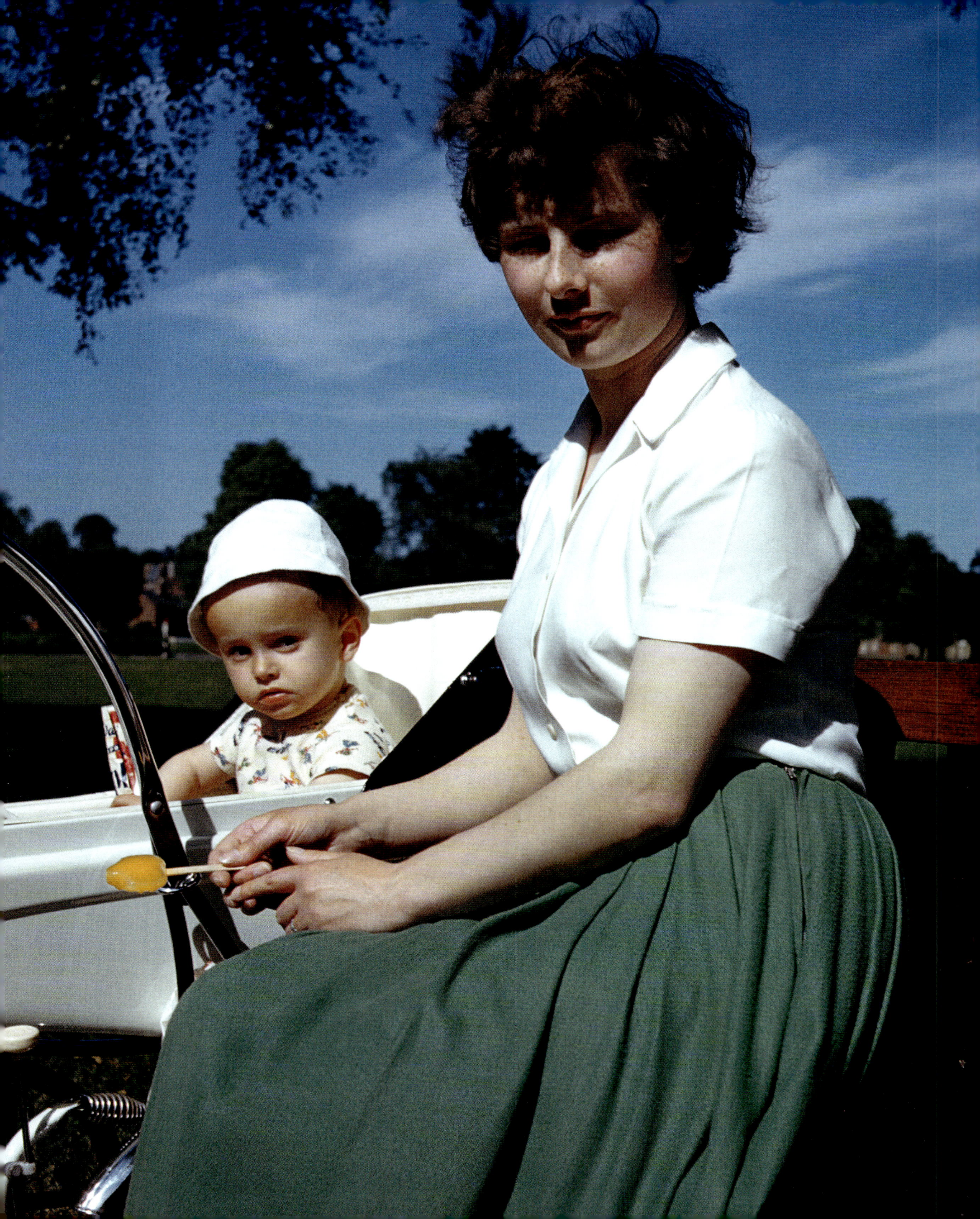

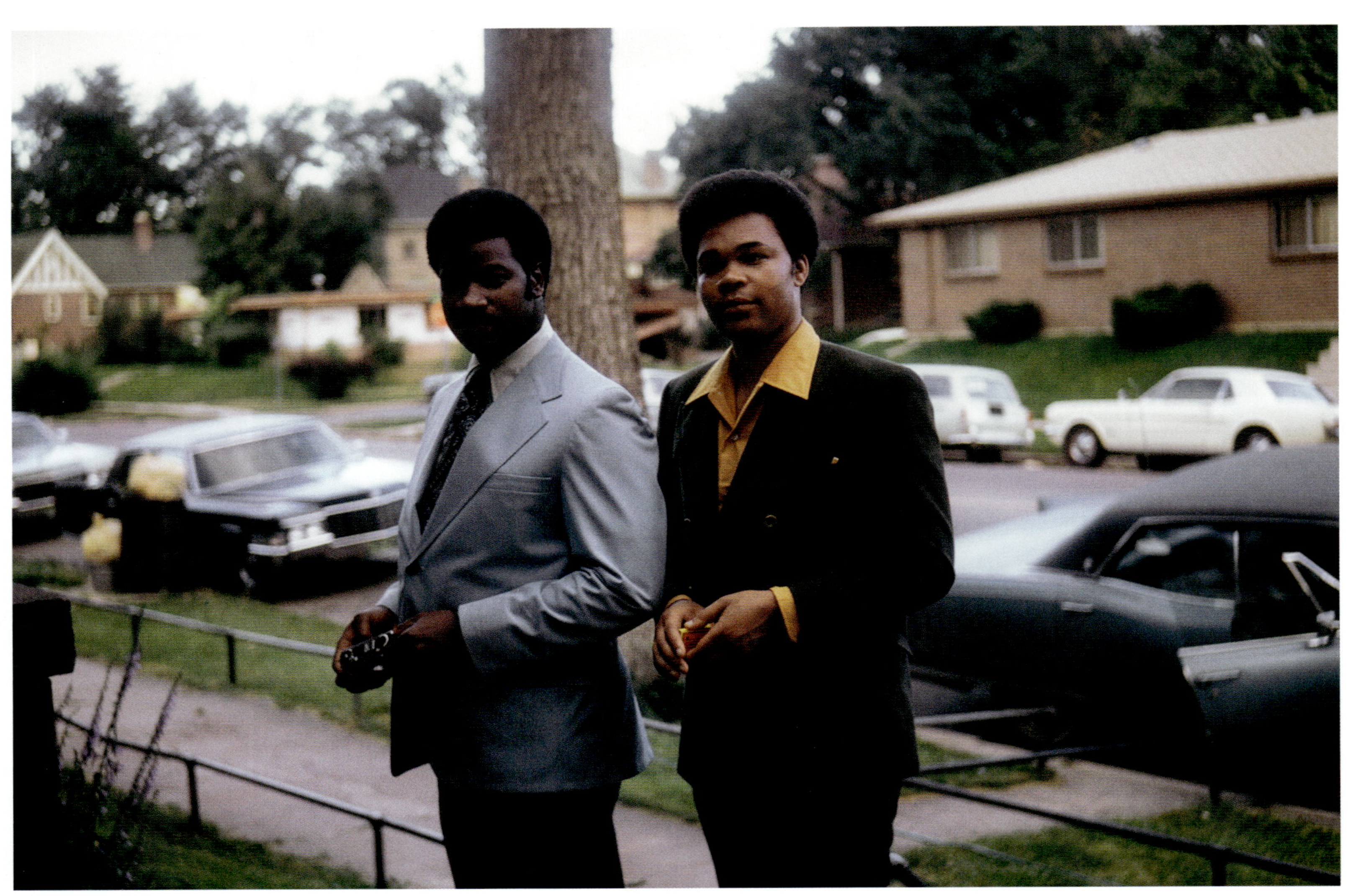

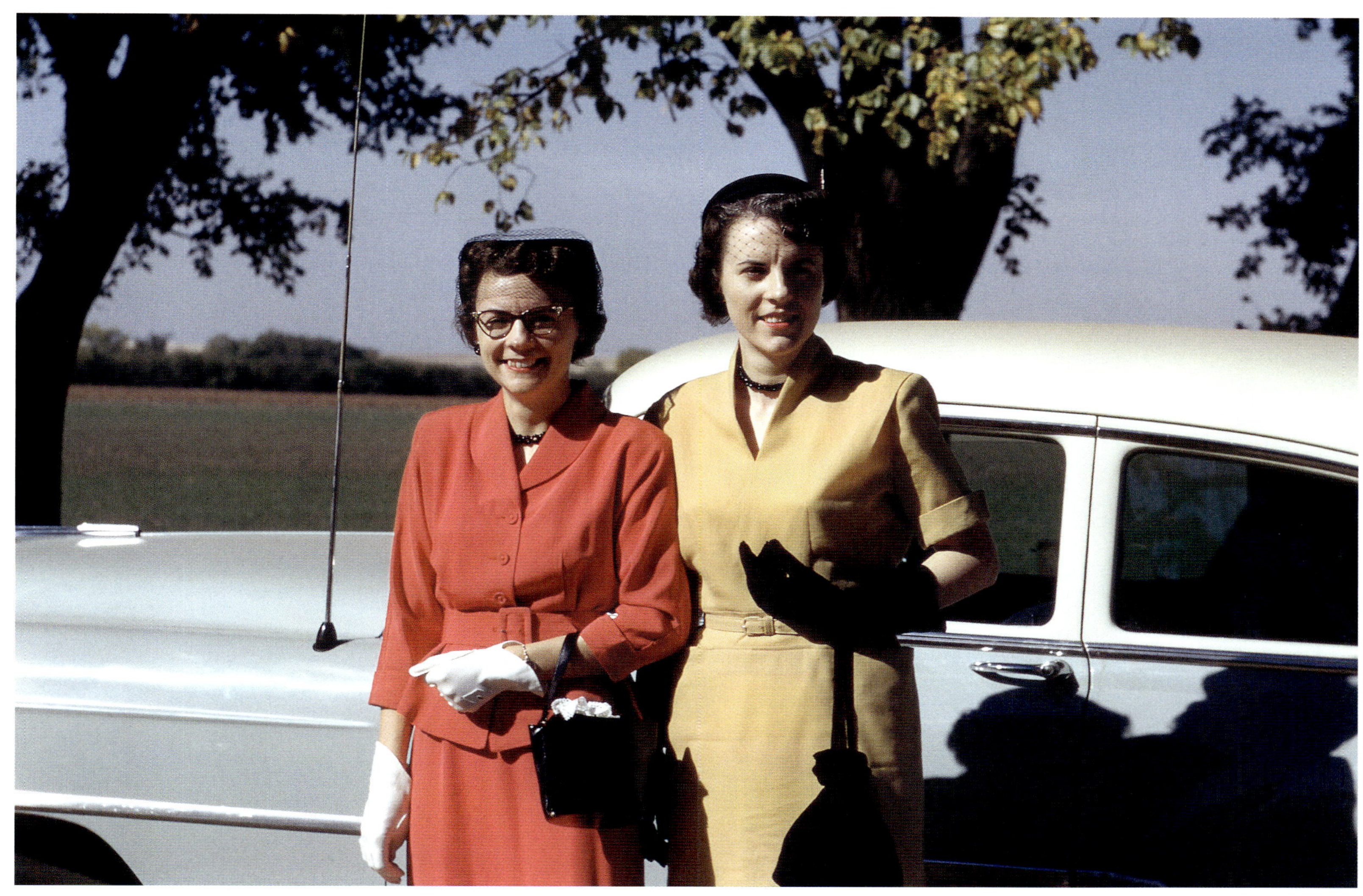

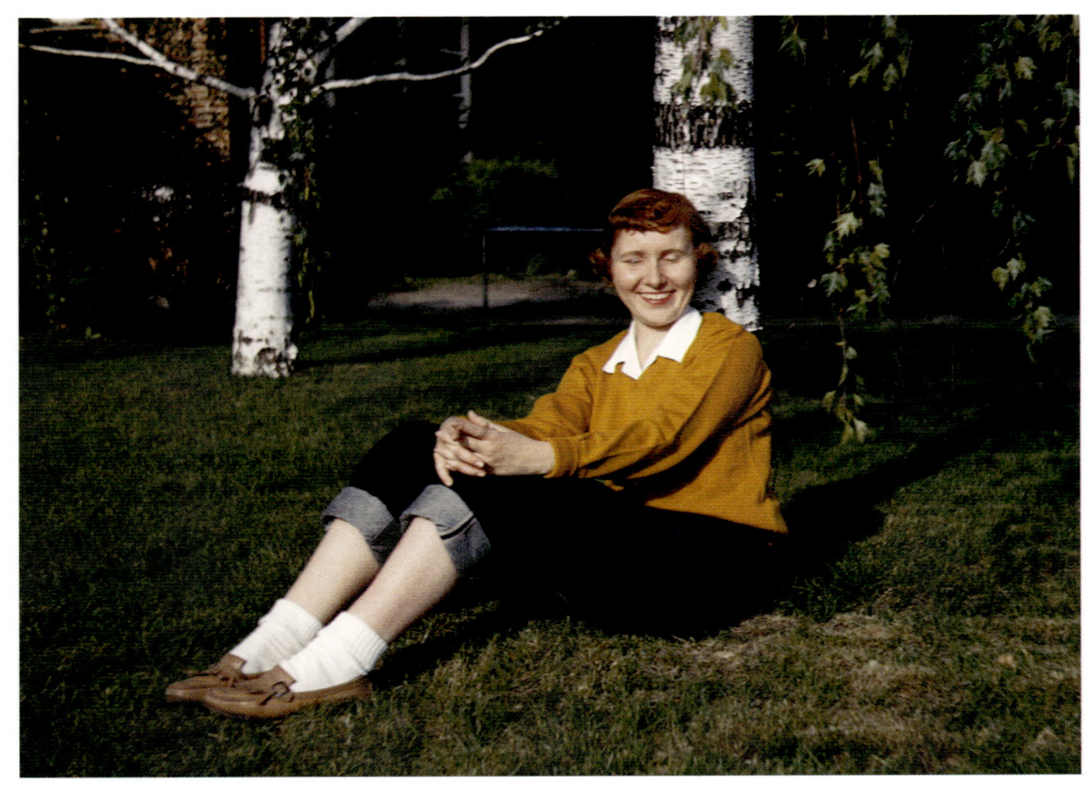

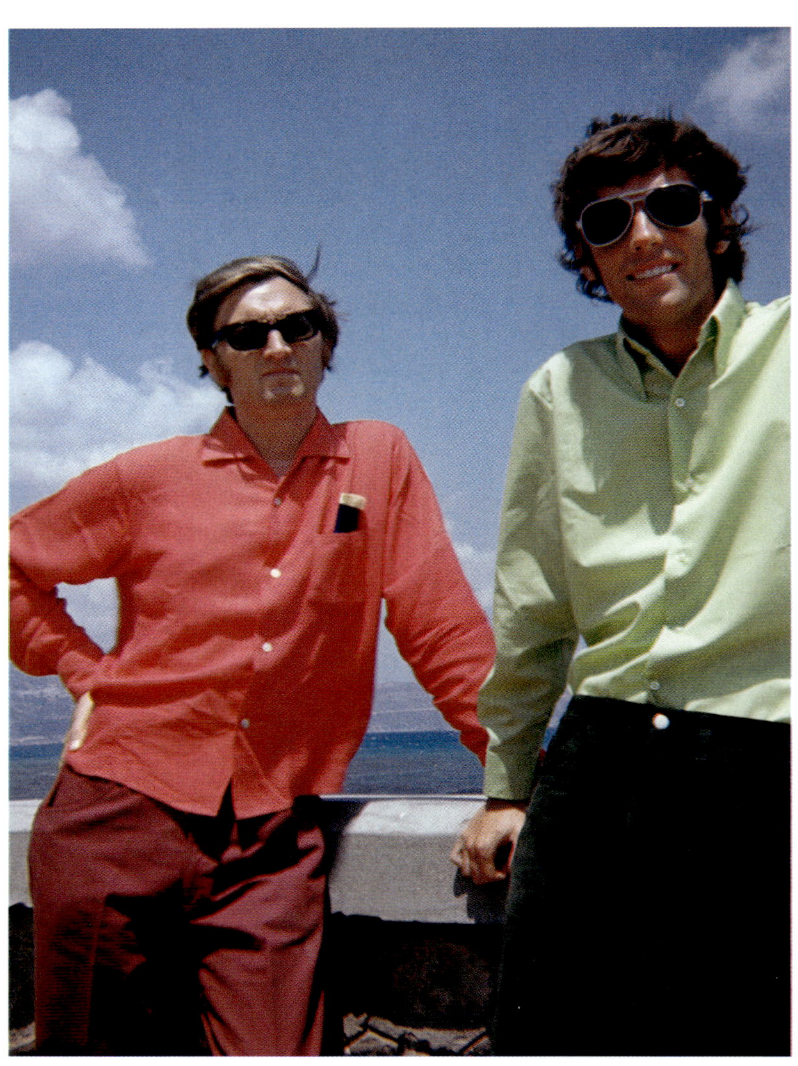

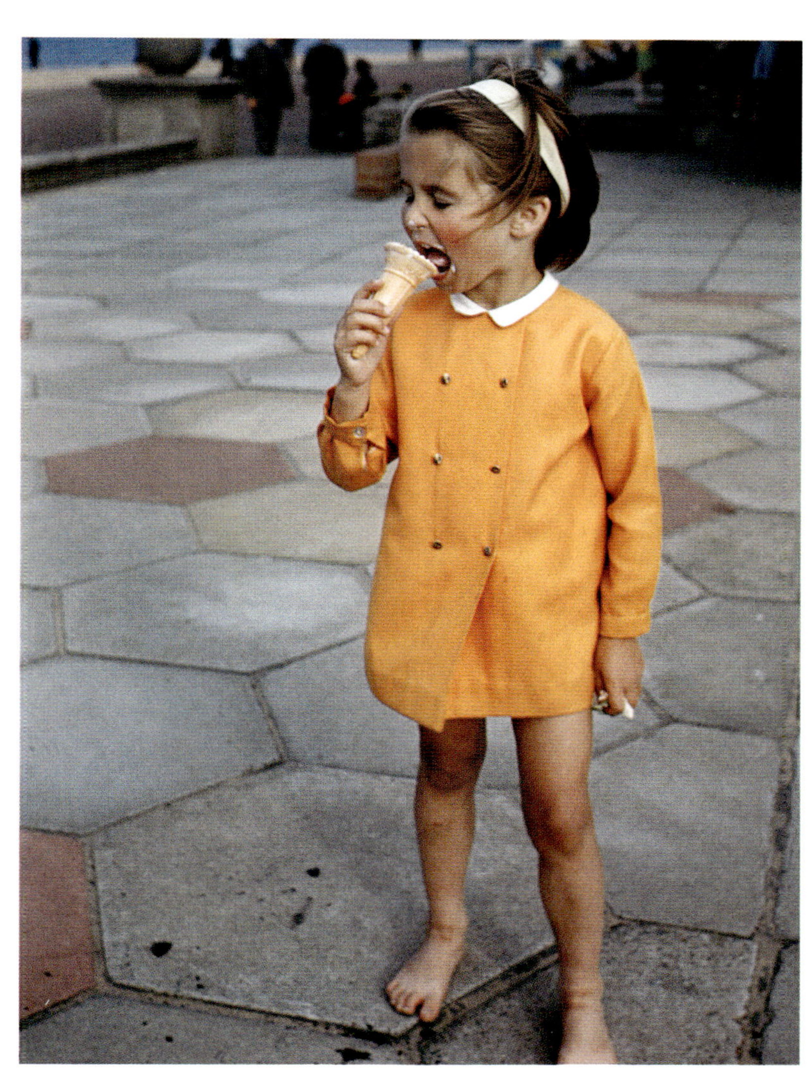

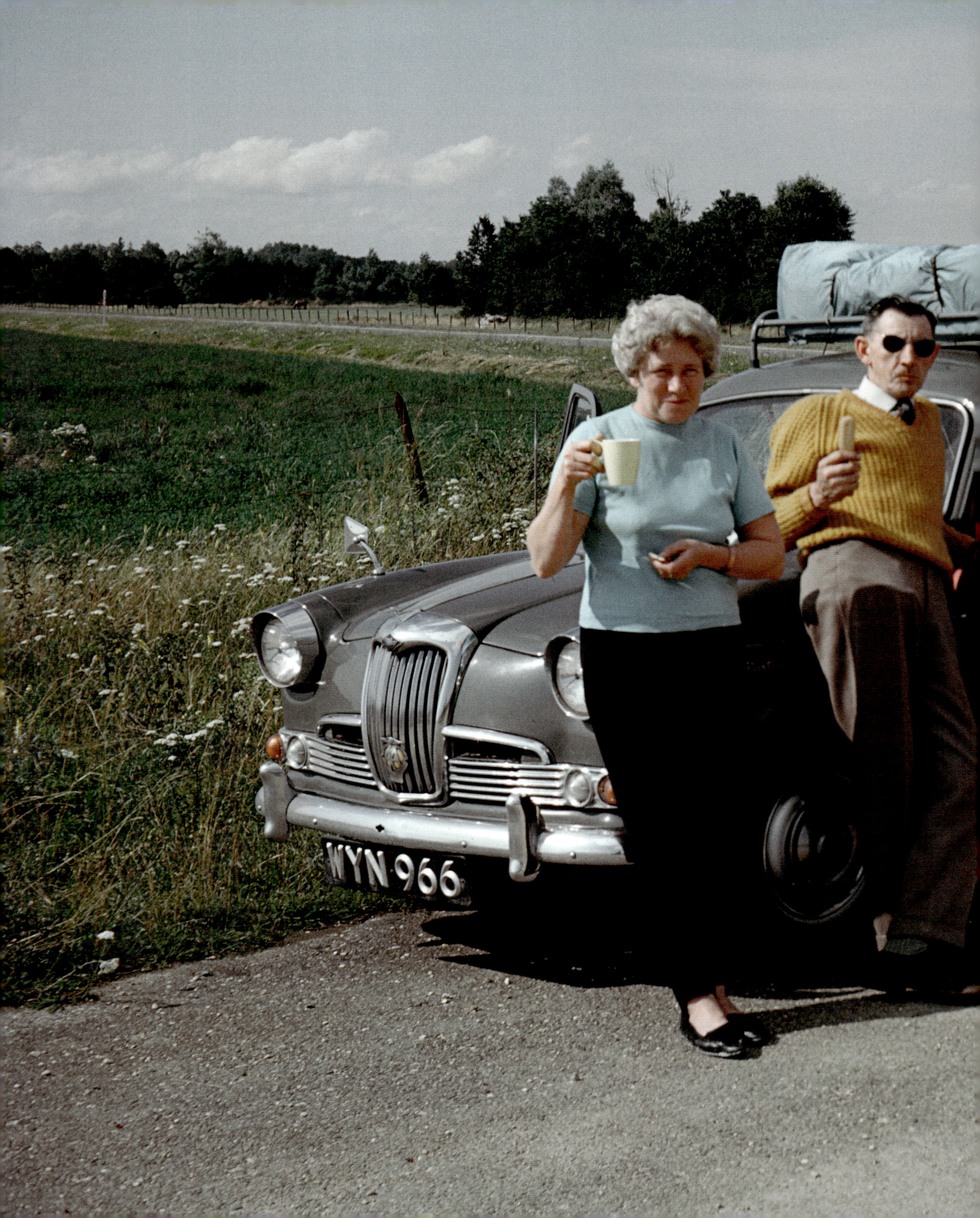
WYN 966

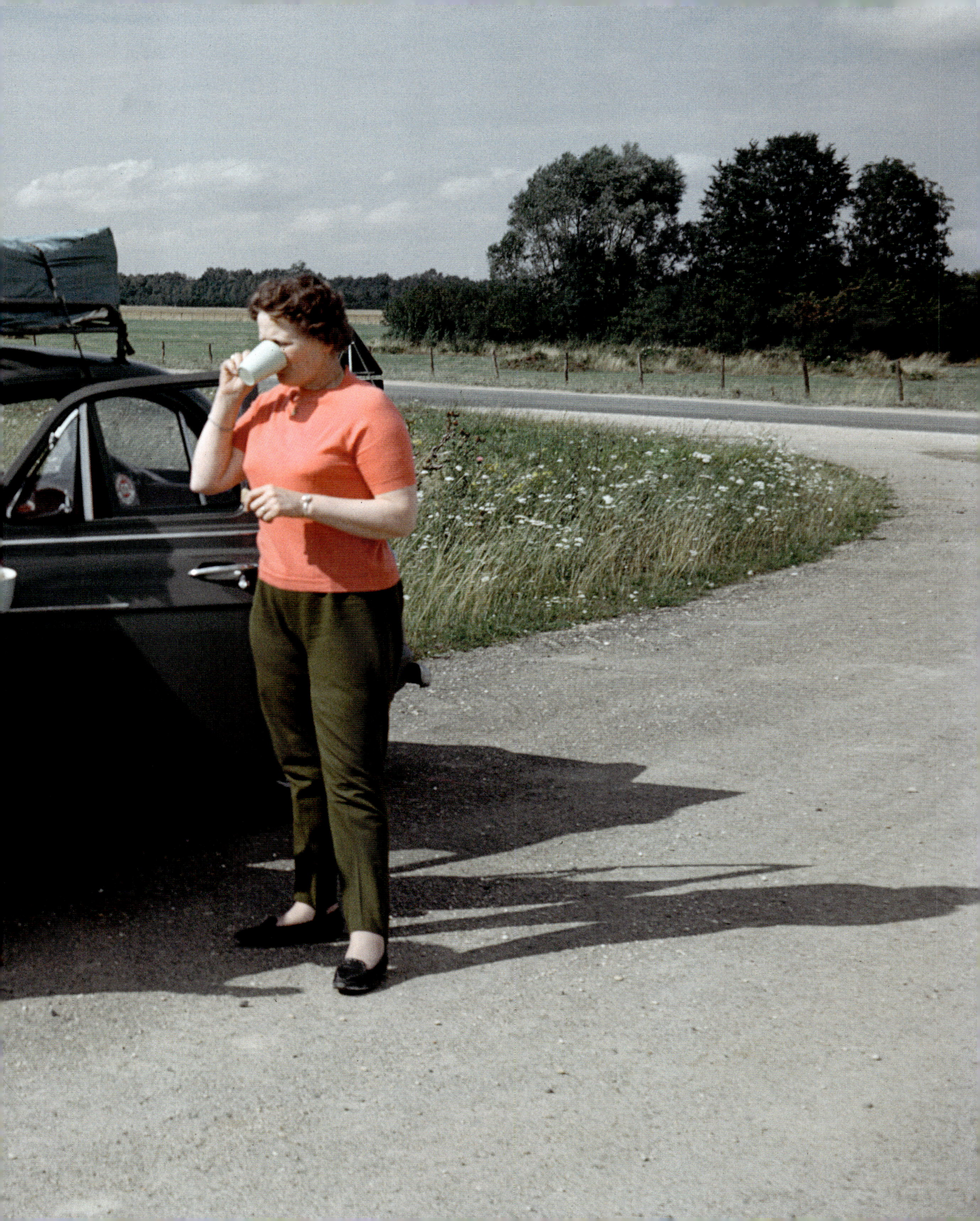

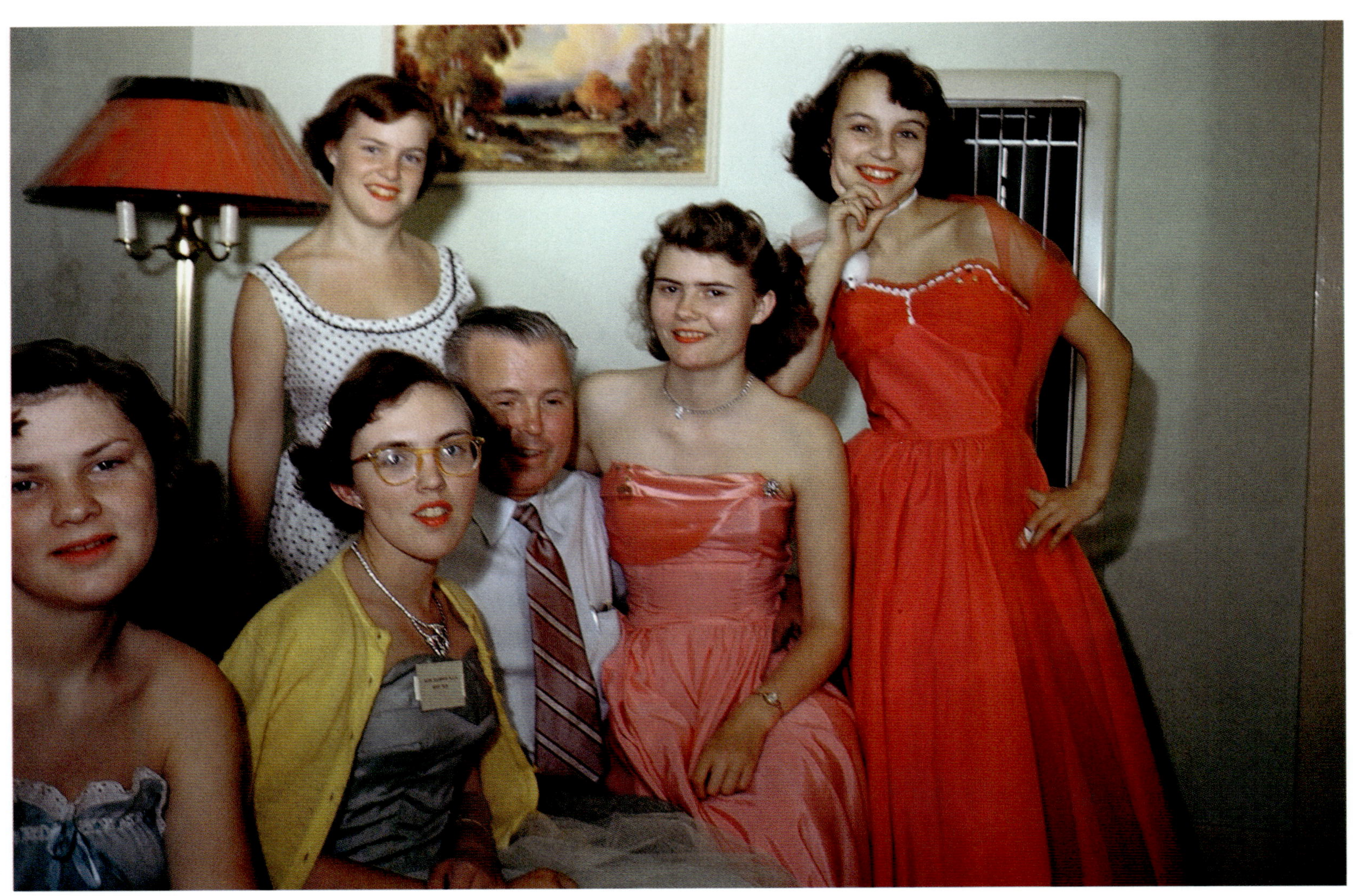

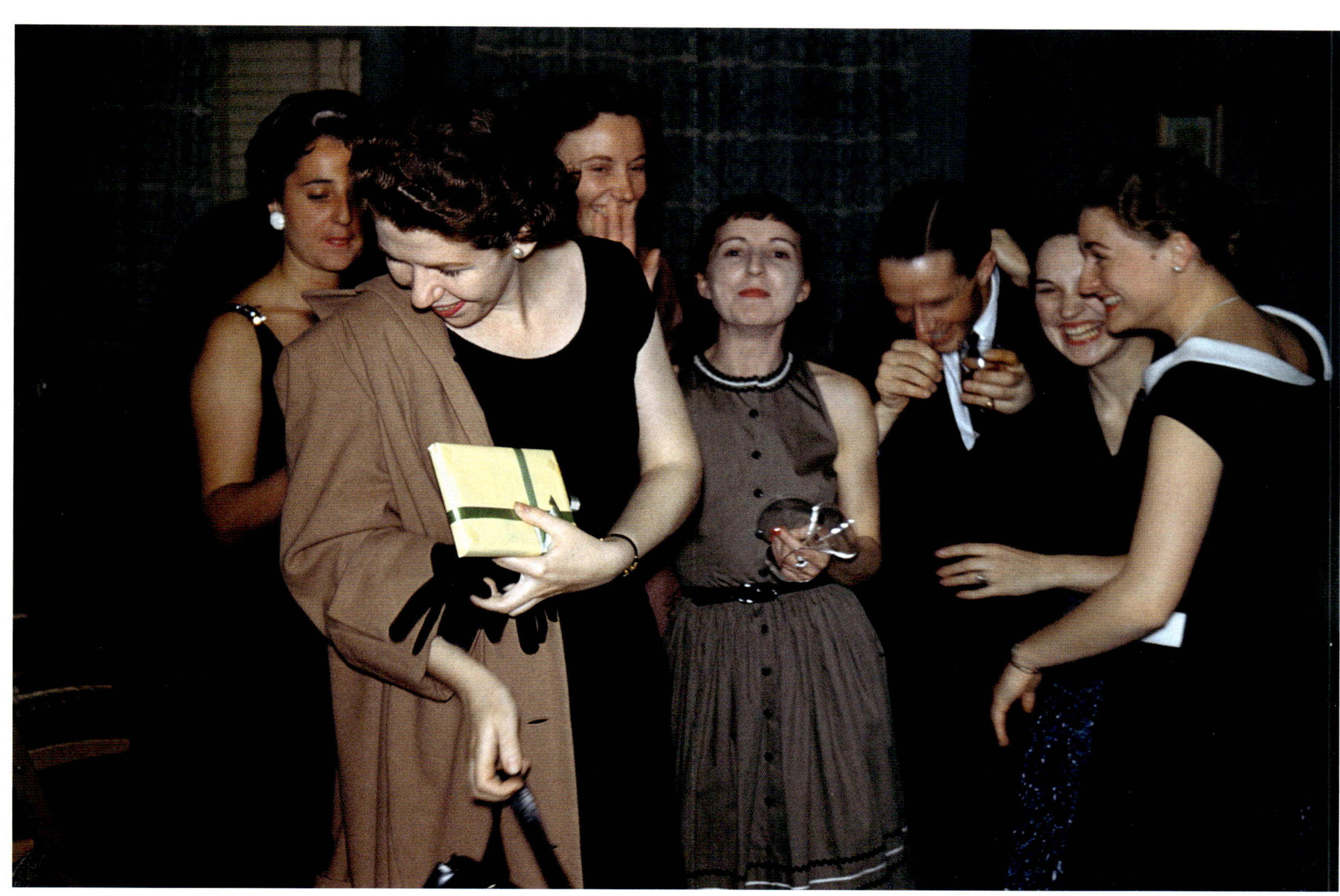

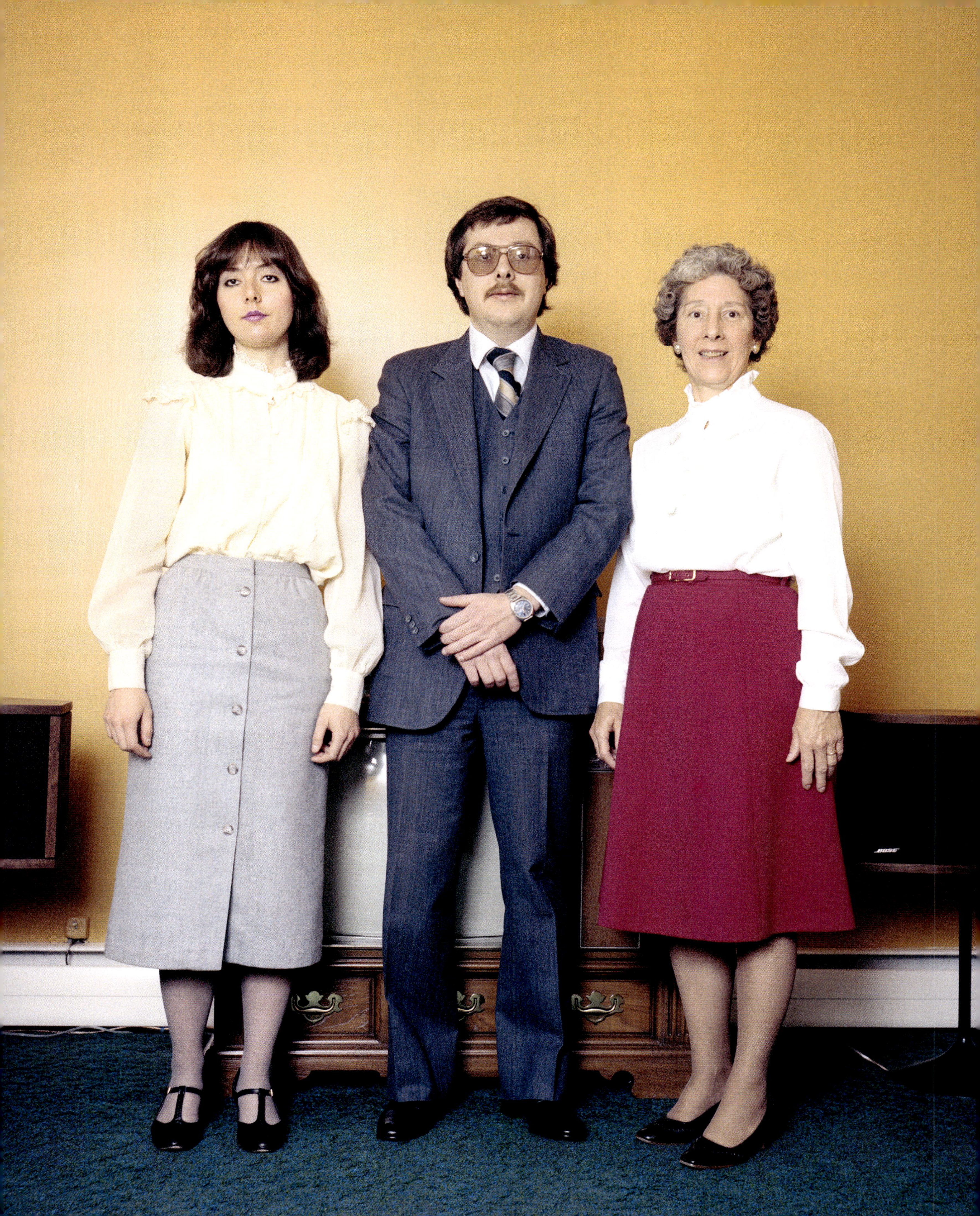

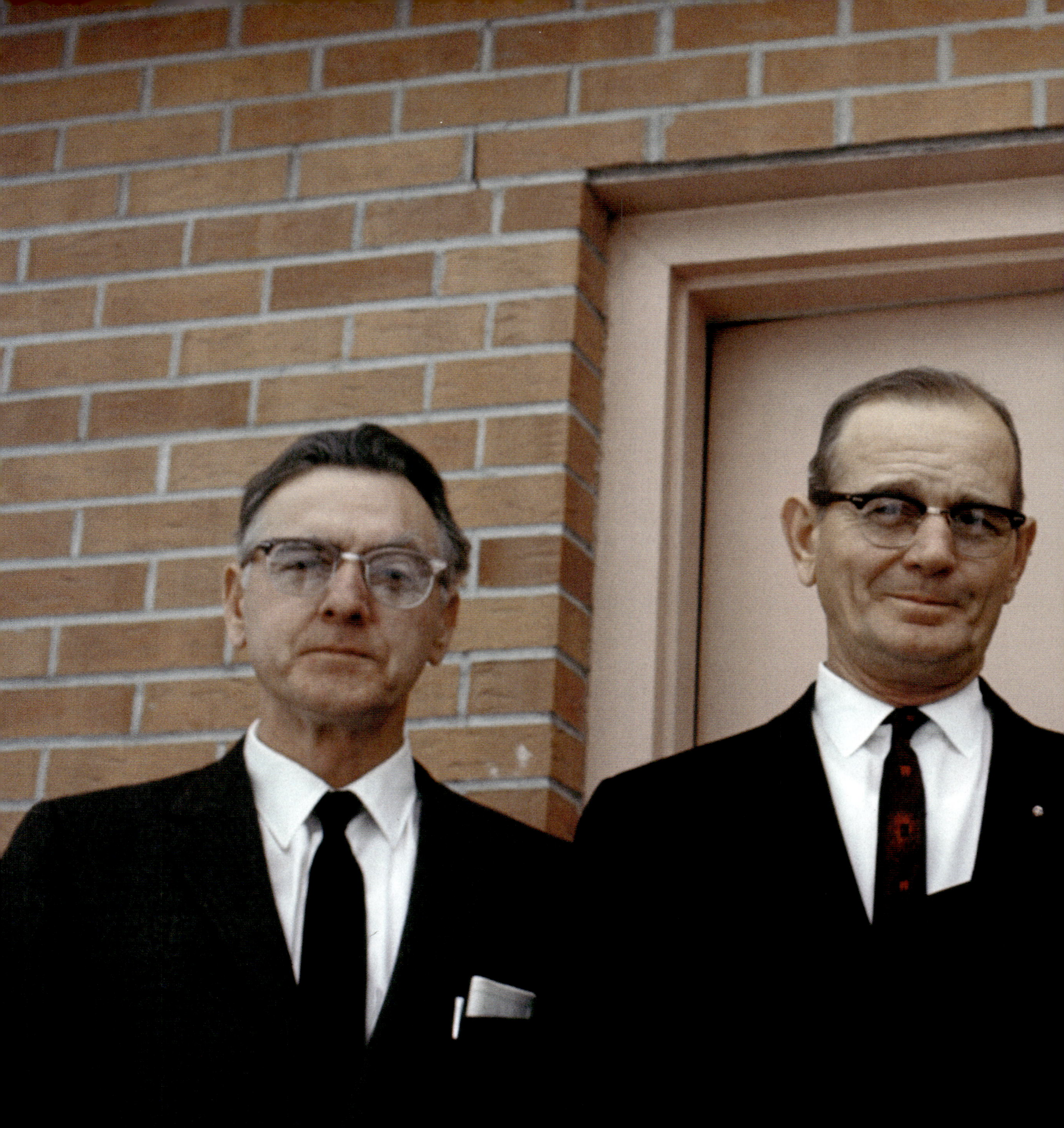

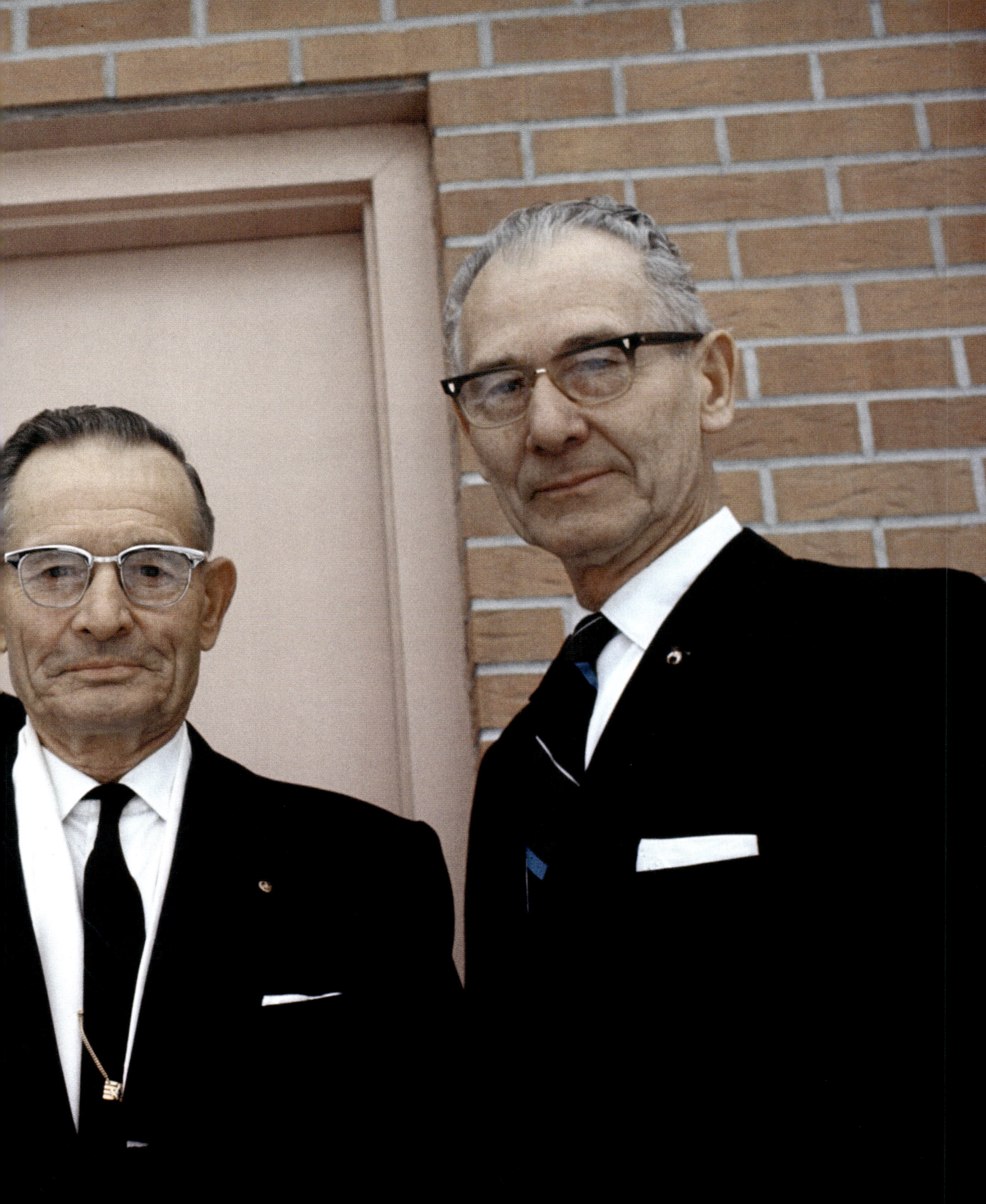

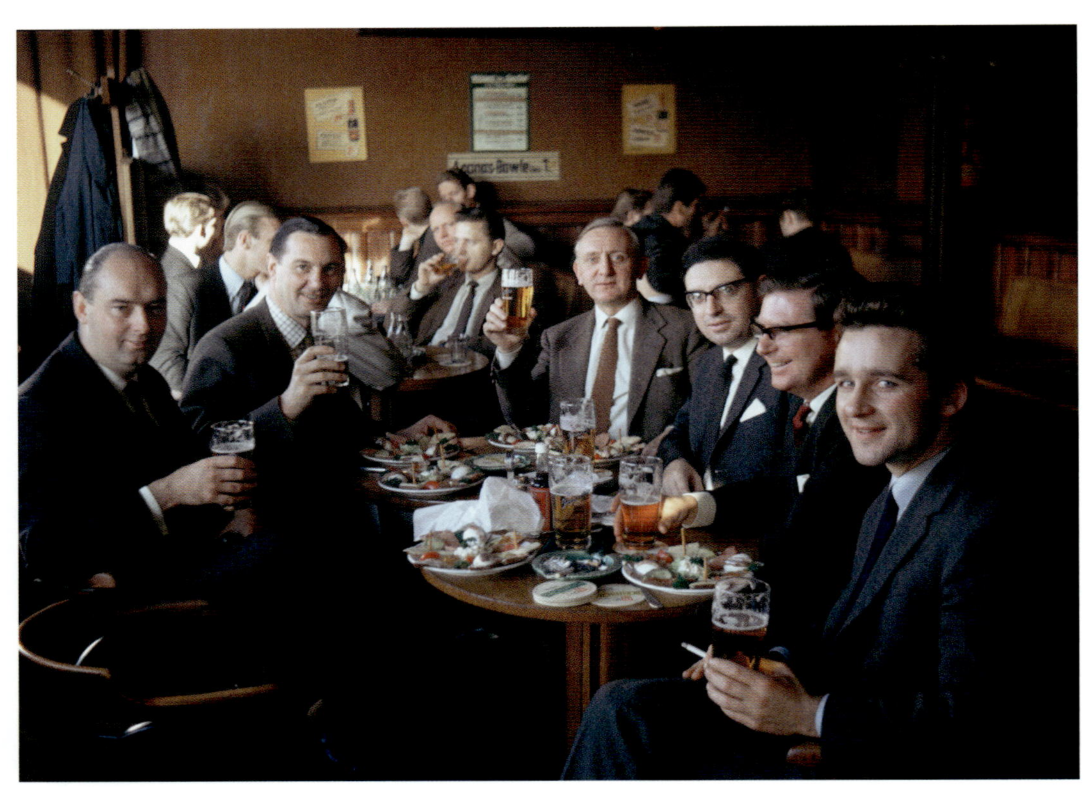

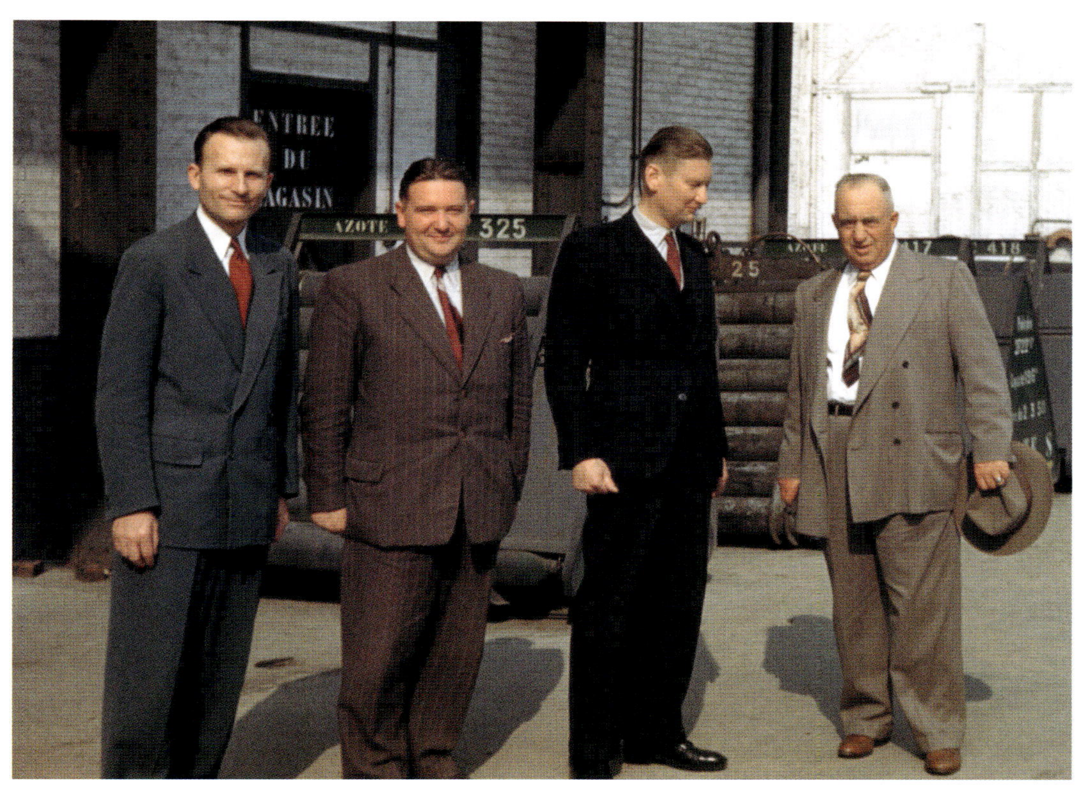
ENTREE
DU
AGASIN
AZOTE
325
418

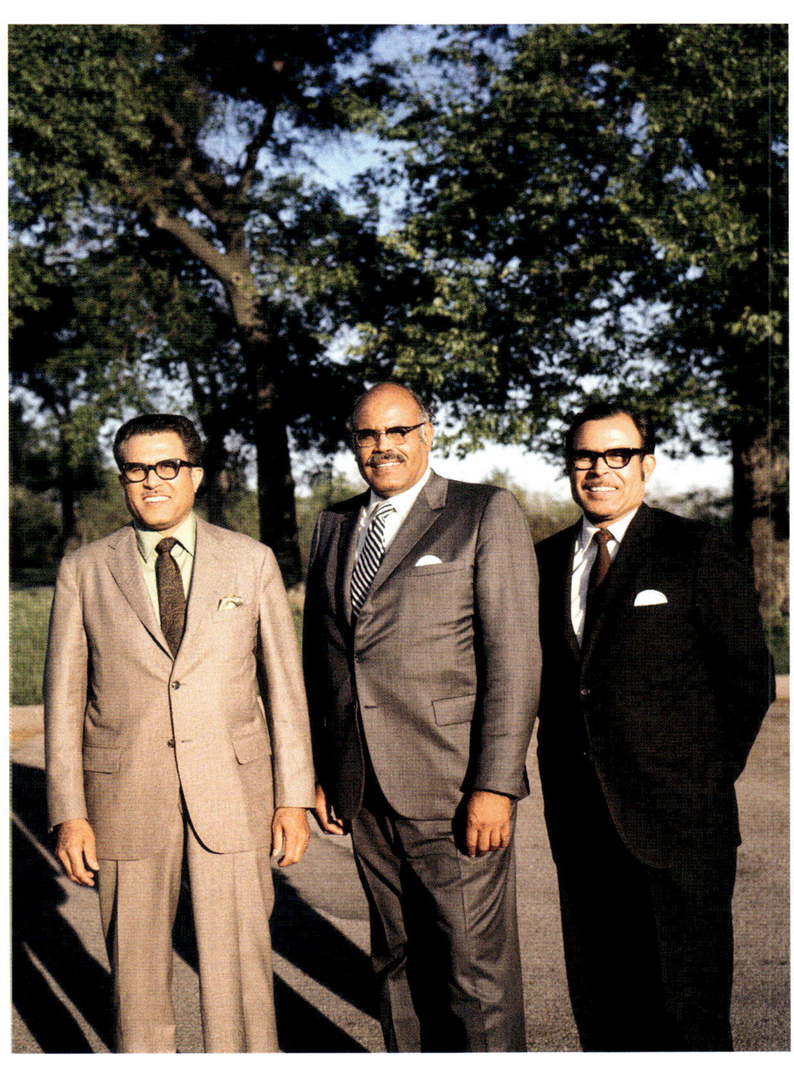

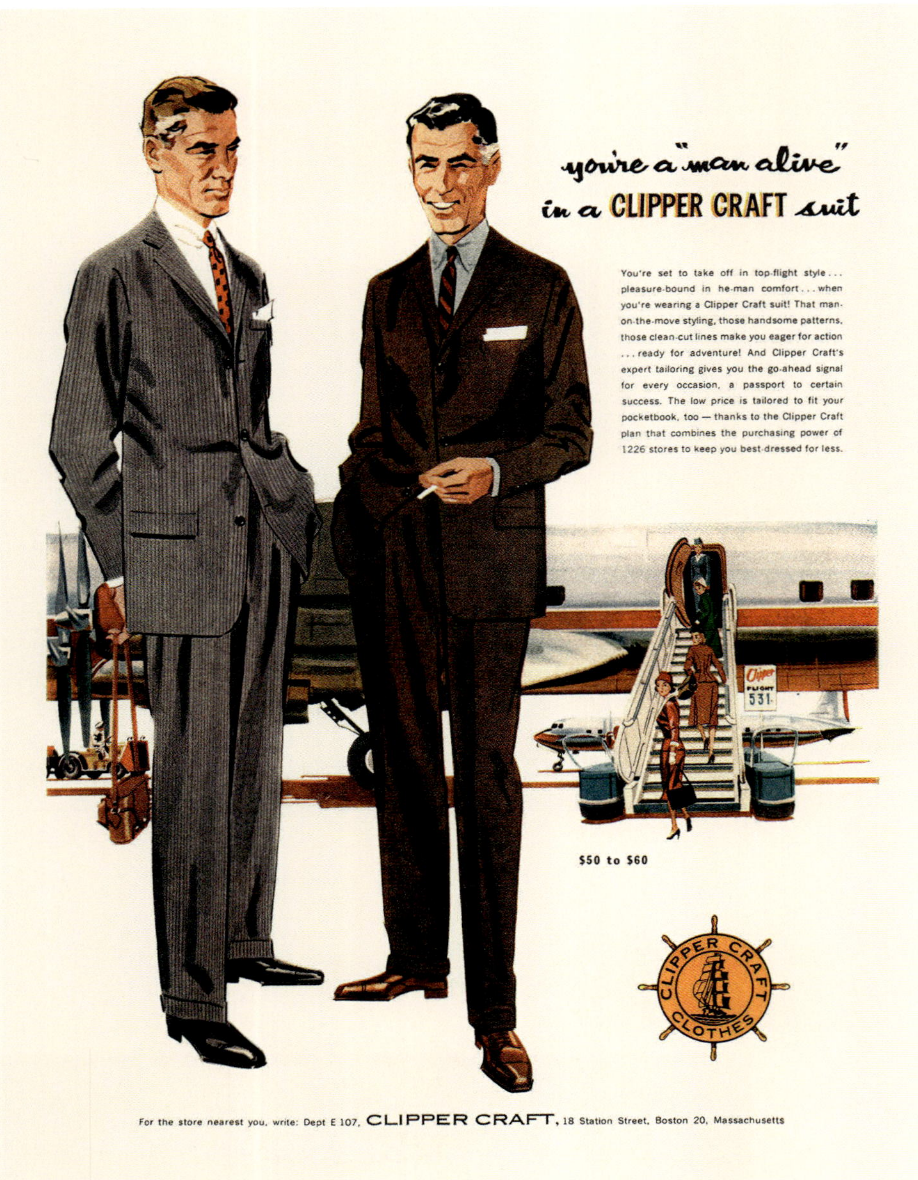
you're a "man alive"
in a CLIPPER CRAFT suit
You're set to take off in top-flight style... pleasure-bound in he-man comfort... when you're wearing a Clipper Craft suit! That man-on-the-move styling, those handsome patterns, those clean-cut lines make you eager for action ... ready for adventure! And Clipper Craft's expert tailoring gives you the go-ahead signal for every occasion, a passport to certain success. The low price is tailored to fit your pocketbook, too — thanks to the Clipper Craft plan that combines the purchasing power of 1226 stores to keep you best-dressed for less.
Clipper
FLIGHT
531
$50 to $60
CLIPPER CRAFT CLOTHES
For the store nearest you, write: Dept E 107, CLIPPER CRAFT, 18 Station Street, Boston 20, Massachusetts

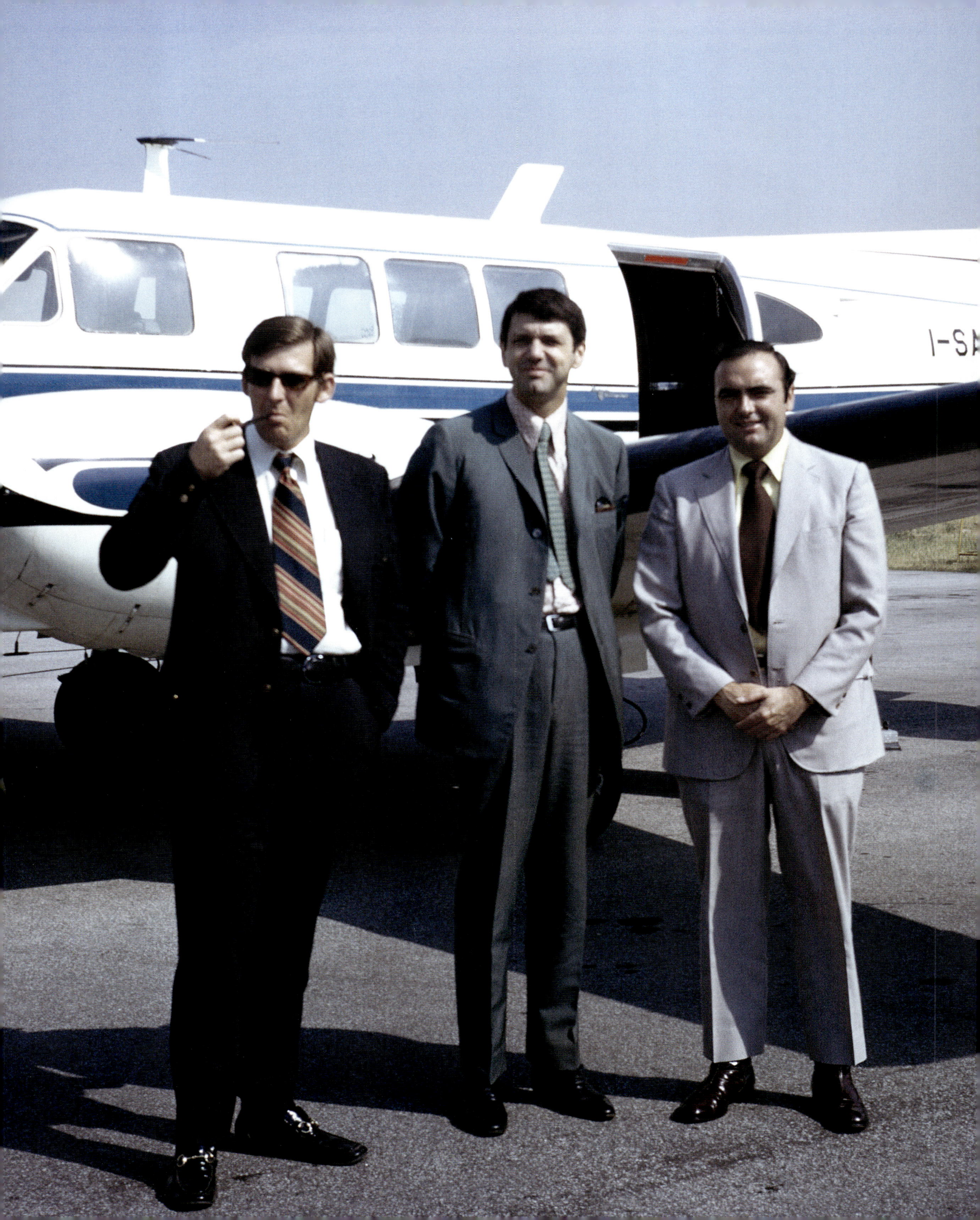
I-SA

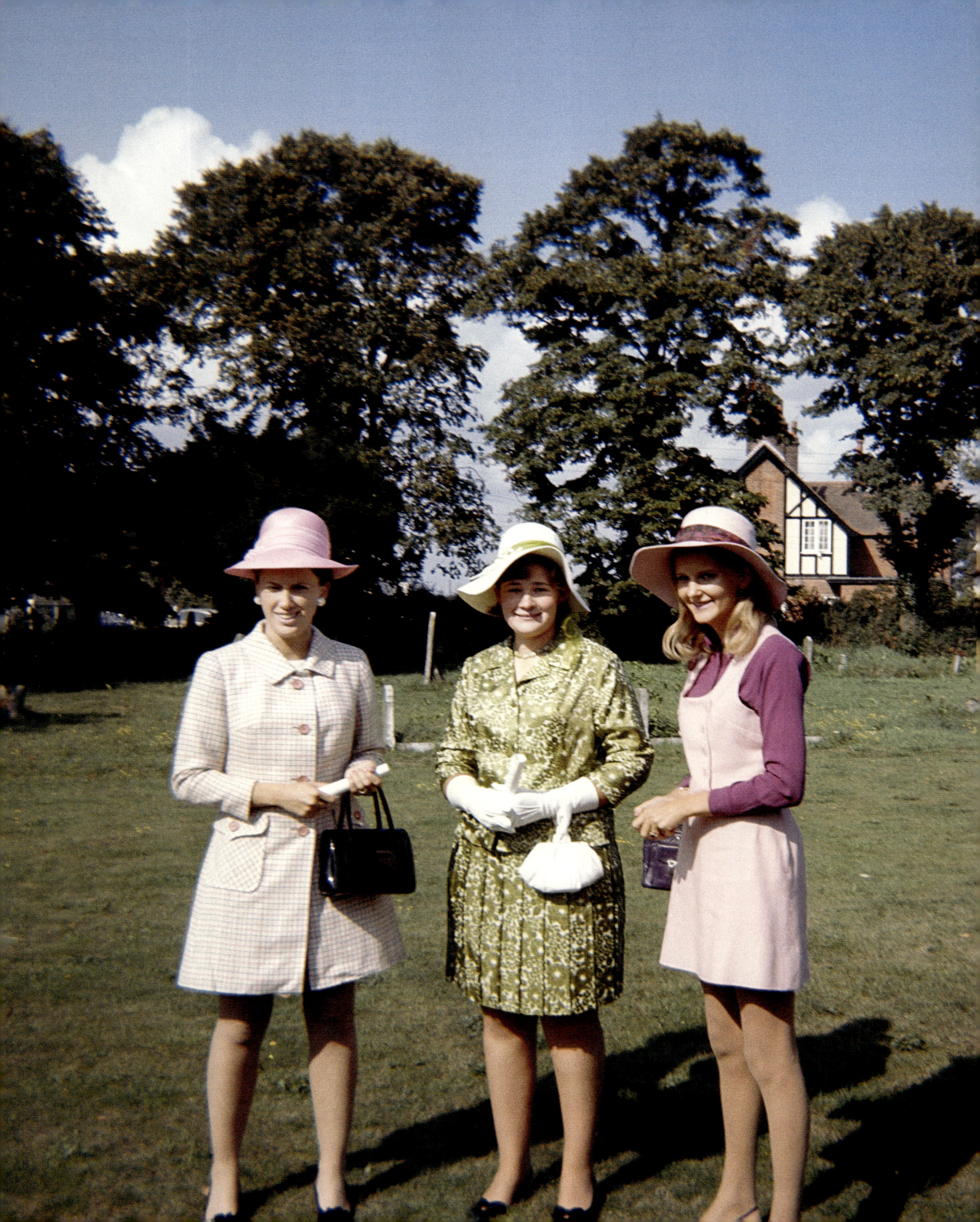

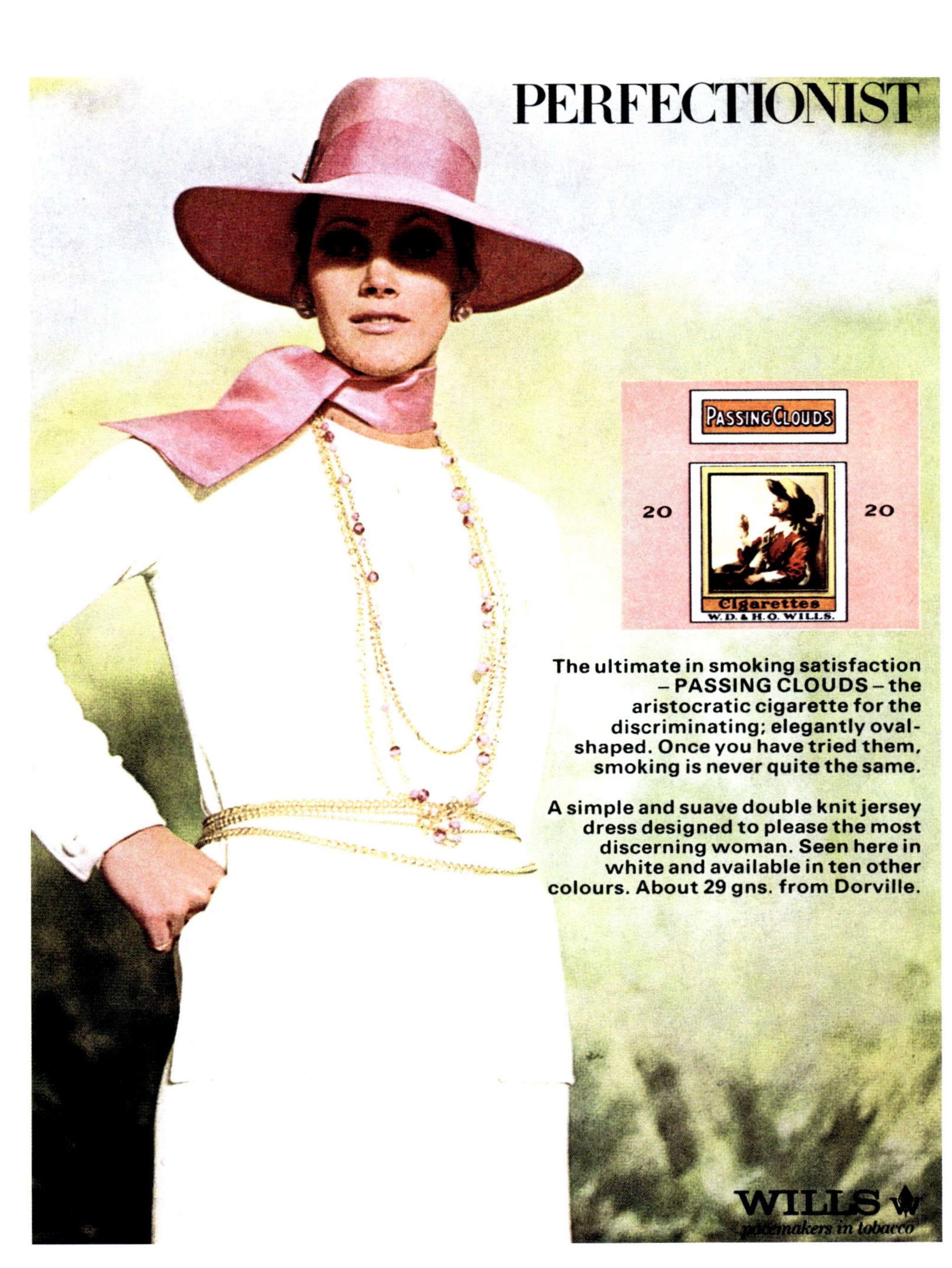
PERFECTIONIST
PASSING CLOUDS
20
20
Cigarettes
W.D. & H.O. WILLS.
The ultimate in smoking satisfaction – PASSING CLOUDS – the aristocratic cigarette for the discriminating; elegantly oval-shaped. Once you have tried them, smoking is never quite the same.
A simple and suave double knit jersey dress designed to please the most discerning woman. Seen here in white and available in ten other colours. About 29 gns. from Dorville.
WILLS
pacemakers in tobacco

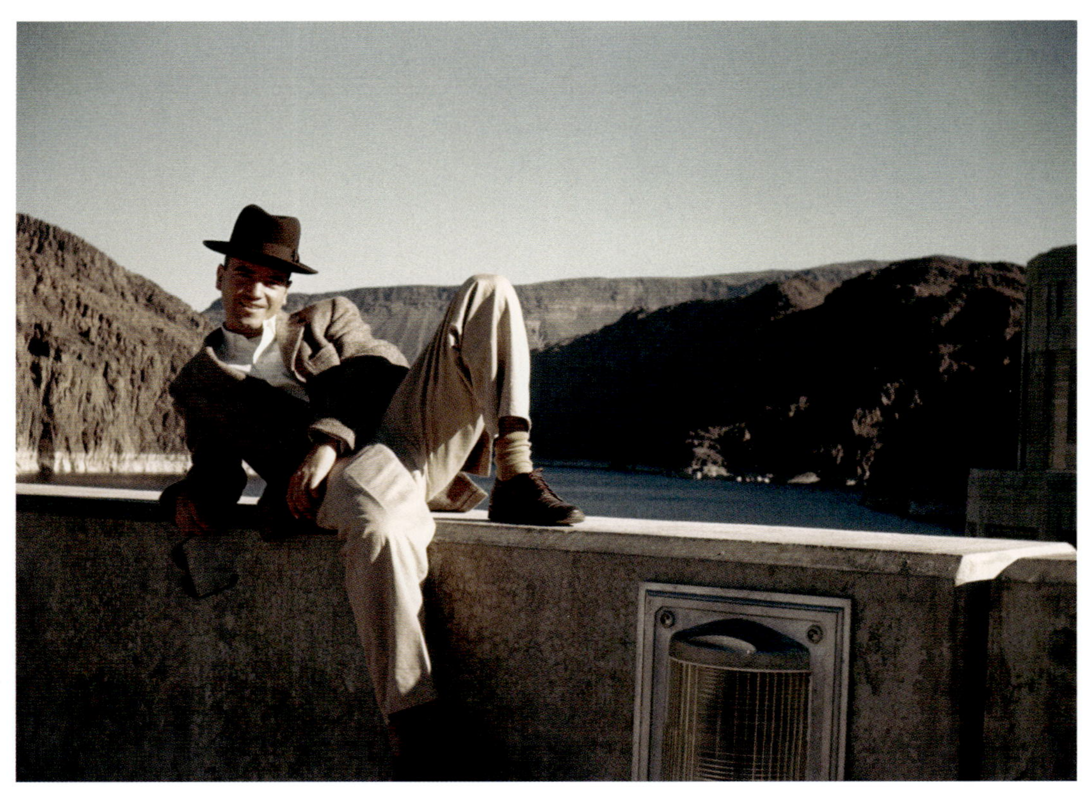

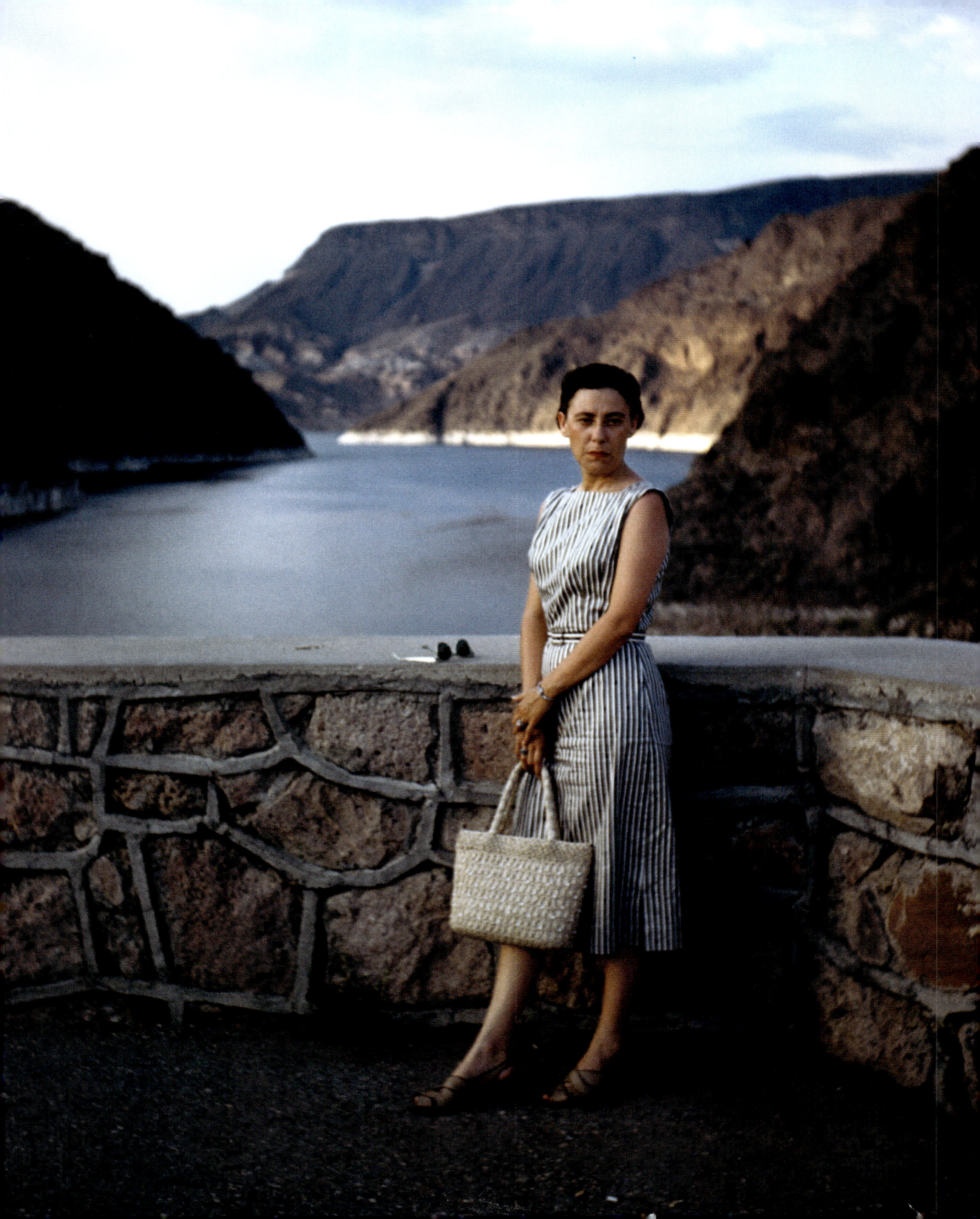

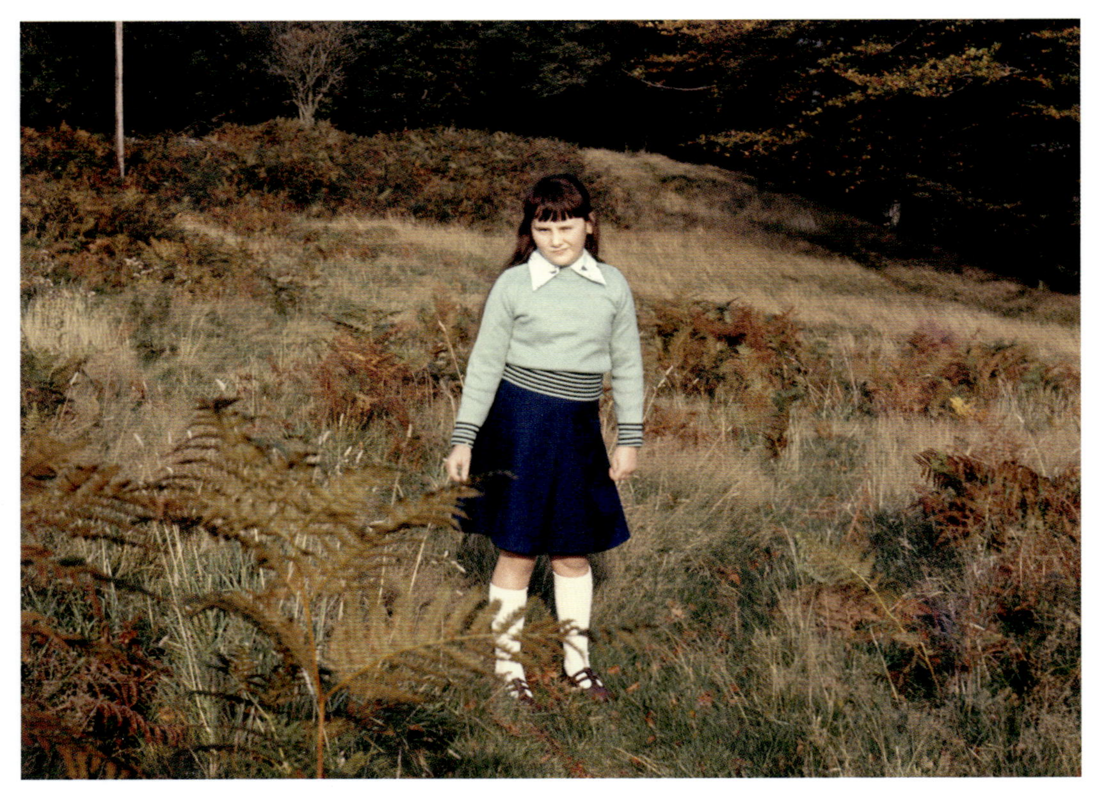

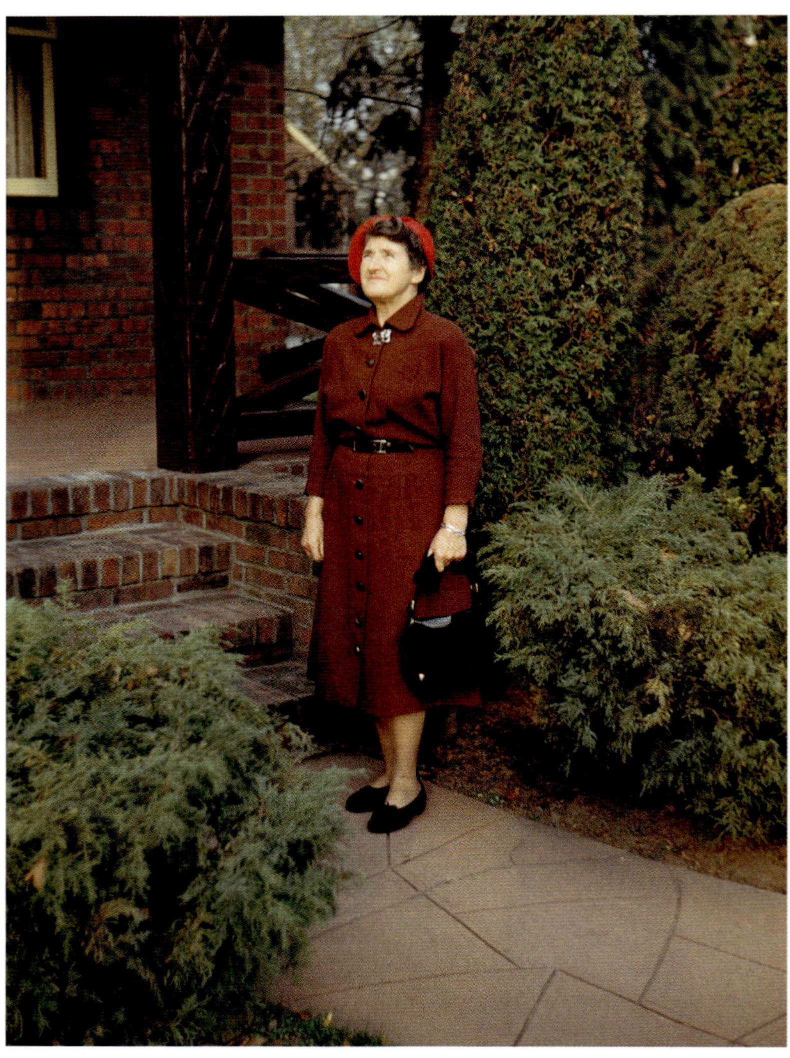

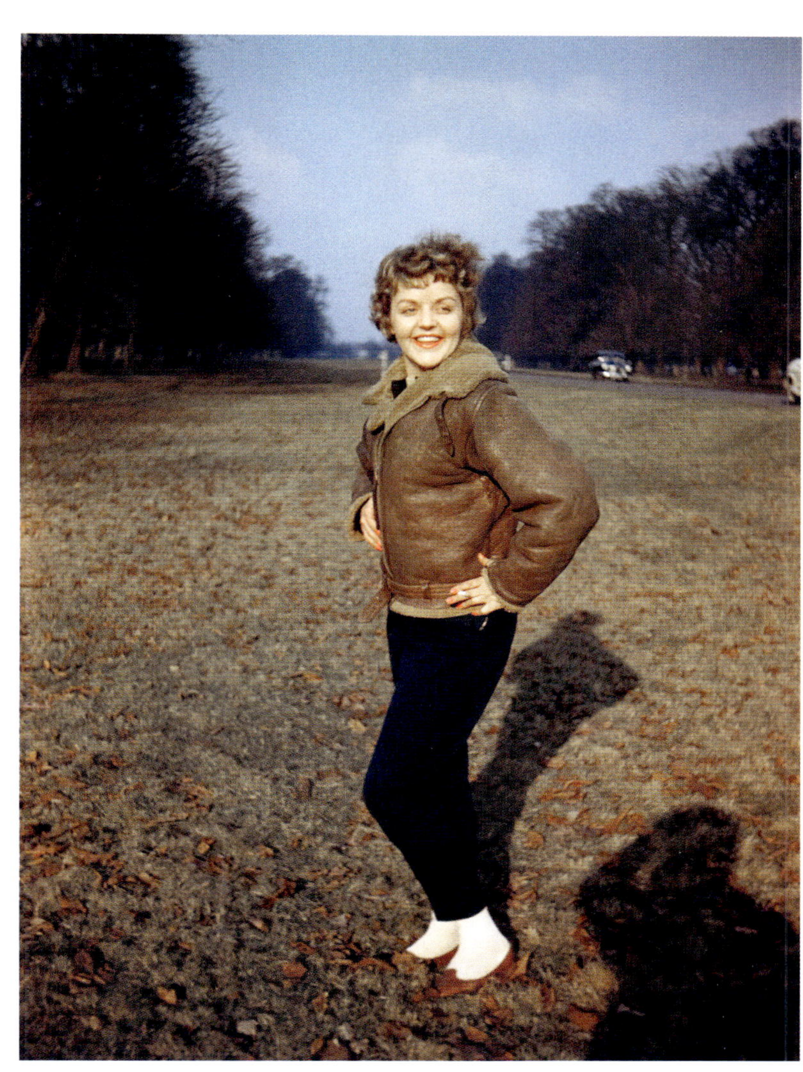

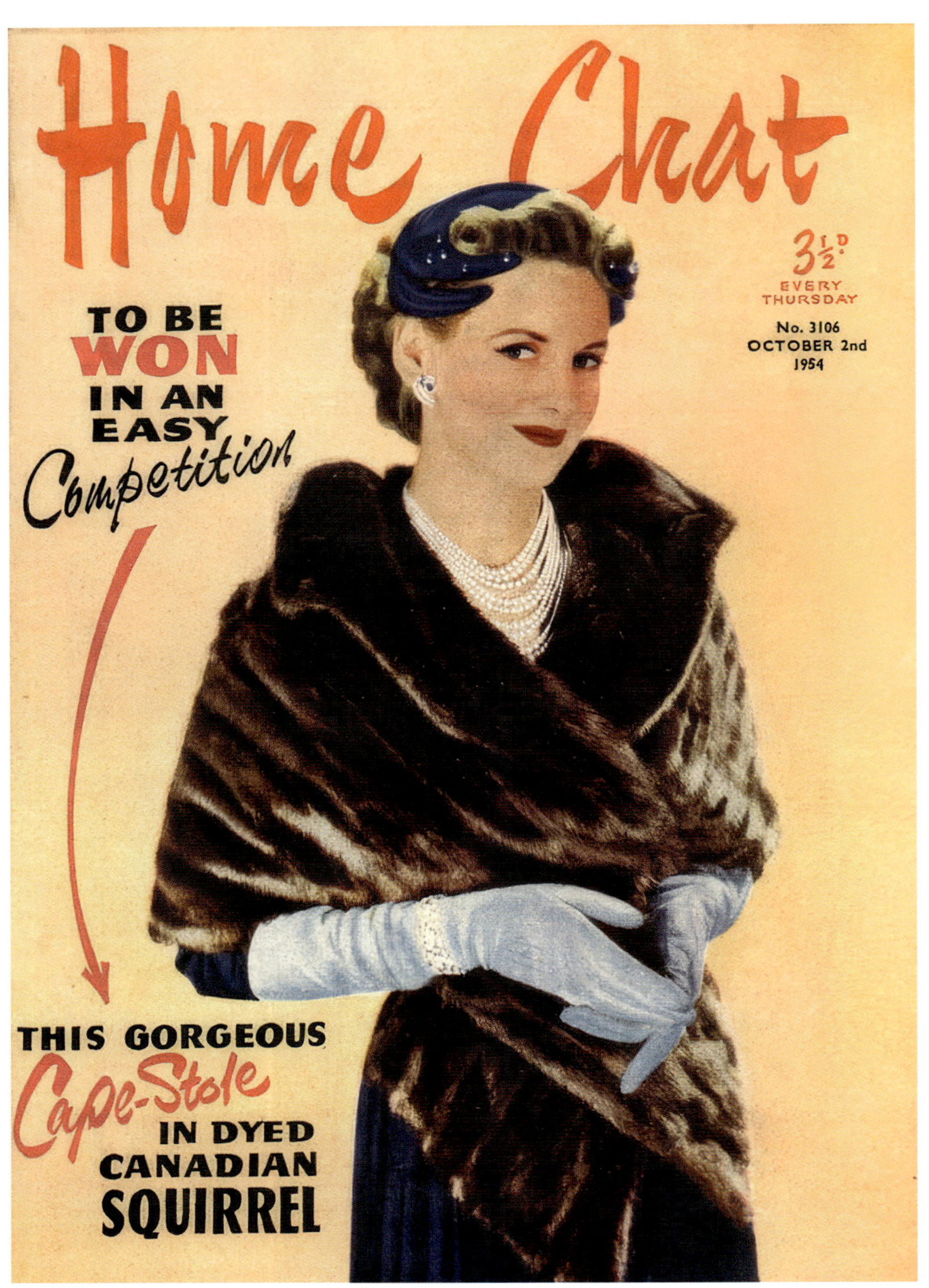
Home Chat
3½D
EVERY THURSDAY
No. 3106
OCTOBER 2nd
1954
TO BE
WON
IN AN
EASY
Competition
THIS GORGEOUS
Cape-Stole
IN DYED
CANADIAN
SQUIRREL

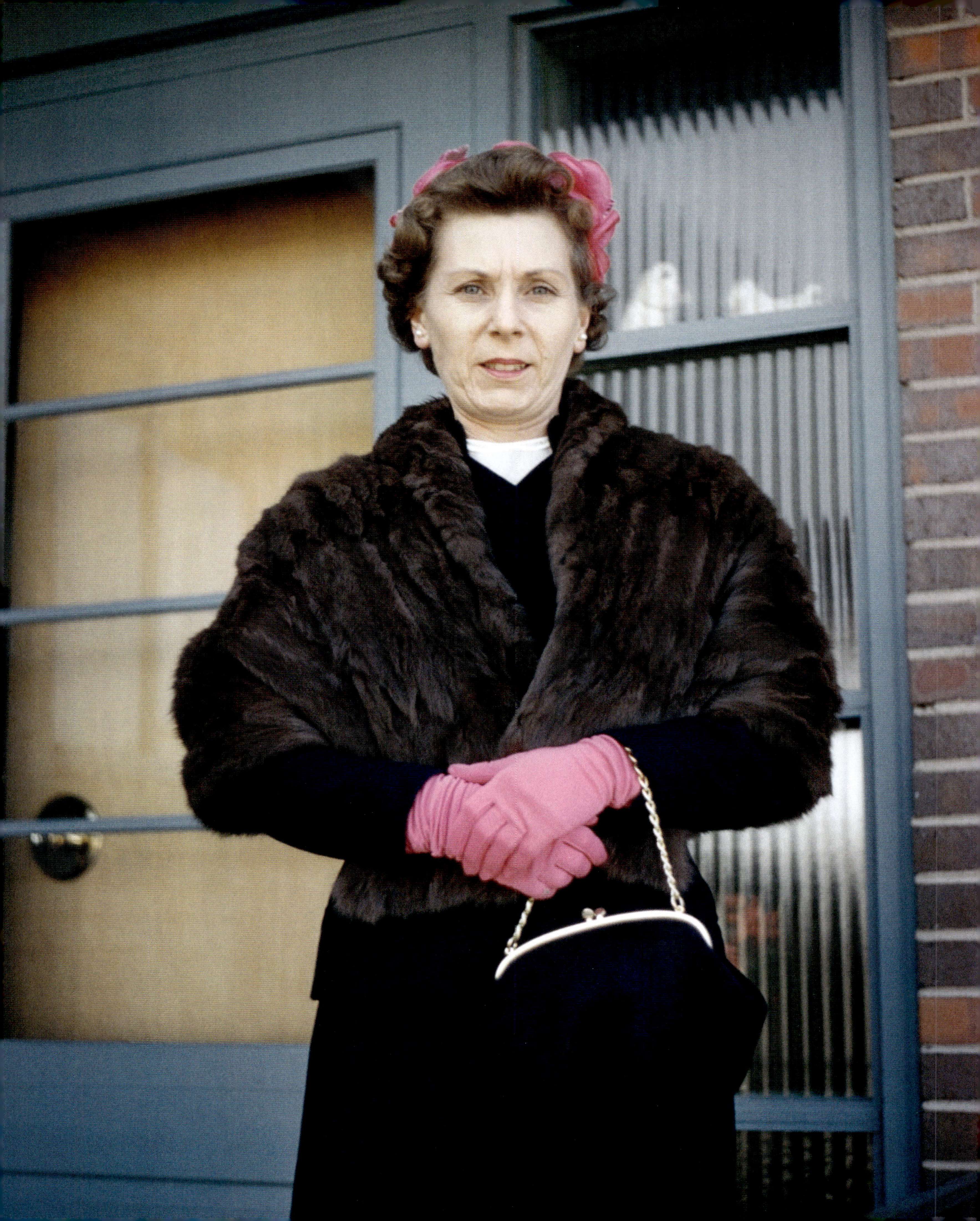

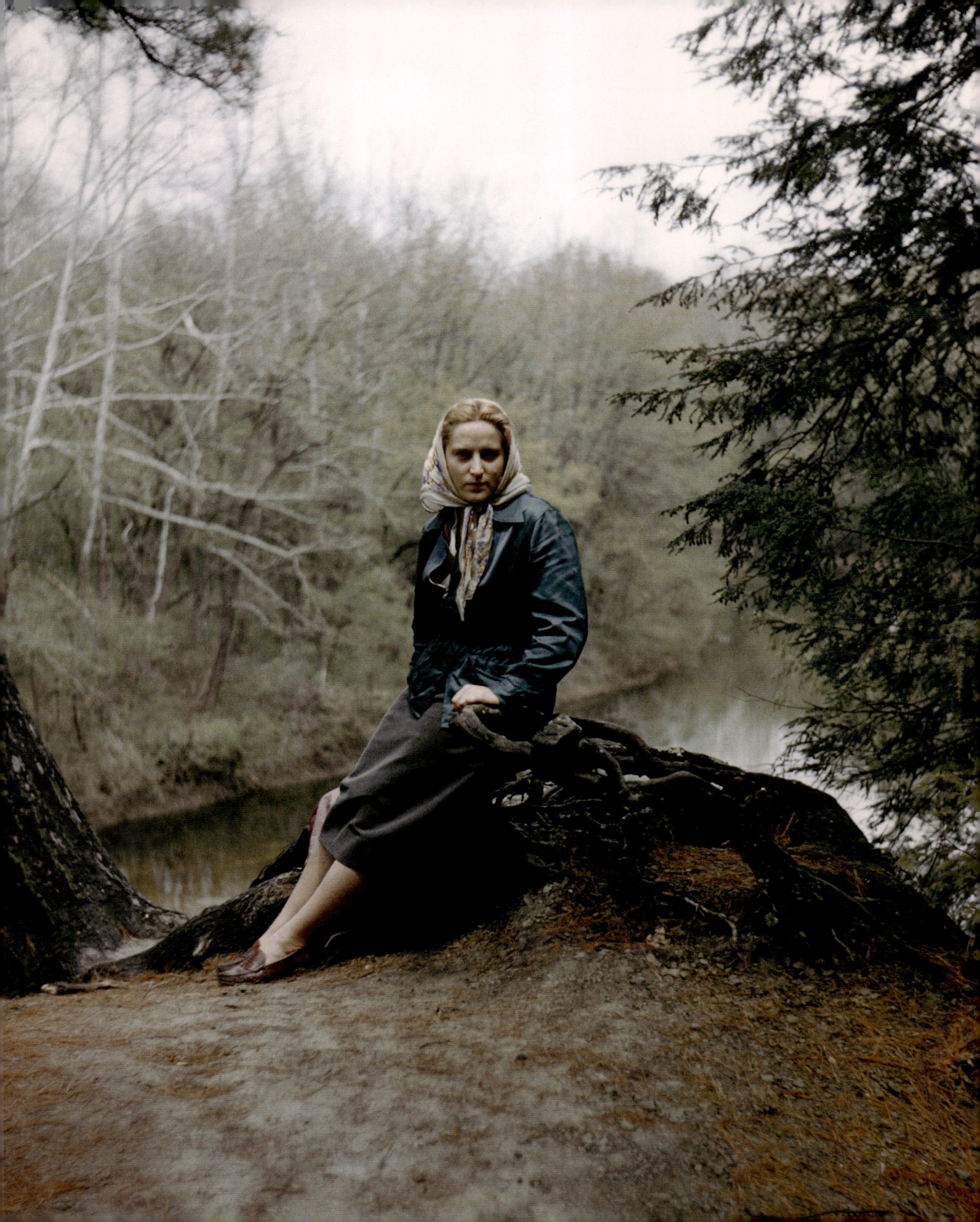

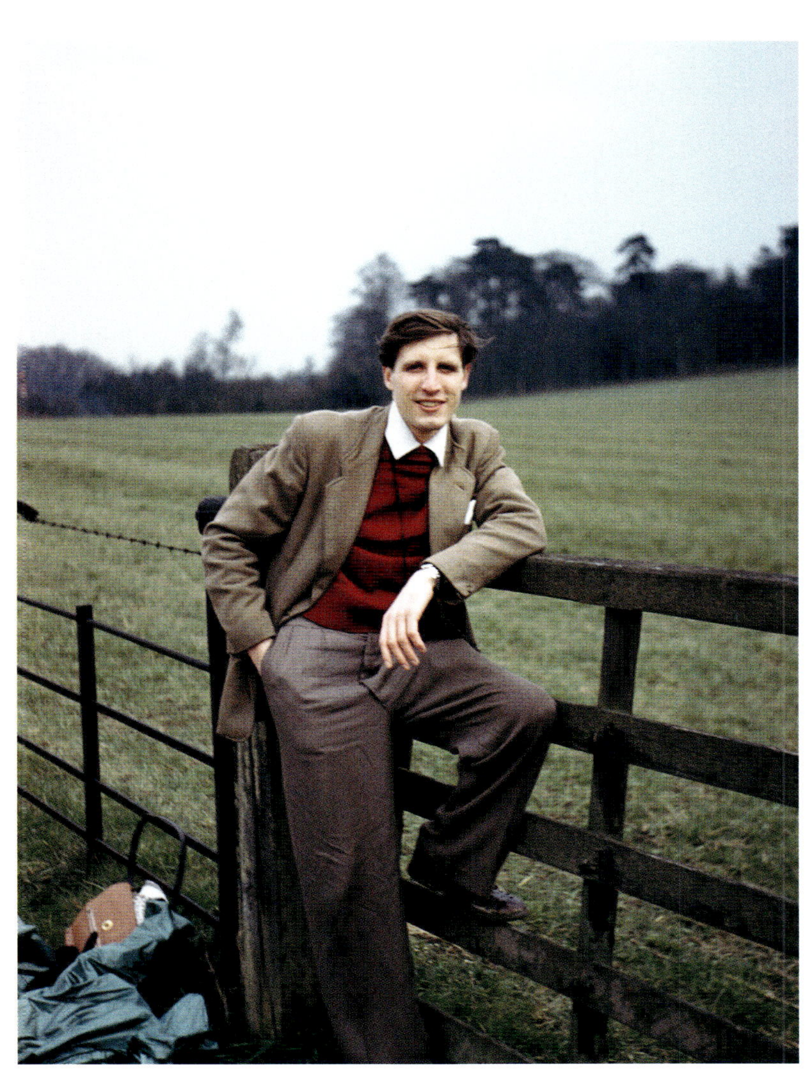

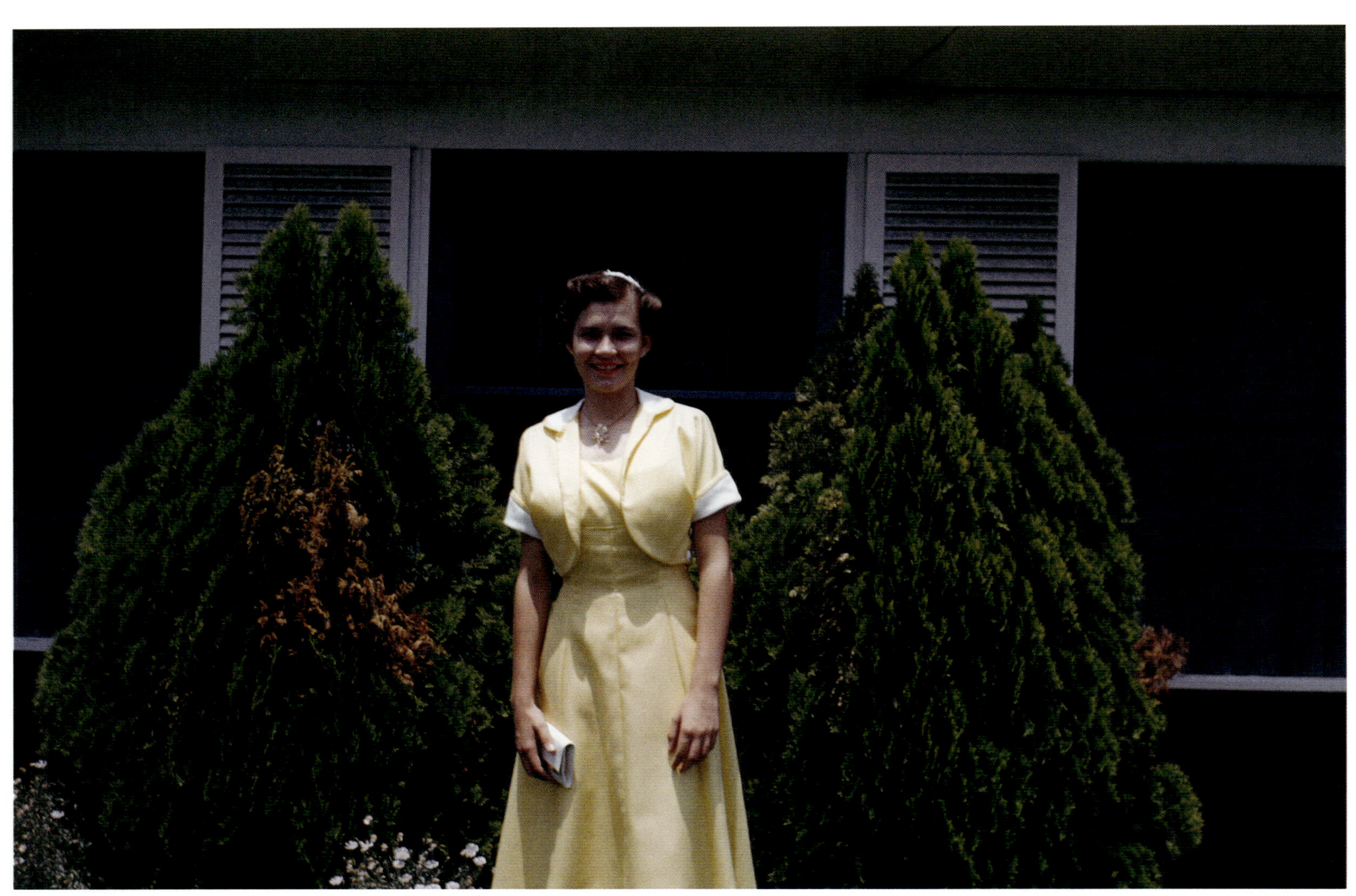

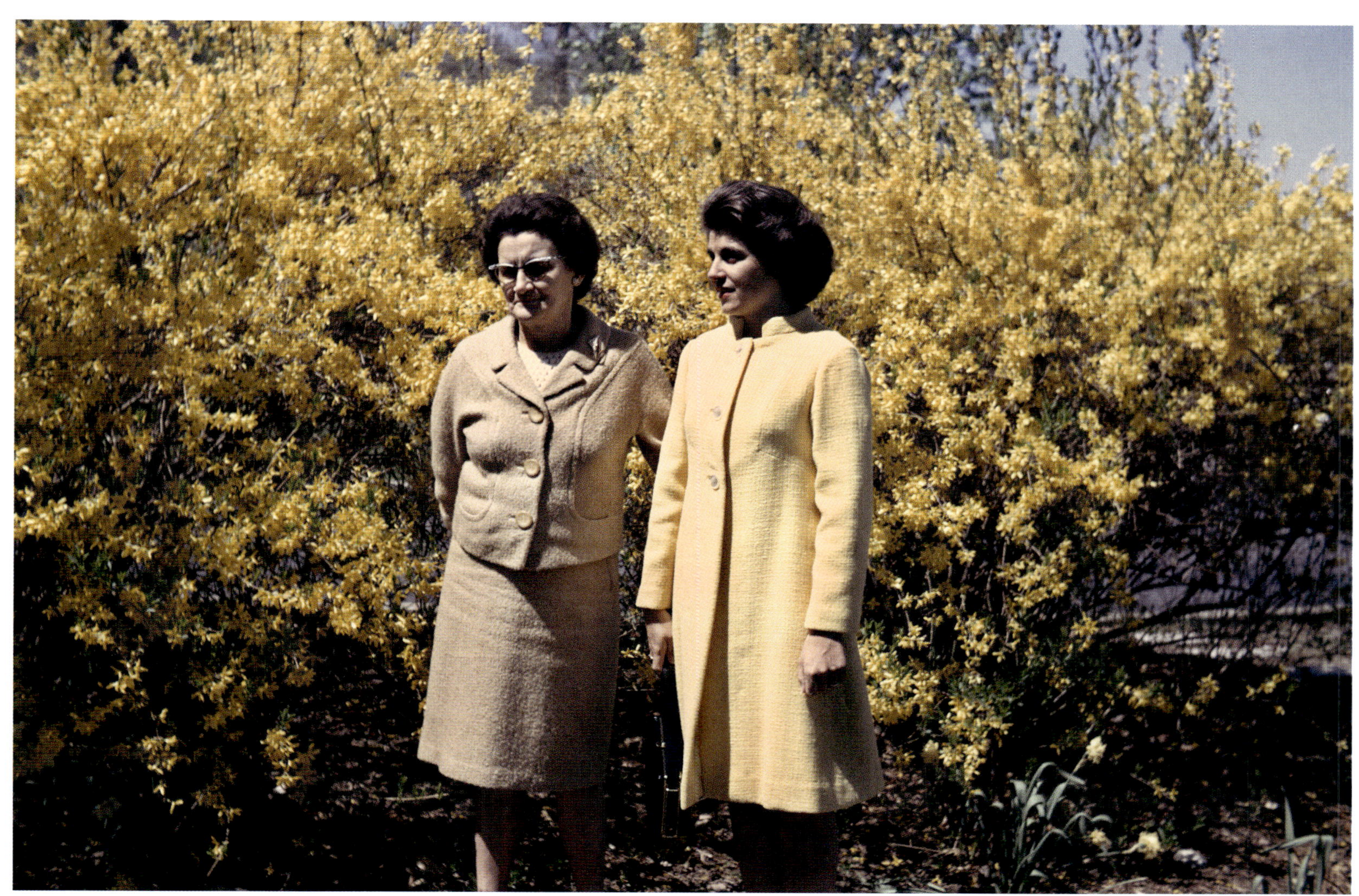

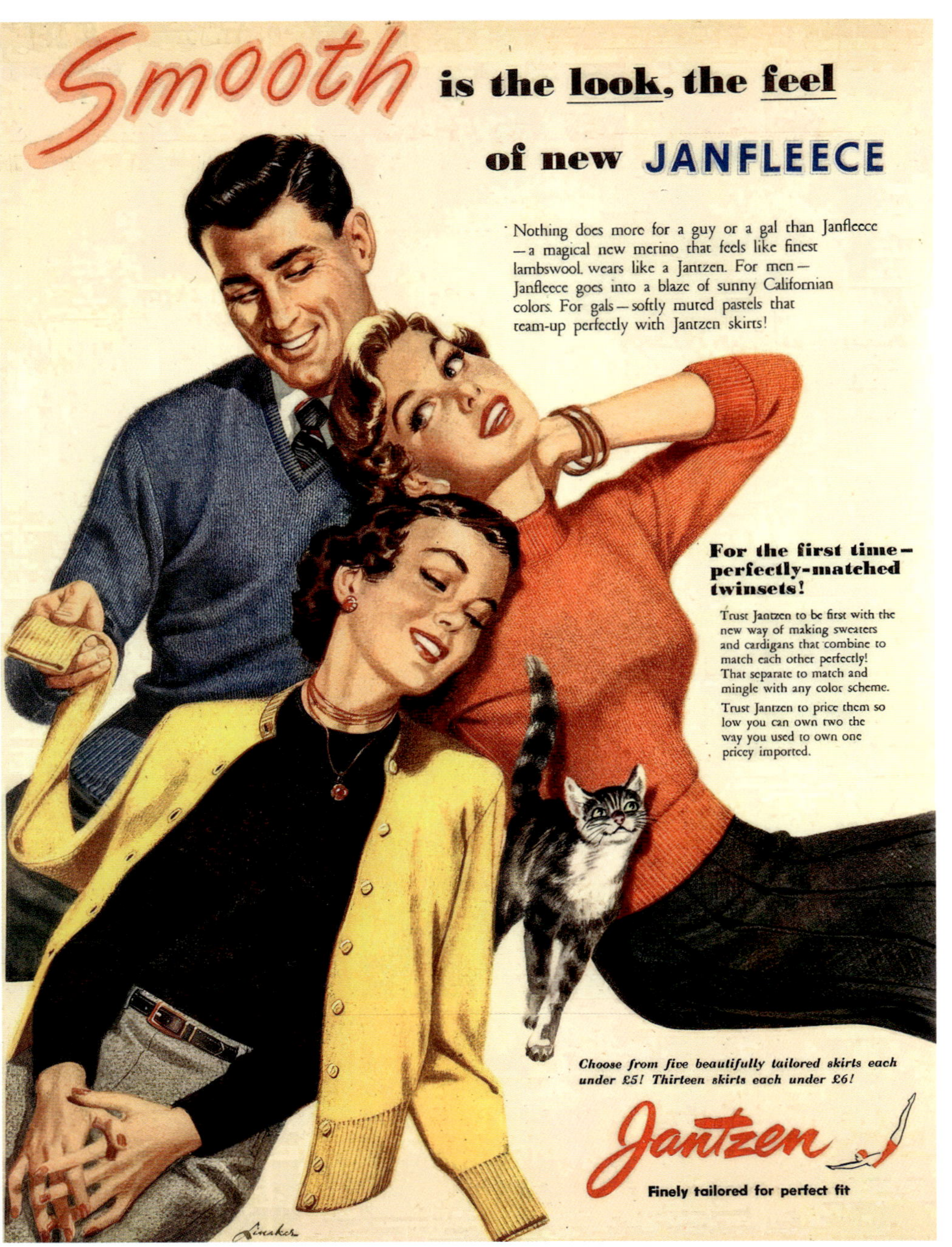
Smooth is the look, the feel
of new JANFLEECE
Nothing does more for a guy or a gal than Janfleece —a magical new merino that feels like finest lambswool. wears like a Jantzen. For men— Janfleece goes into a blaze of sunny Californian colors. For gals—softly muted pastels that team-up perfectly with Jantzen skirts!
For the first time— perfectly-matched twinsets!
Trust Jantzen to be first with the new way of making sweaters and cardigans that combine to match each other perfectly! That separate to match and mingle with any color scheme.
Trust Jantzen to price them so low you can own two the way you used to own one pricey imported.
Choose from five beautifully tailored skirts each under £5! Thirteen skirts each under £6!
Jantzen
Finely tailored for perfect fit

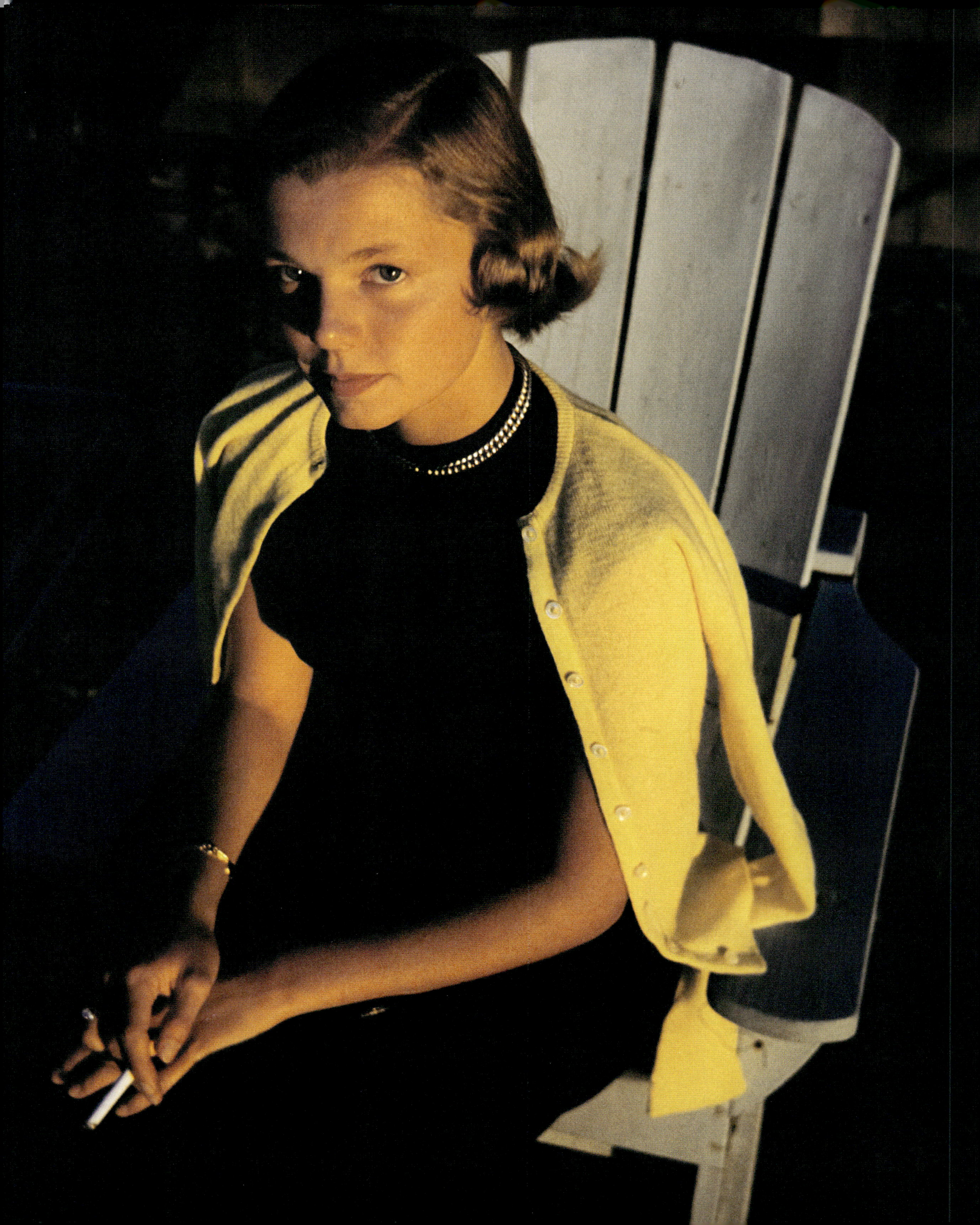

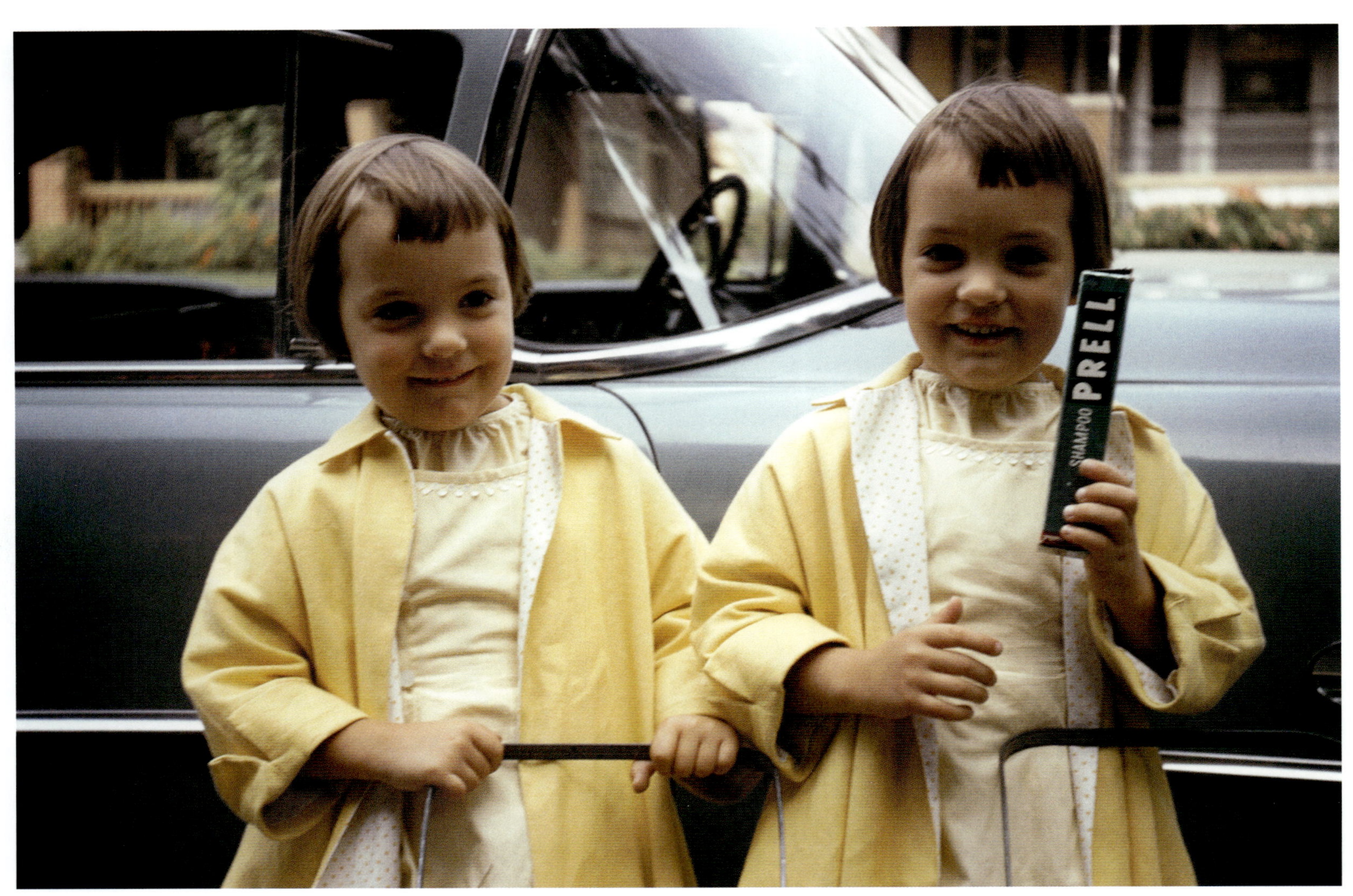
SHAMPOO
PRELL

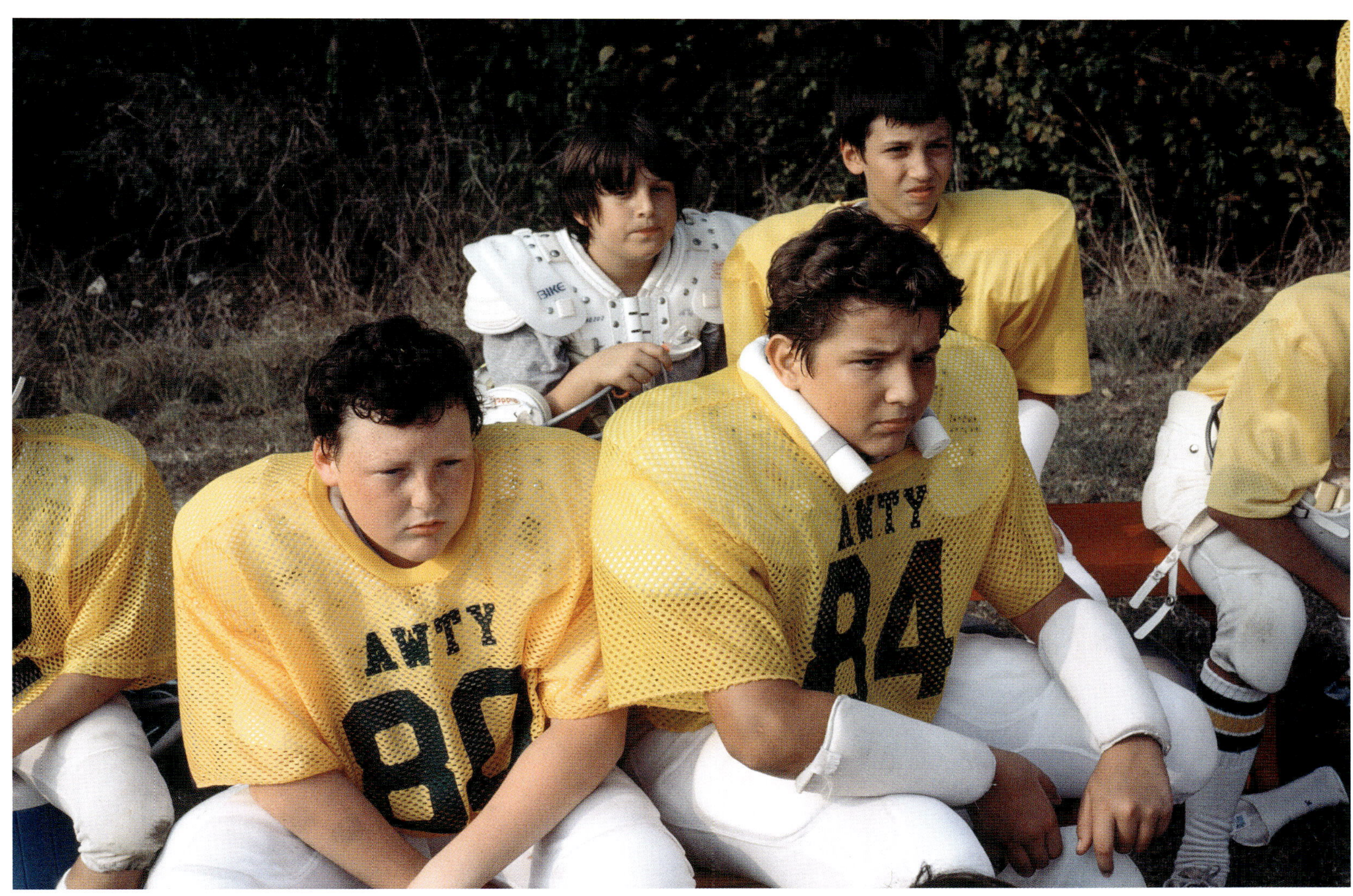
AWTY
AWTY
84

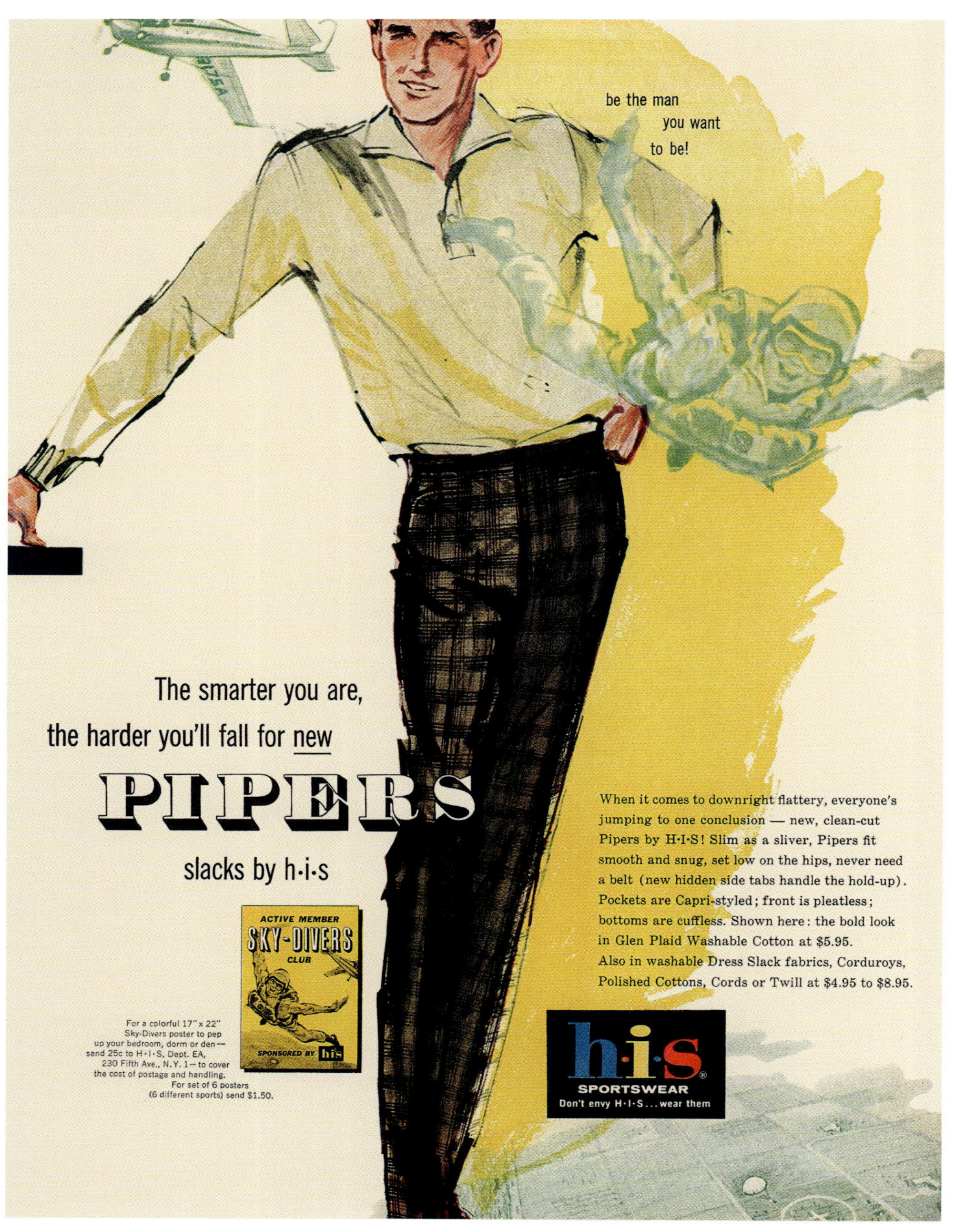
be the man
you want
to be!
The smarter you are,
the harder you'll fall for new
PIPERS
slacks by h·i·s
ACTIVE MEMBER
SKY-DIVERS
CLUB
SPONSORED BY his
For a colorful 17" x 22" Sky-Divers poster to pep up your bedroom, dorm or den — send 25c to H·I·S, Dept. EA, 230 Fifth Ave., N.Y. 1 — to cover the cost of postage and handling. For set of 6 posters (6 different sports) send $1.50.
When it comes to downright flattery, everyone's jumping to one conclusion — new, clean-cut Pipers by H·I·S! Slim as a sliver, Pipers fit smooth and snug, set low on the hips, never need a belt (new hidden side tabs handle the hold-up). Pockets are Capri-styled; front is pleatless; bottoms are cuffless. Shown here: the bold look in Glen Plaid Washable Cotton at $5.95.
Also in washable Dress Slack fabrics, Corduroys, Polished Cottons, Cords or Twill at $4.95 to $8.95.
h·i·s
SPORTSWEAR
Don't envy H·I·S... wear them

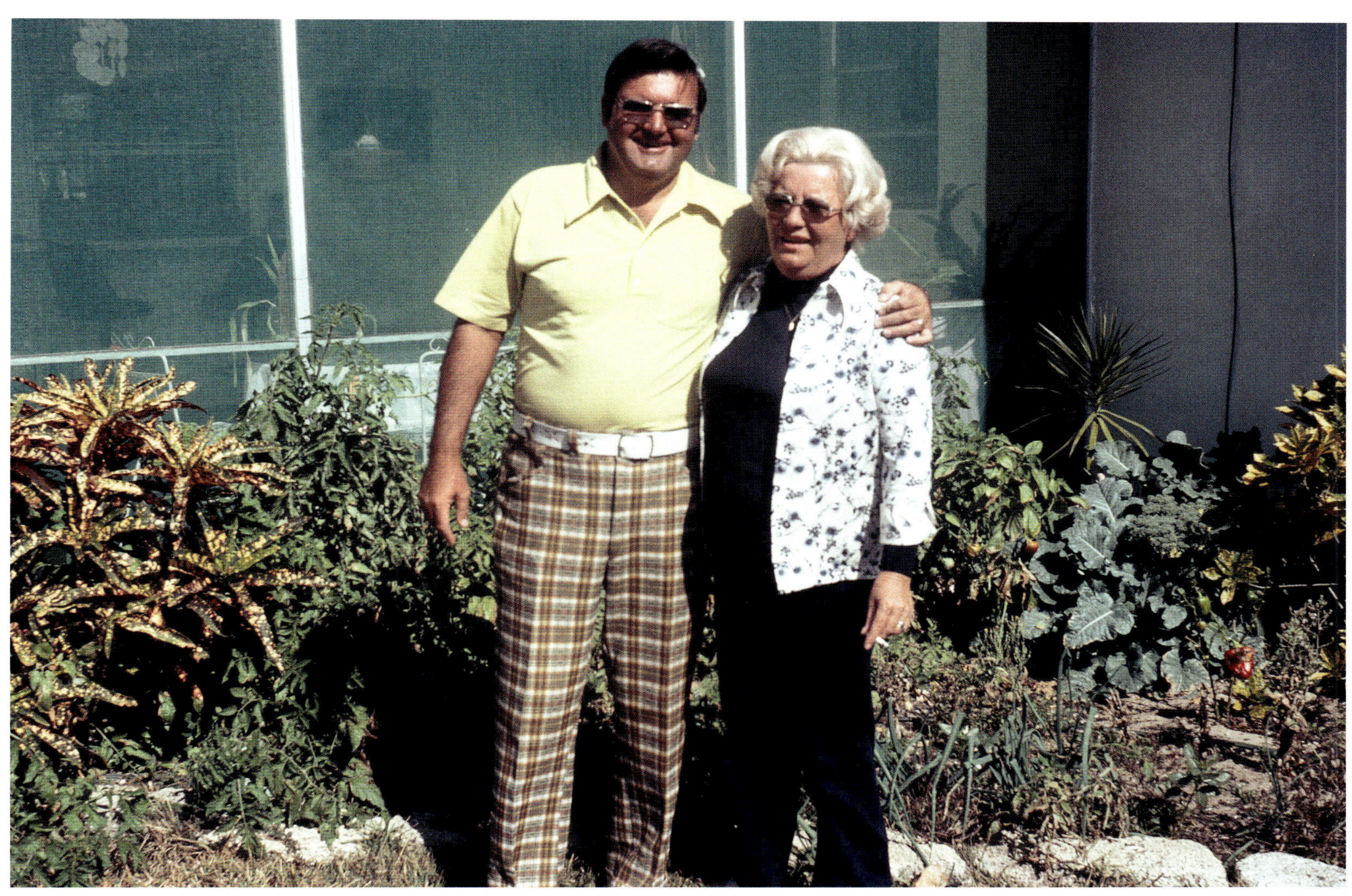

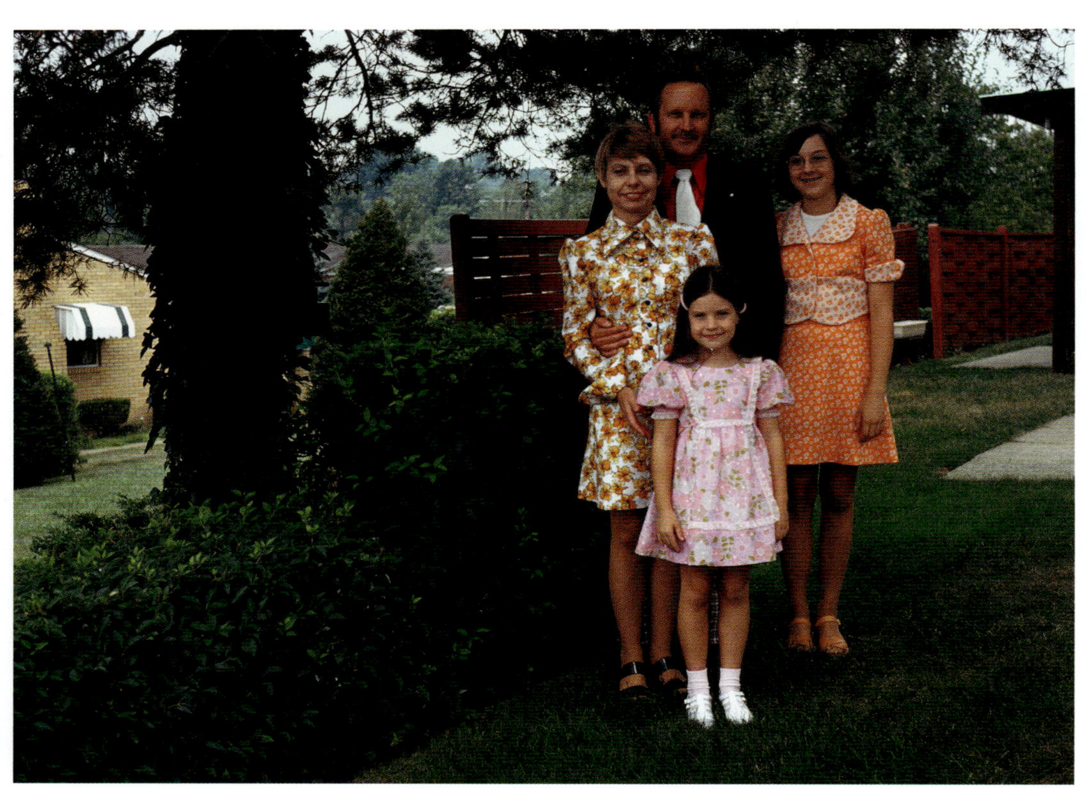

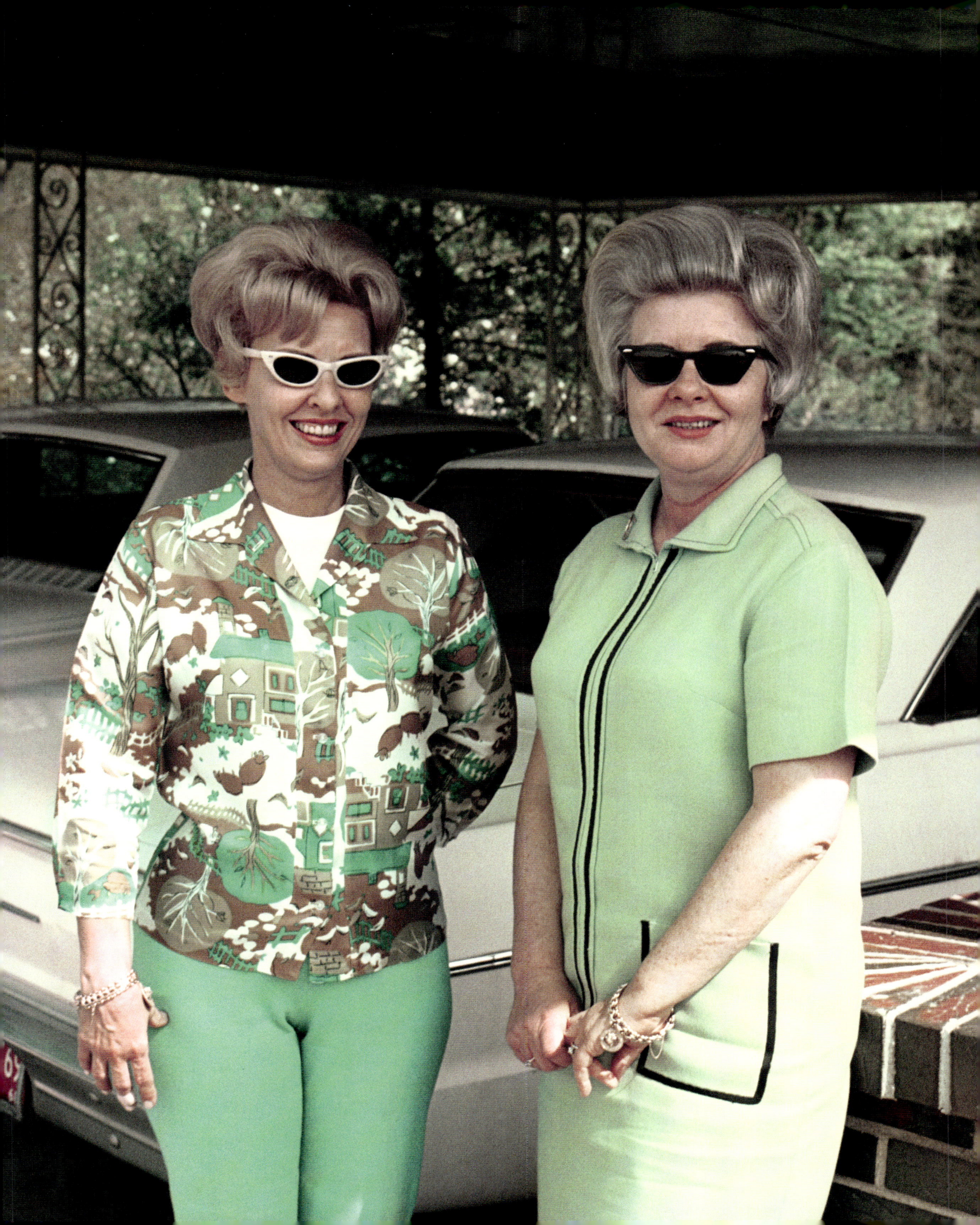

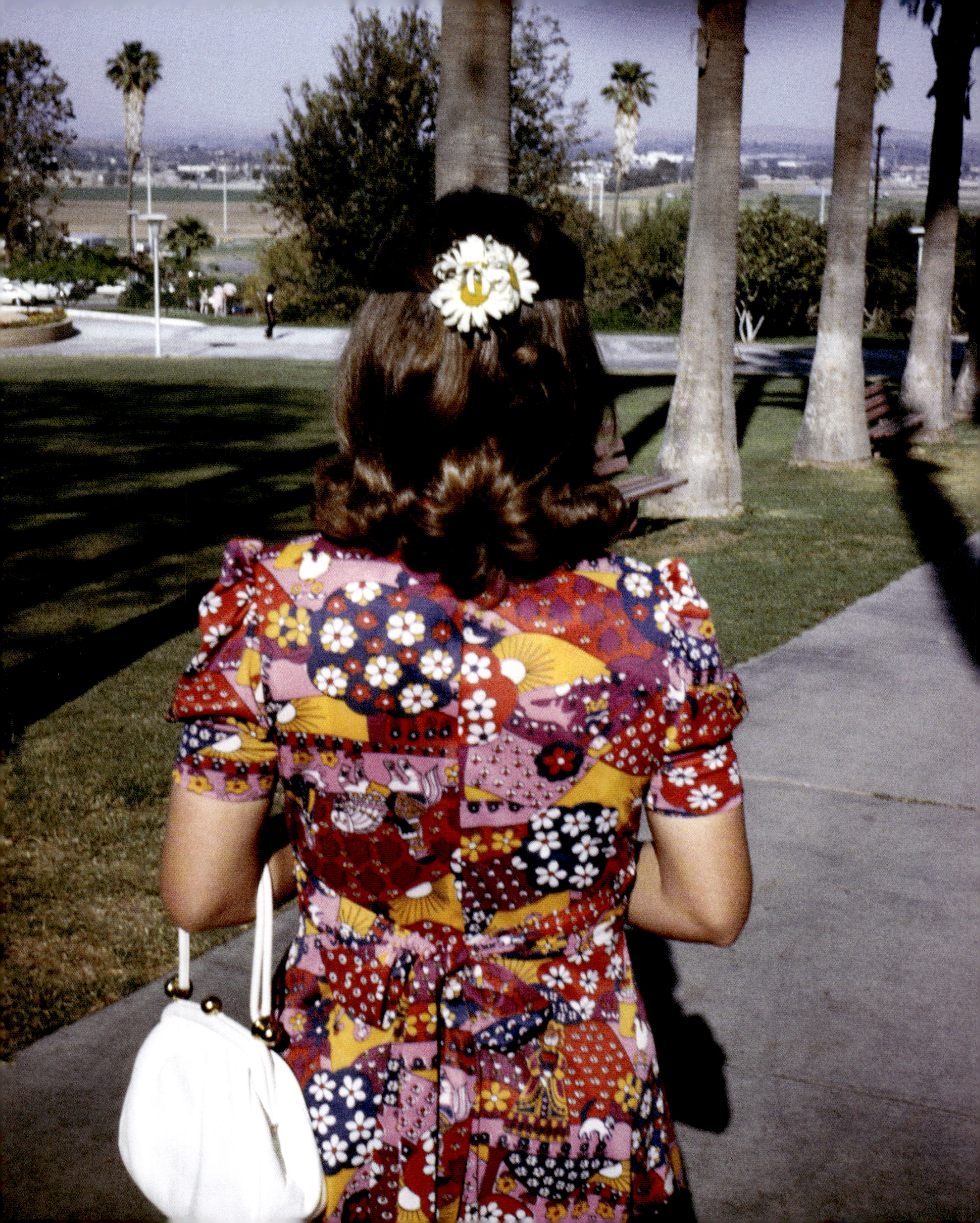

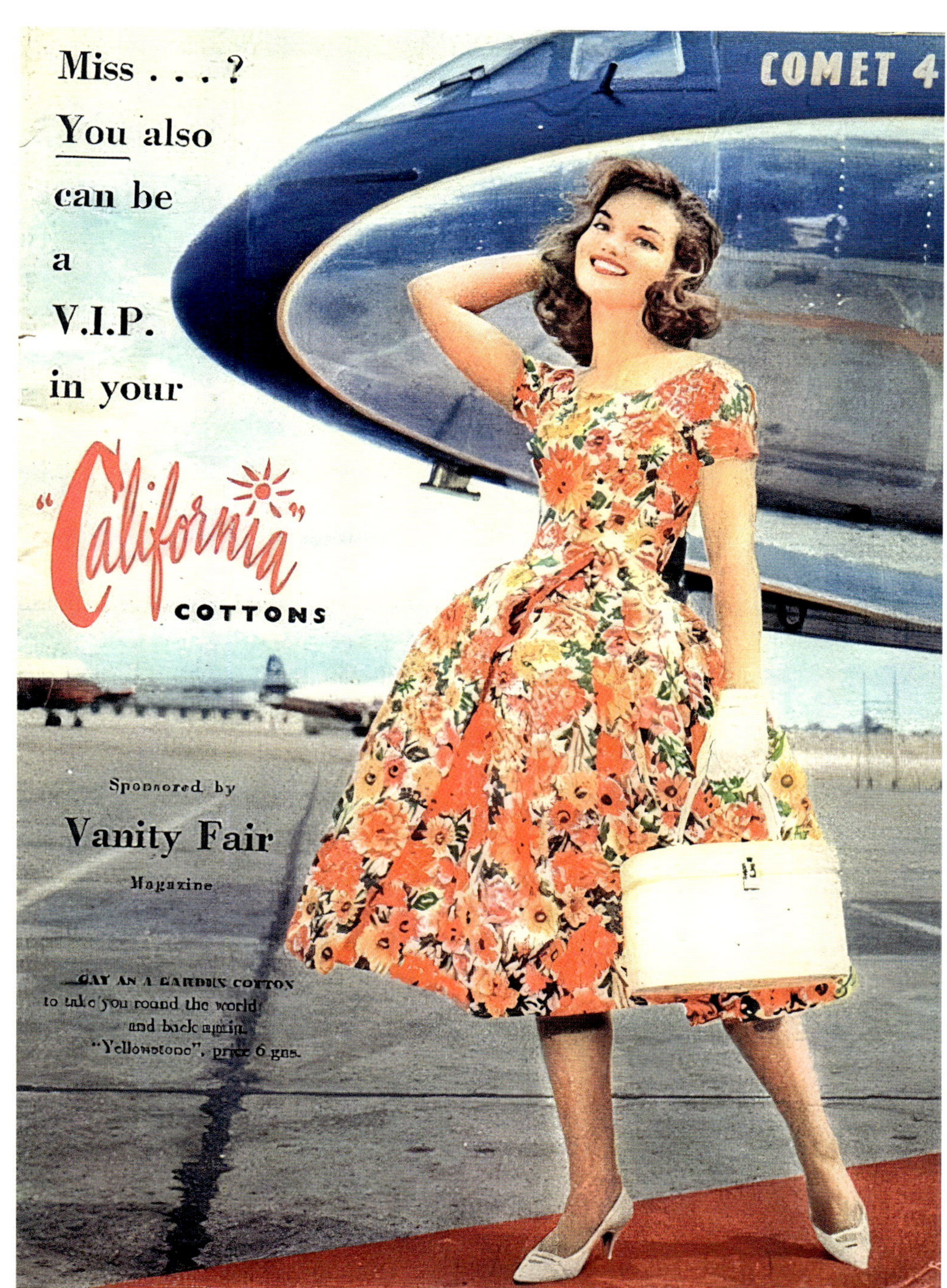
COMET 4
Miss . . . ?
You also
can be
a
V.I.P.
in your
"California"
COTTONS
Sponsored by
Vanity Fair
Magazine
—GAY AS A GARDEN COTTON
to take you round the world
and back again.
"Yellowstone", price 6 gns.

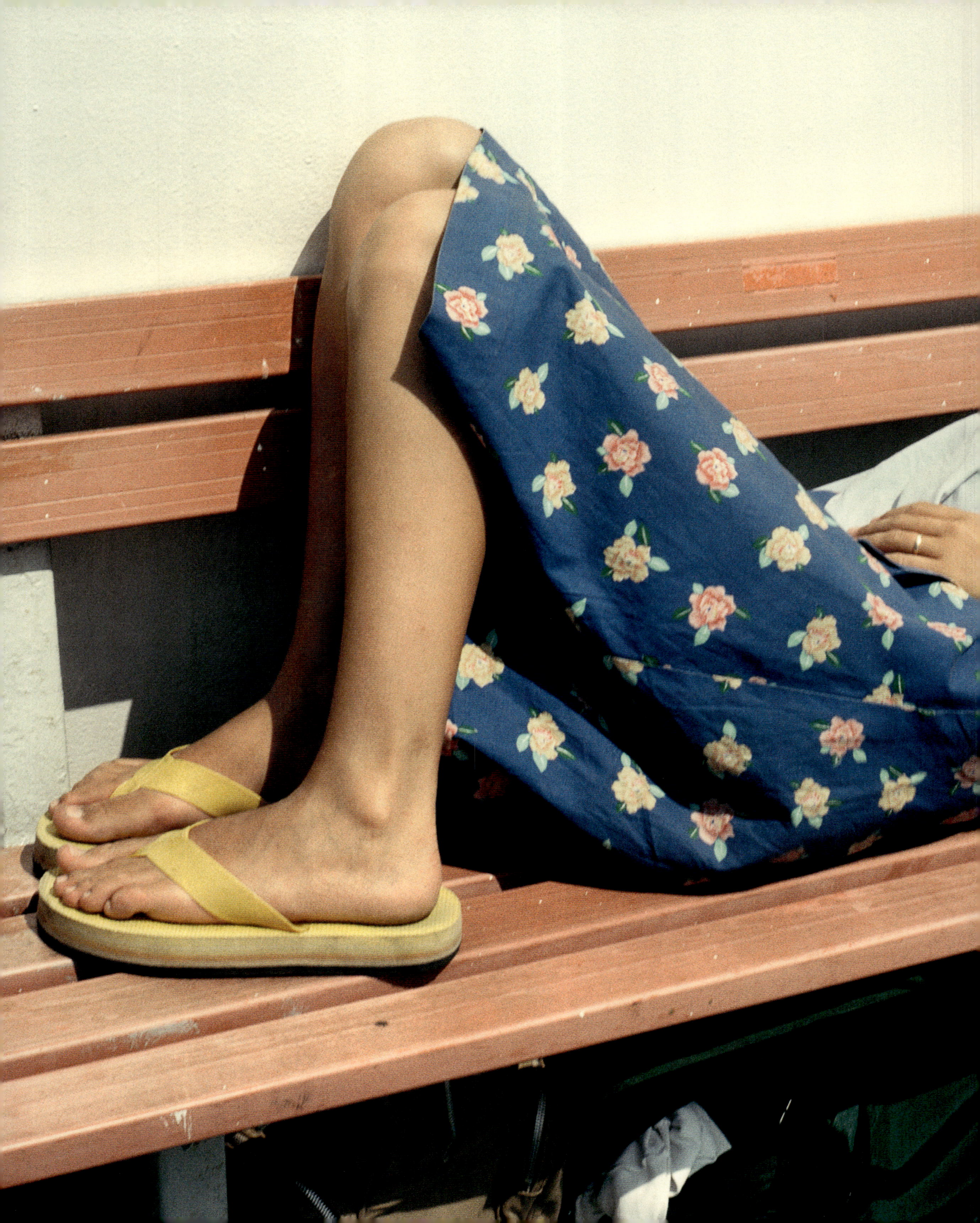

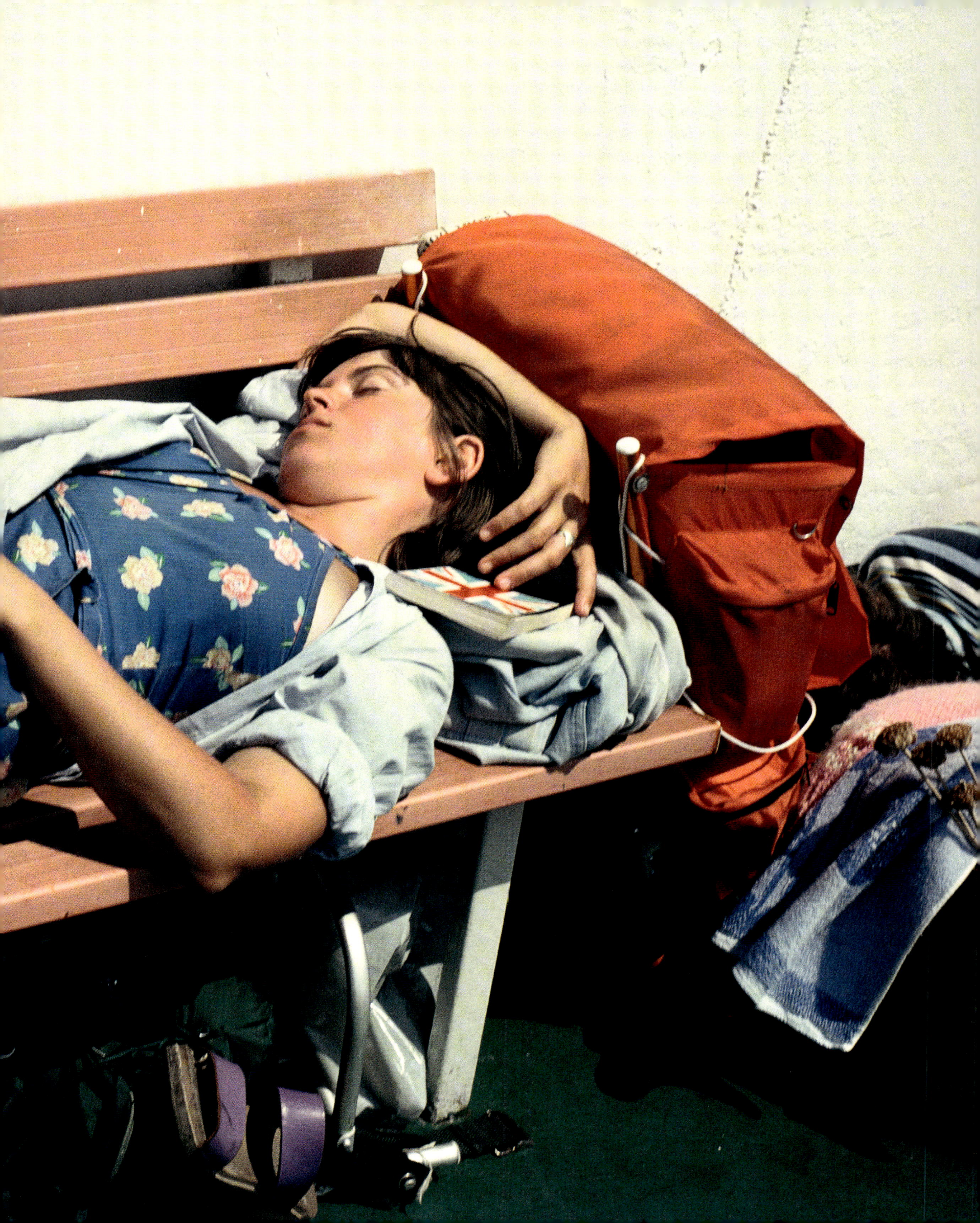

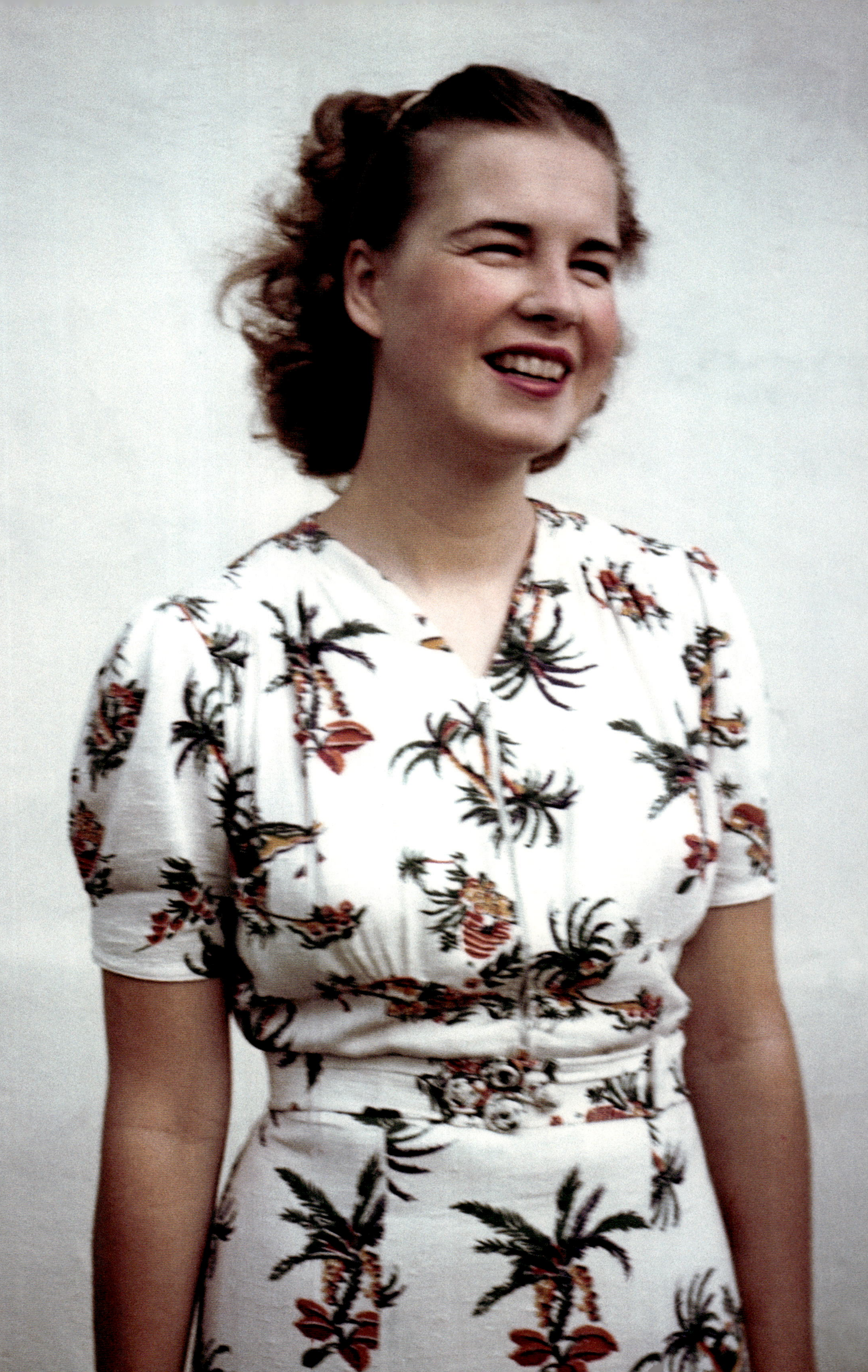

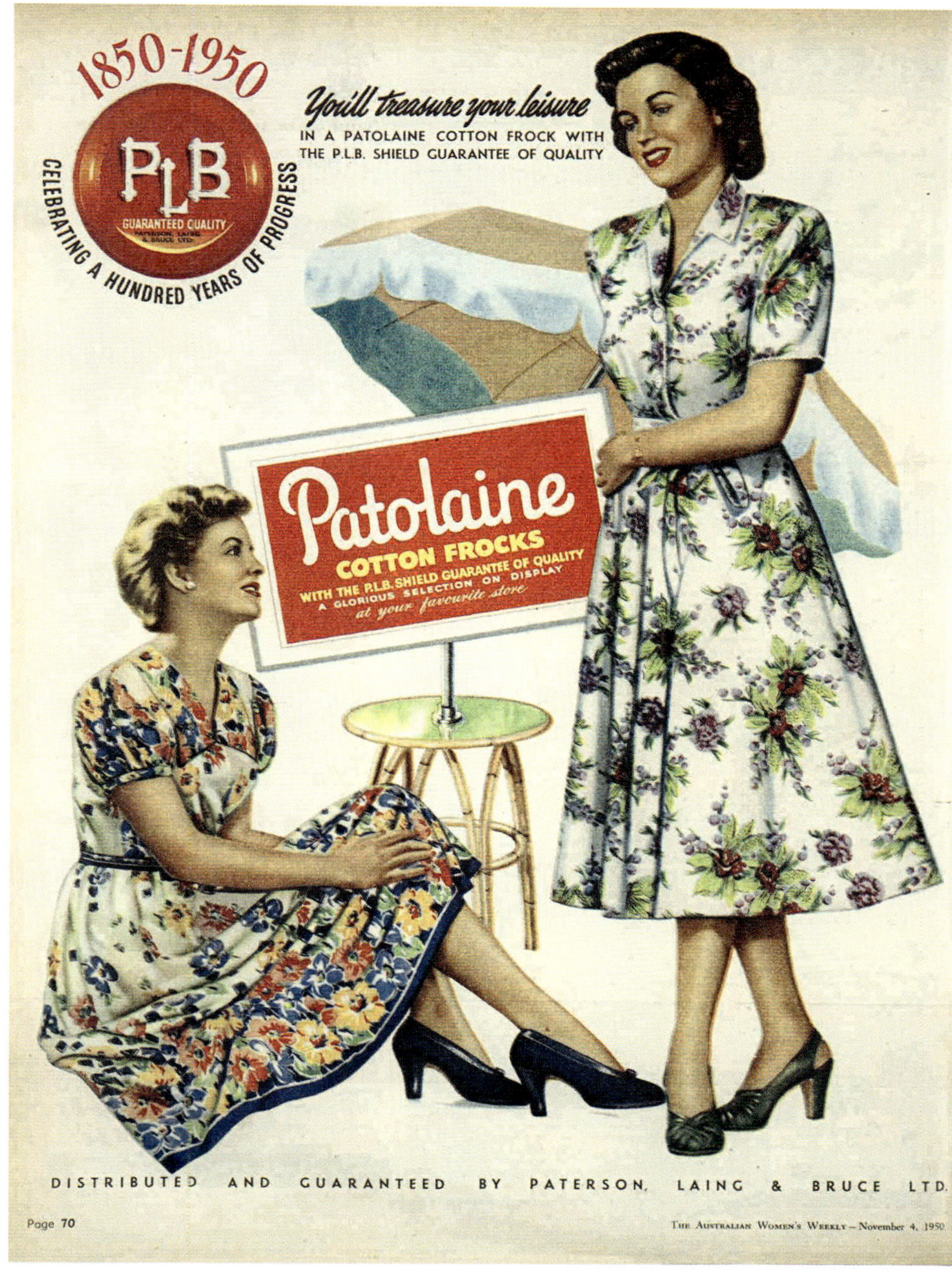
1850-1950
PLB
GUARANTEED QUALITY
CELEBRATING A HUNDRED YEARS OF PROGRESS
You'll treasure your leisure
IN A PATOLAINE COTTON FROCK WITH
THE P.L.B. SHIELD GUARANTEE OF QUALITY
Patolaine
COTTON FROCKS
WITH THE P.L.B. SHIELD GUARANTEE OF QUALITY
A GLORIOUS SELECTION ON DISPLAY
at your favourite store
DISTRIBUTED AND GUARANTEED BY PATERSON, LAING & BRUCE LTD.
Page 70
The Australian Women's Weekly – November 4, 1950

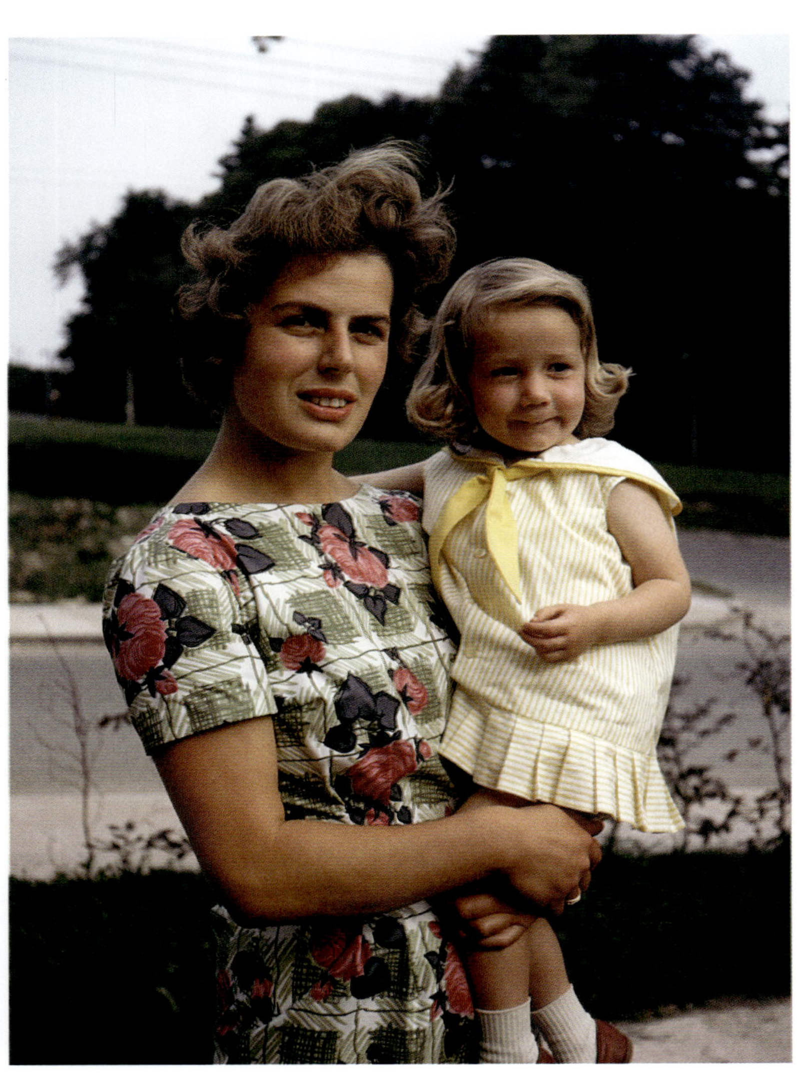

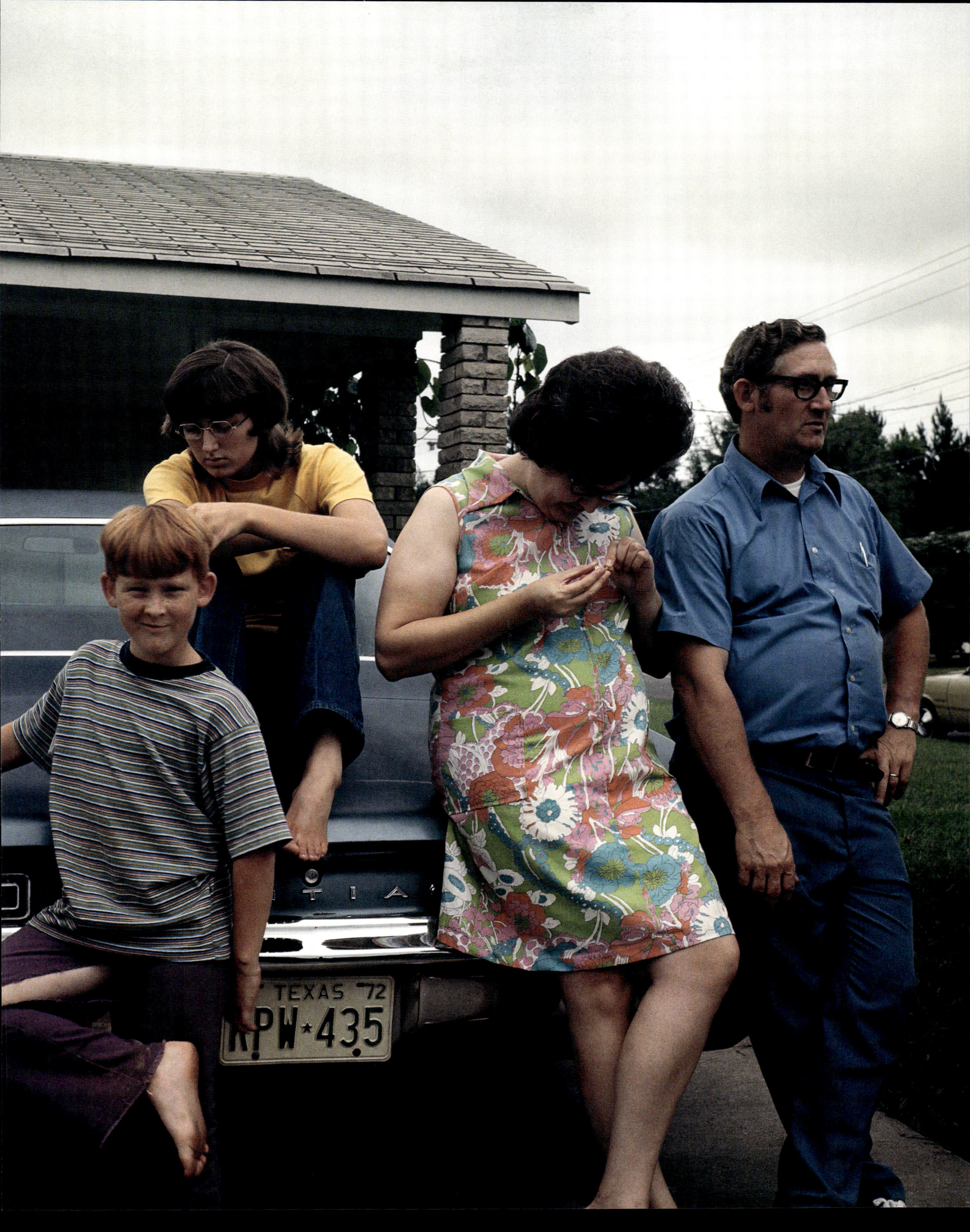
TEXAS 72
PW★435

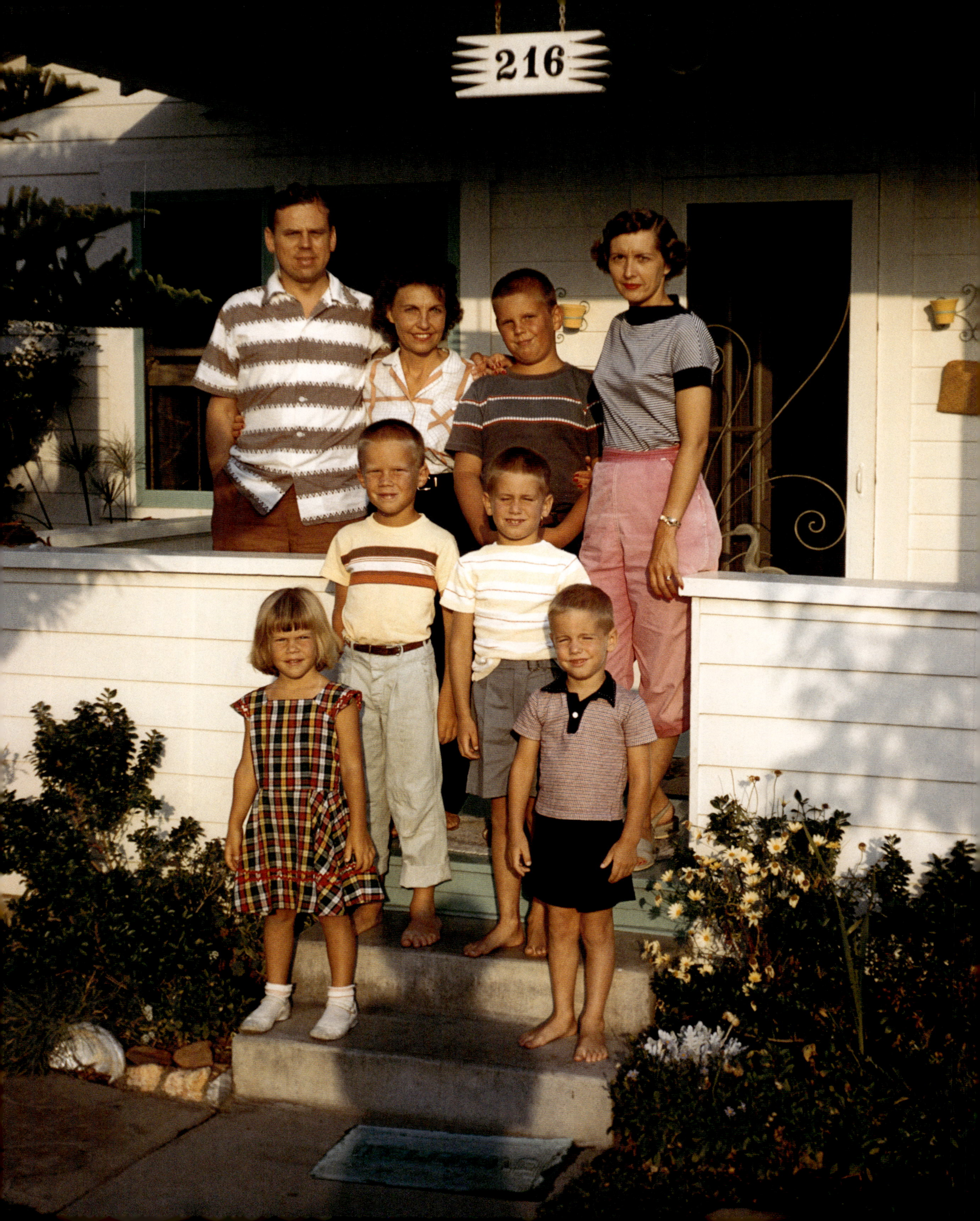
216

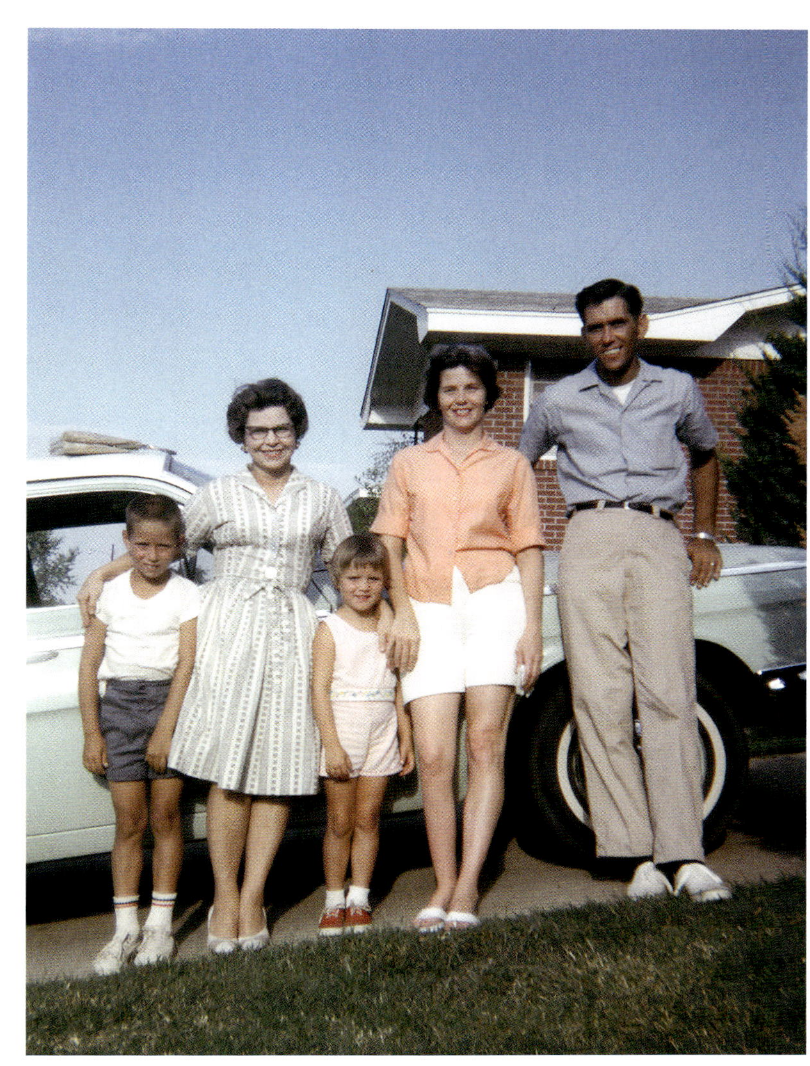

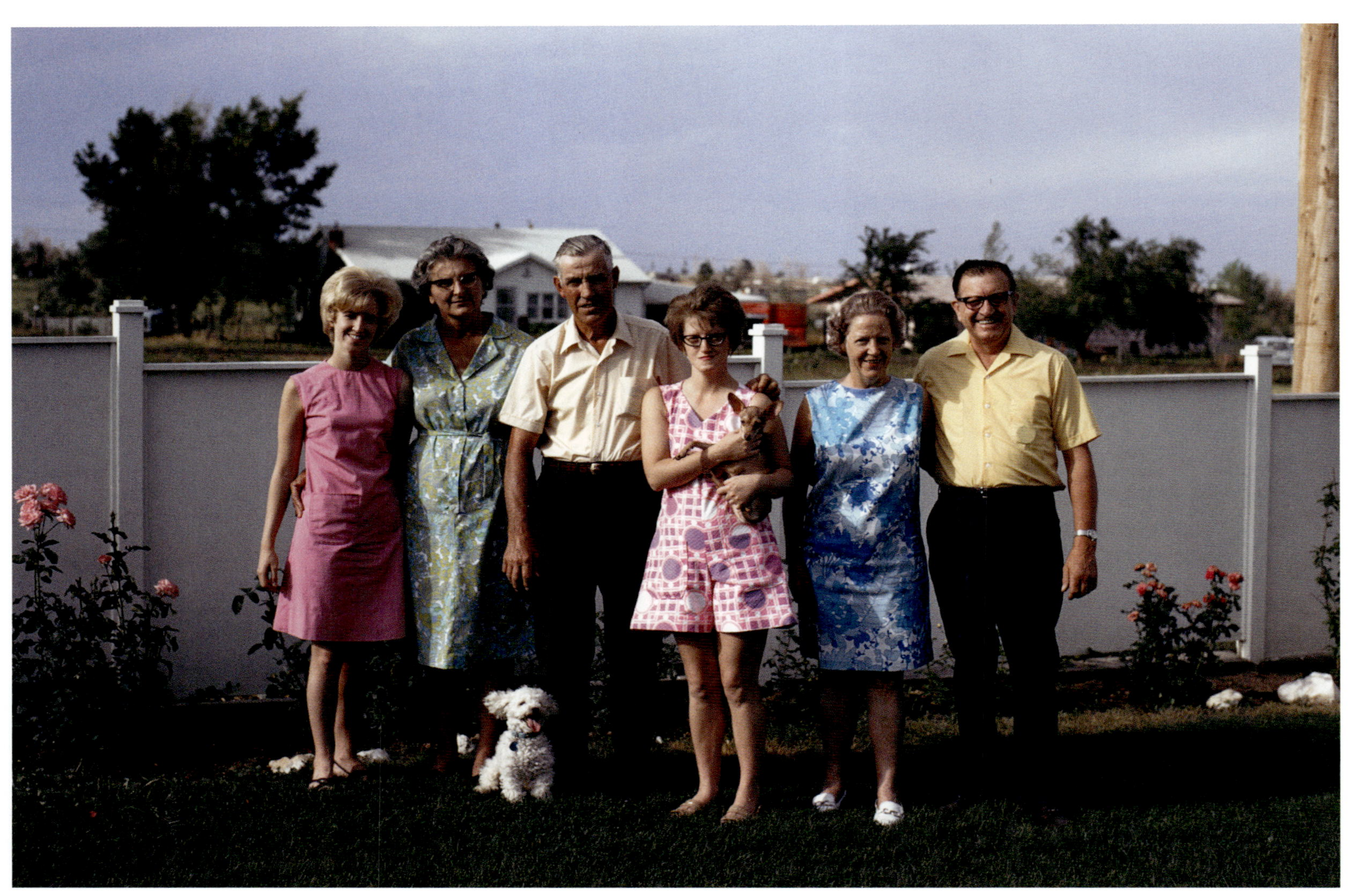

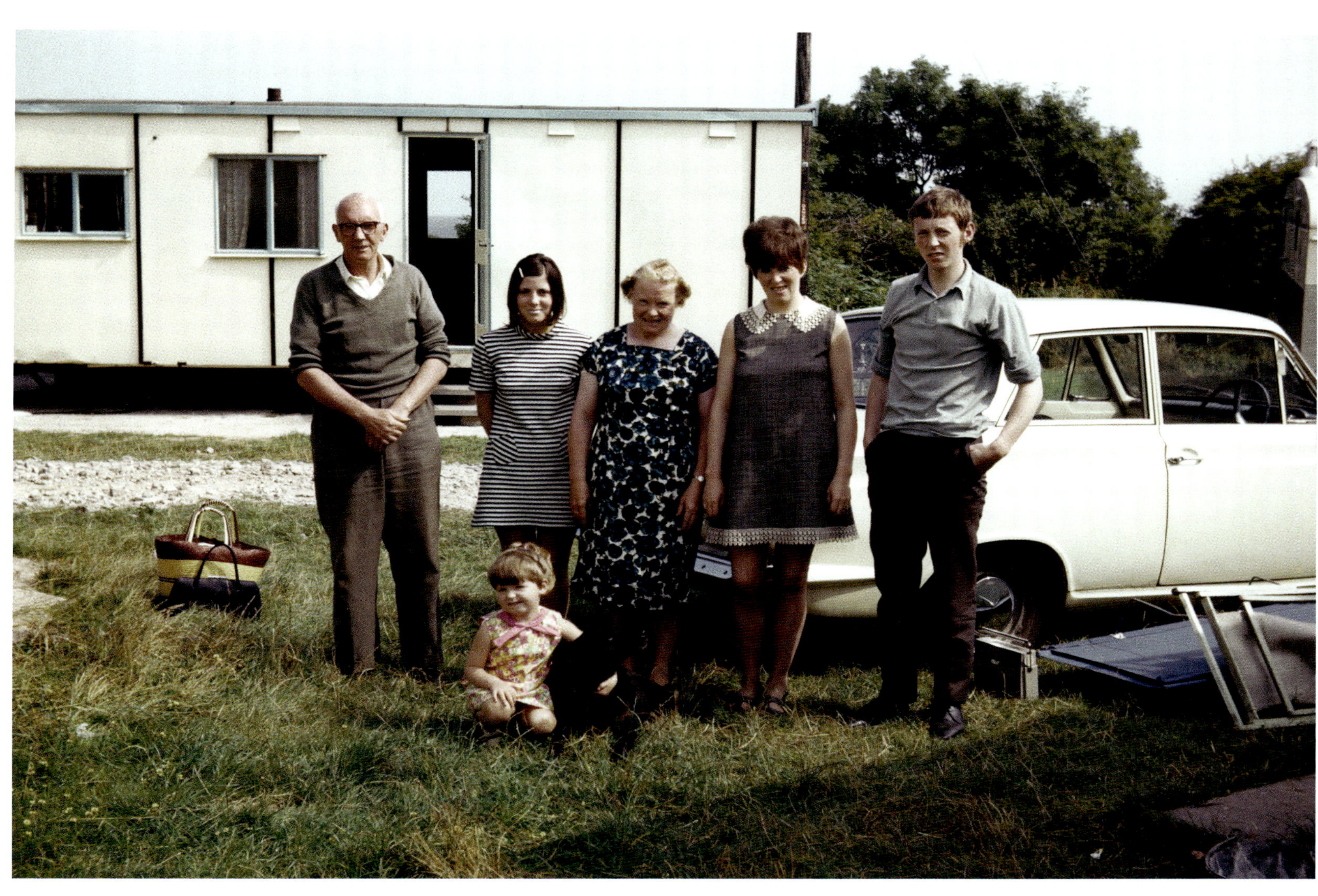

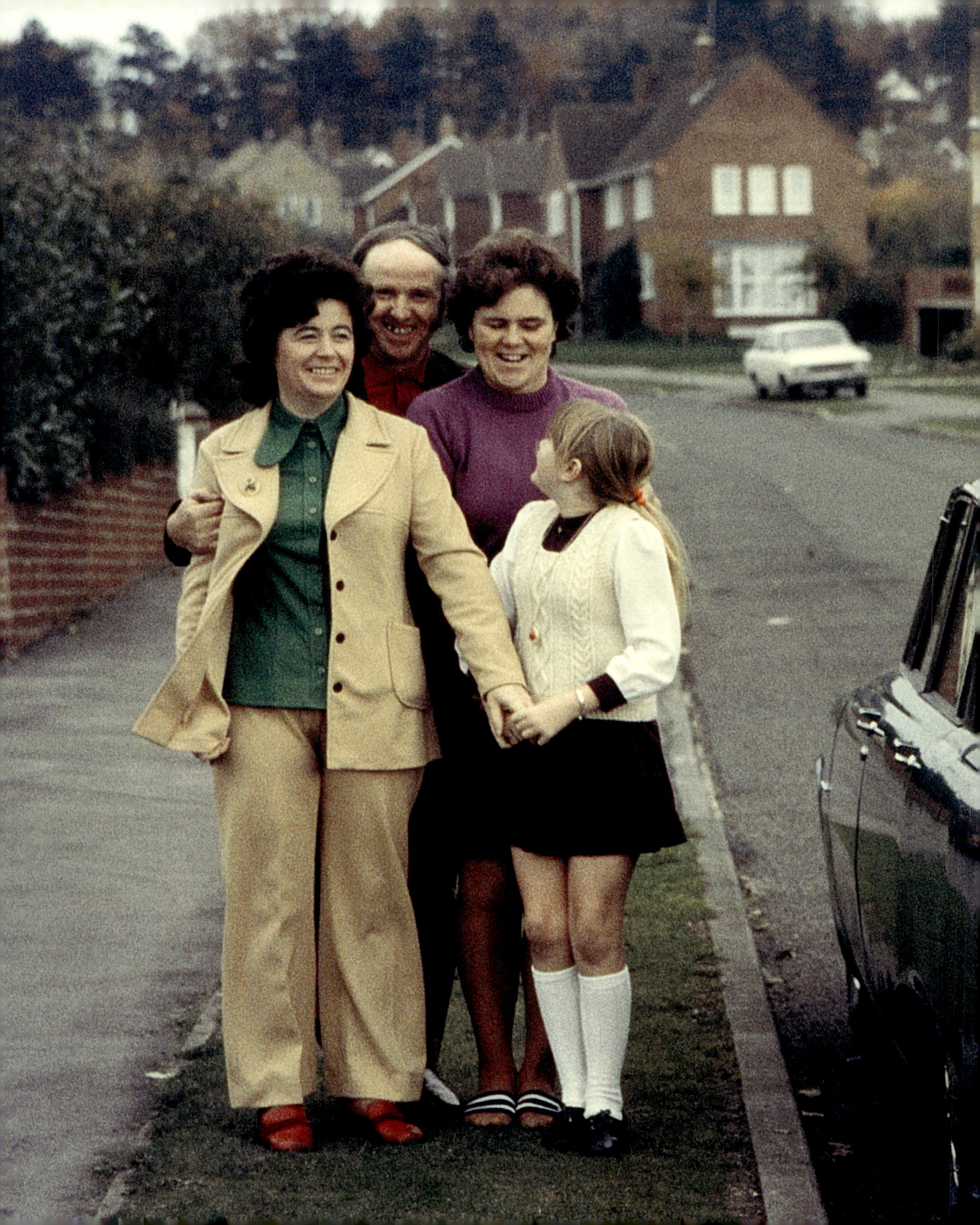

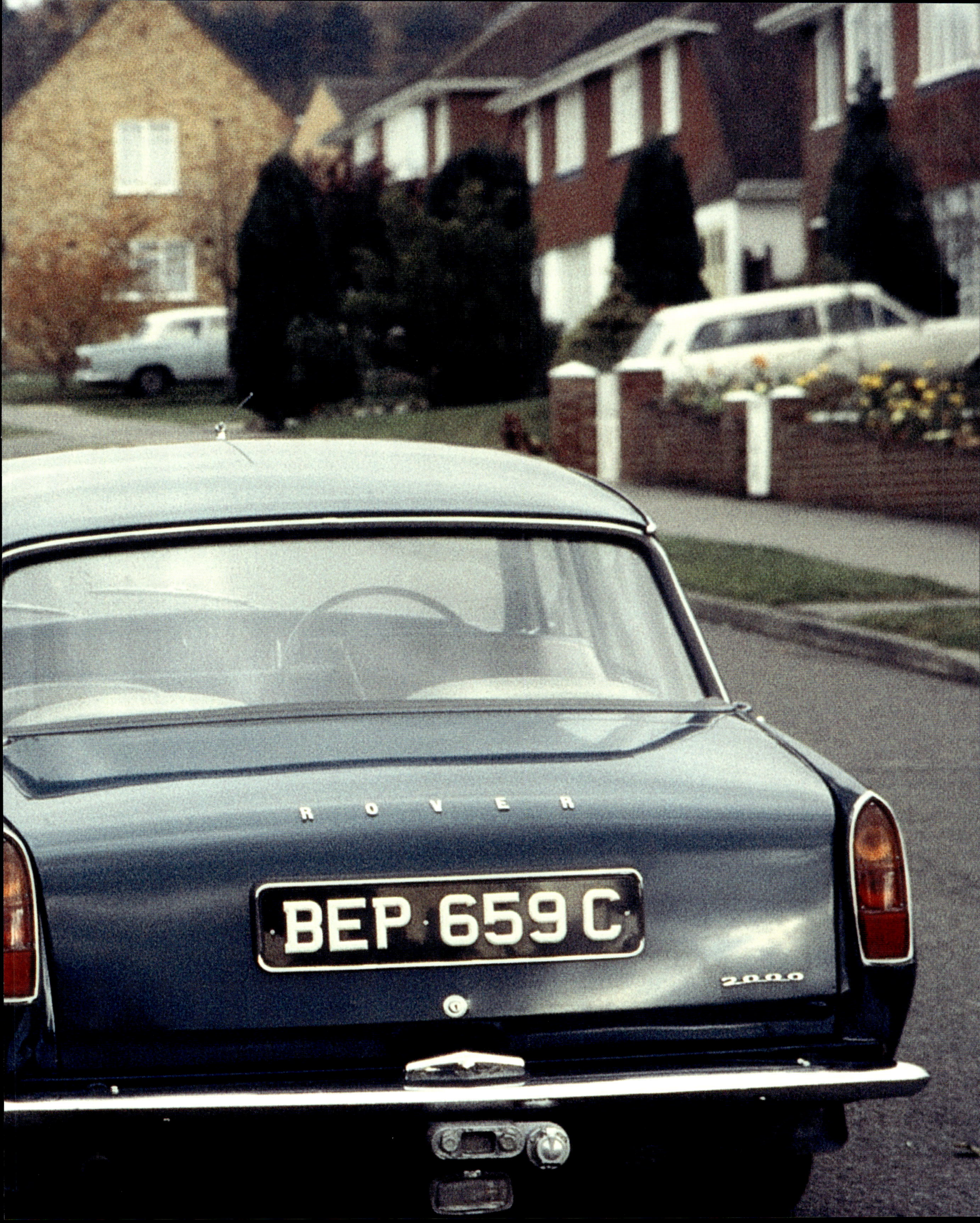
ROVER
BEP 659 C
2000

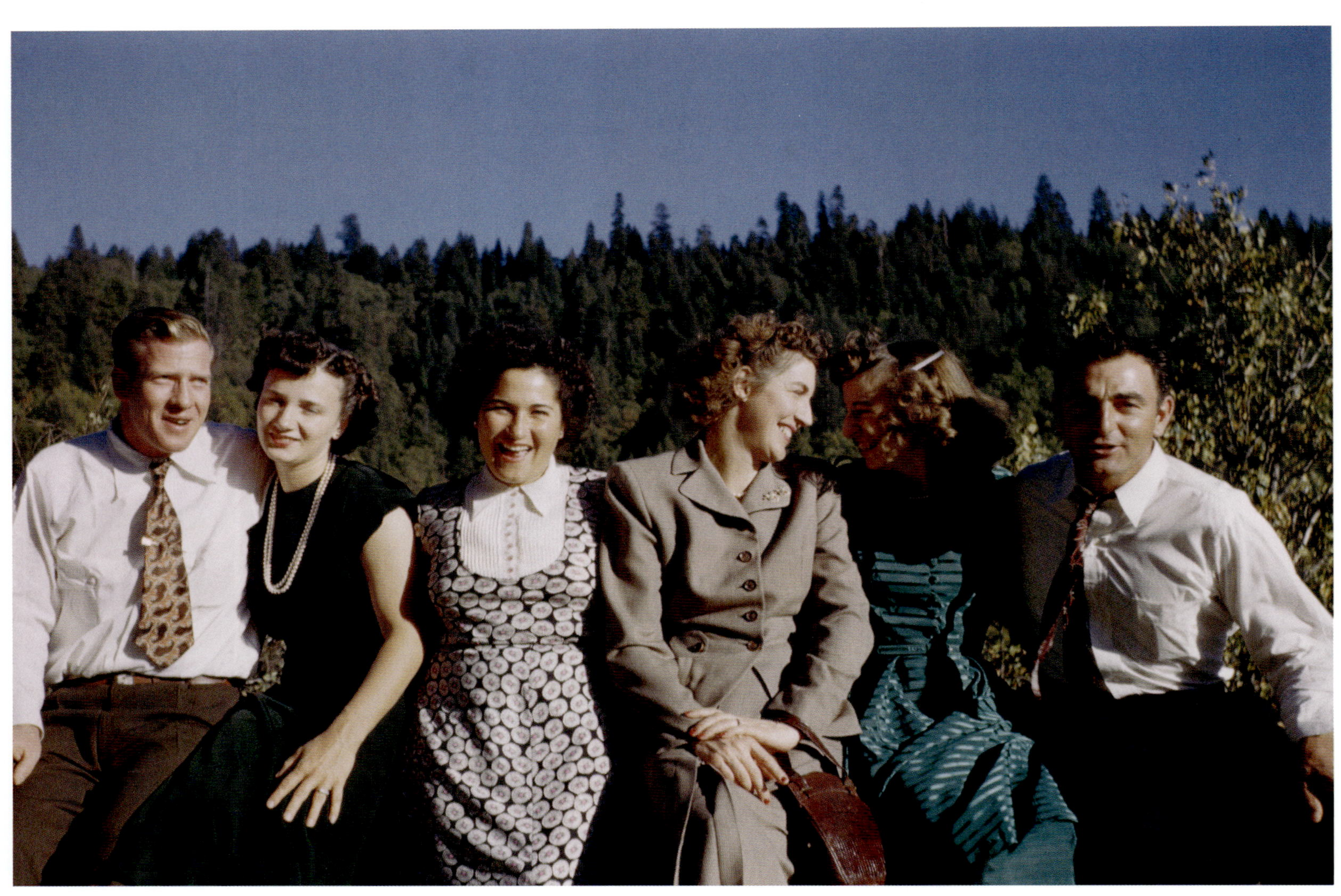

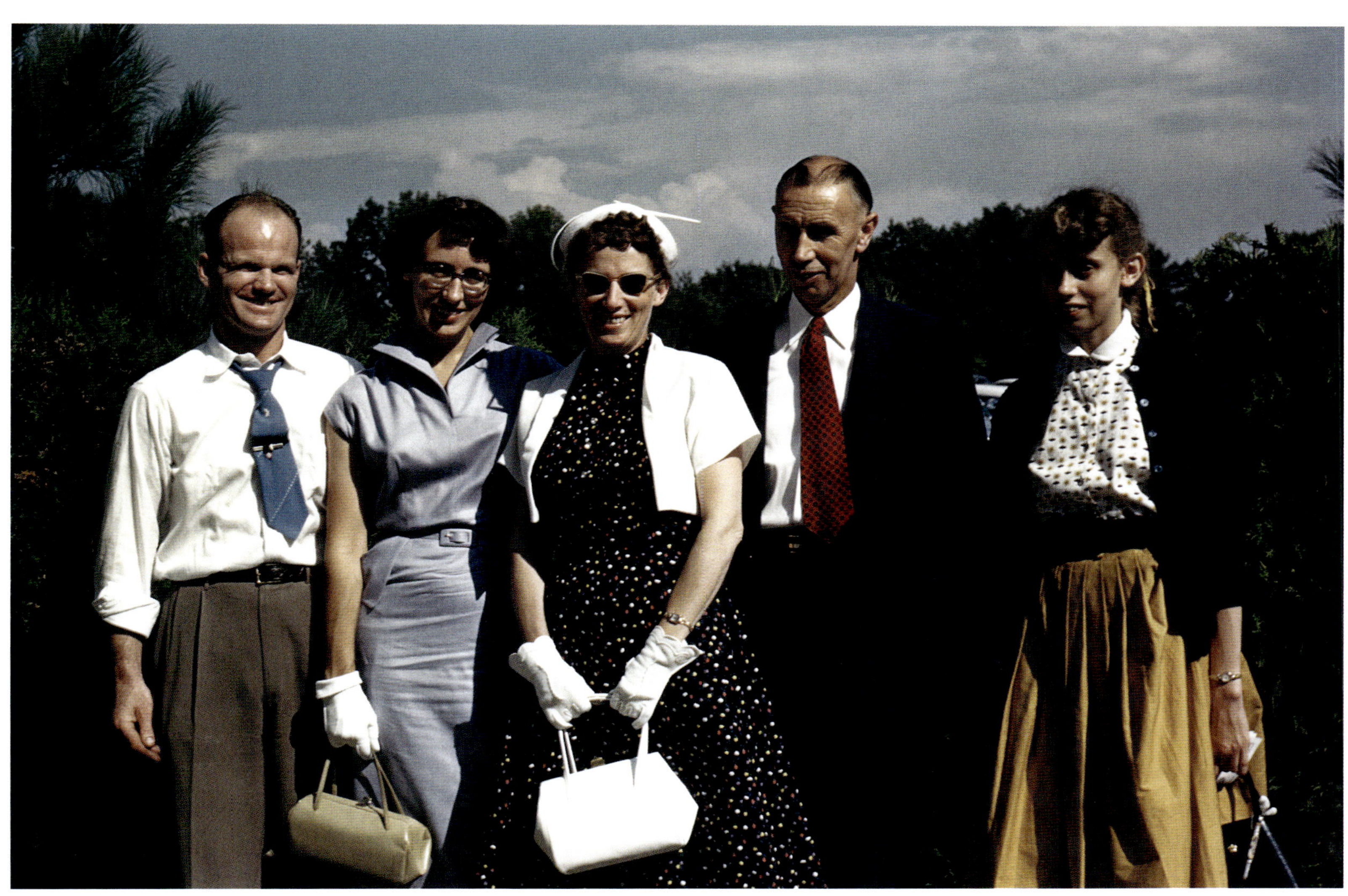

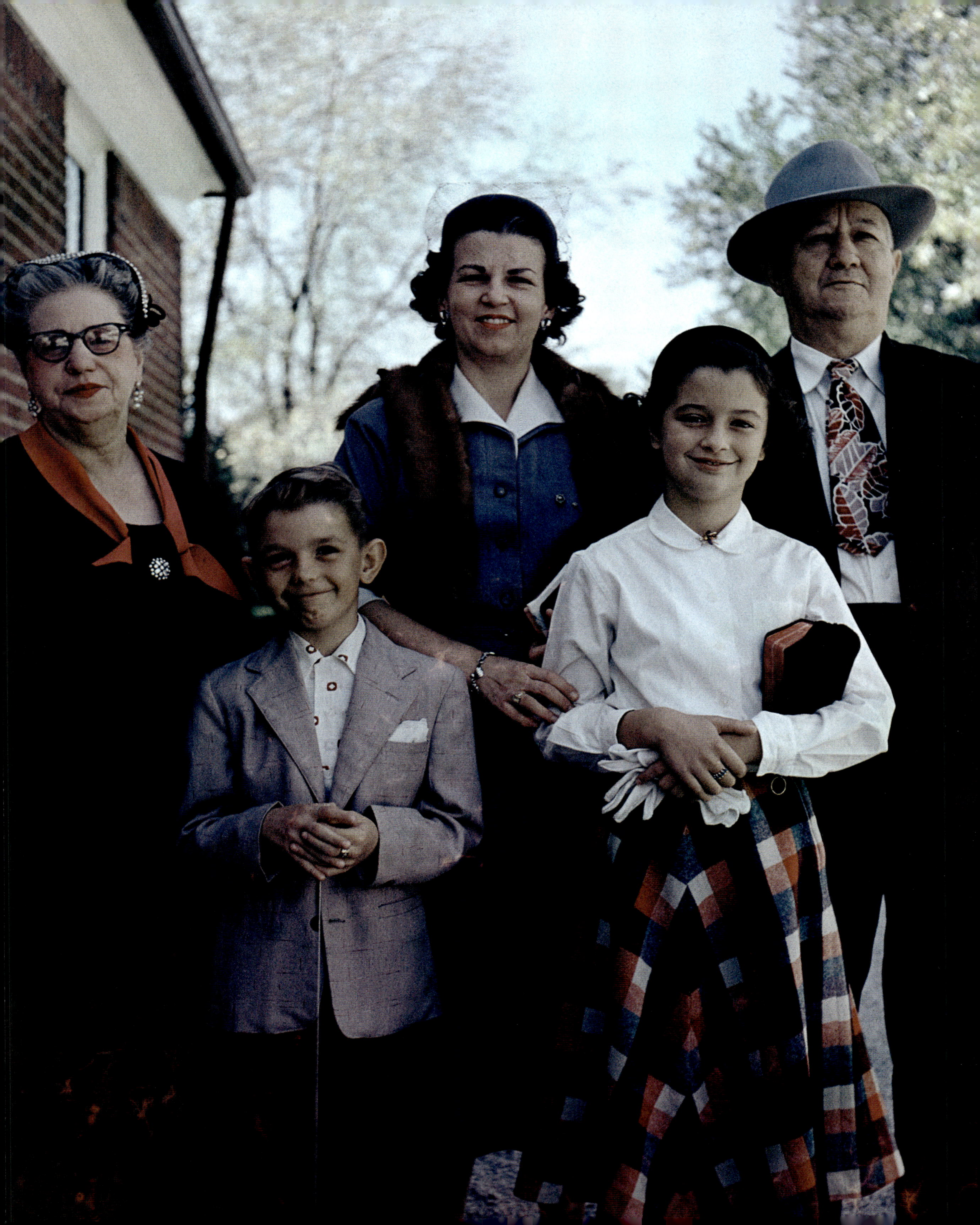

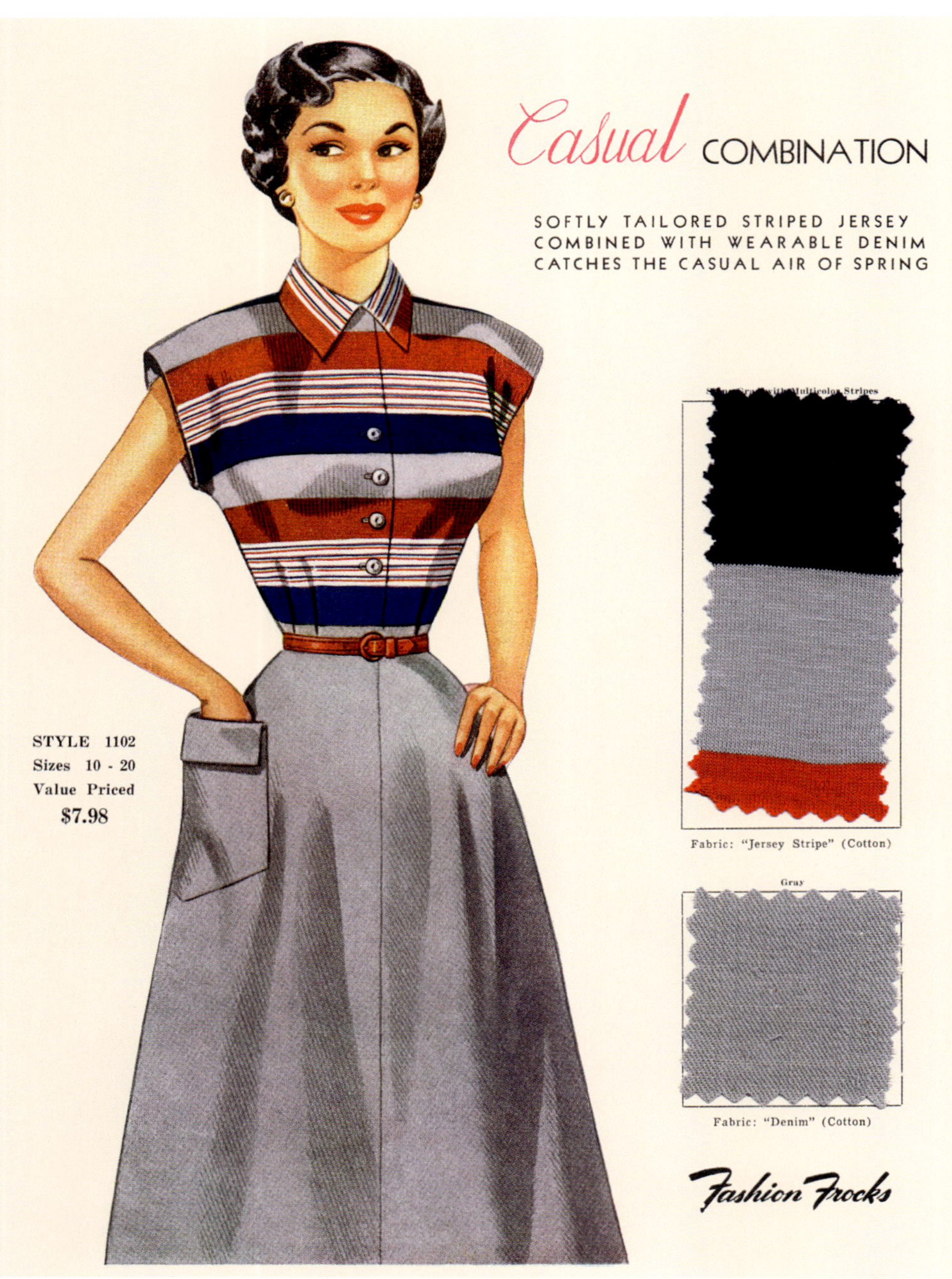
Casual COMBINATION
SOFTLY TAILORED STRIPED JERSEY
COMBINED WITH WEARABLE DENIM
CATCHES THE CASUAL AIR OF SPRING
STYLE 1102
Sizes 10 - 20
Value Priced
$7.98
Fabric: "Jersey Stripe" (Cotton)
Gray
Fabric: "Denim" (Cotton)
Fashion Frocks

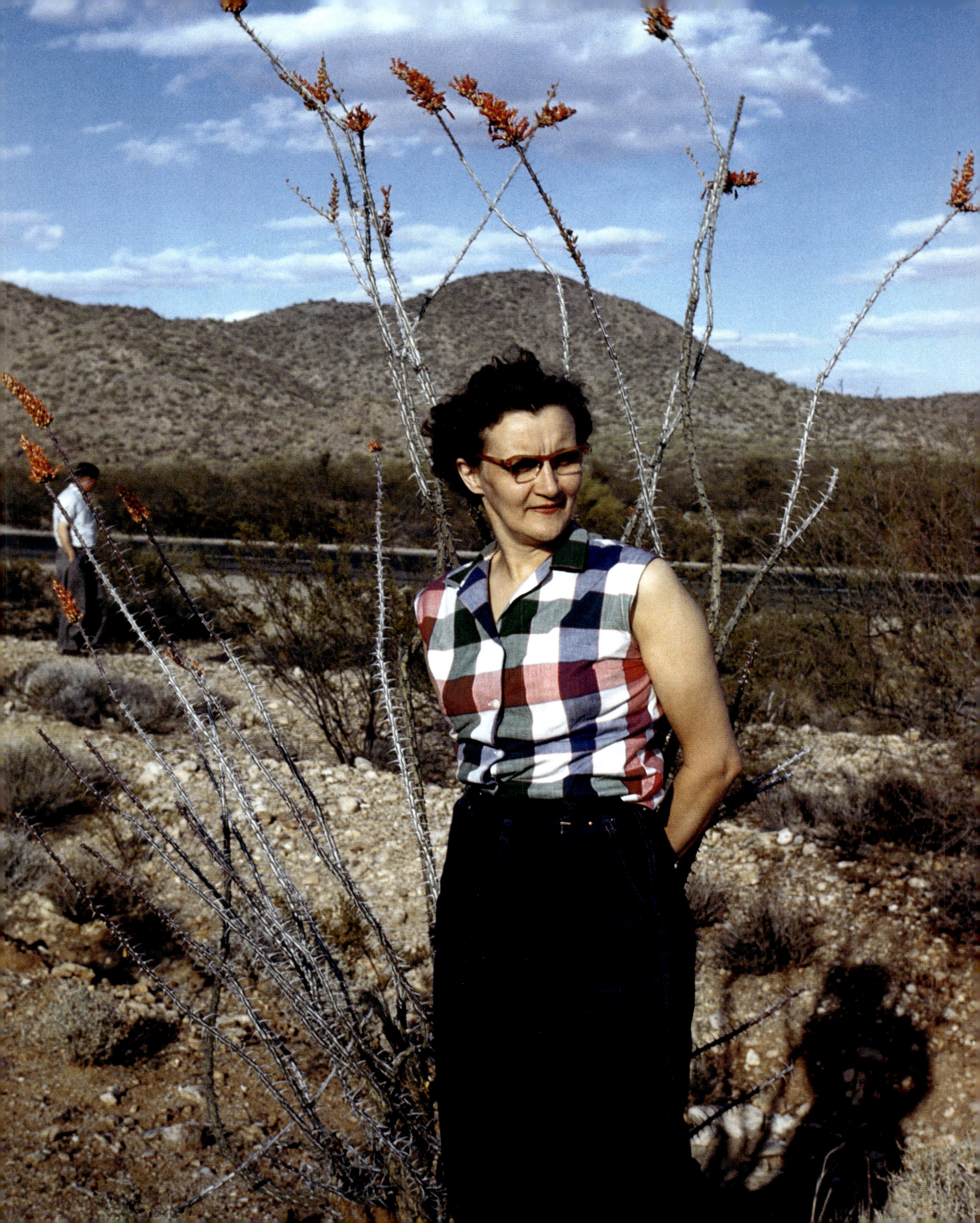

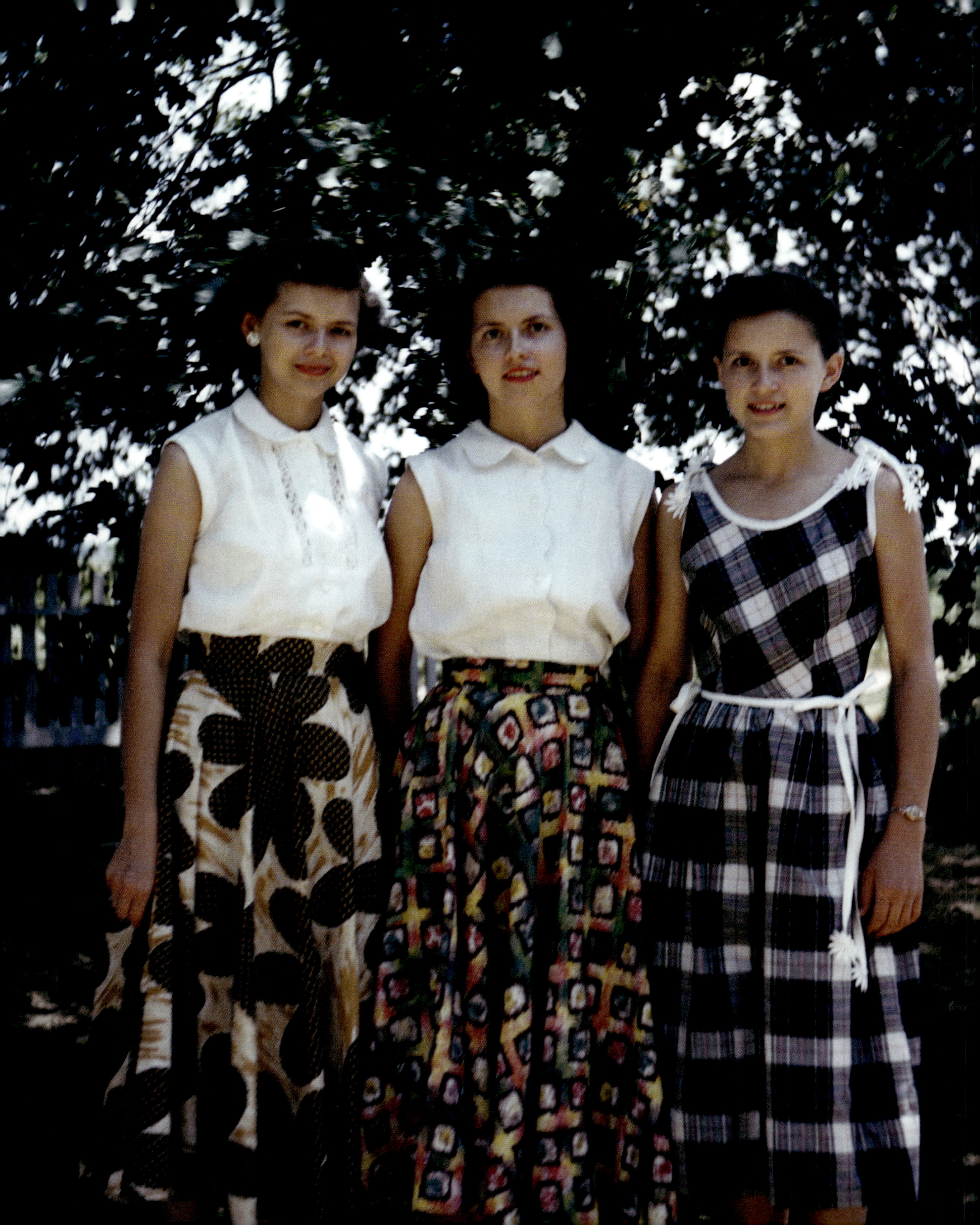

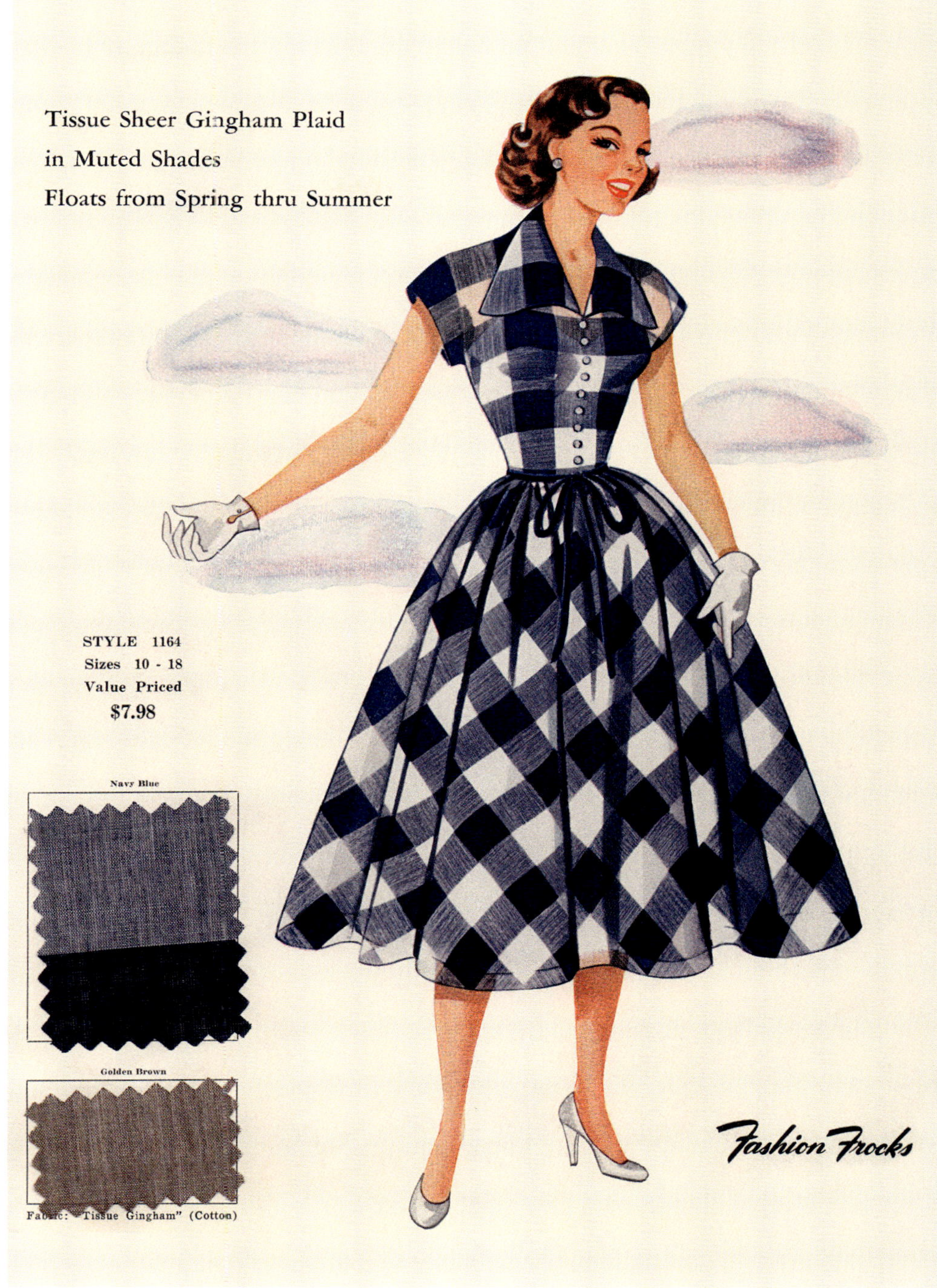

Tissue Sheer Gingham Plaid
in Muted Shades
Floats from Spring thru Summer
STYLE 1164
Sizes 10 - 18
Value Priced
$7.98
Navy Blue
Golden Brown
Tissue Gingham" (Cotton)
Fashion Frocks

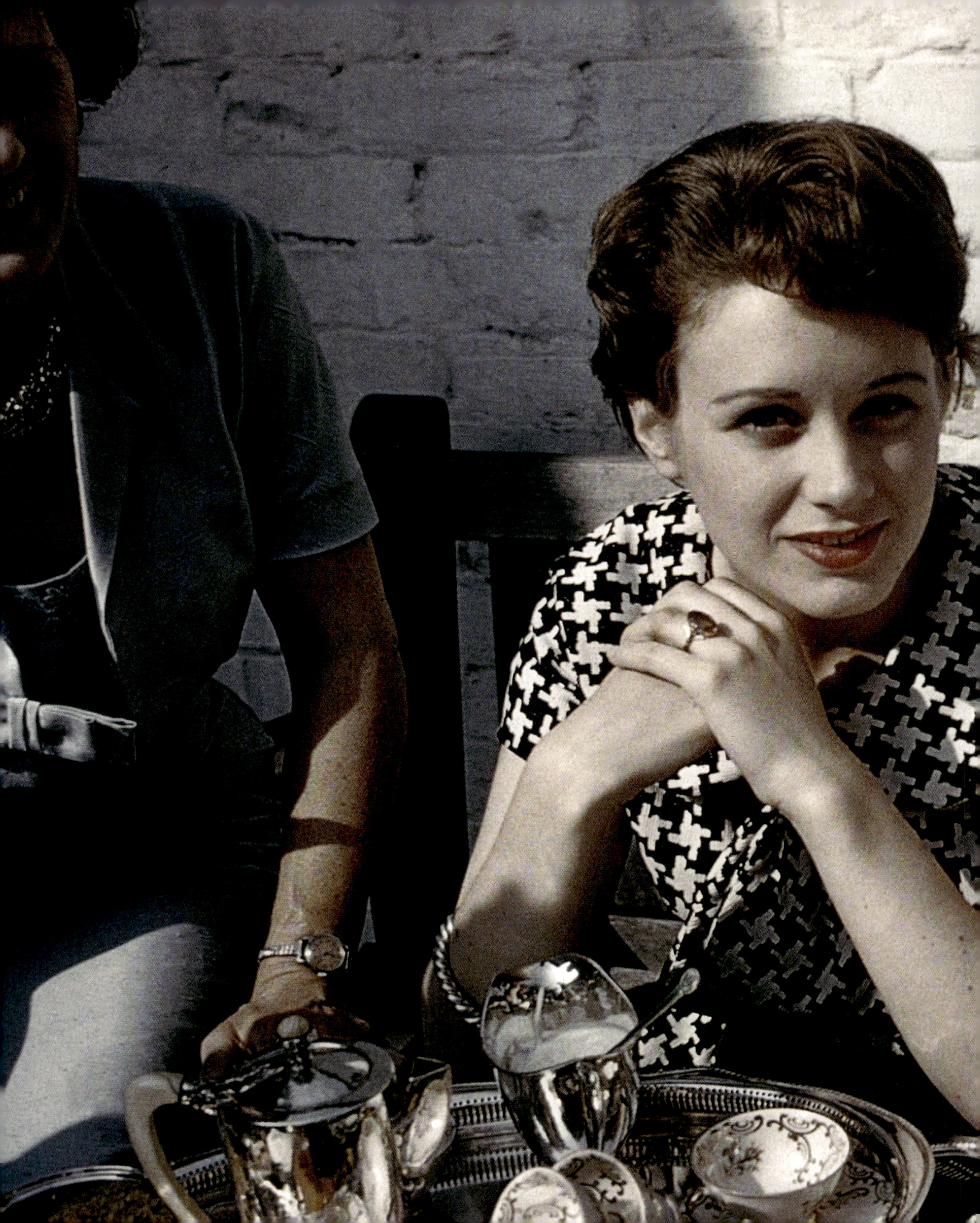

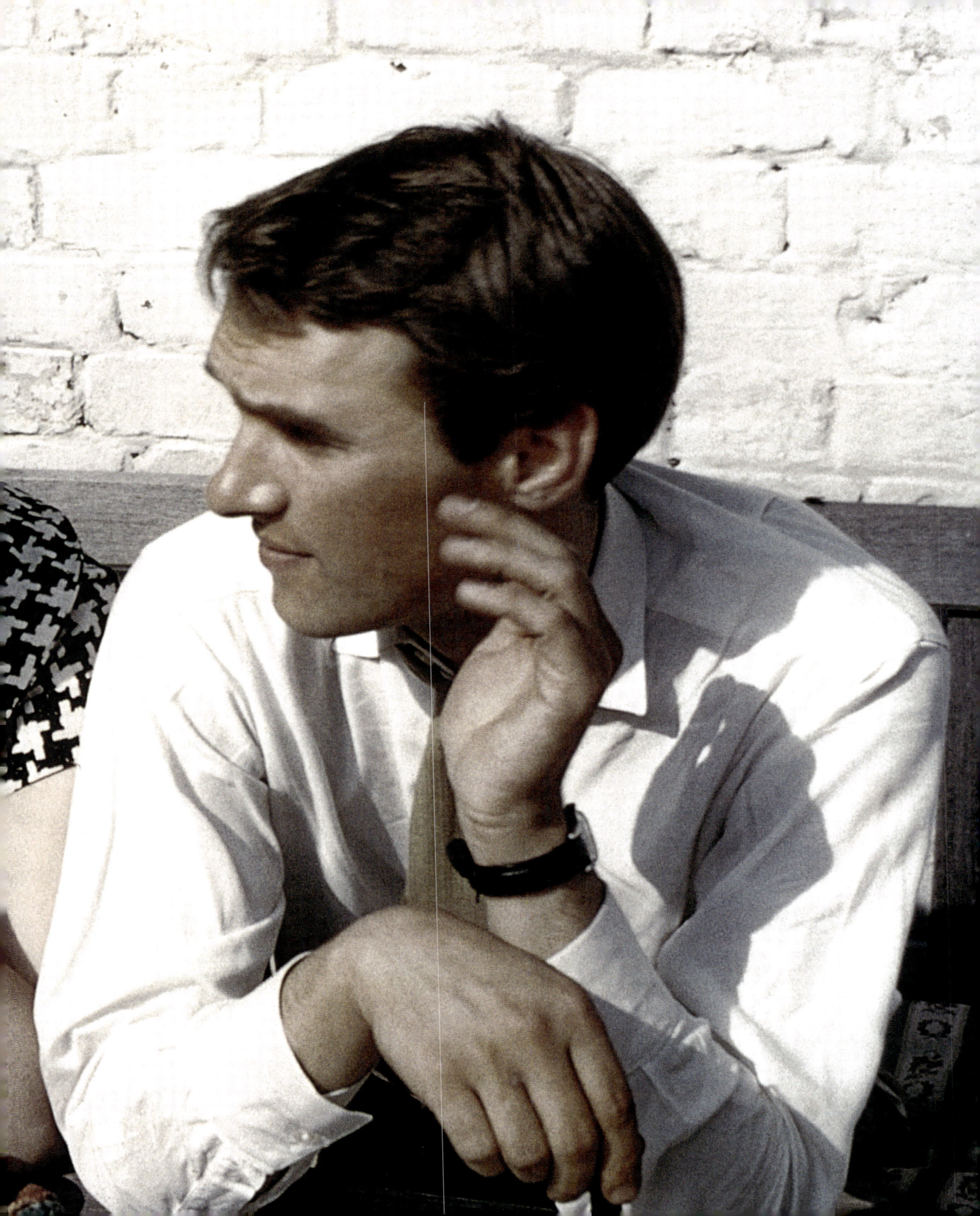

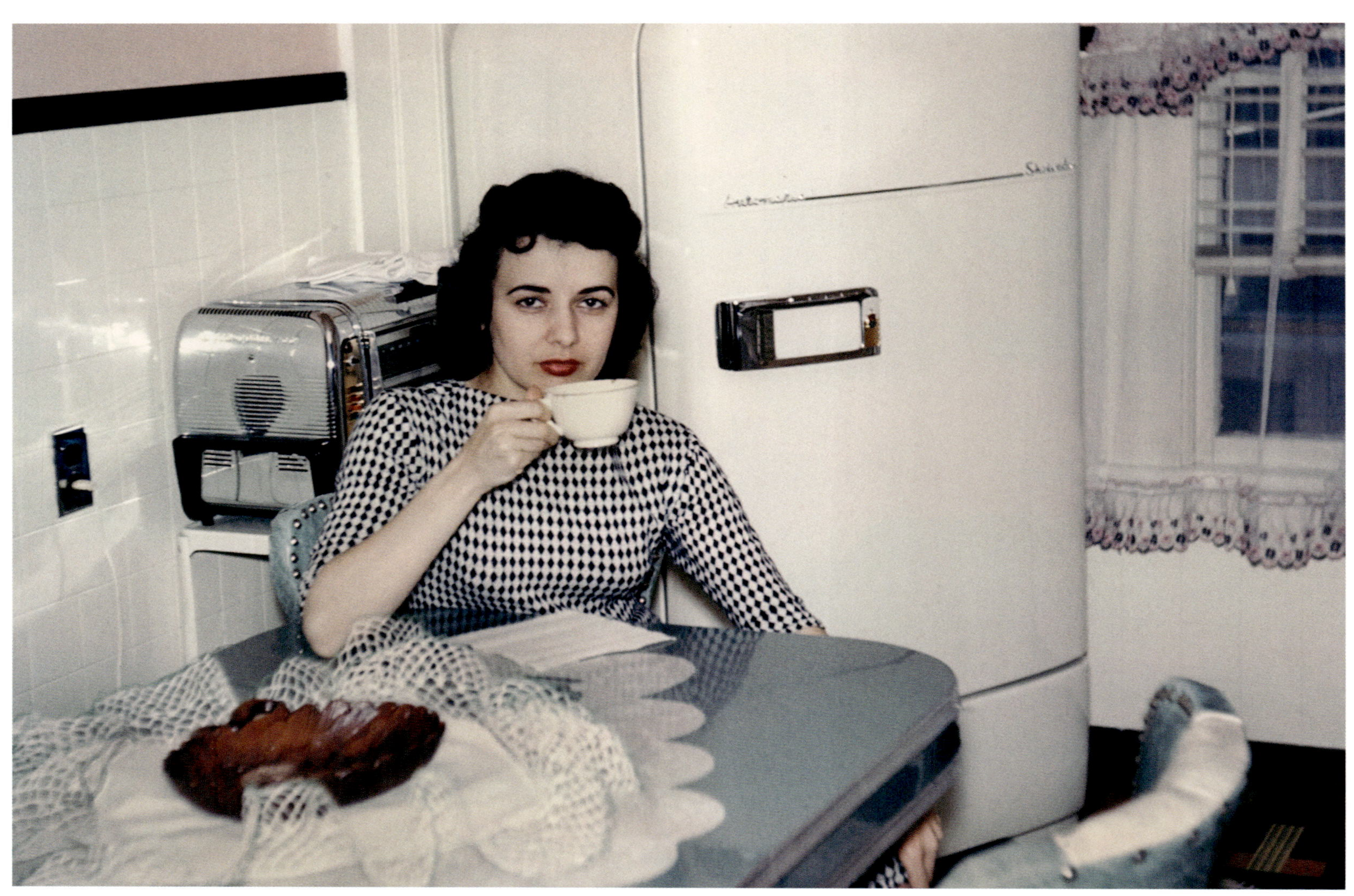

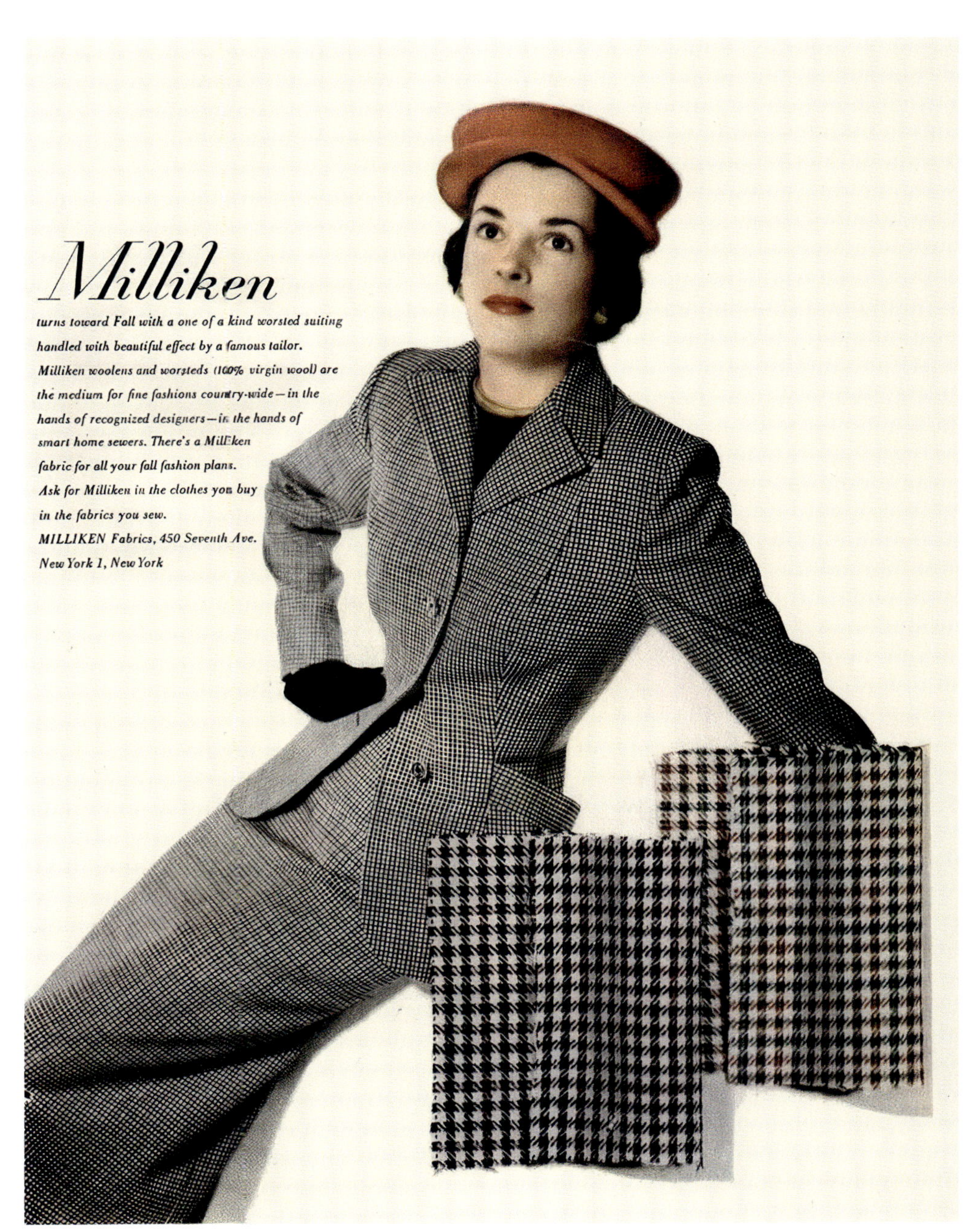
Milliken
turns toward Fall with a one of a kind worsted suiting
handled with beautiful effect by a famous tailor.
Milliken woolens and worsteds (100% virgin wool) are
the medium for fine fashions country-wide—in the
hands of recognized designers—in the hands of
smart home sewers. There's a Milliken
fabric for all your fall fashion plans.
Ask for Milliken in the clothes you buy
in the fabrics you sew.
MILLIKEN Fabrics, 450 Seventh Ave.
New York 1, New York

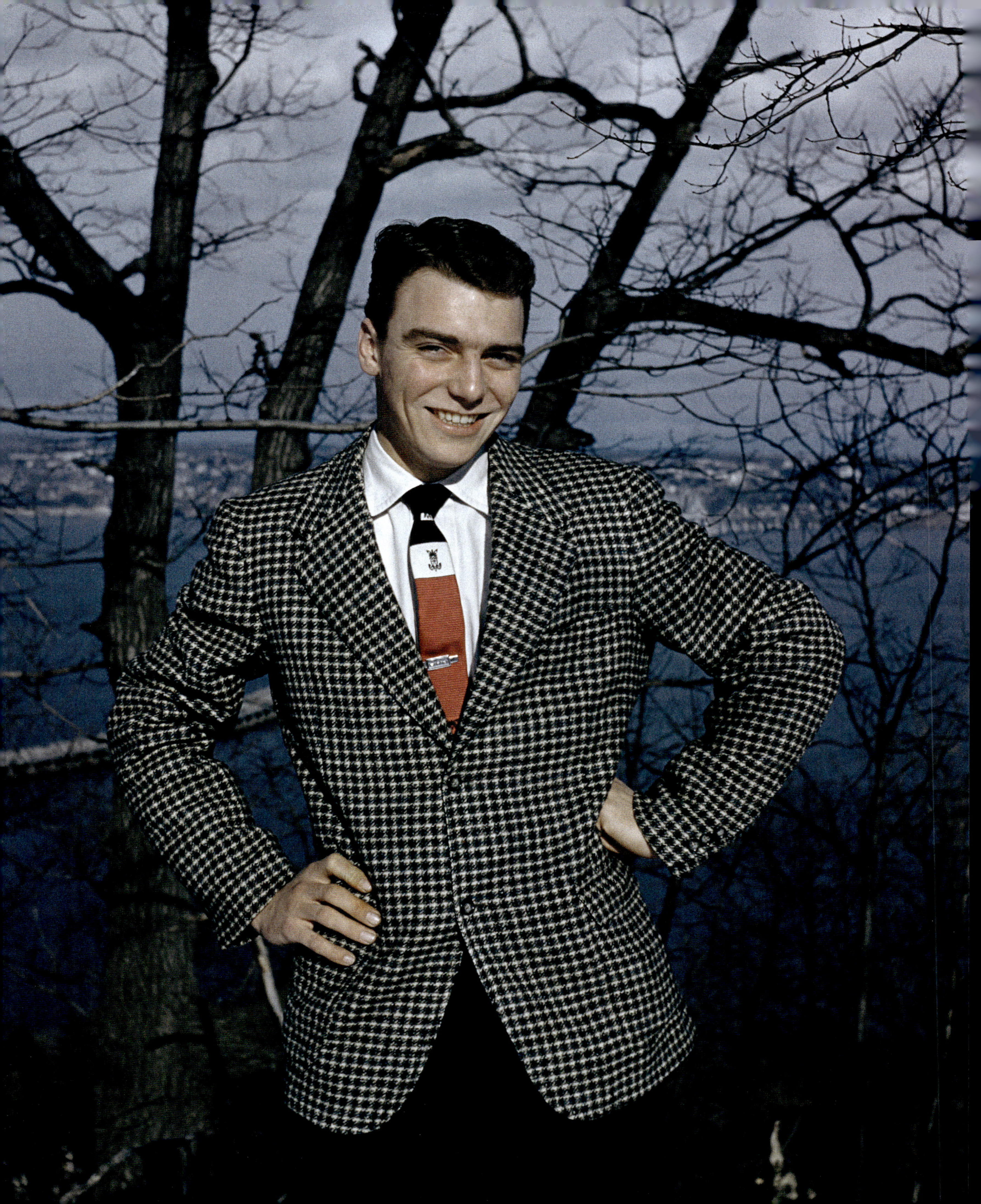

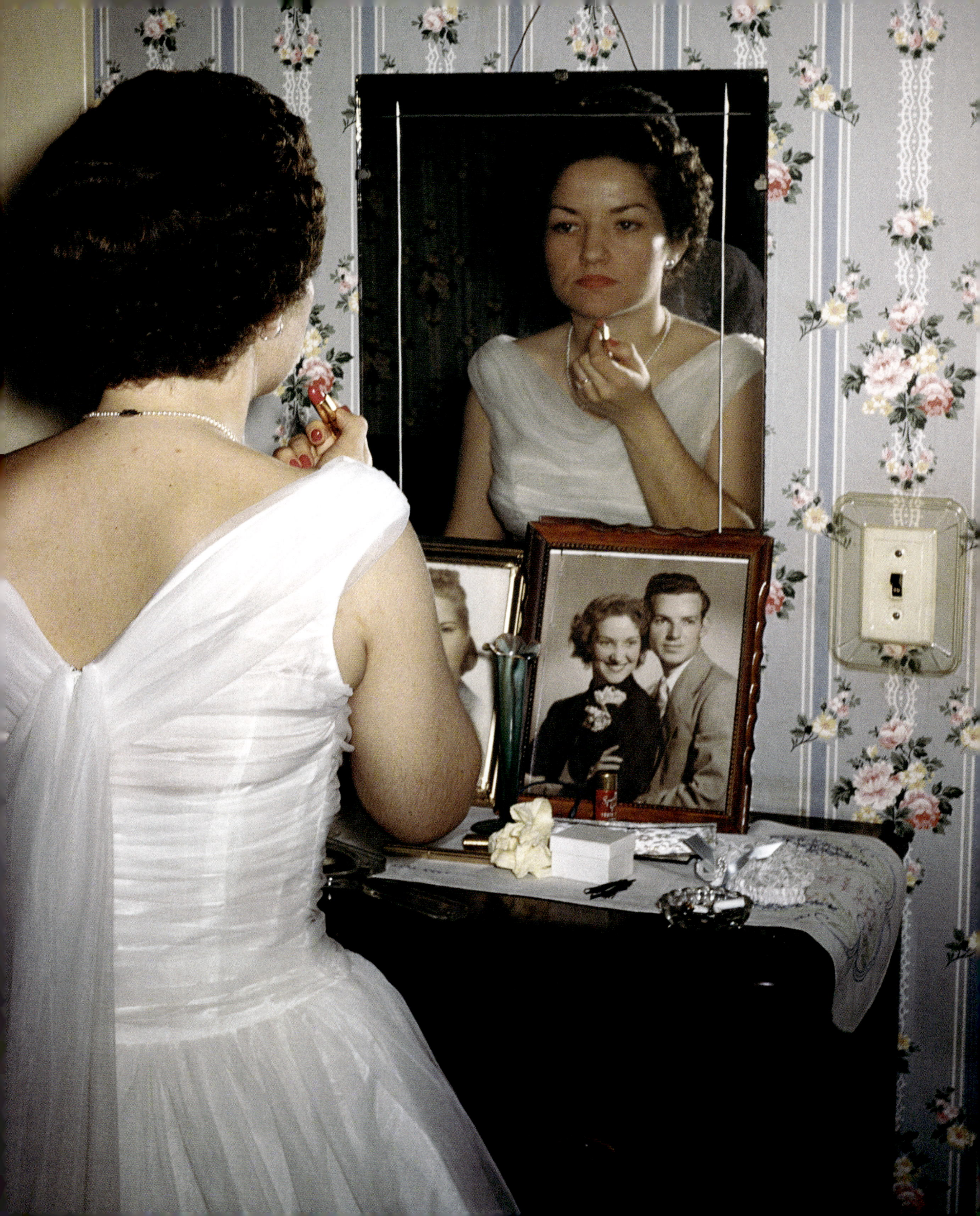

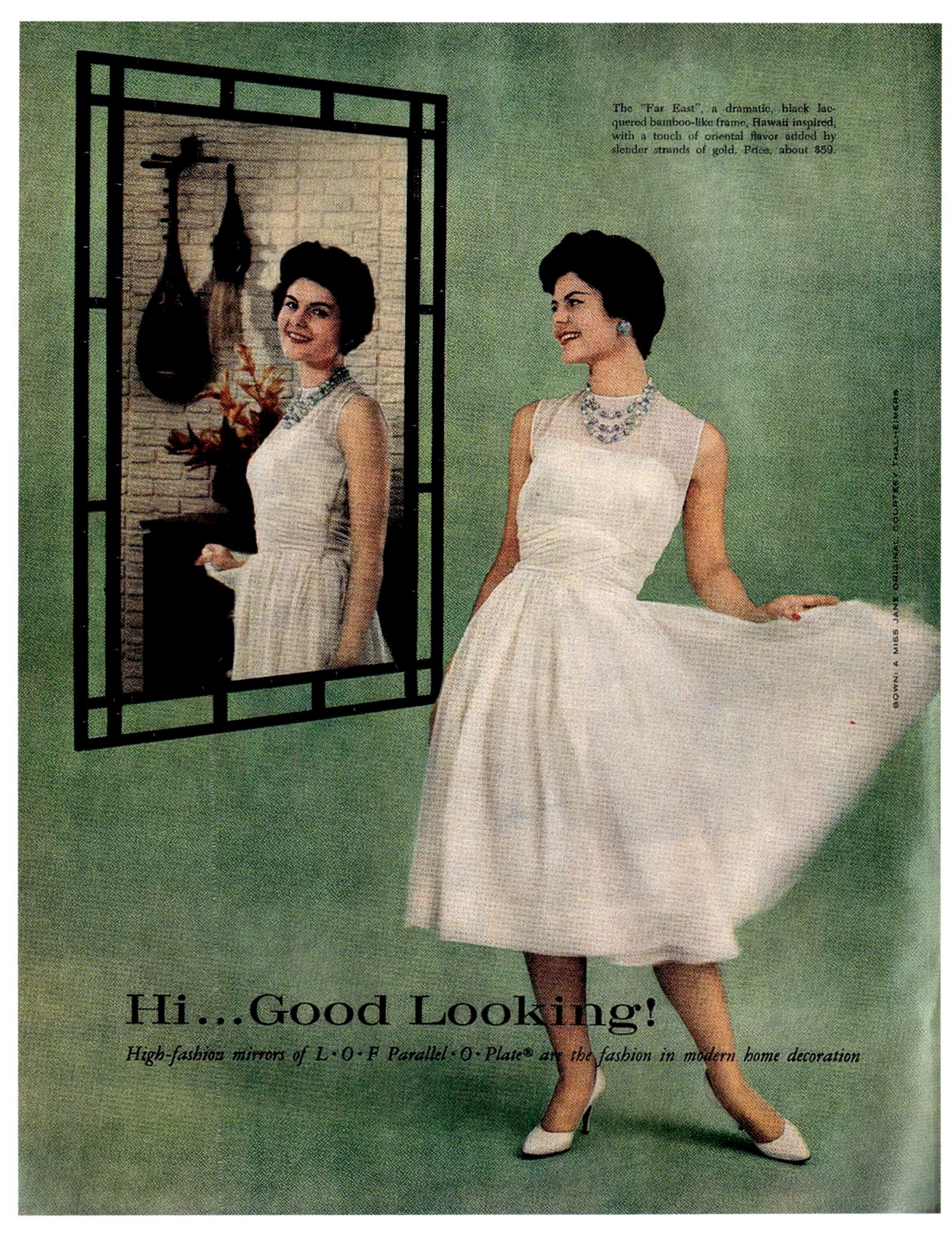
The "Far East", a dramatic, black lacquered bamboo-like frame, Hawaii inspired, with a touch of oriental flavor added by slender strands of gold. Price, about $59.
GOWN: A MISS JANE ORIGINAL COURTESY THALHEIMERS
Hi...Good Looking!
High-fashion mirrors of L·O·F Parallel·O·Plate® are the fashion in modern home decoration

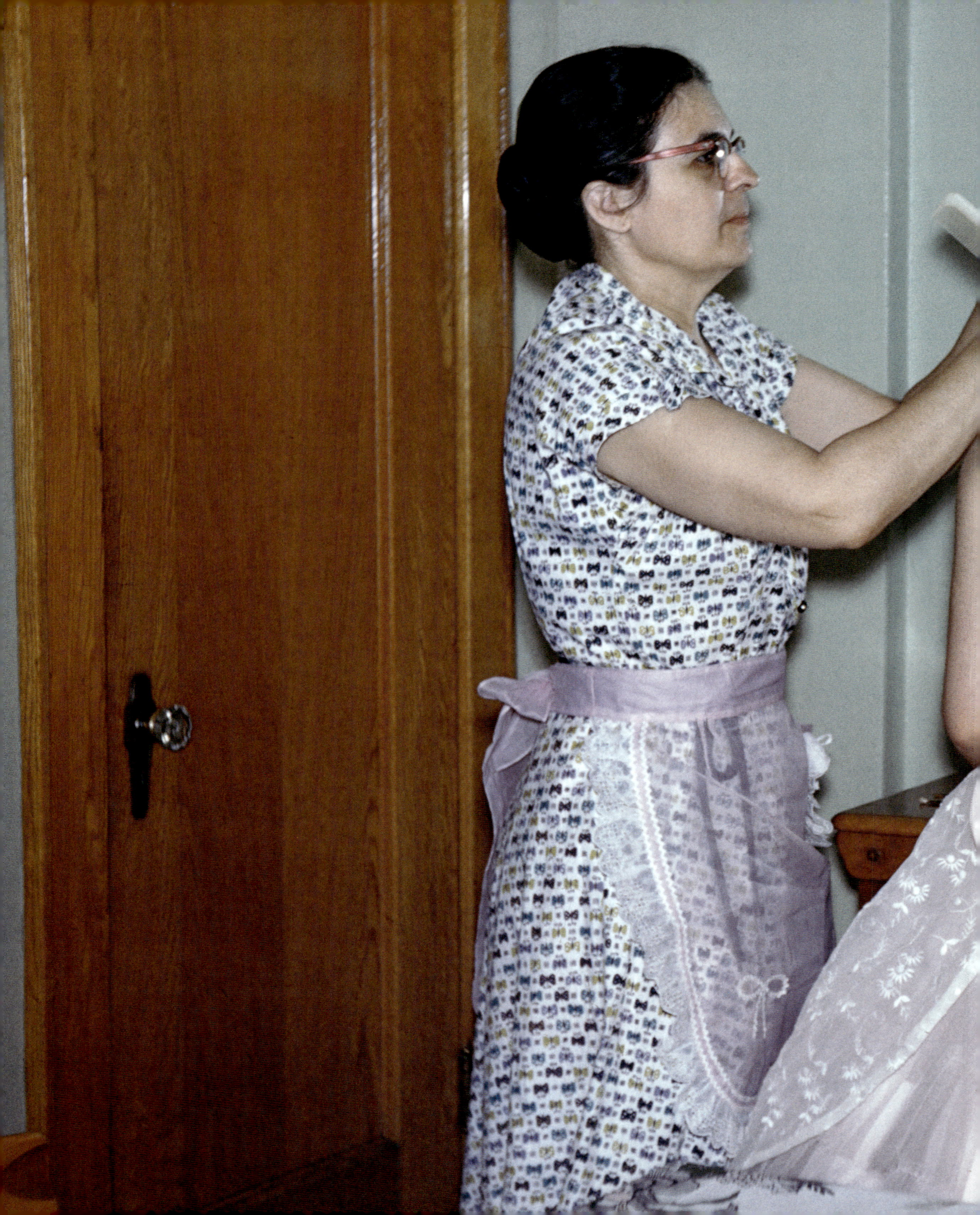

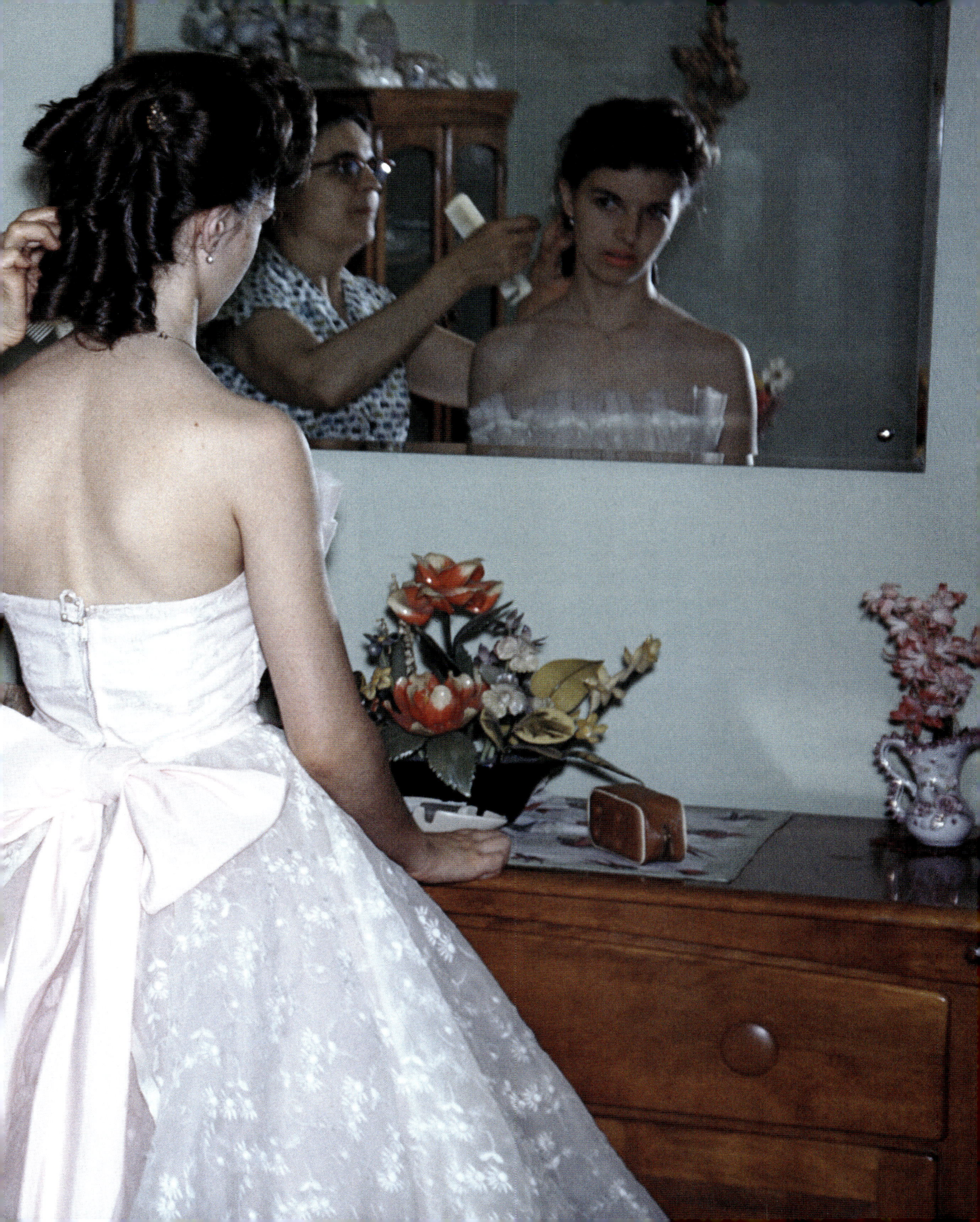

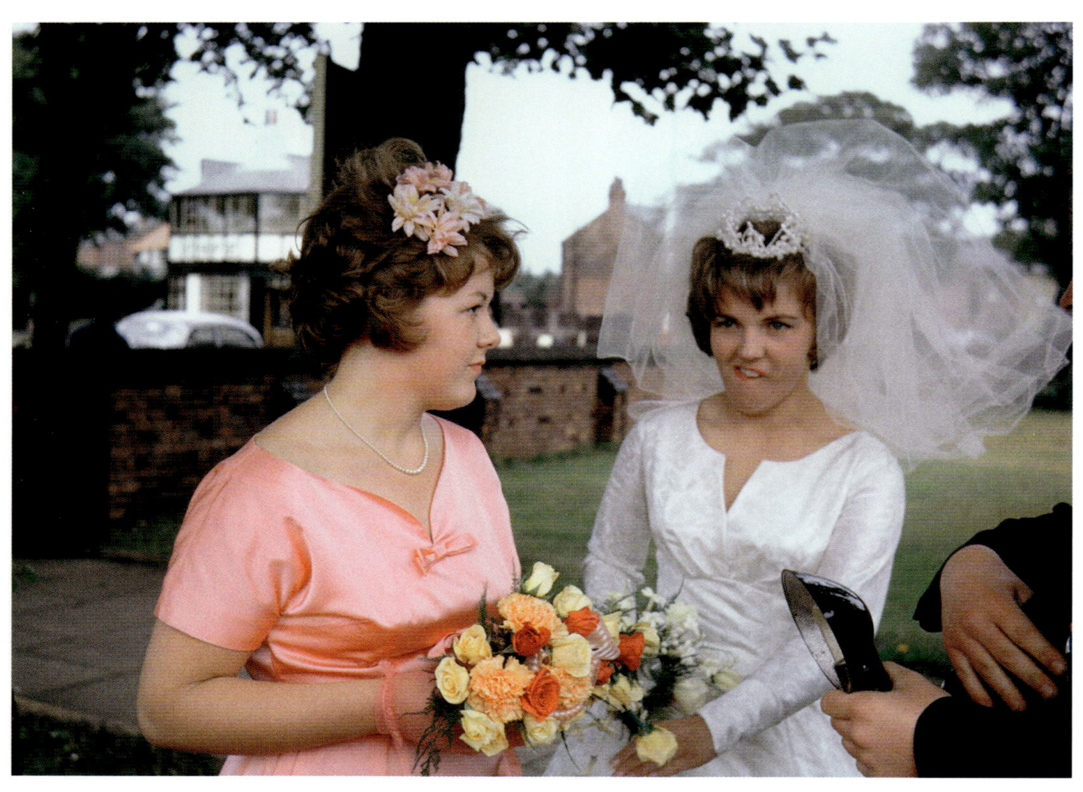

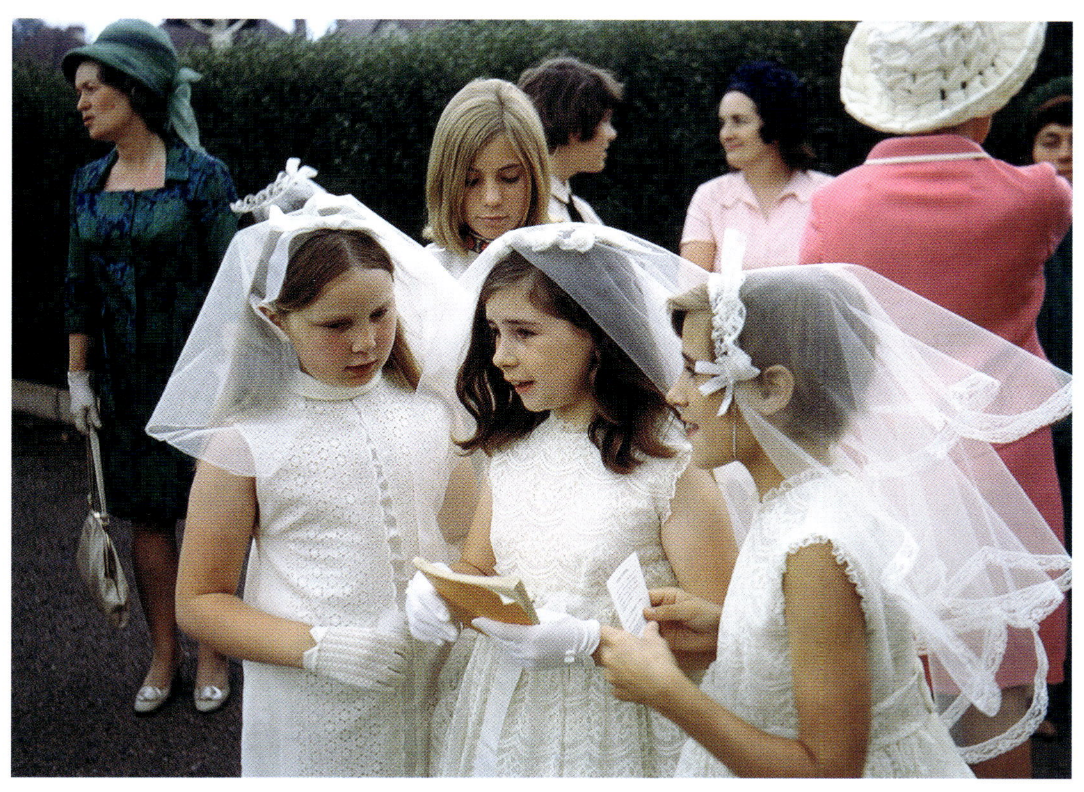

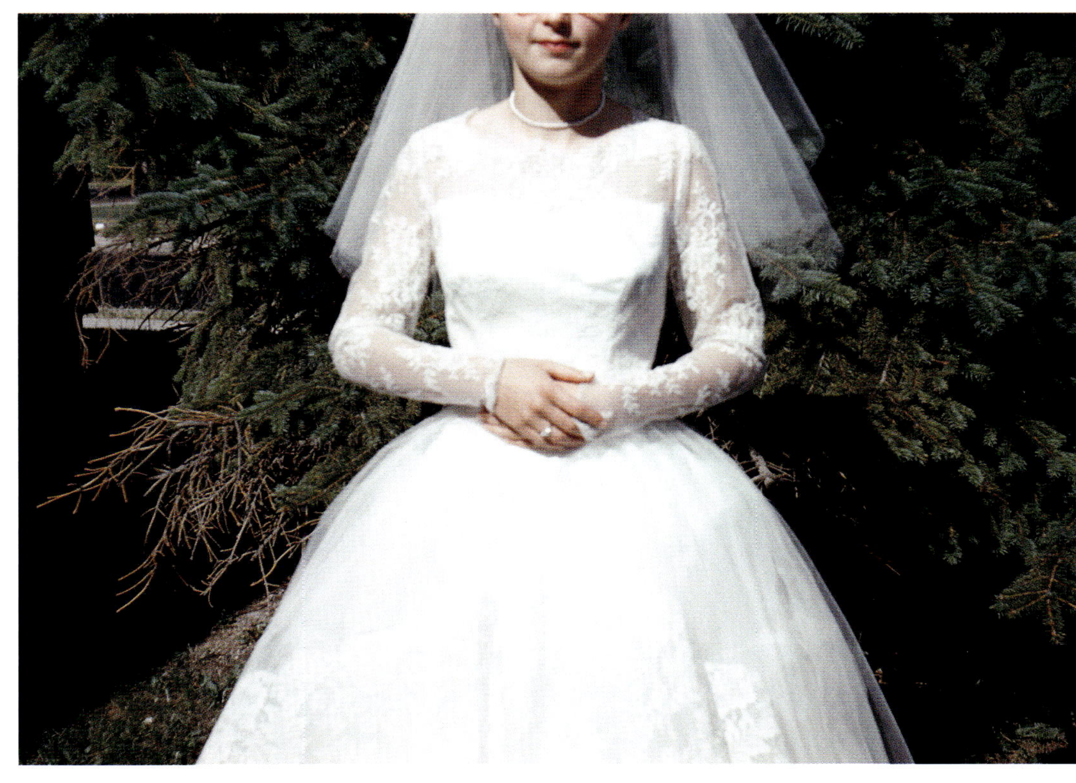

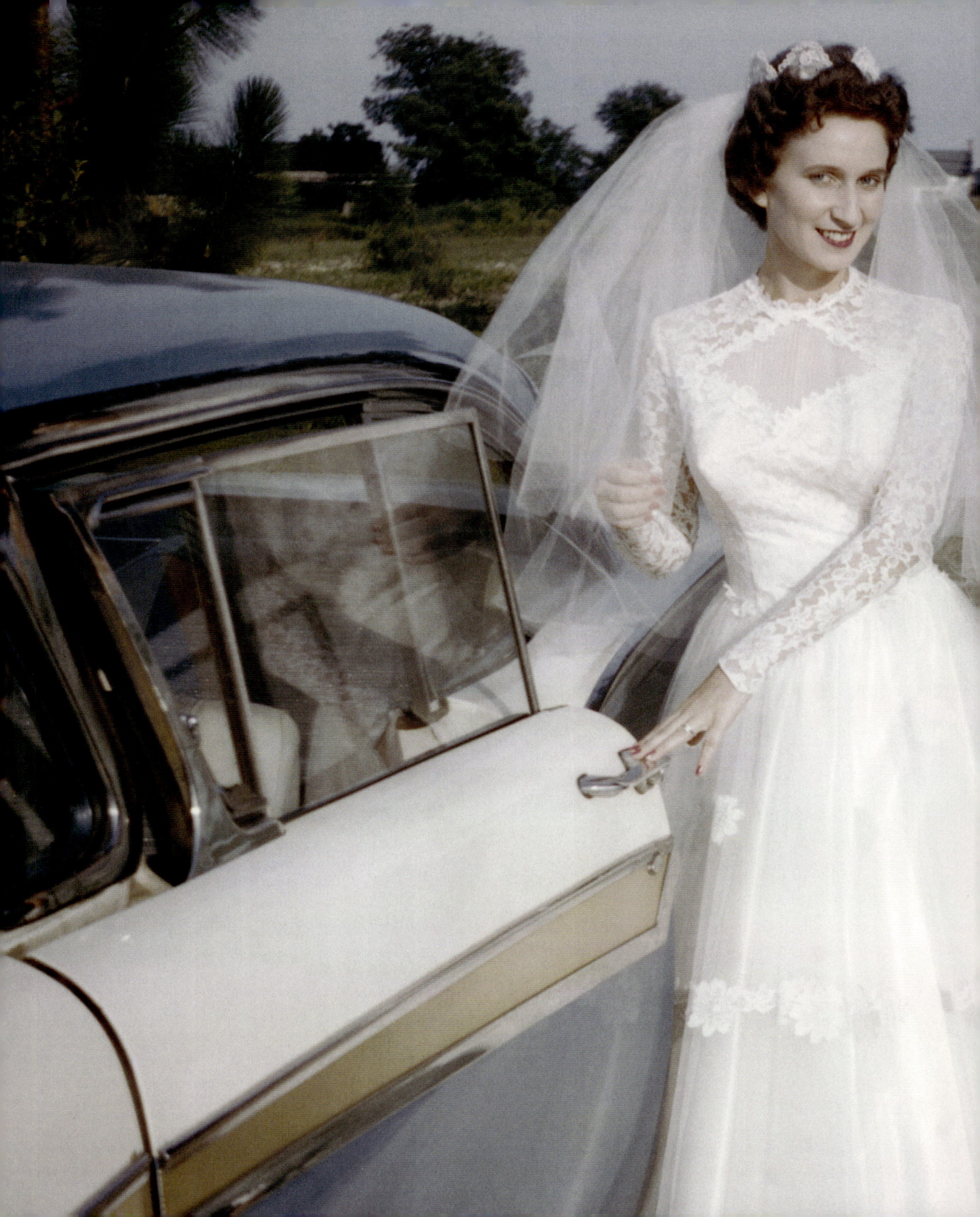

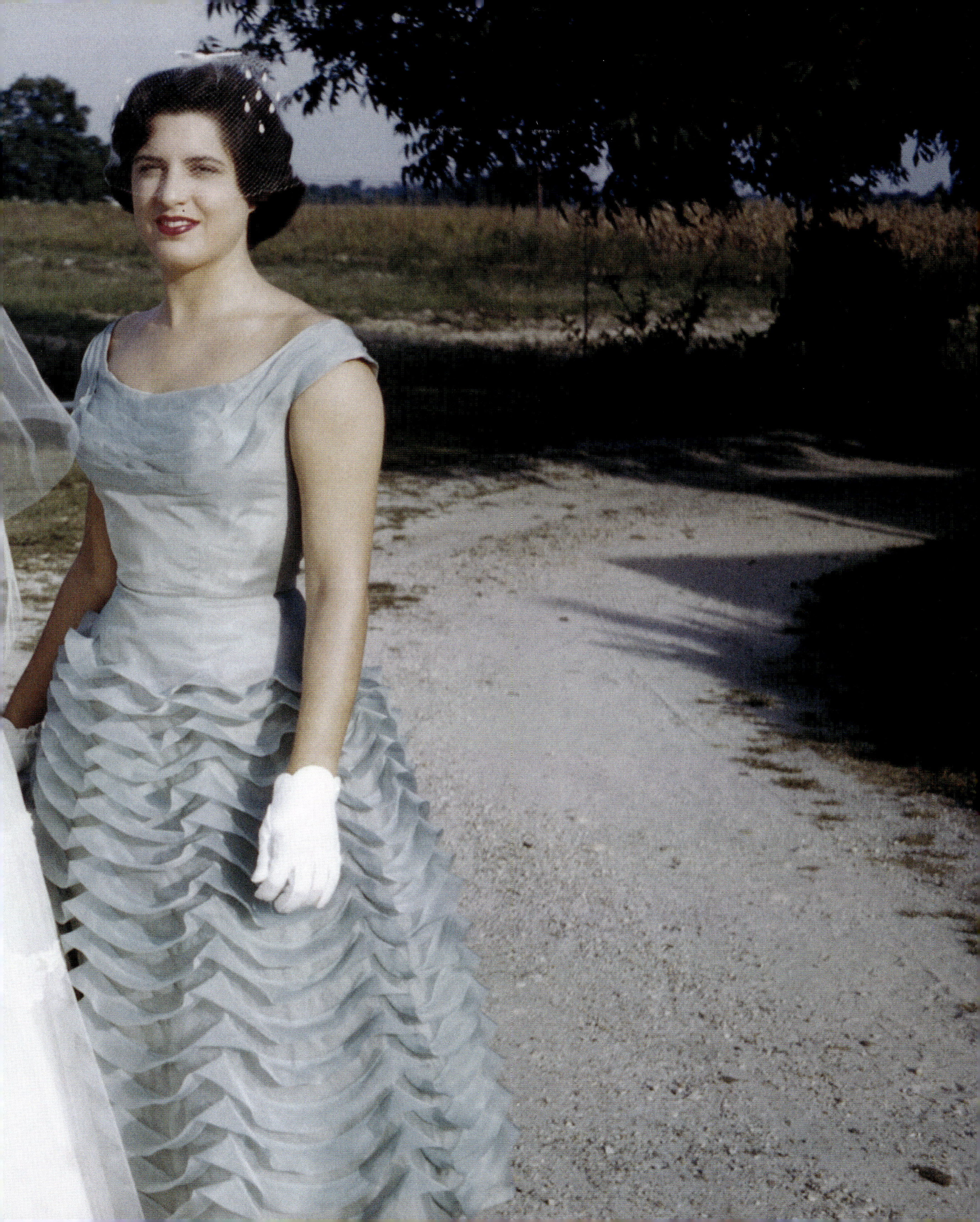

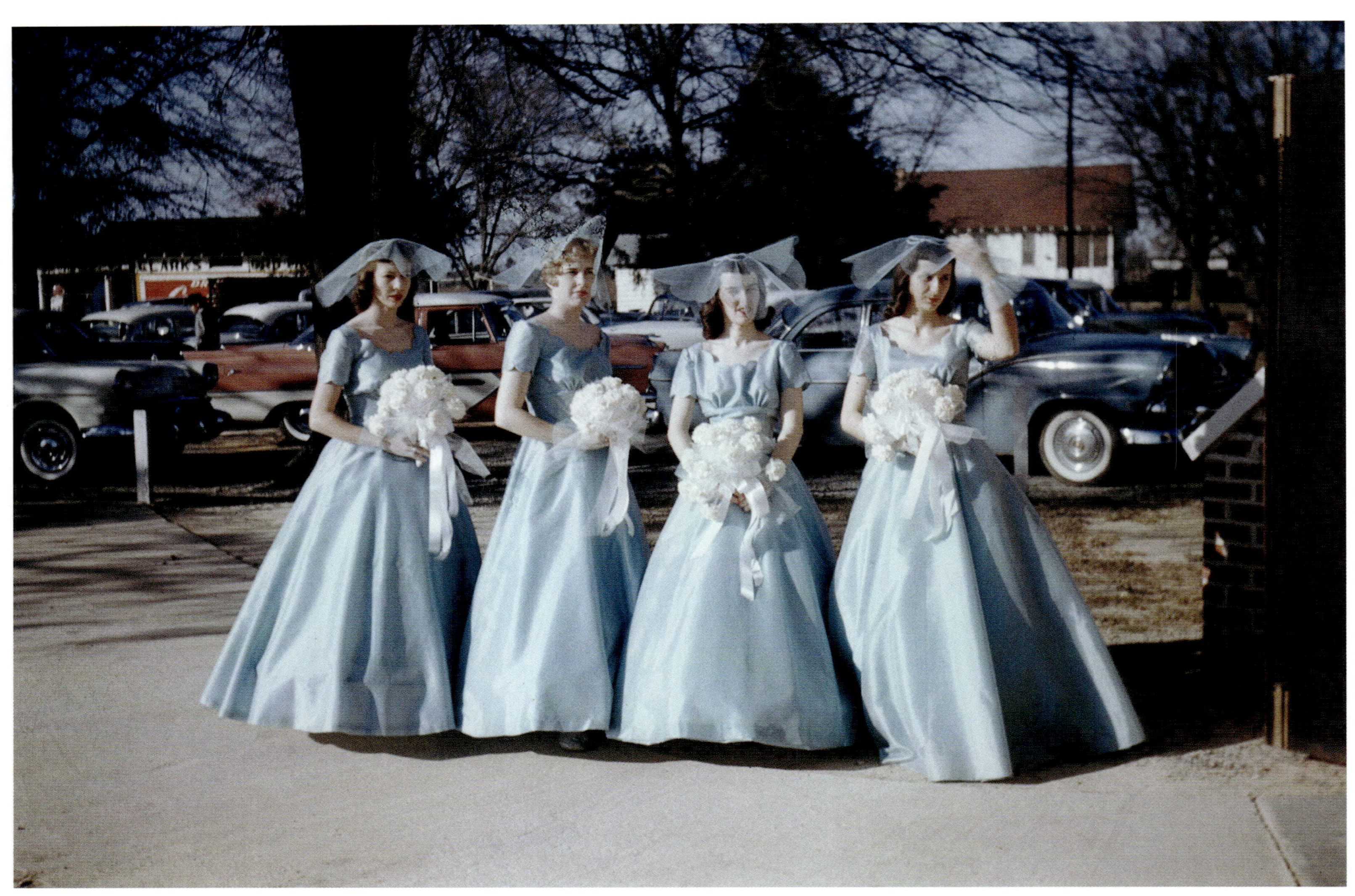

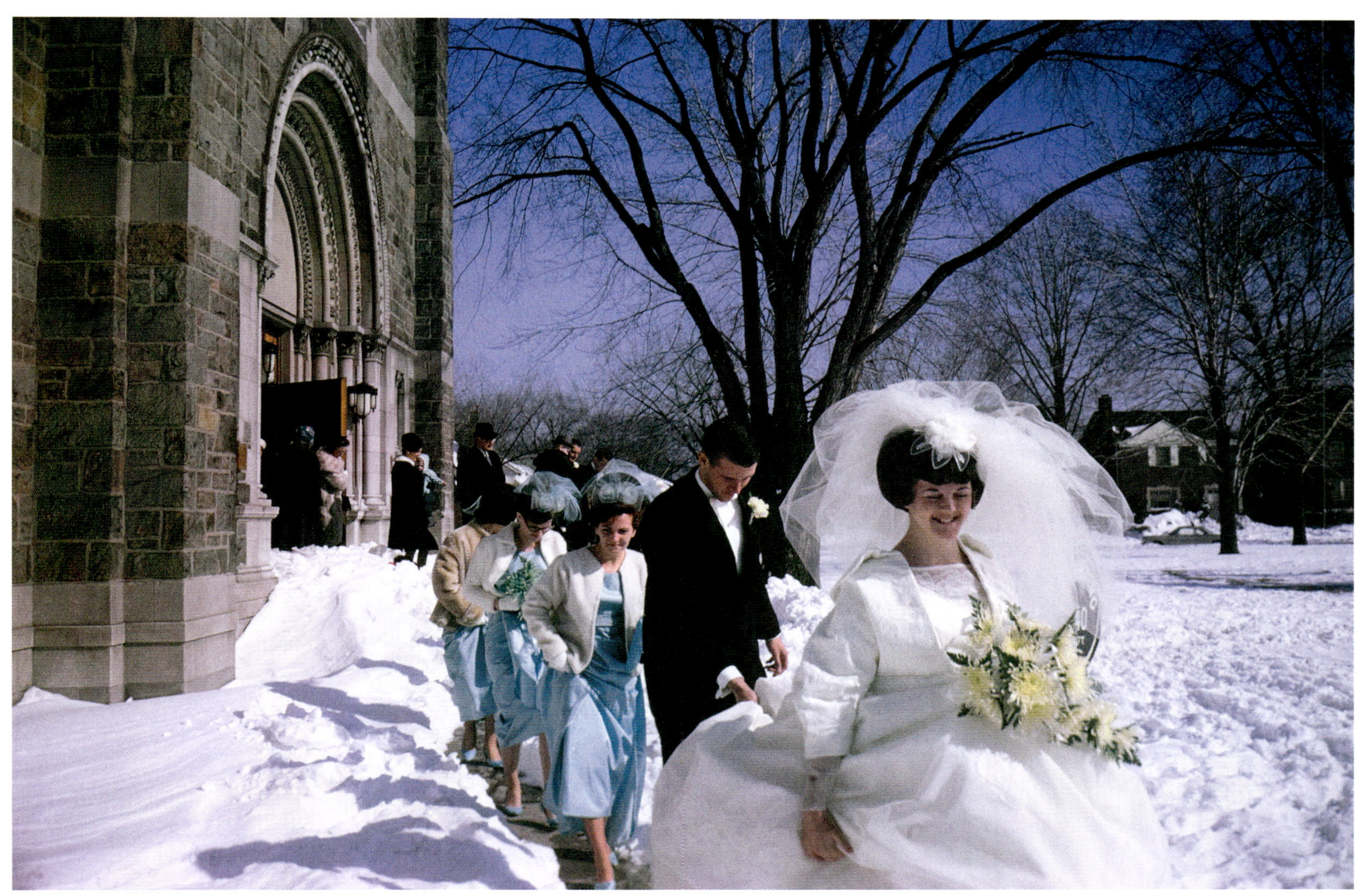

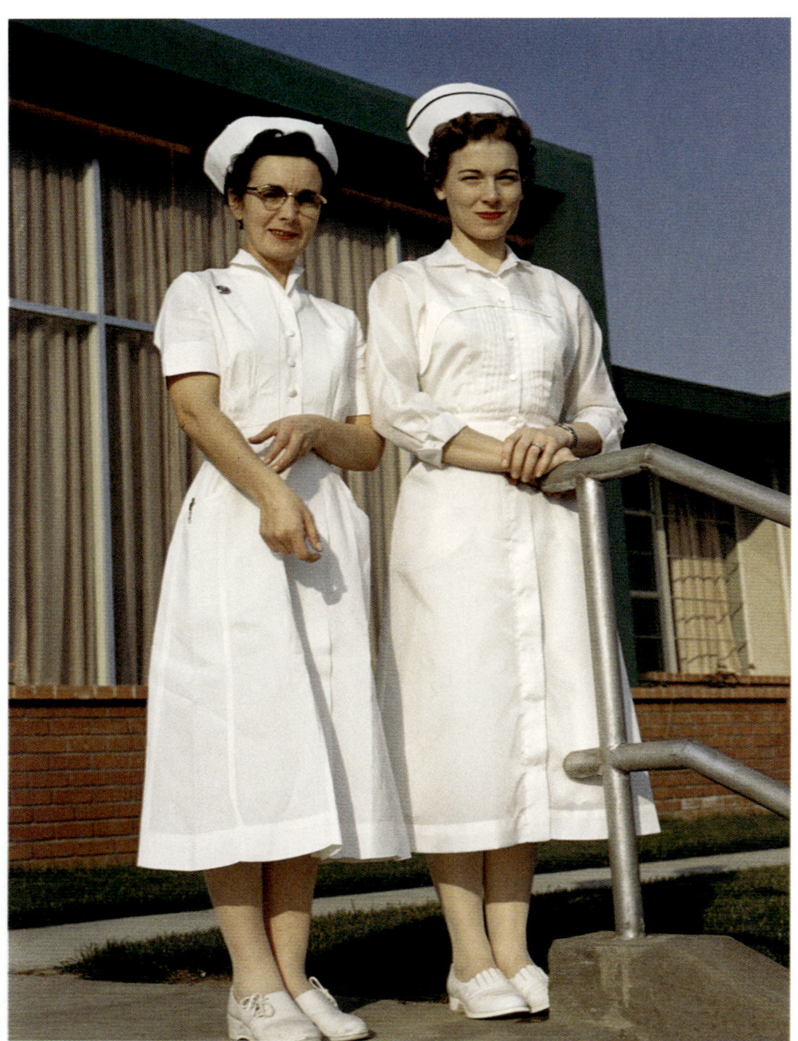

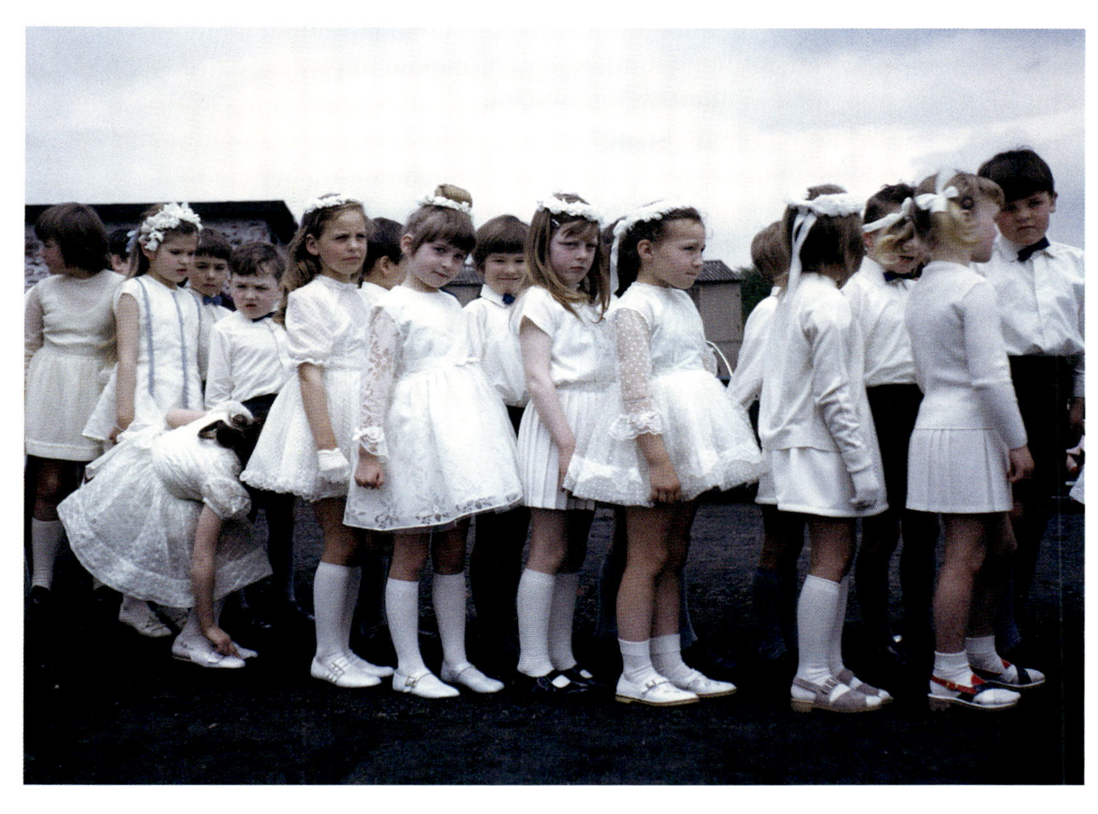

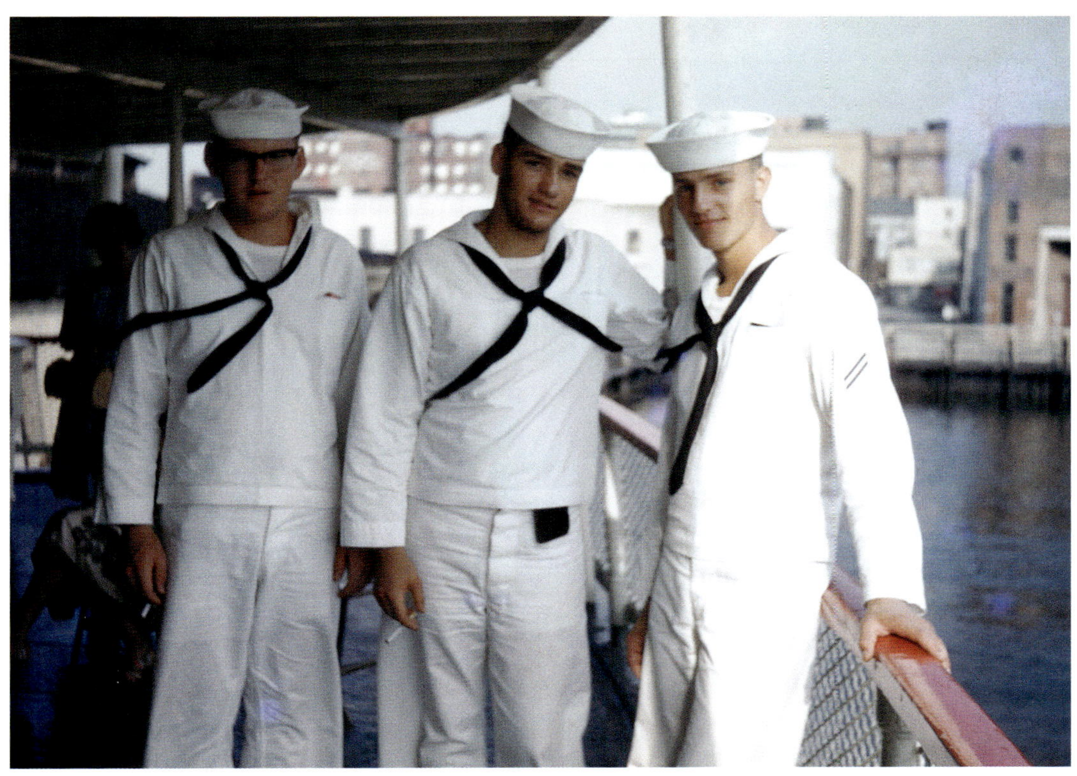

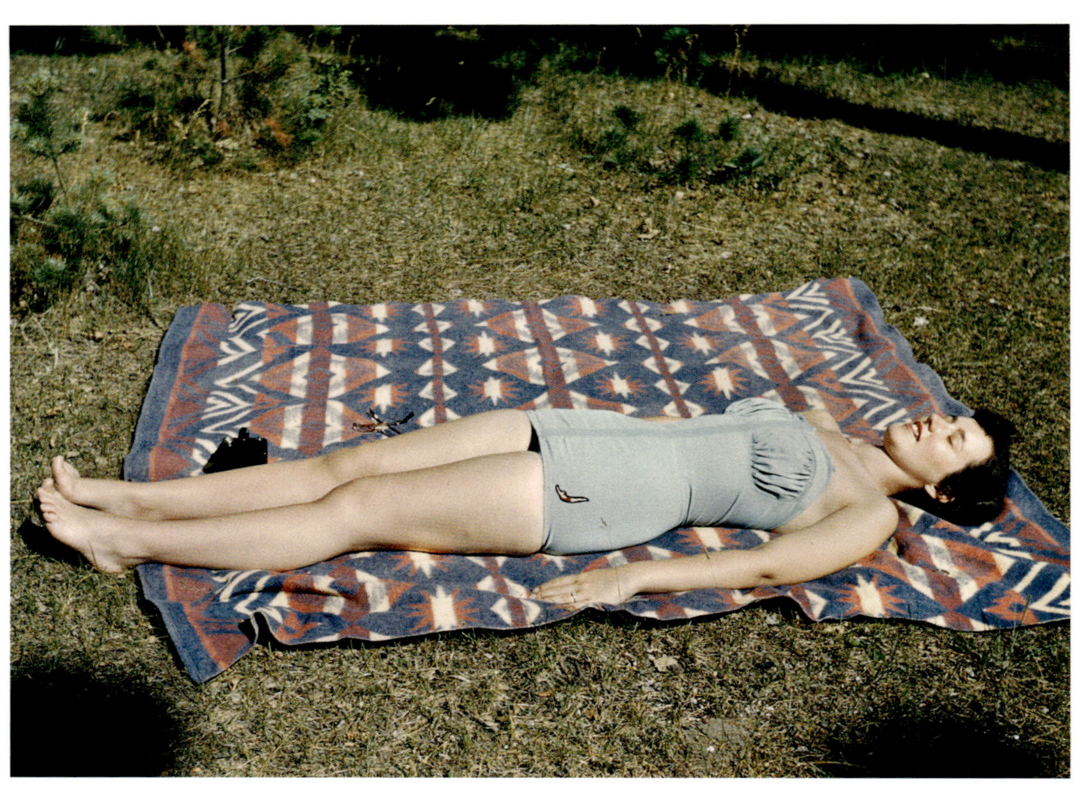

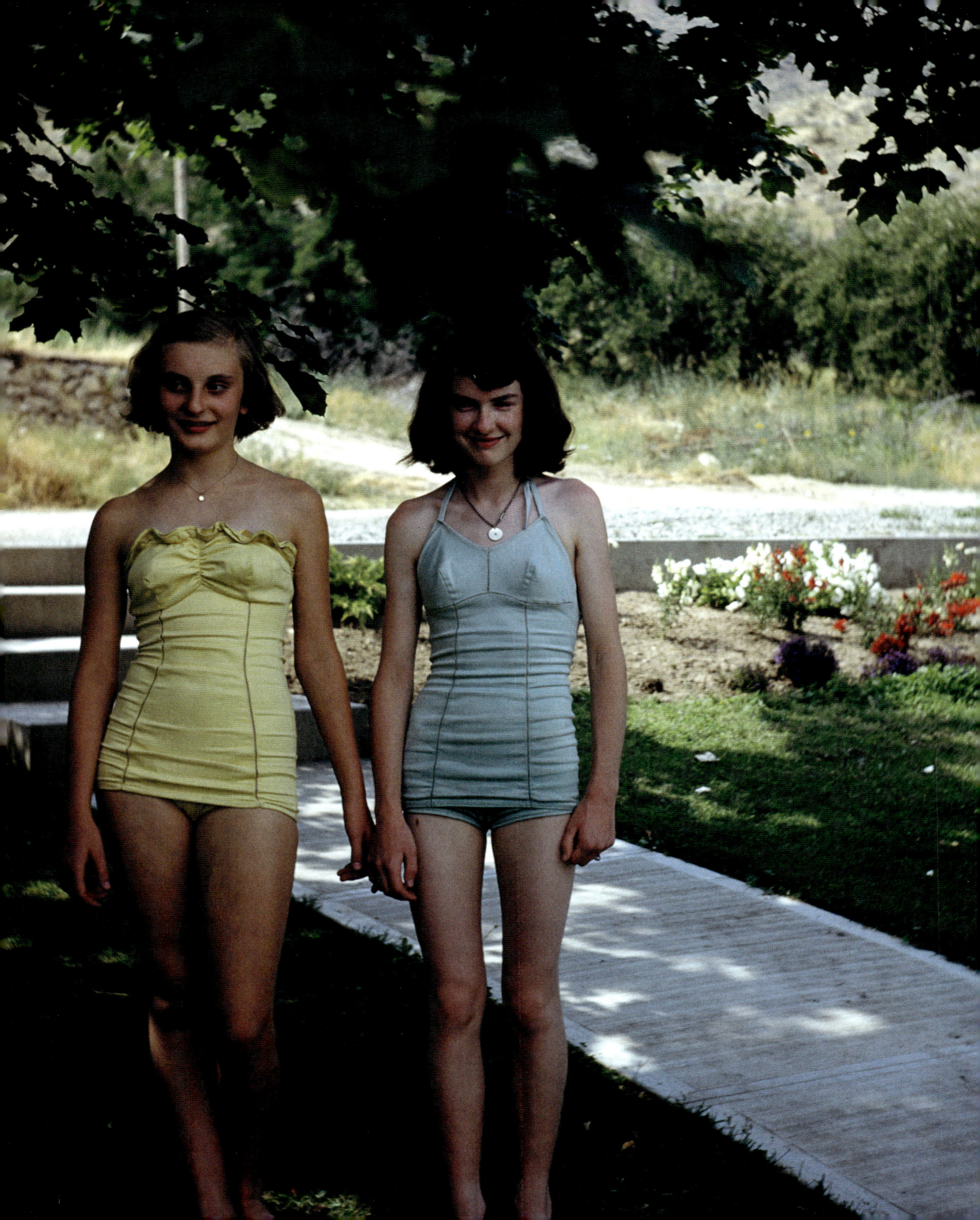

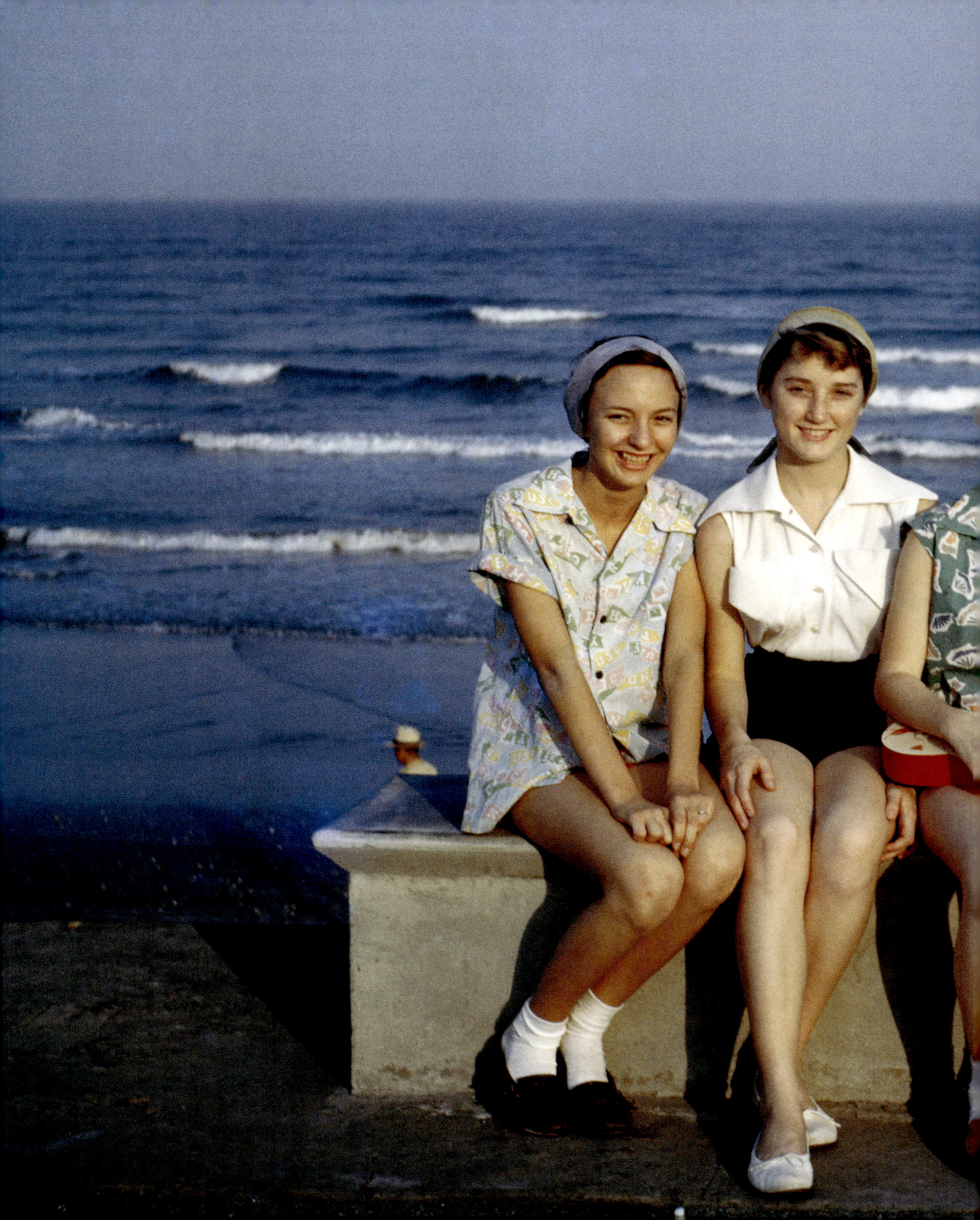

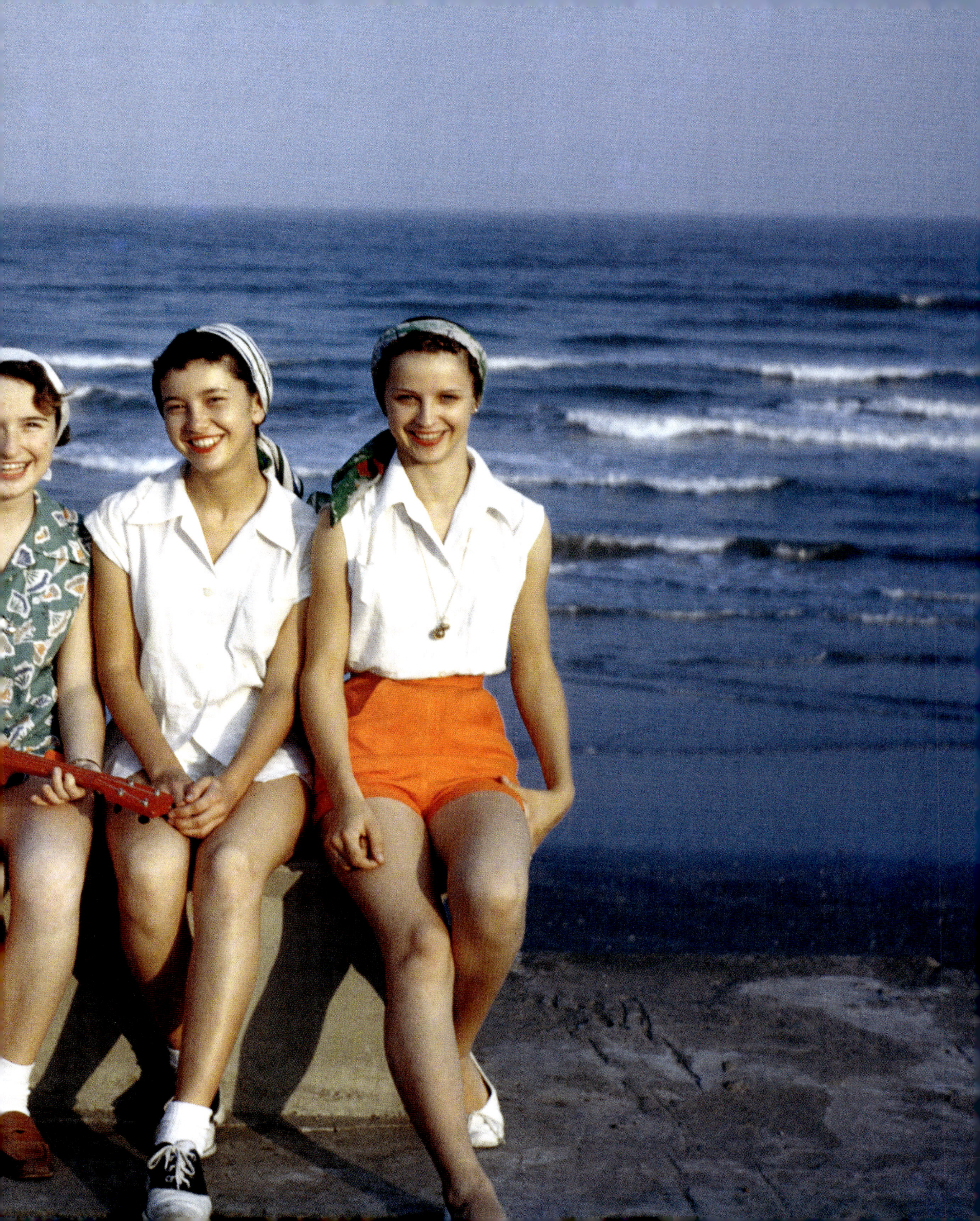

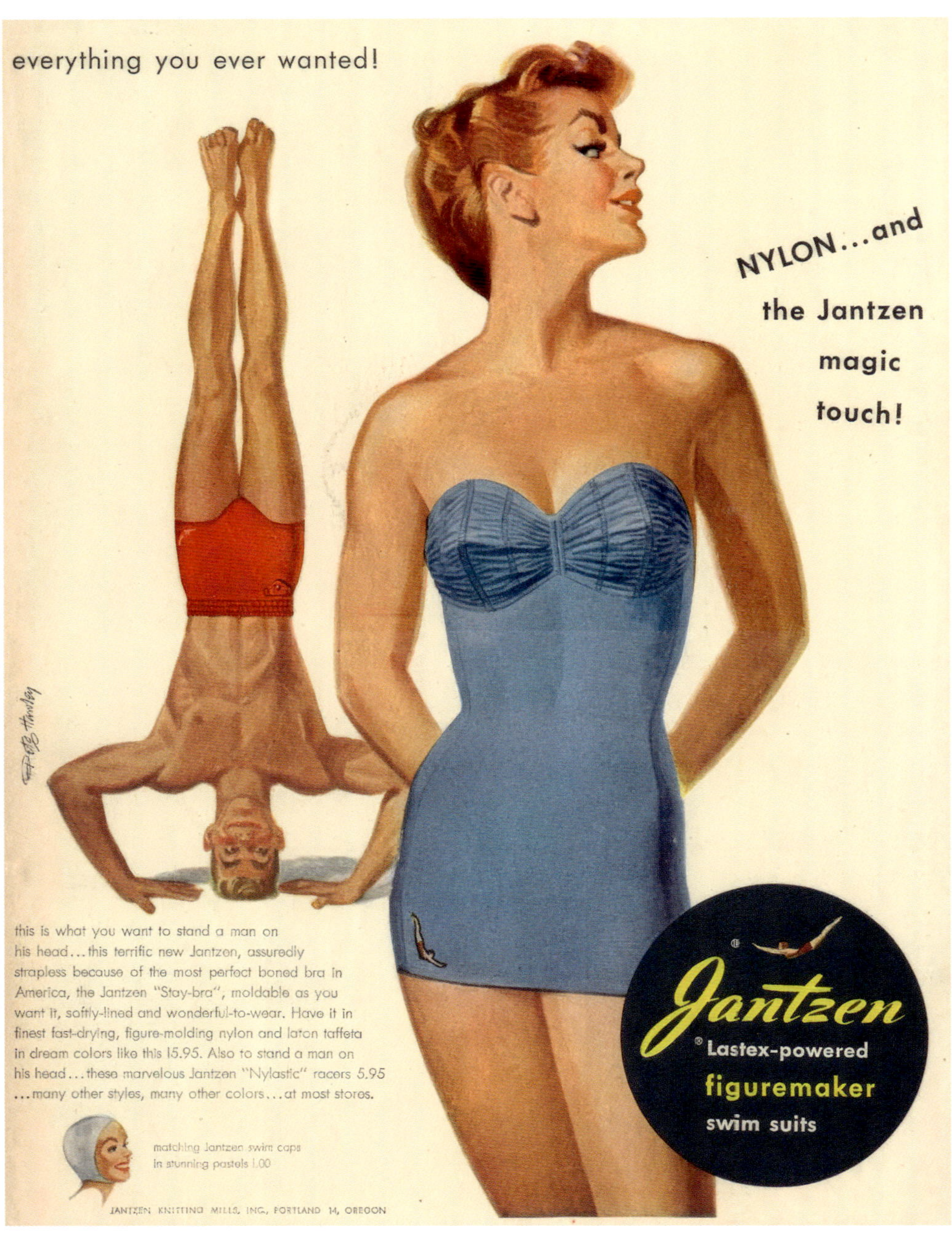

everything you ever wanted!
NYLON...and
the Jantzen
magic
touch!
this is what you want to stand a man on
his head...this terrific new Jantzen, assuredly
strapless because of the most perfect boned bra in
America, the Jantzen "Stay-bra", moldable as you
want it, softly-lined and wonderful-to-wear. Have it in
finest fast-drying, figure-molding nylon and laton taffeta
in dream colors like this 15.95. Also to stand a man on
his head...these marvelous Jantzen "Nylastic" racers 5.95
...many other styles, many other colors...at most stores.
matching Jantzen swim caps
in stunning pastels 1.00
JANTZEN KNITTING MILLS, INC., PORTLAND 14, OREGON
Jantzen
Lastex-powered
figuremaker
swim suits

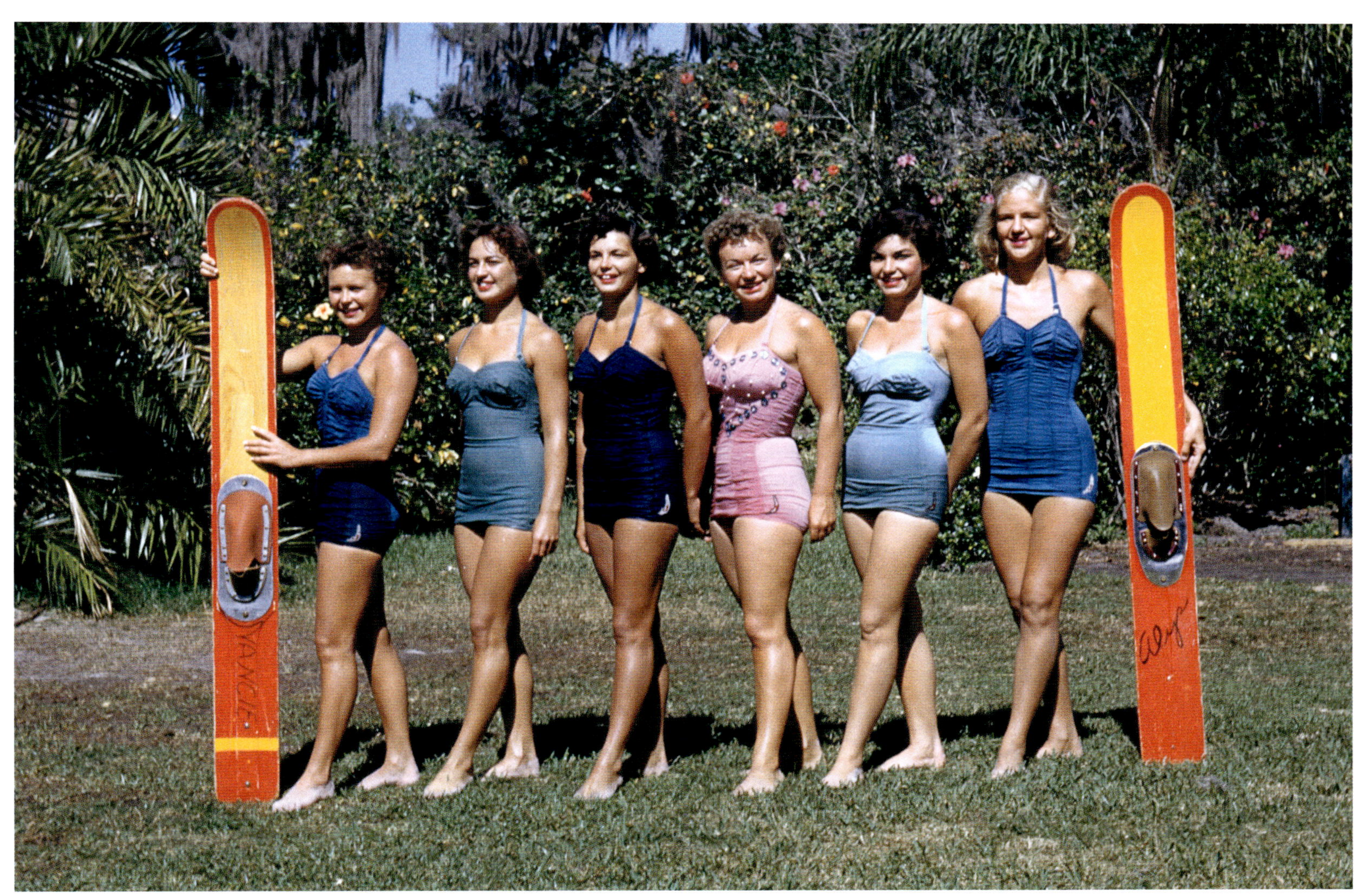

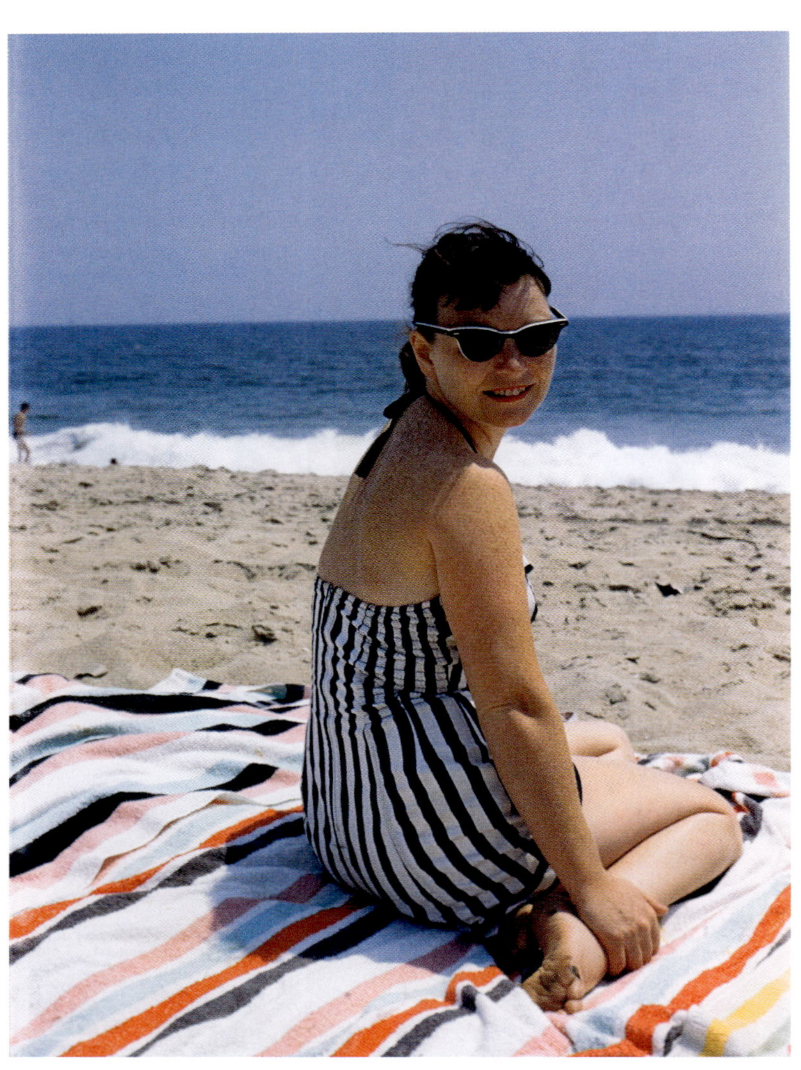

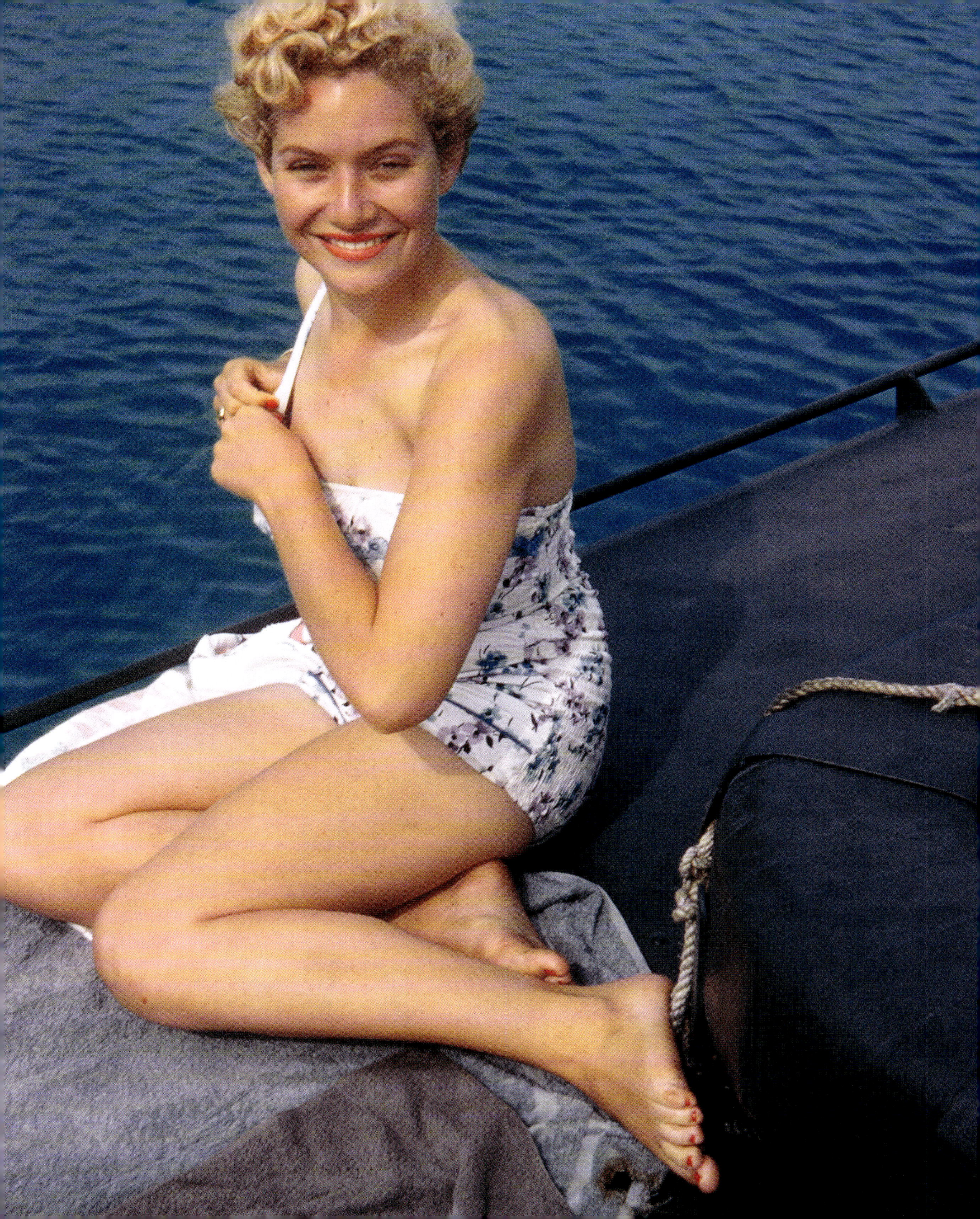

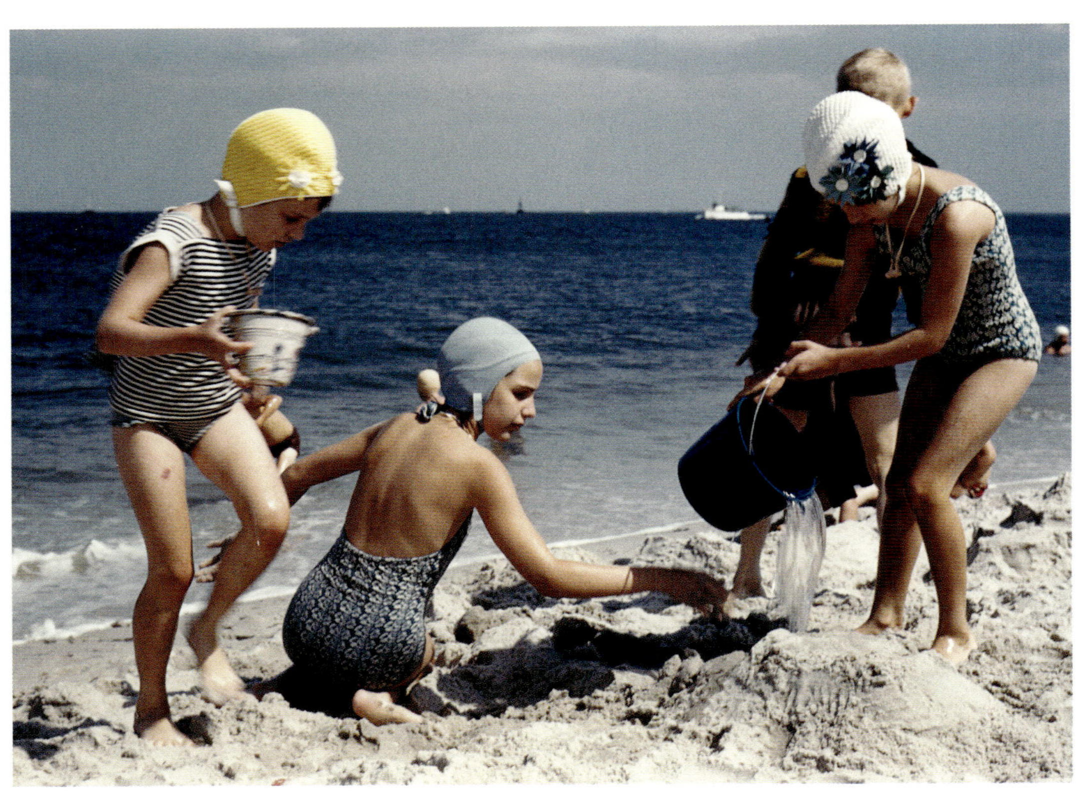

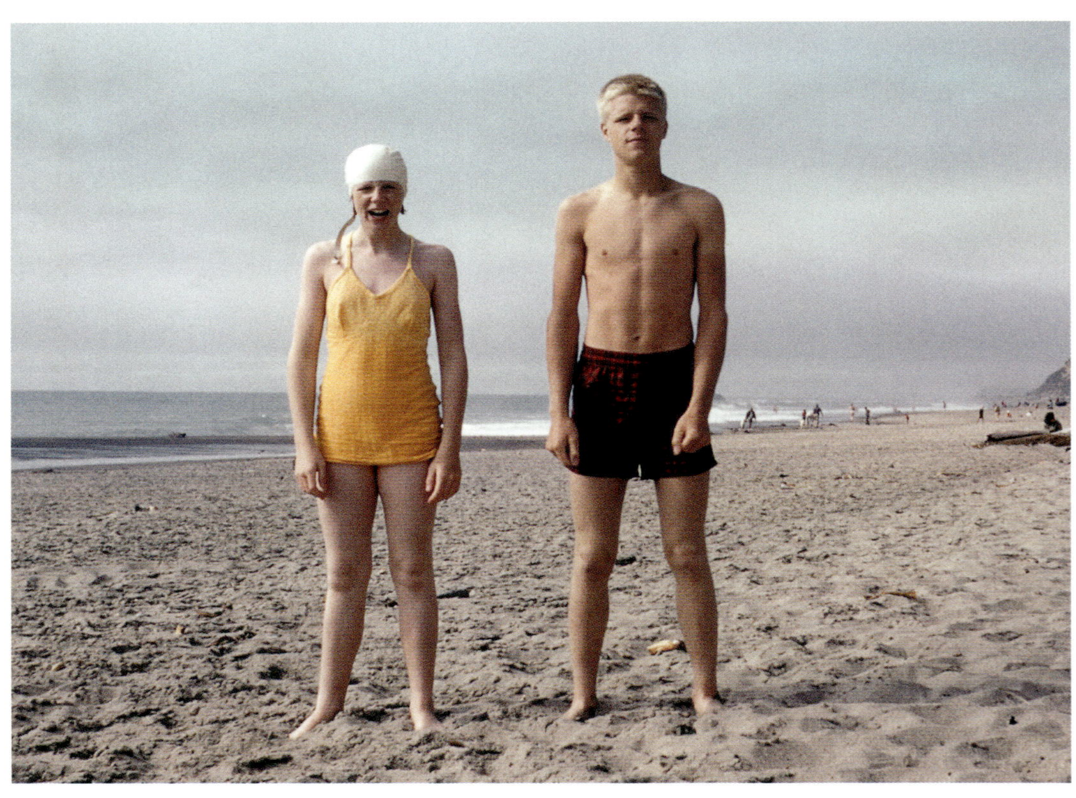

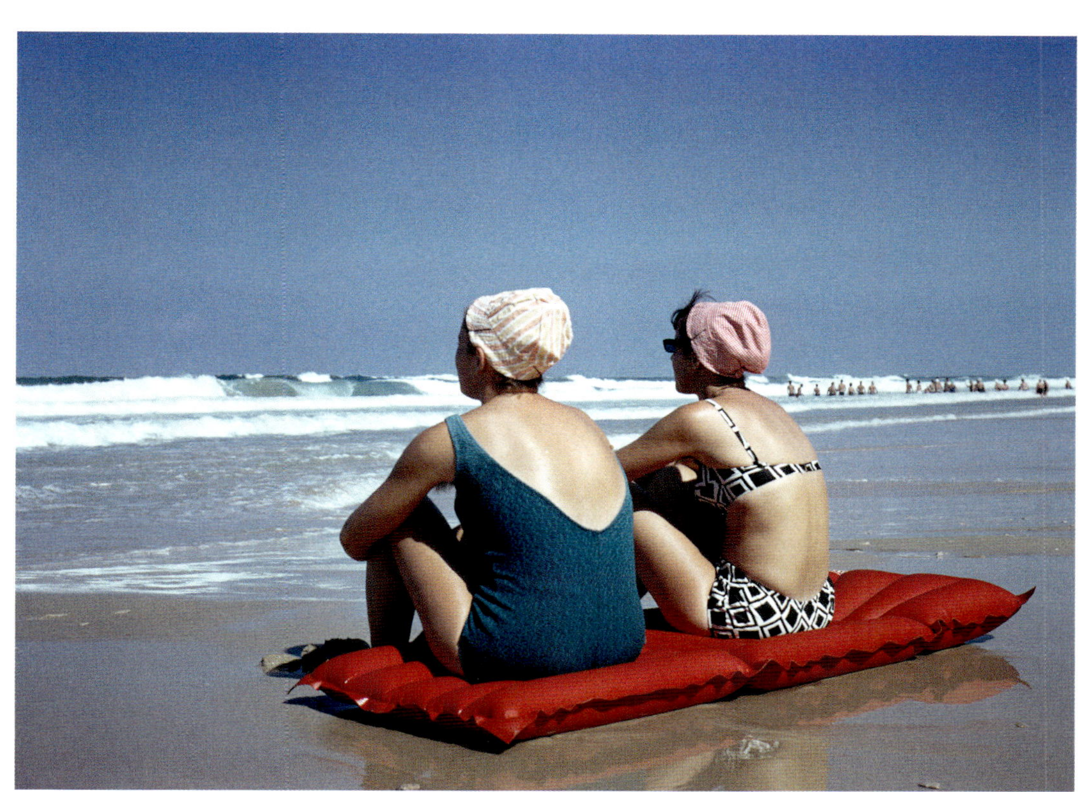

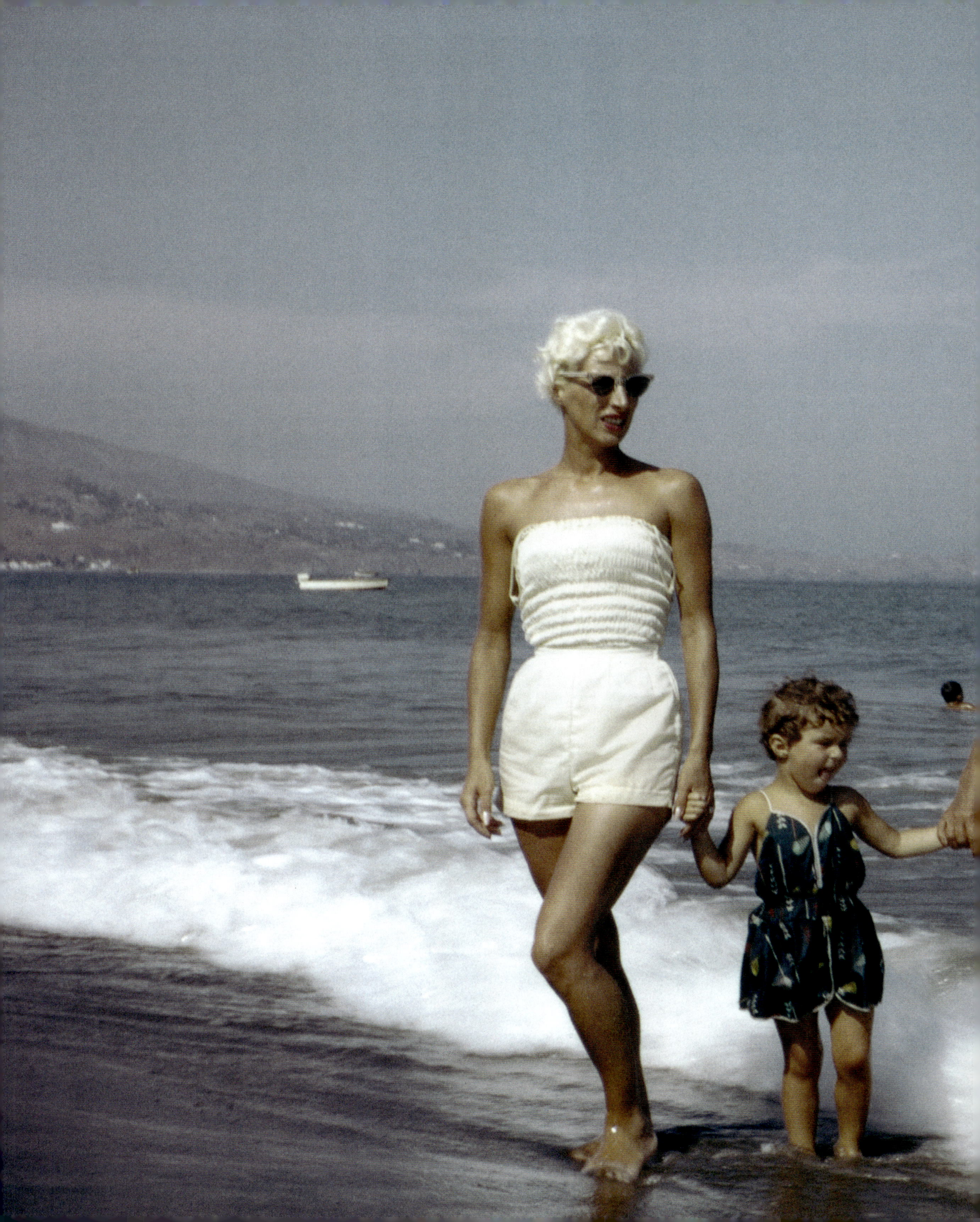

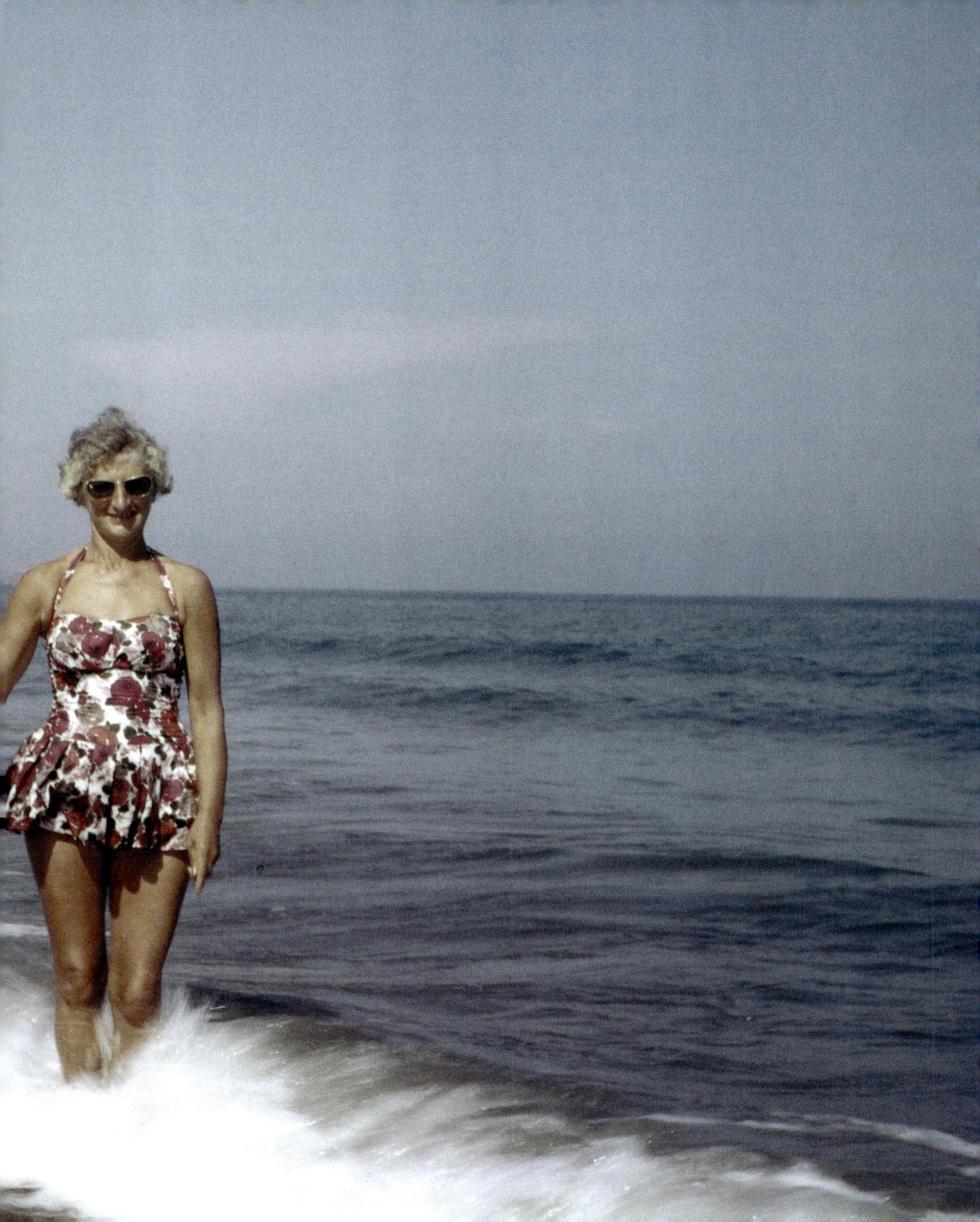

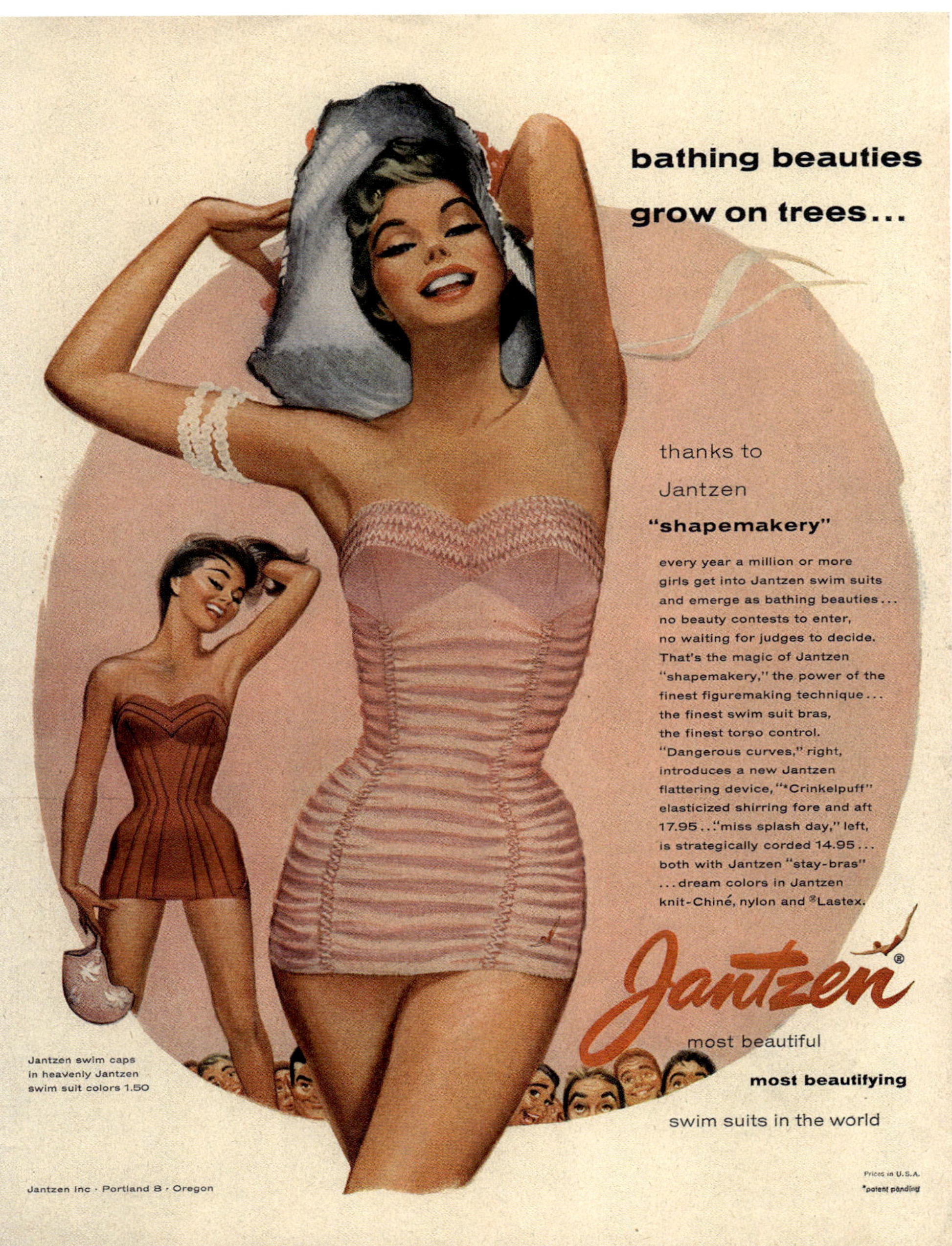
bathing beauties
grow on trees...
thanks to
Jantzen
"shapemakery"
every year a million or more girls get into Jantzen swim suits and emerge as bathing beauties... no beauty contests to enter, no waiting for judges to decide. That's the magic of Jantzen "shapemakery," the power of the finest figuremaking technique... the finest swim suit bras, the finest torso control. "Dangerous curves," right, introduces a new Jantzen flattering device, "*Crinkelpuff" elasticized shirring fore and aft 17.95..."miss splash day," left, is strategically corded 14.95... both with Jantzen "stay-bras" ...dream colors in Jantzen knit-Chiné, nylon and ®Lastex.
Jantzen®
most beautiful
most beautifying
swim suits in the world
Jantzen swim caps in heavenly Jantzen swim suit colors 1.50
Jantzen inc · Portland 8 · Oregon
Prices in U.S.A.
*patent pending

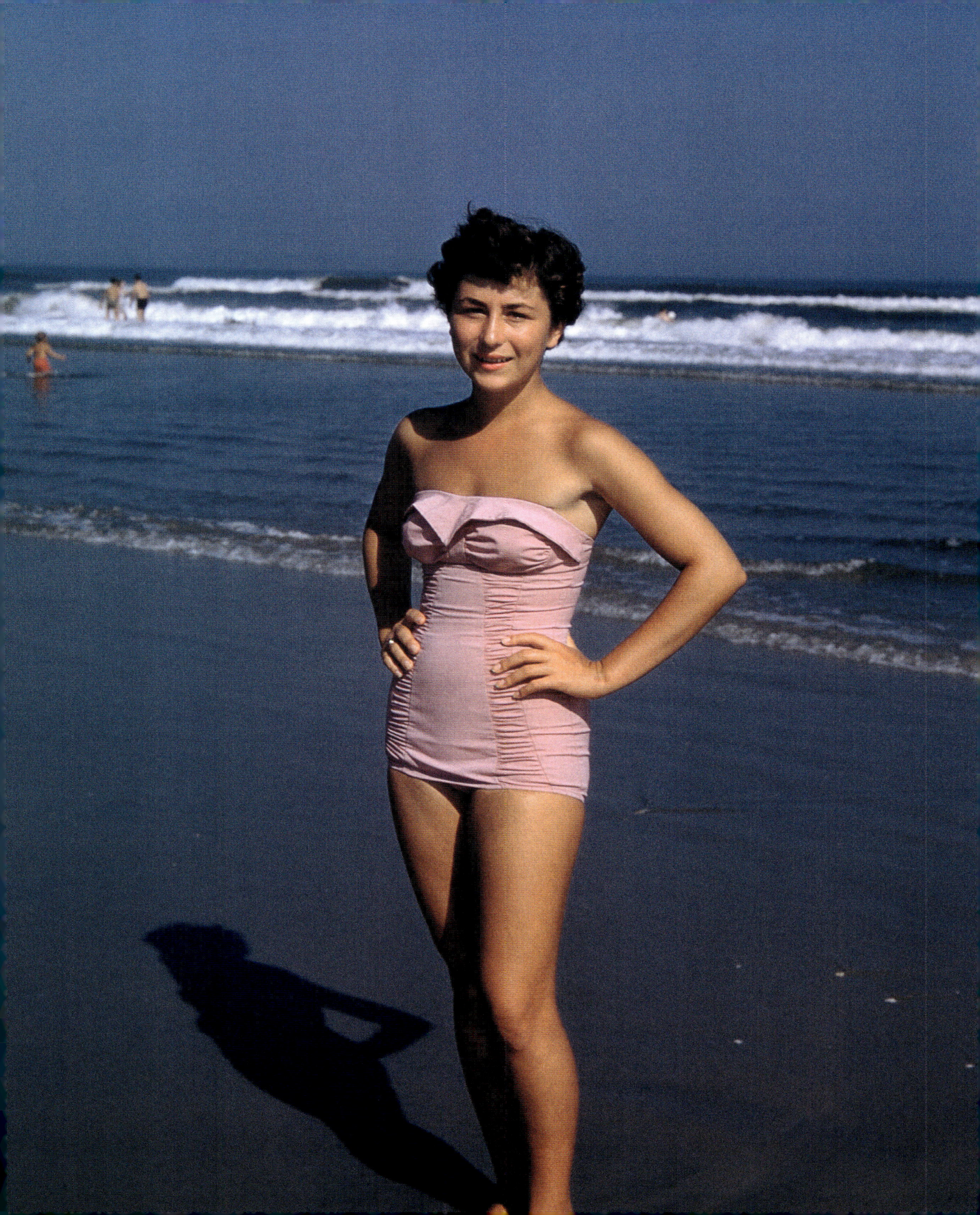

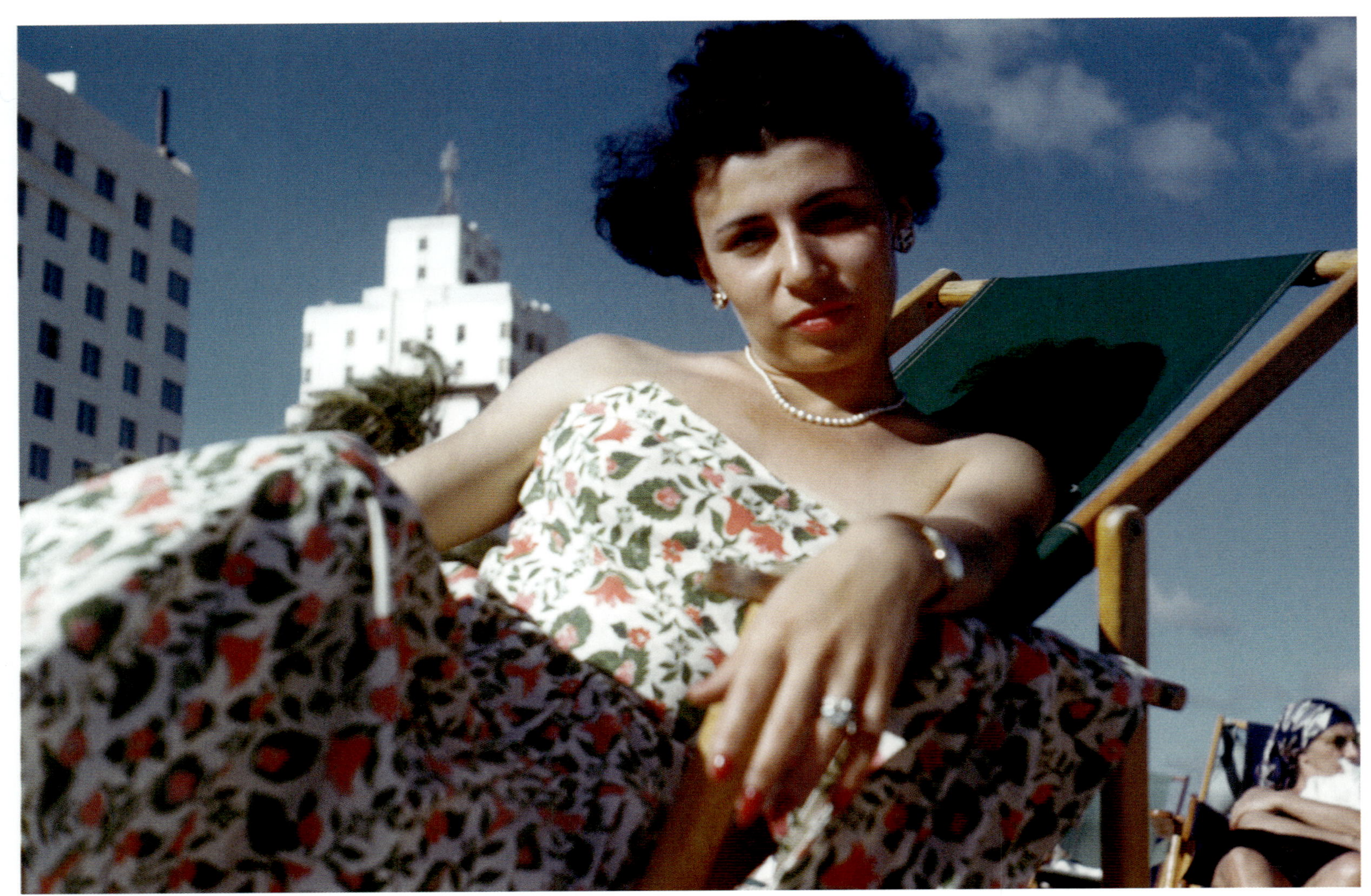

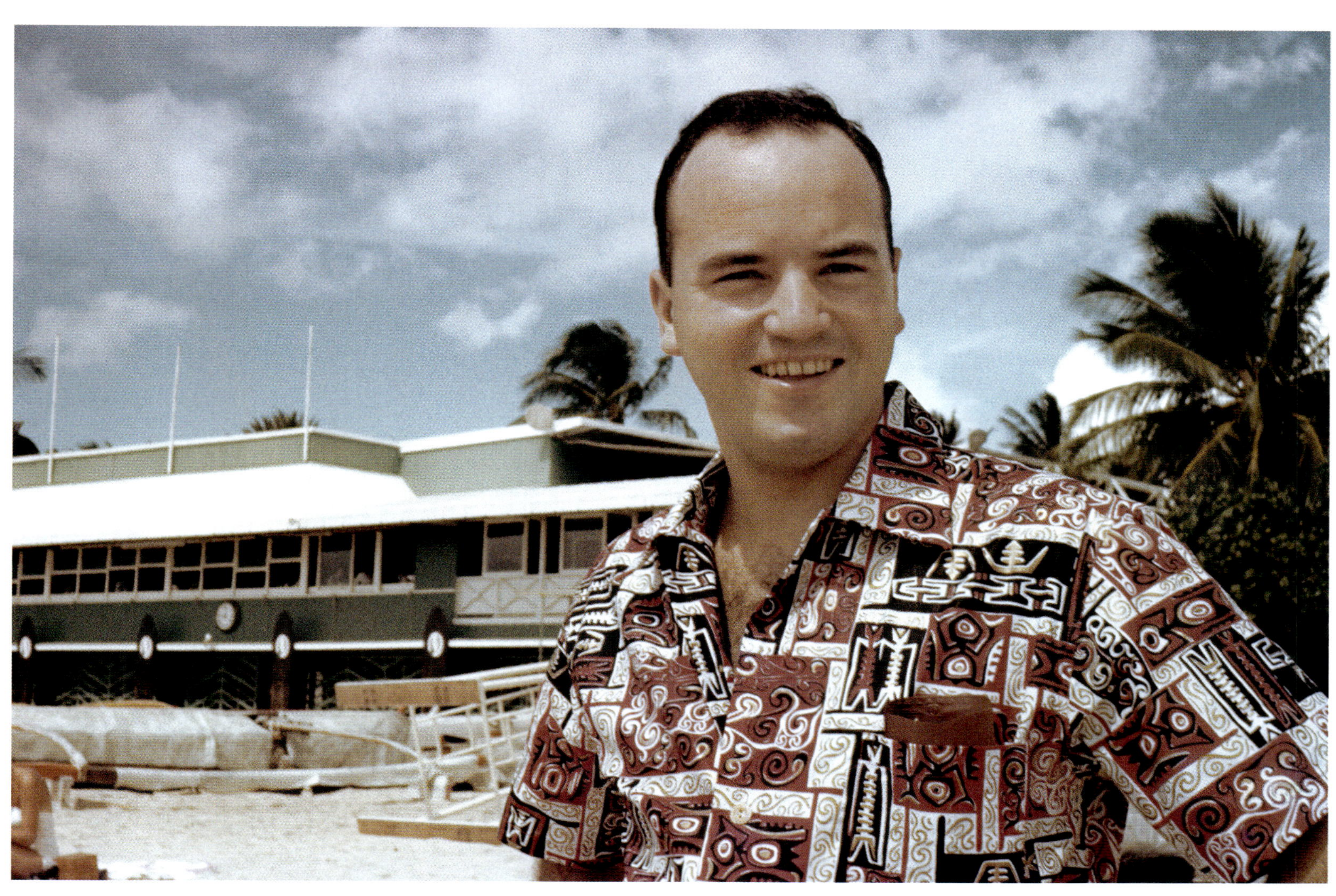

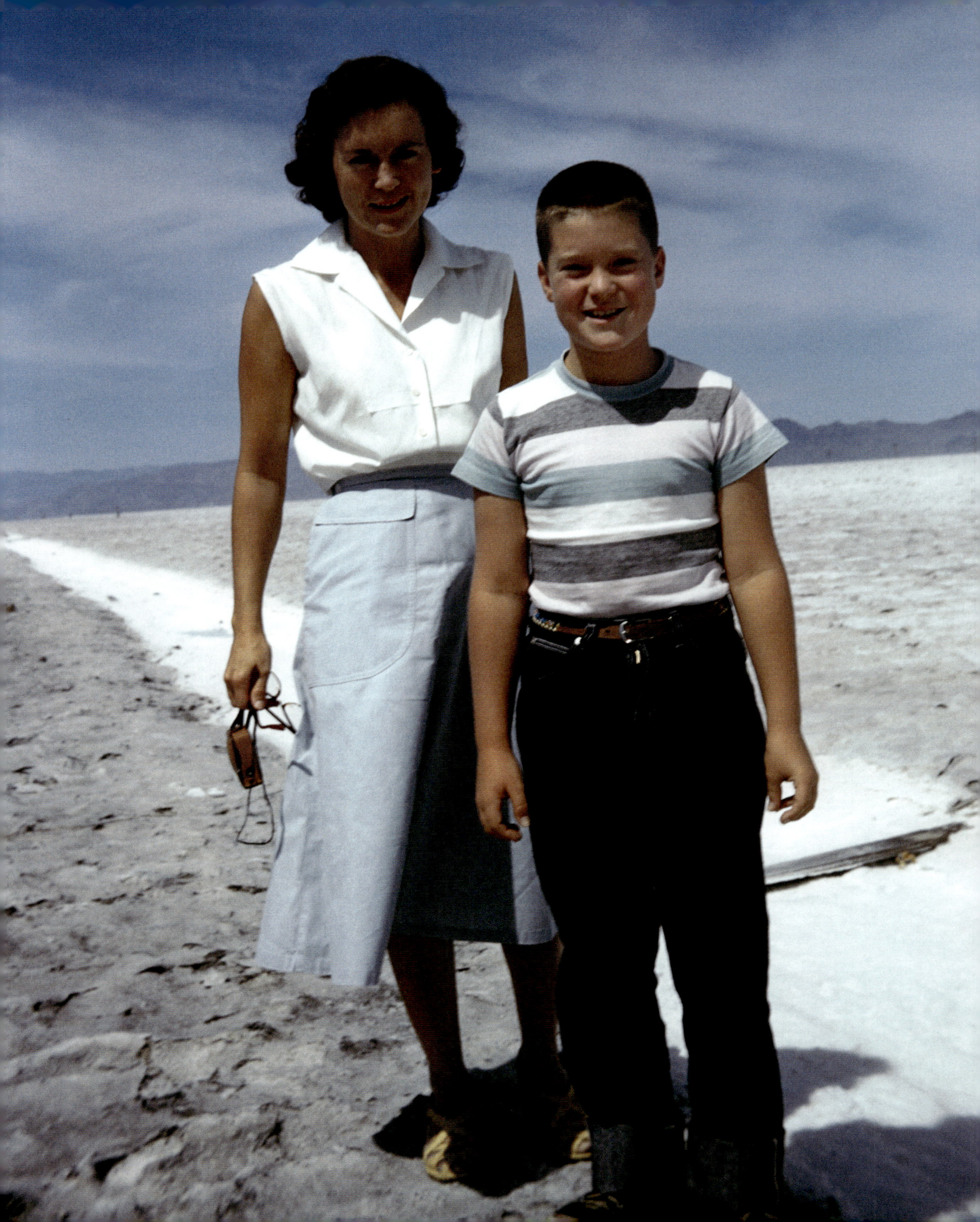

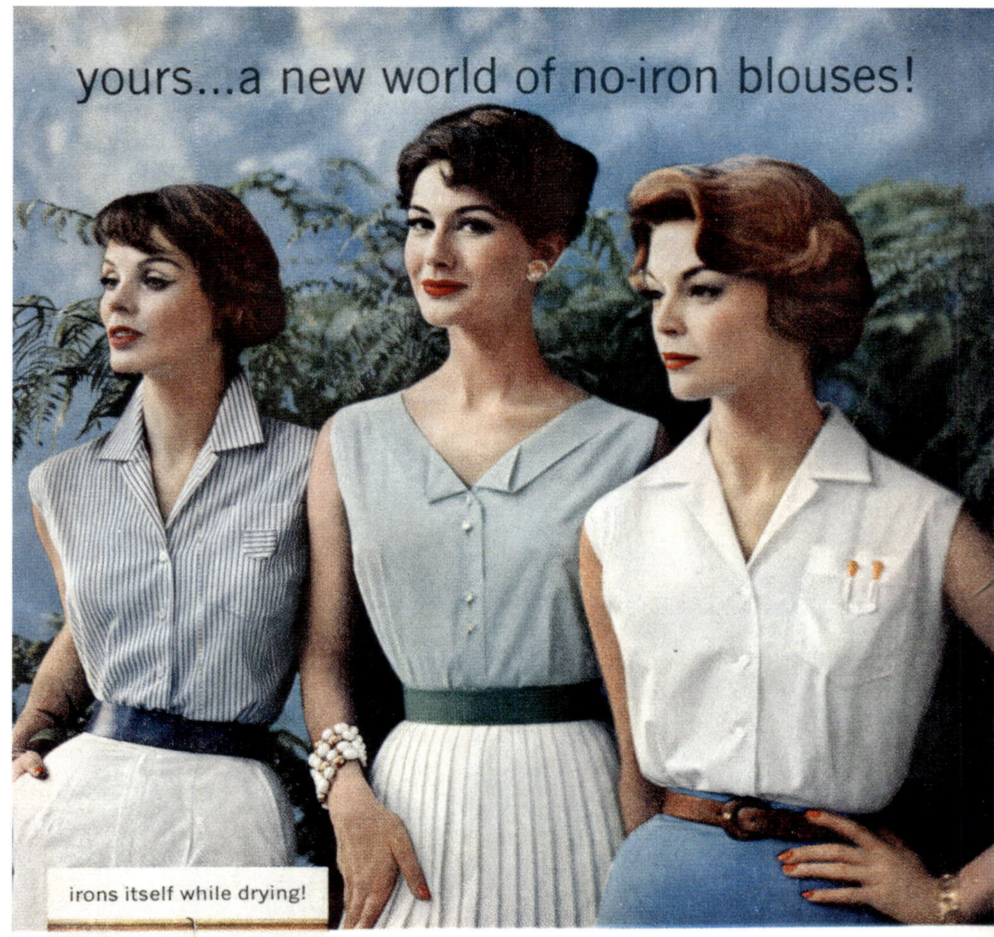

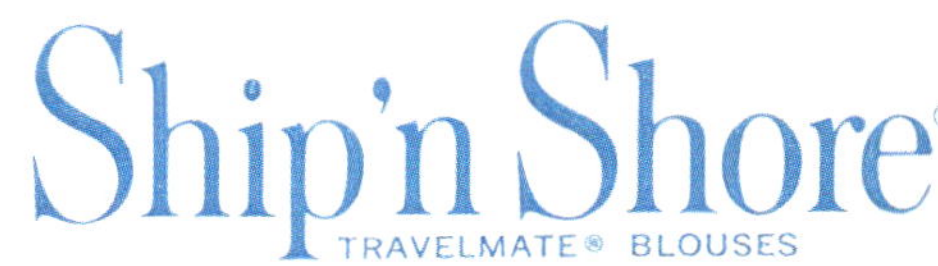

65% Dacron and 35% Fine Cotton

It's a pleasure living in these no-iron blouses. They're refreshing to wear and so free of care! All you ever need do is dip them in suds and hang them for quick drip-drying. This is the fabric of proven perfection! No worry about pilling, fuzzing or shrinking. And it's permanently no-iron! See these lovely Travelmates at your favorite fashion store. The shirts, with exclusive Tee-Tab™ pocket... the scoop blouse, with a new turn-back collar. Sizes 30 to 38. Wonderful buys at 2.98

Other Travelmates in sizes 38 to 44, 3.50 for children, 2.50

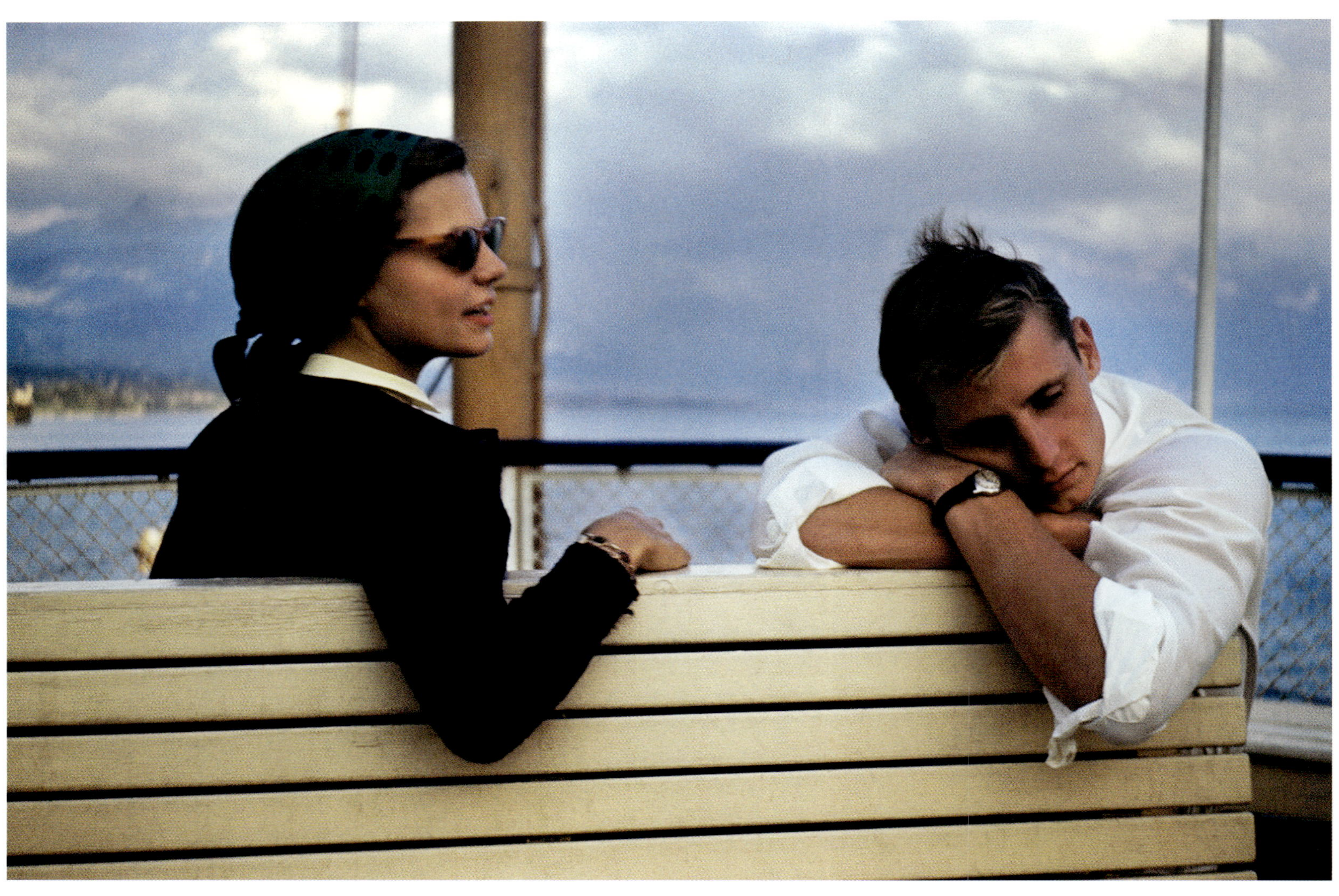

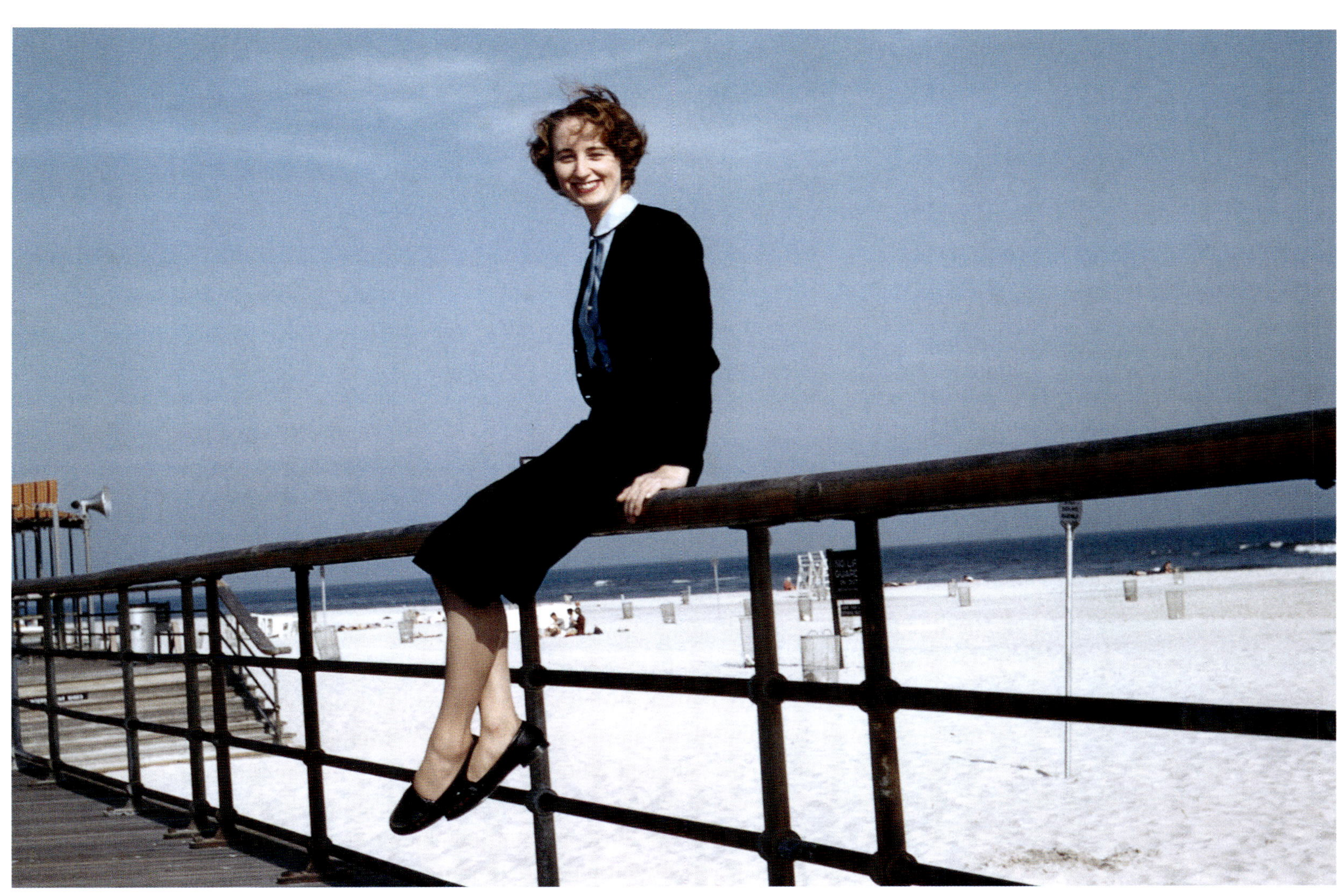

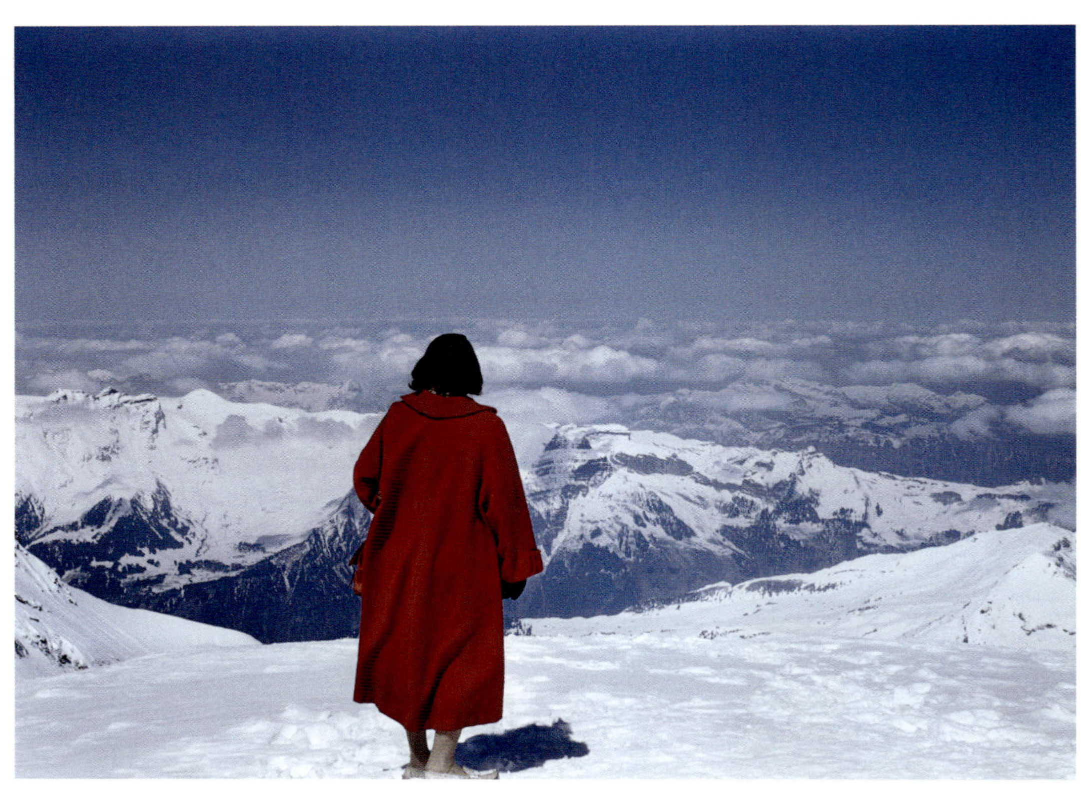

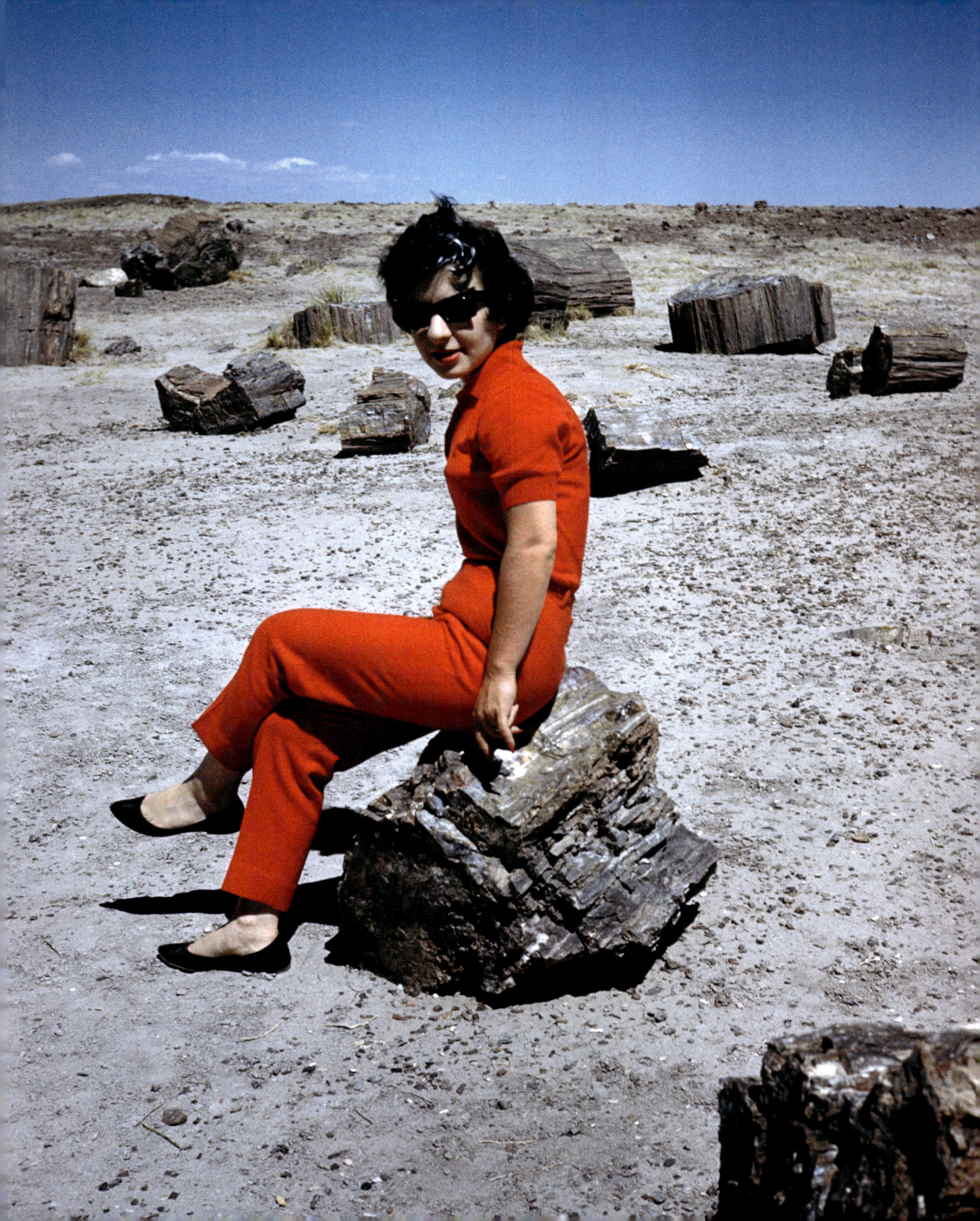

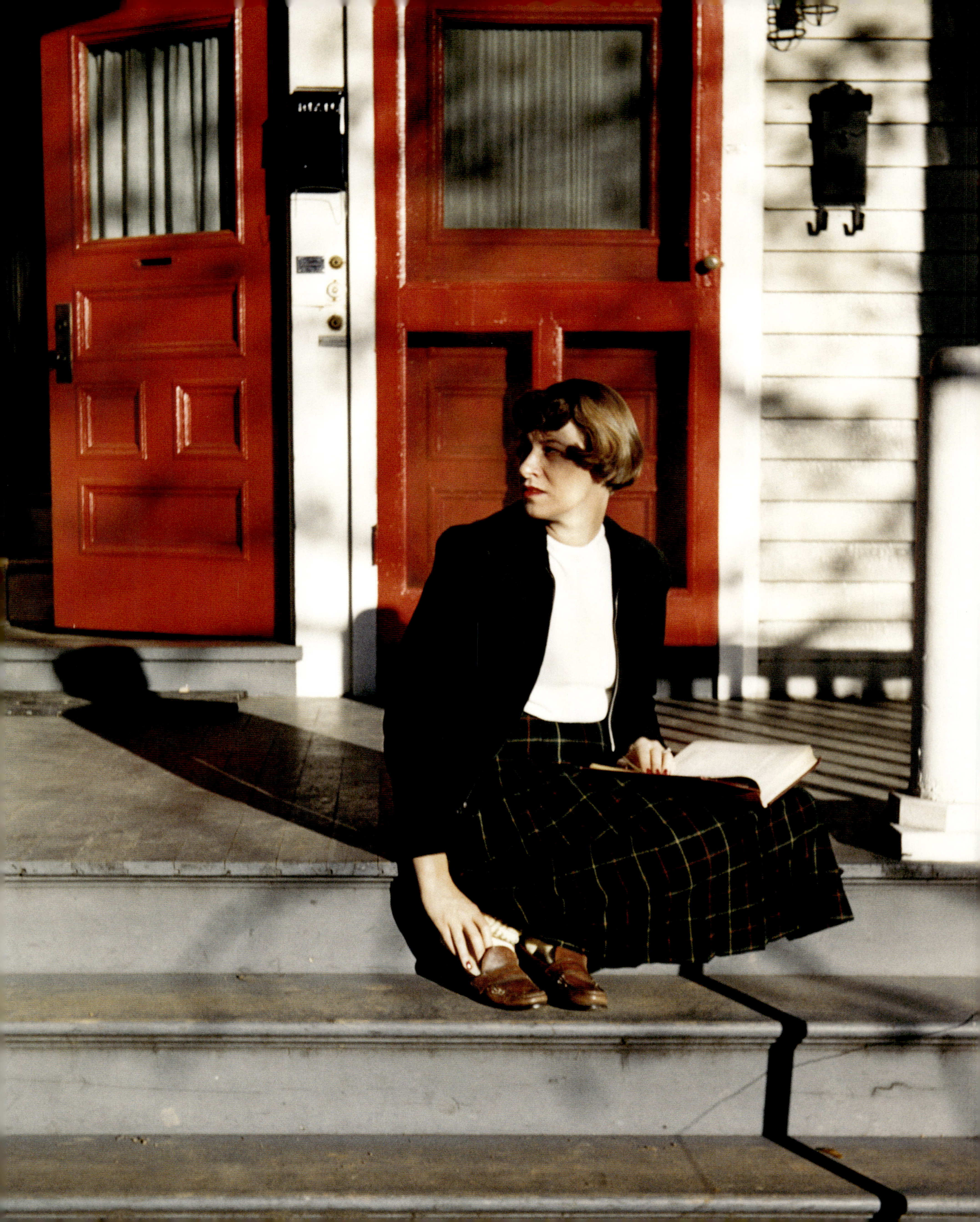

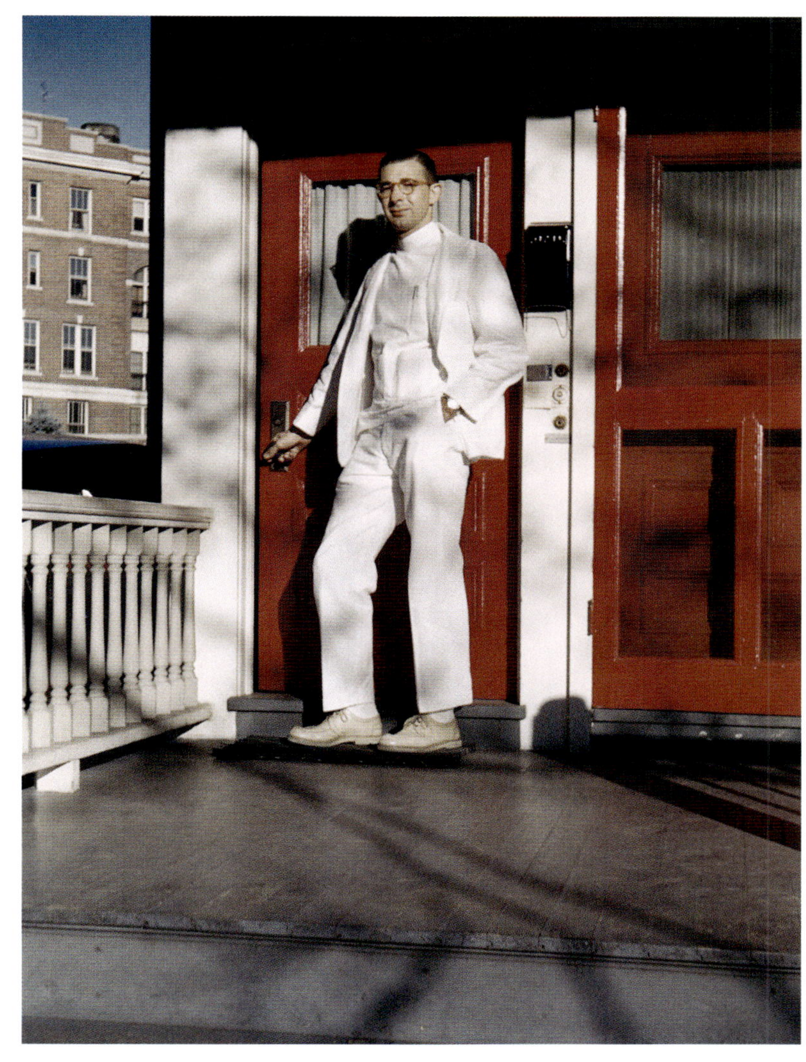

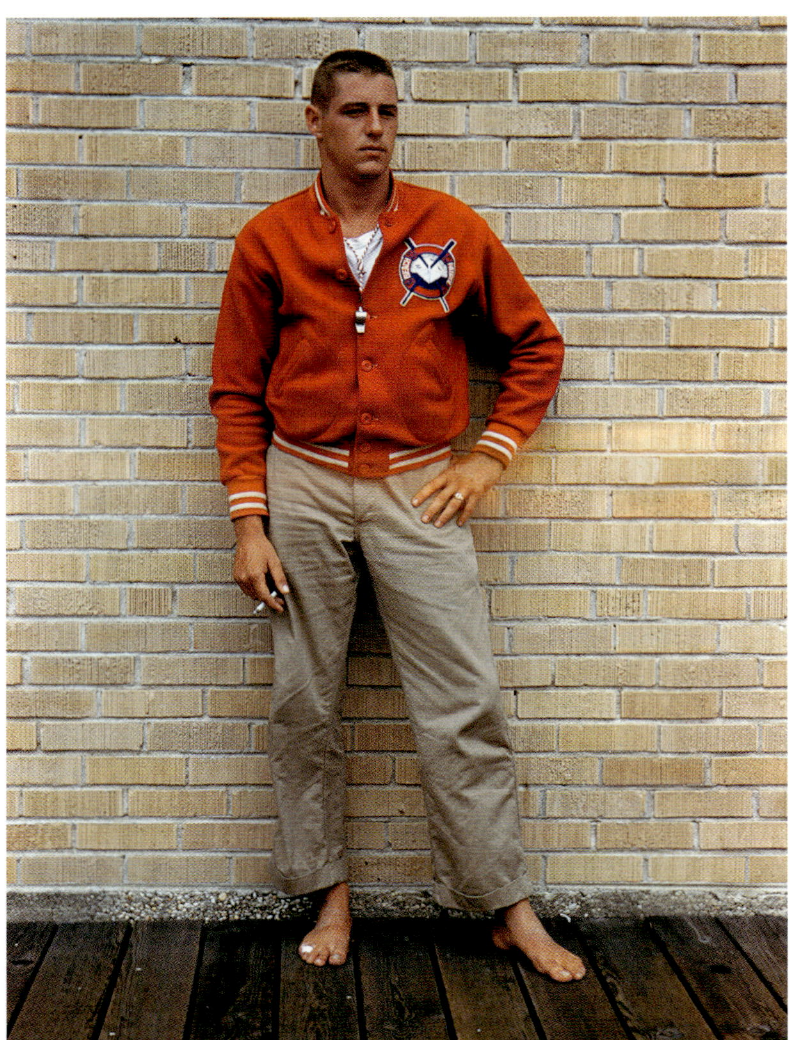

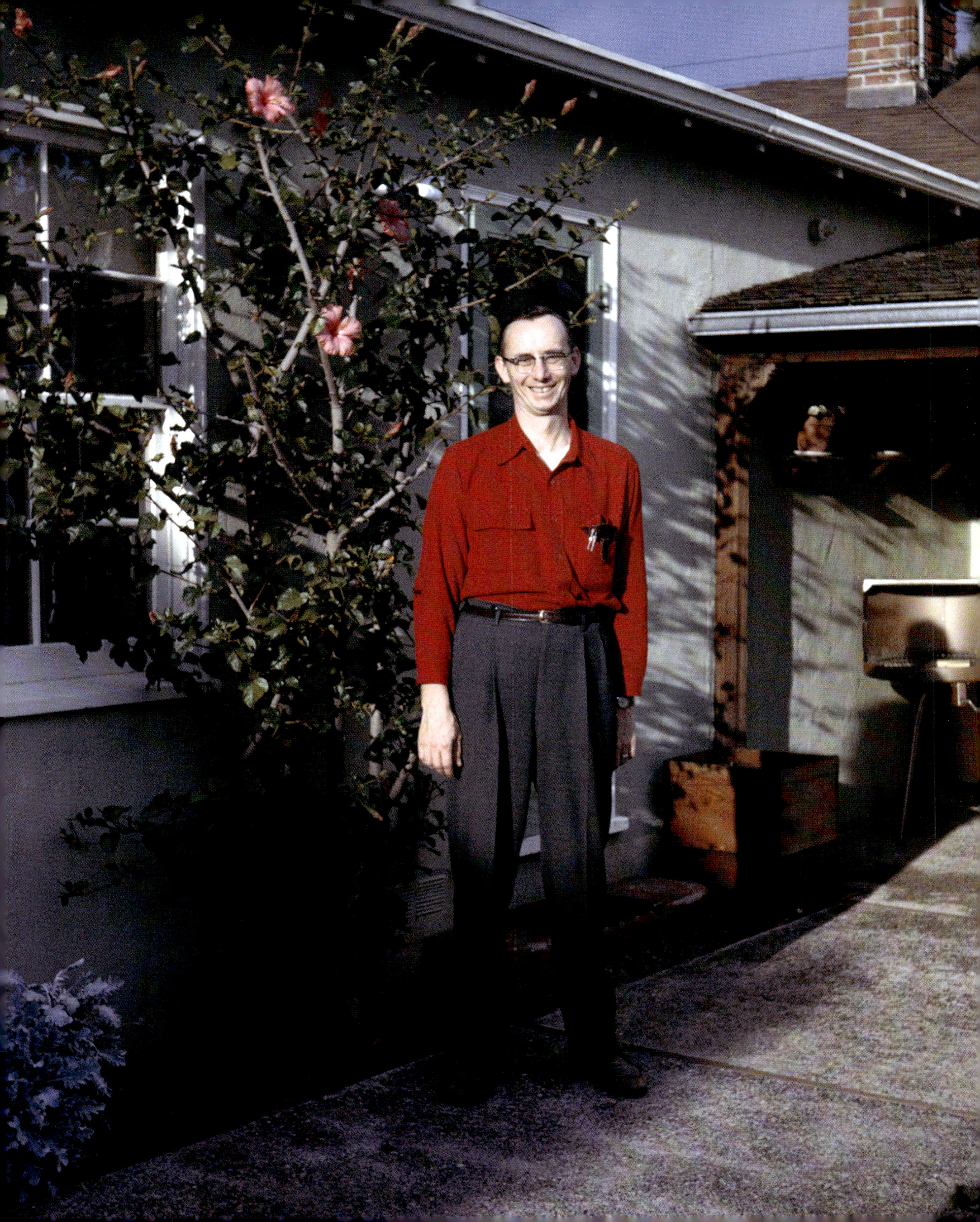

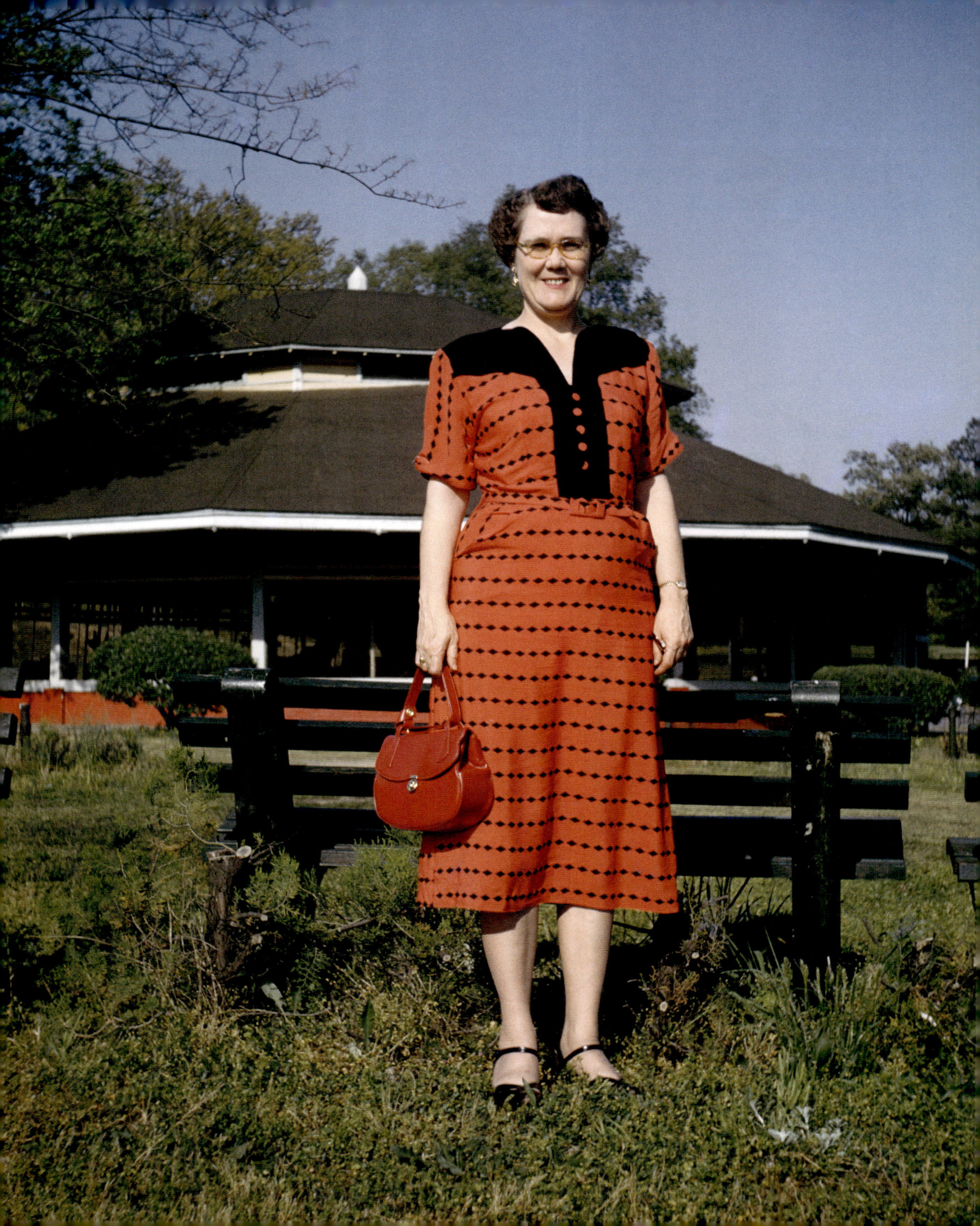

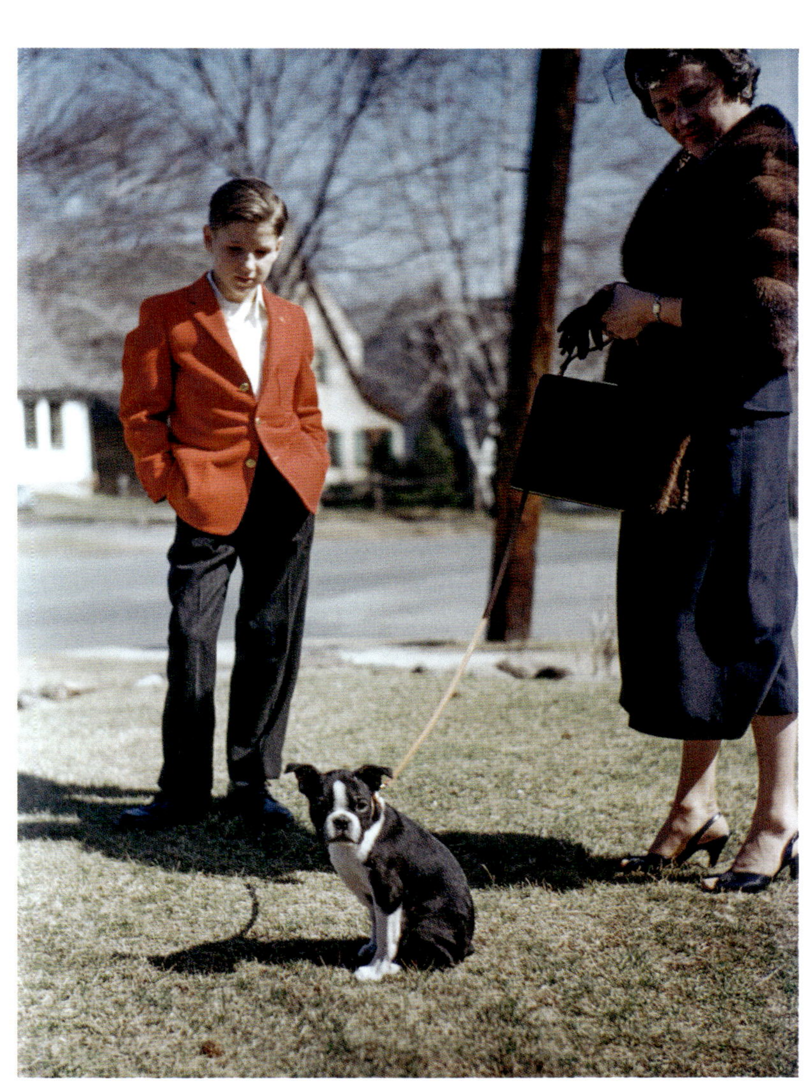

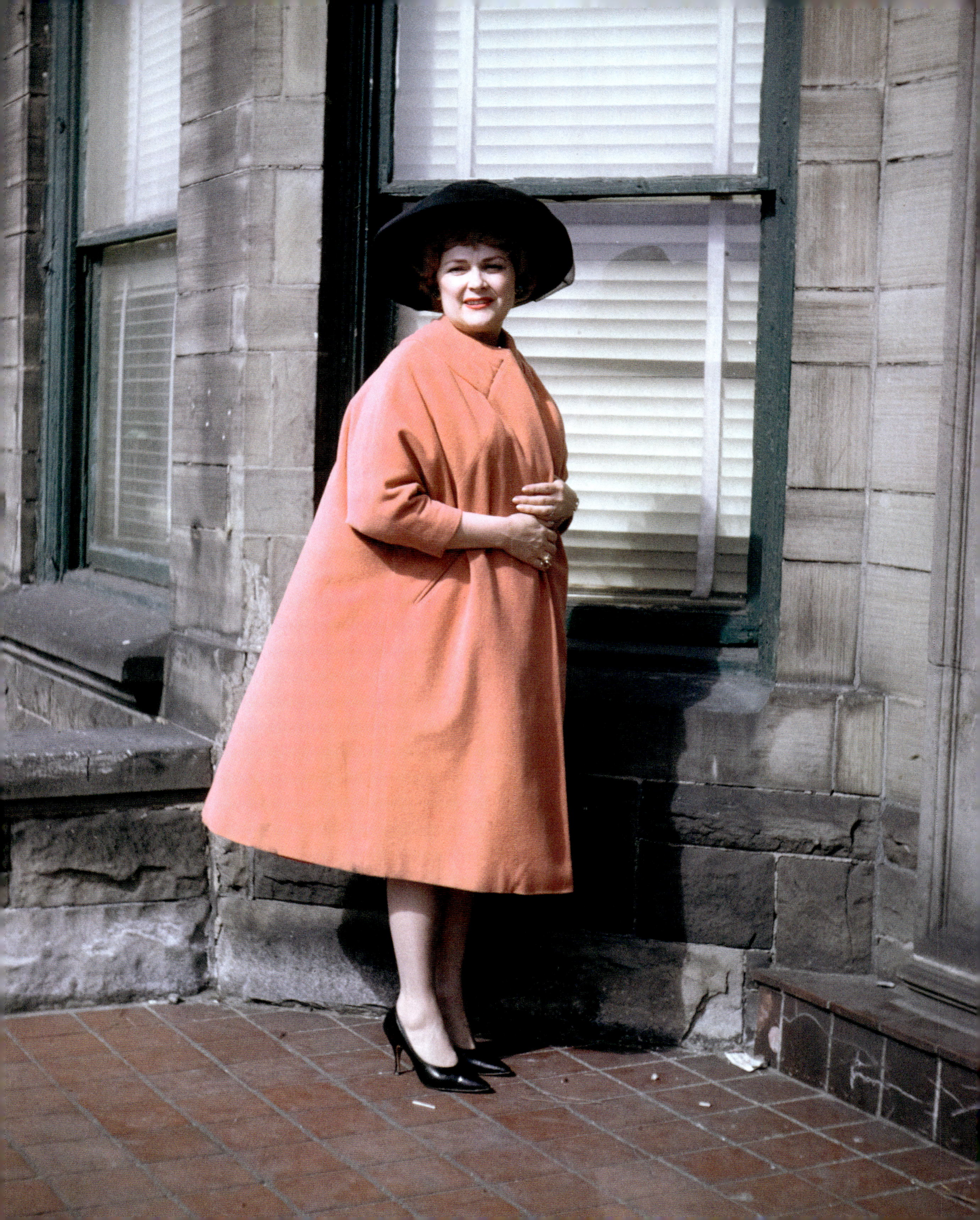

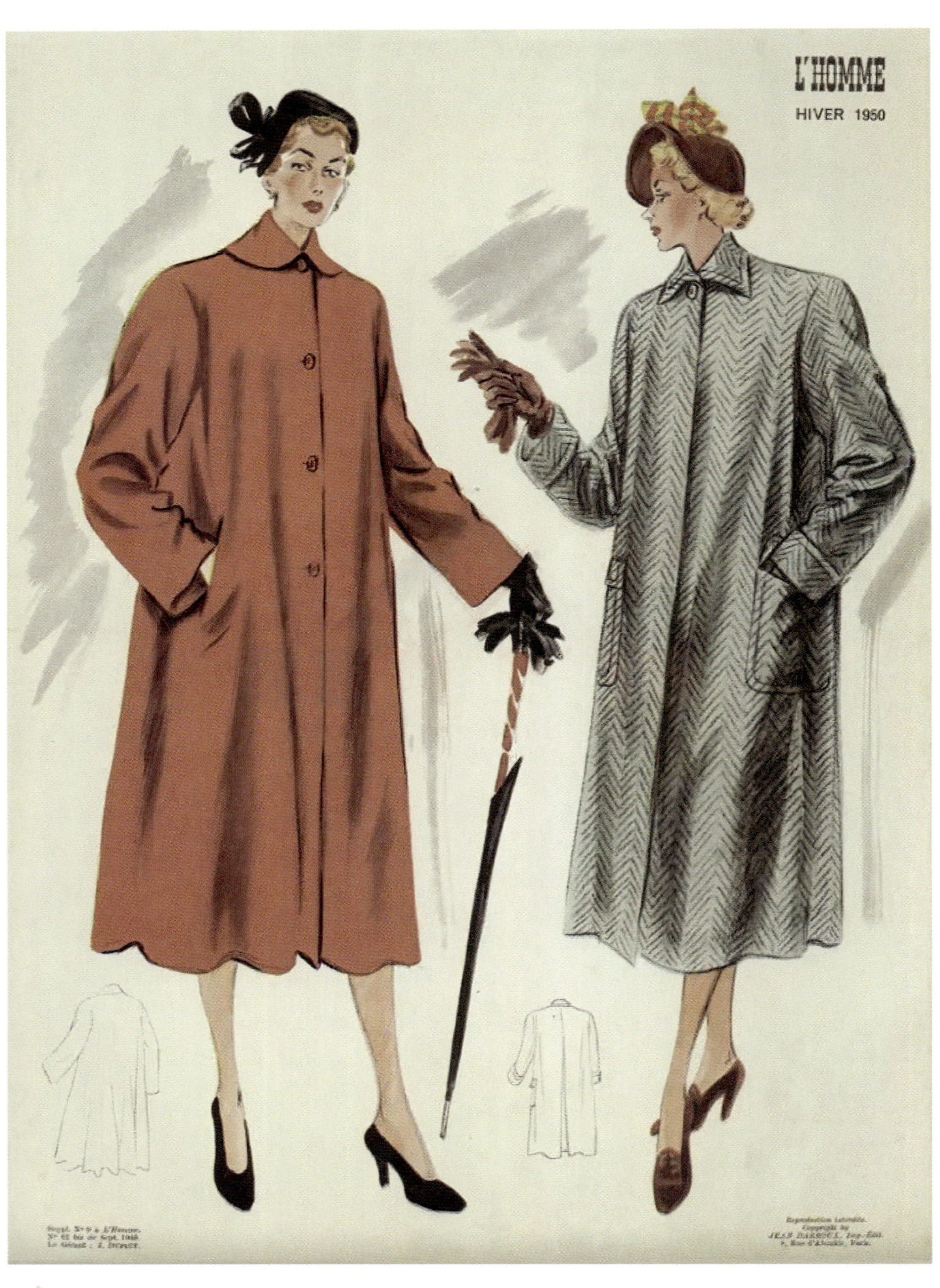
L'HOMME
HIVER 1950

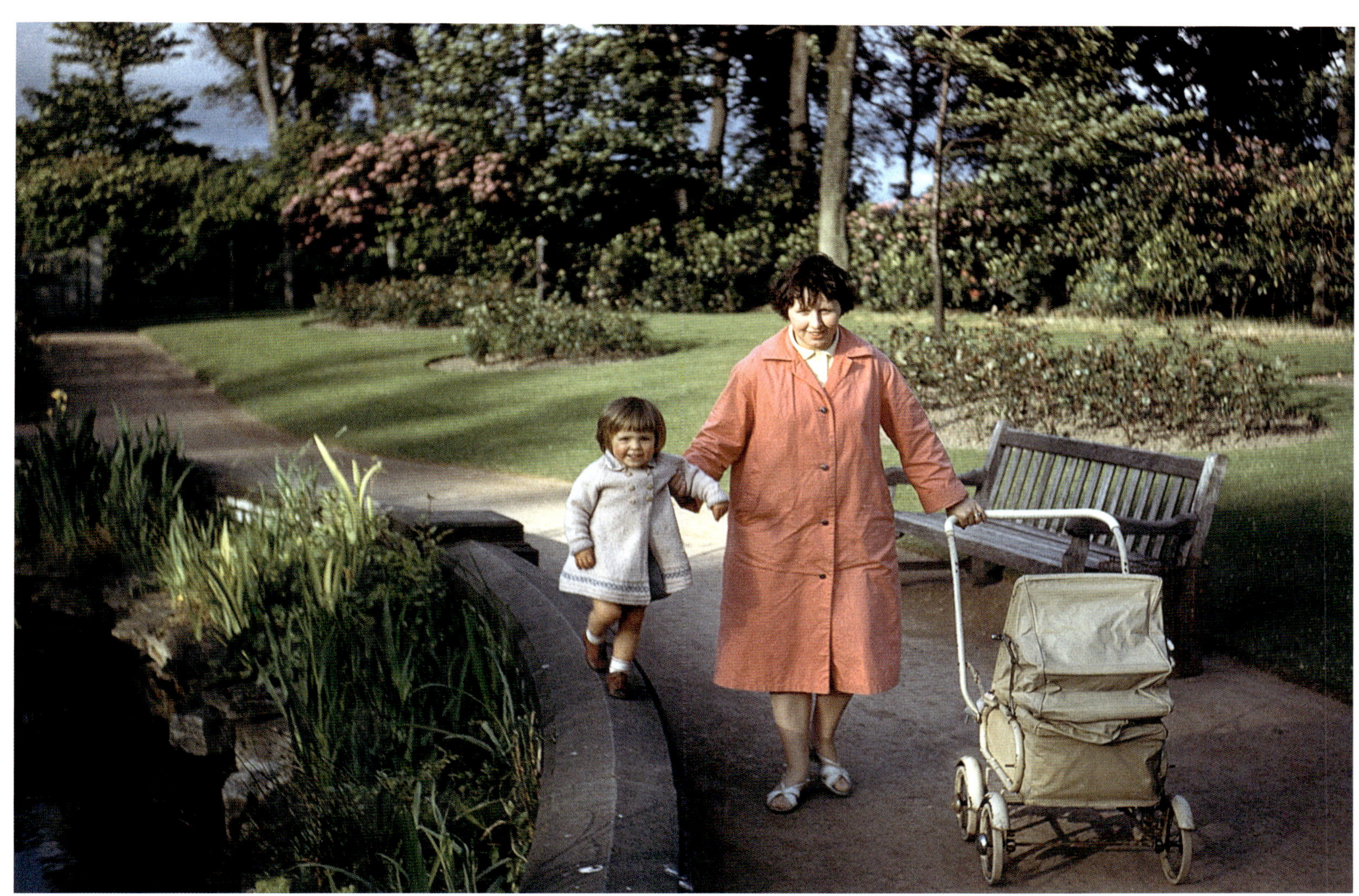

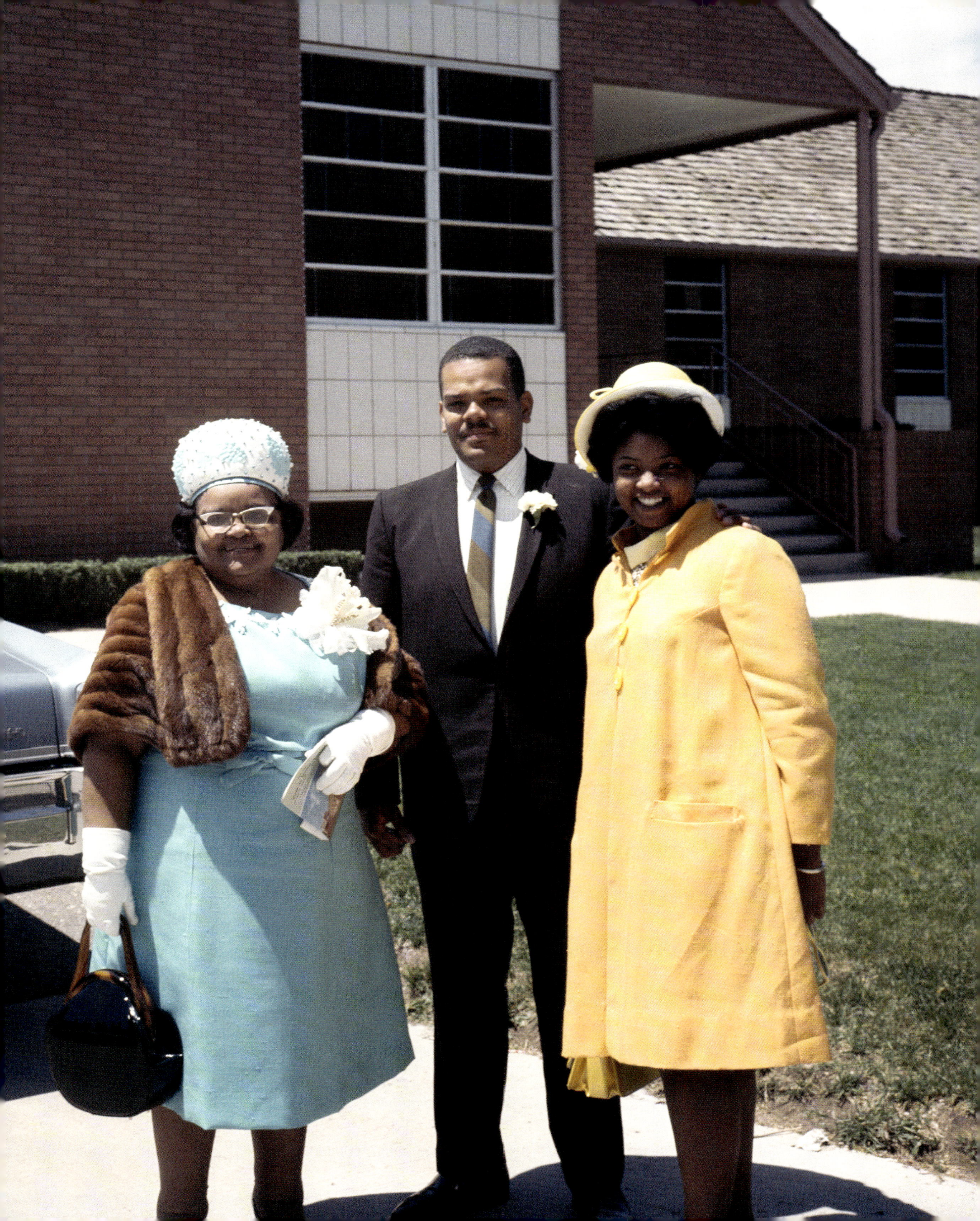

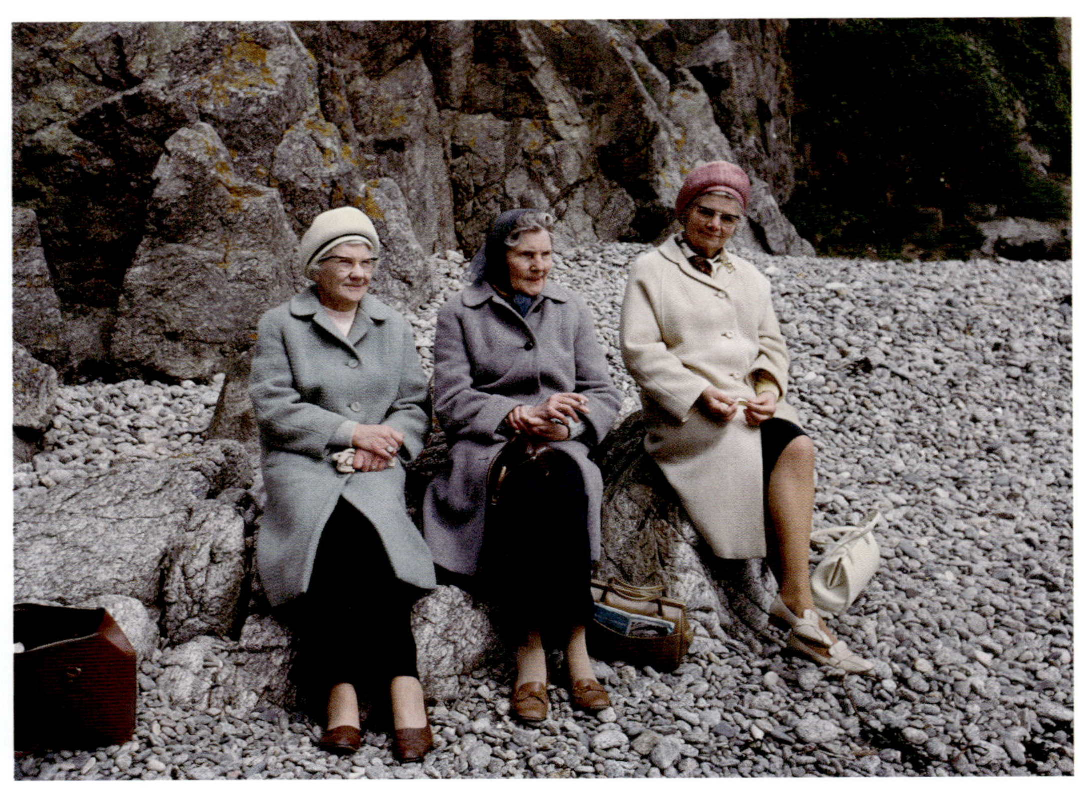

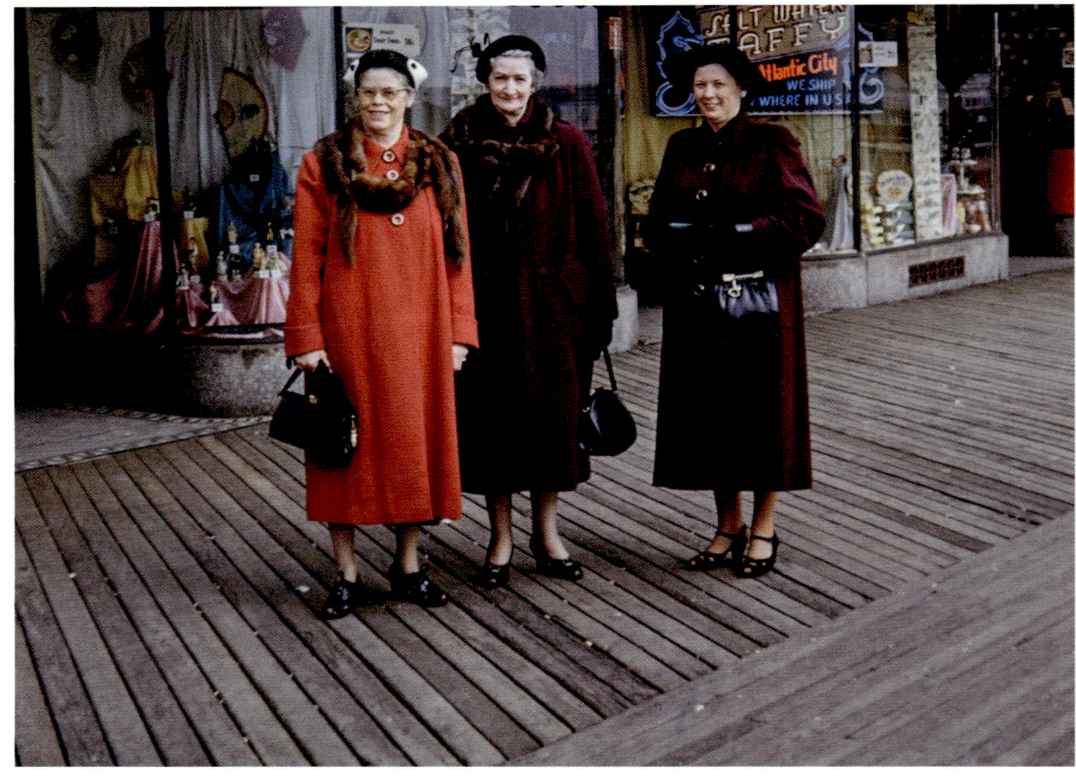
WE SHIP

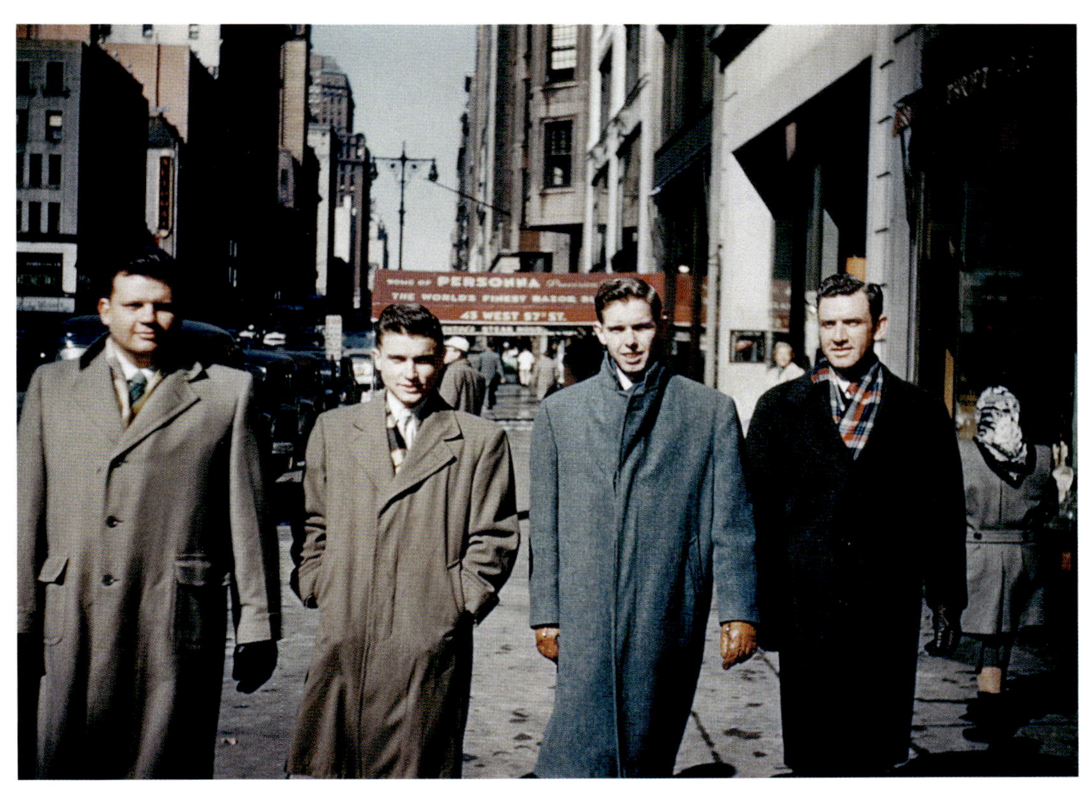
PERSONNA
THE WORLD'S FINEST RAZOR
WEST 57th ST.

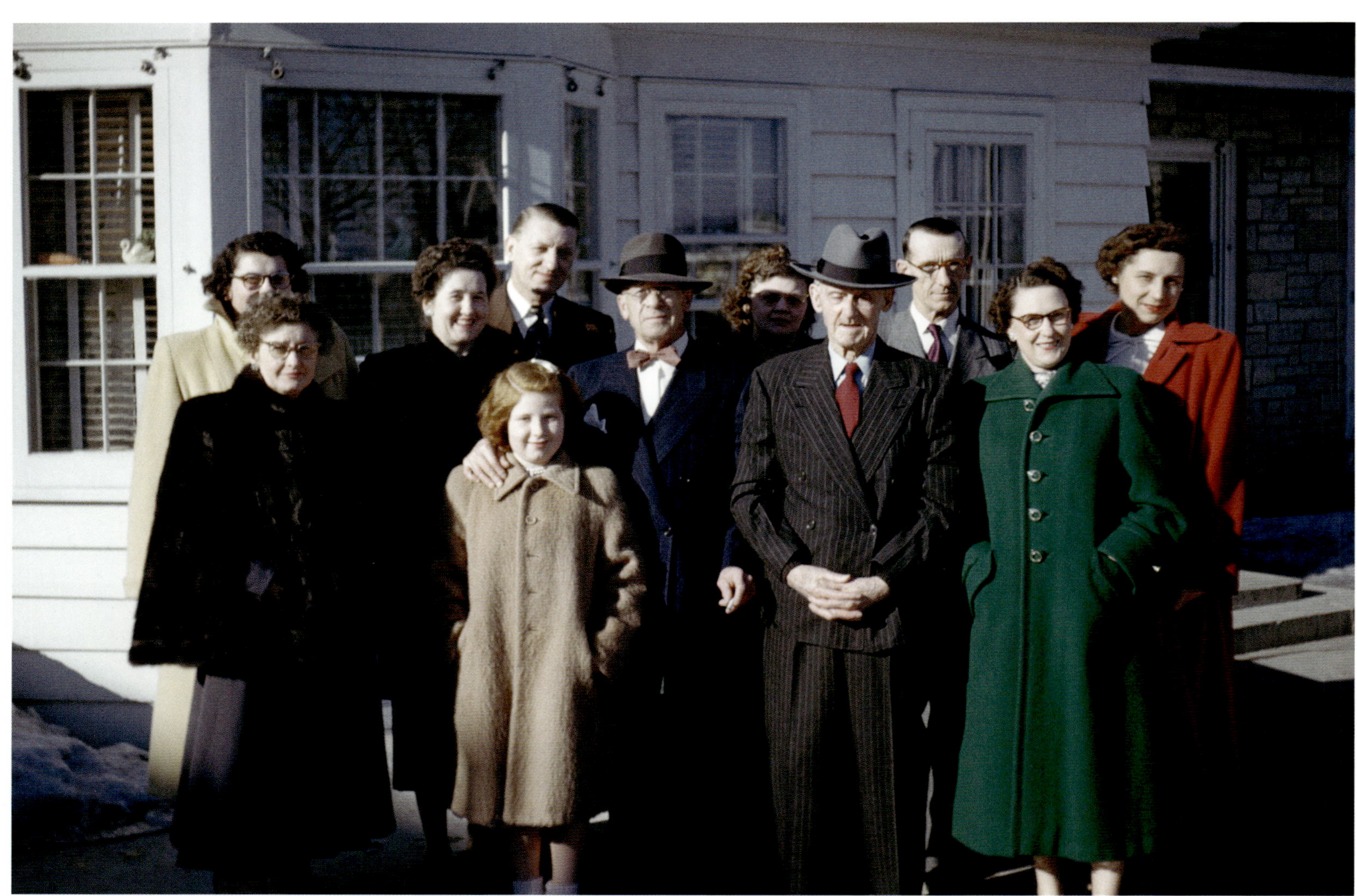

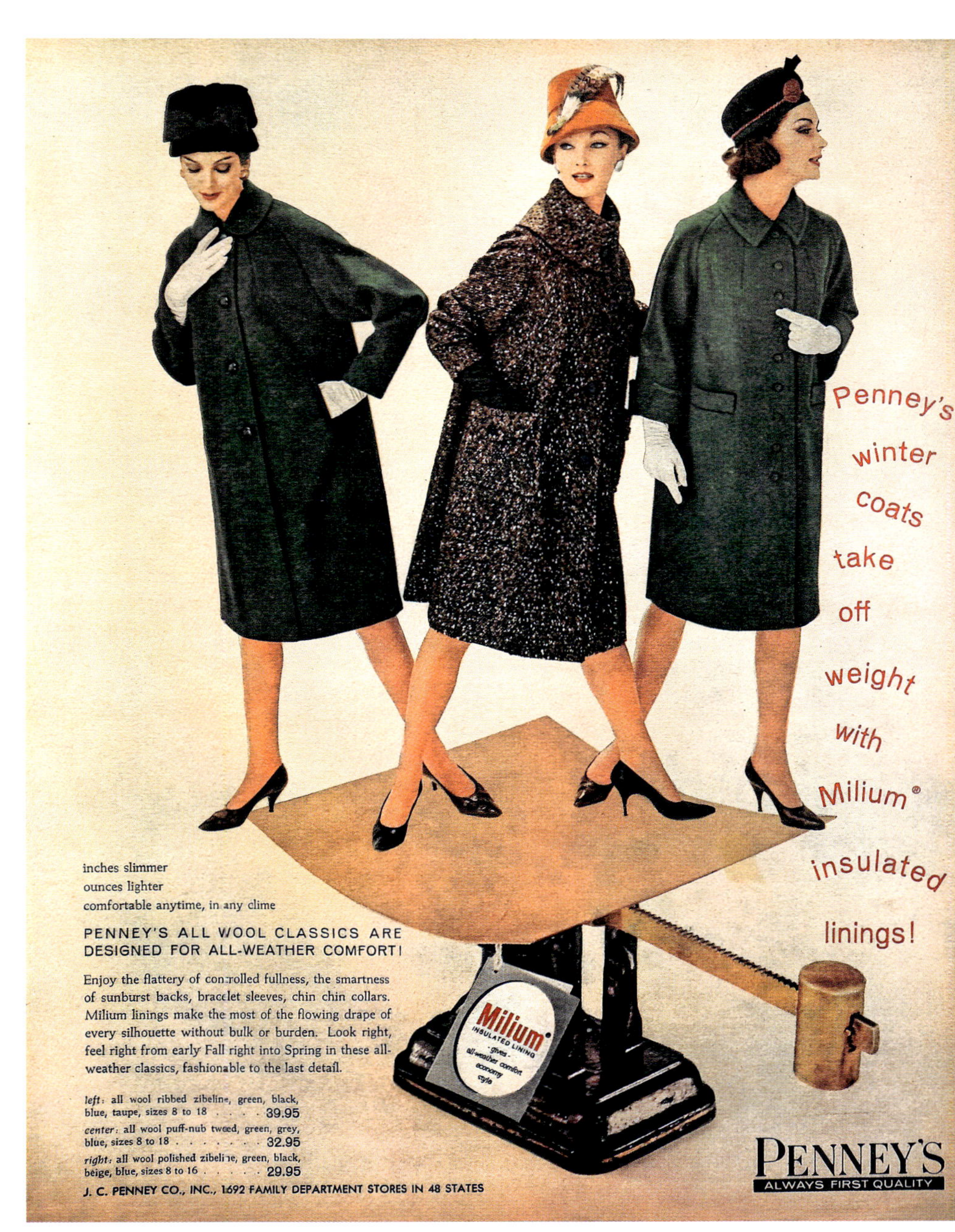

Penney's winter coats take off weight with Milium® insulated linings!
inches slimmer
ounces lighter
comfortable anytime, in any clime
PENNEY'S ALL WOOL CLASSICS ARE DESIGNED FOR ALL-WEATHER COMFORT!
Enjoy the flattery of controlled fullness, the smartness of sunburst backs, bracelet sleeves, chin chin collars. Milium linings make the most of the flowing drape of every silhouette without bulk or burden. Look right, feel right from early Fall right into Spring in these all-weather classics, fashionable to the last detail.
left: all wool ribbed zibeline, green, black, blue, taupe, sizes 8 to 18 . . . . 39.95
center: all wool puff-nub tweed, green, grey, blue, sizes 8 to 18 . . . . 32.95
right: all wool polished zibeline, green, black, beige, blue, sizes 8 to 16 . . . . . 29.95
J. C. PENNEY CO., INC., 1692 FAMILY DEPARTMENT STORES IN 48 STATES
Milium® INSULATED LINING
-gives- all-weather comfort economy style
PENNEY'S
ALWAYS FIRST QUALITY

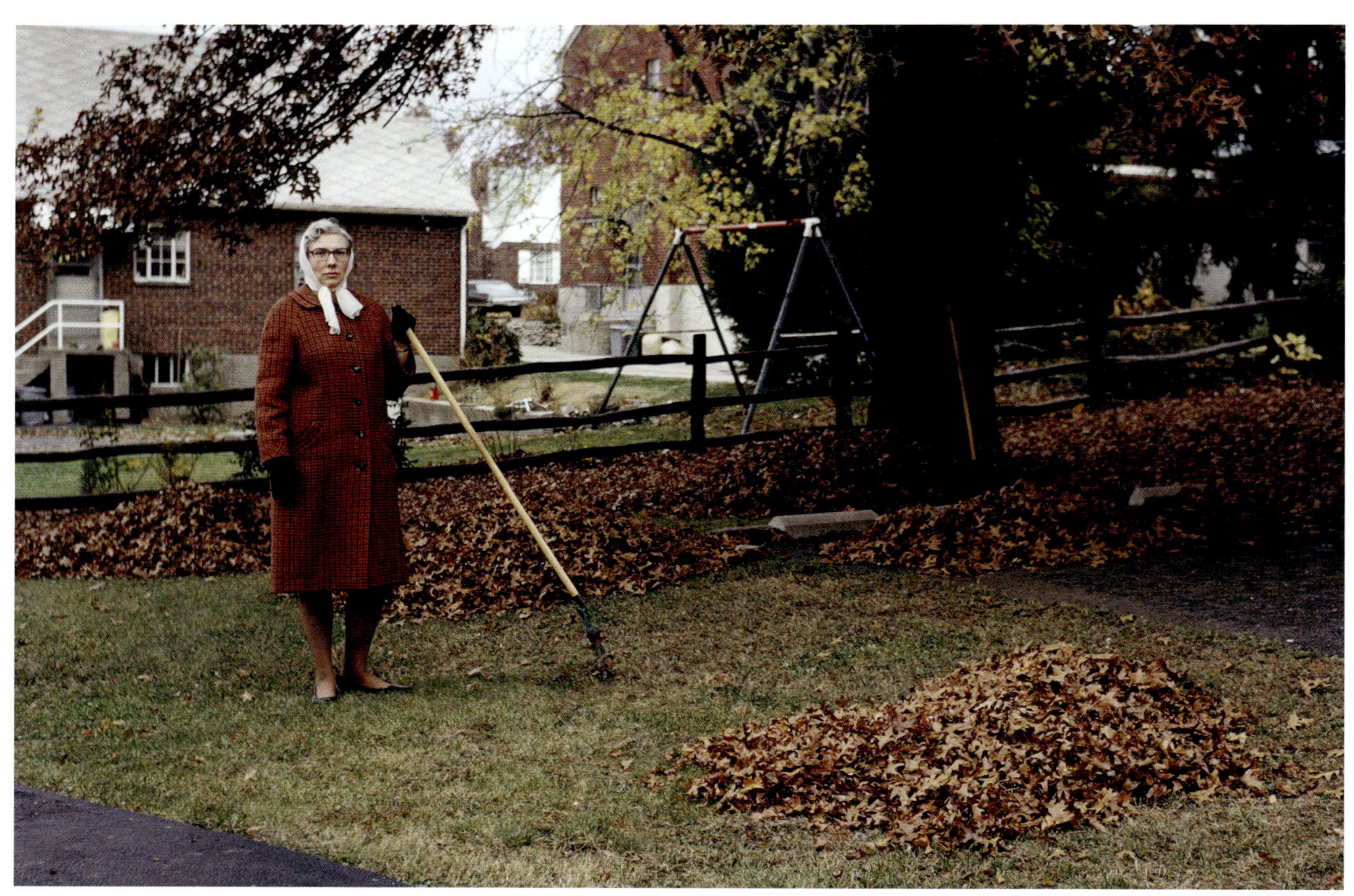

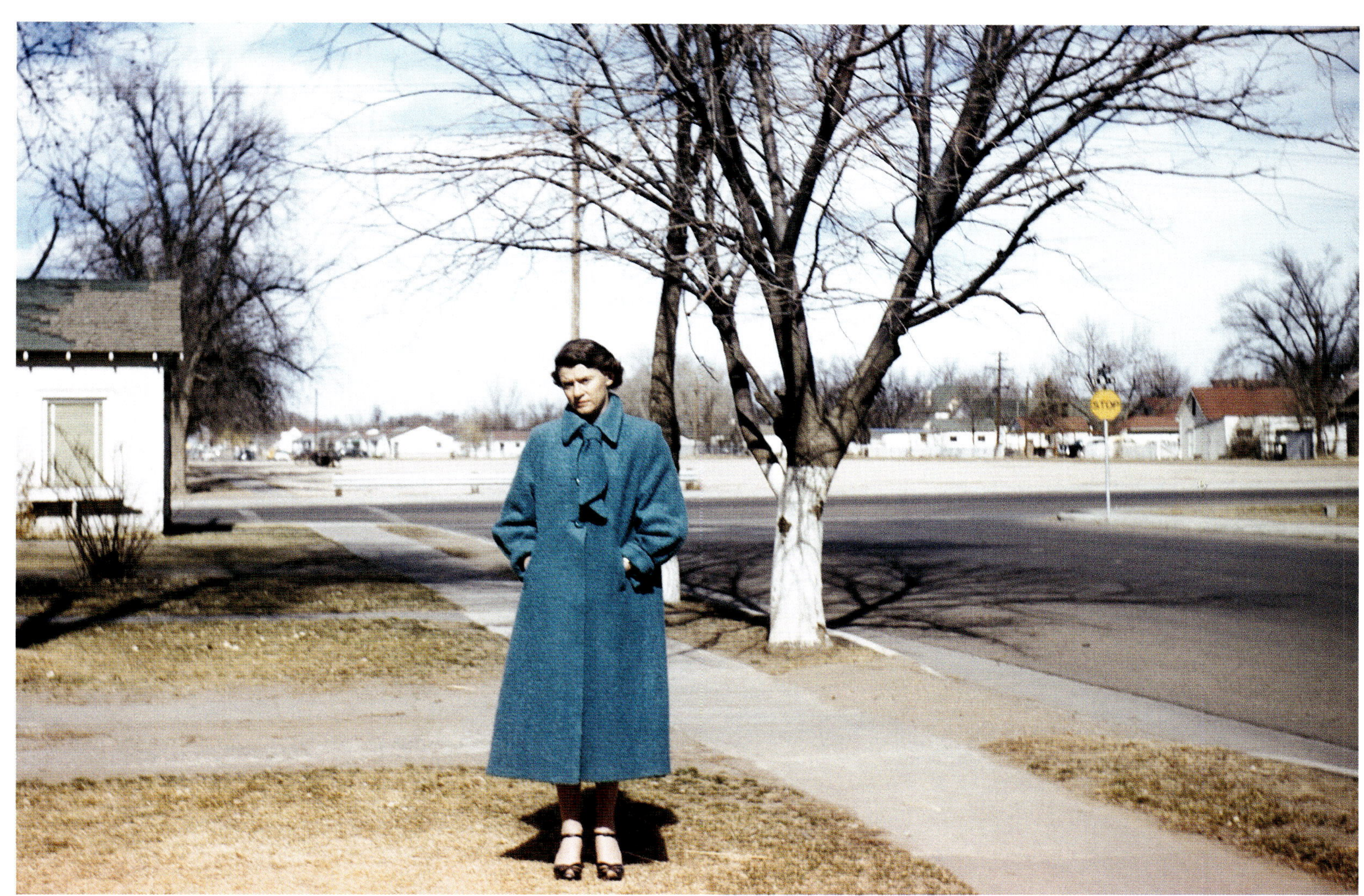

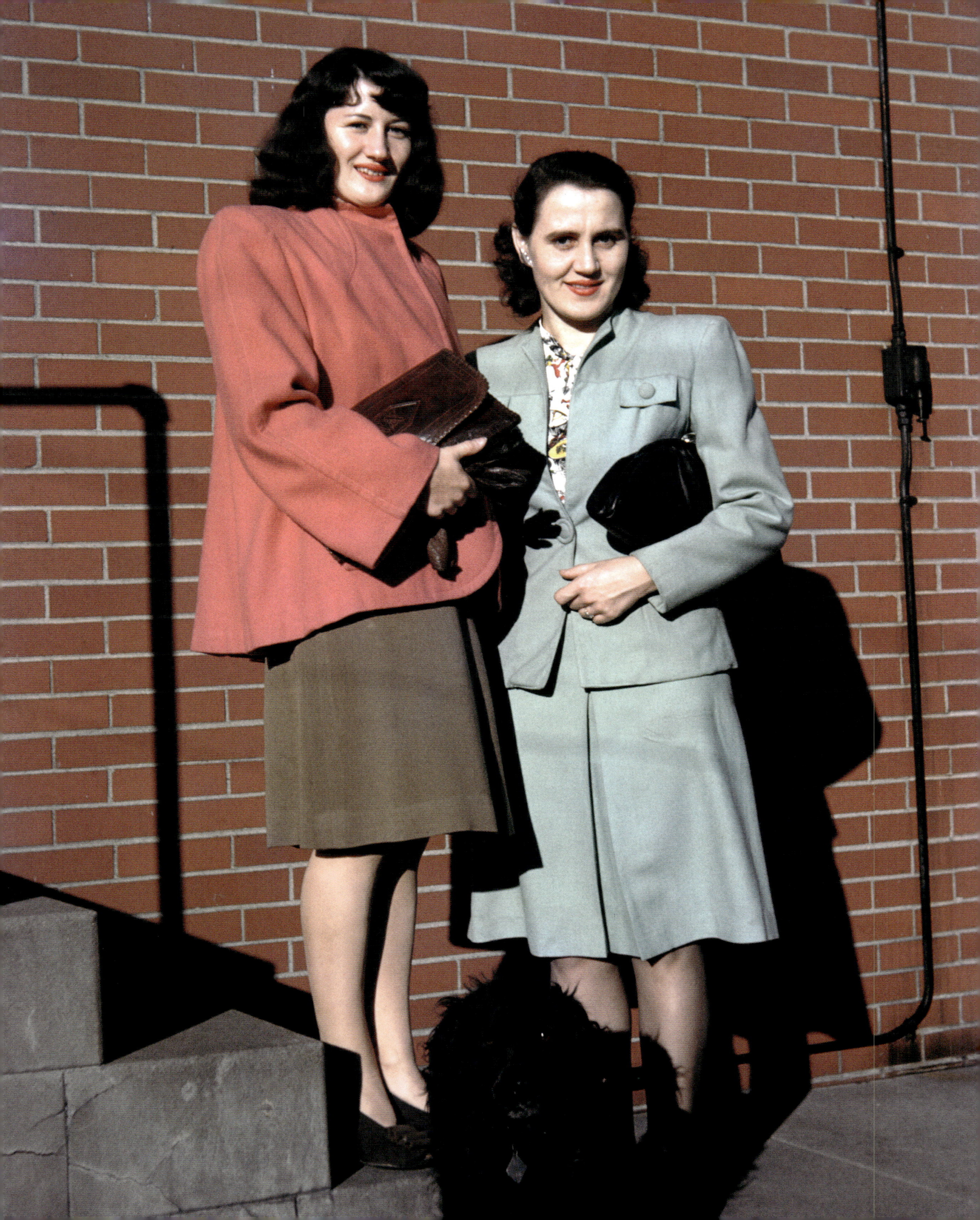

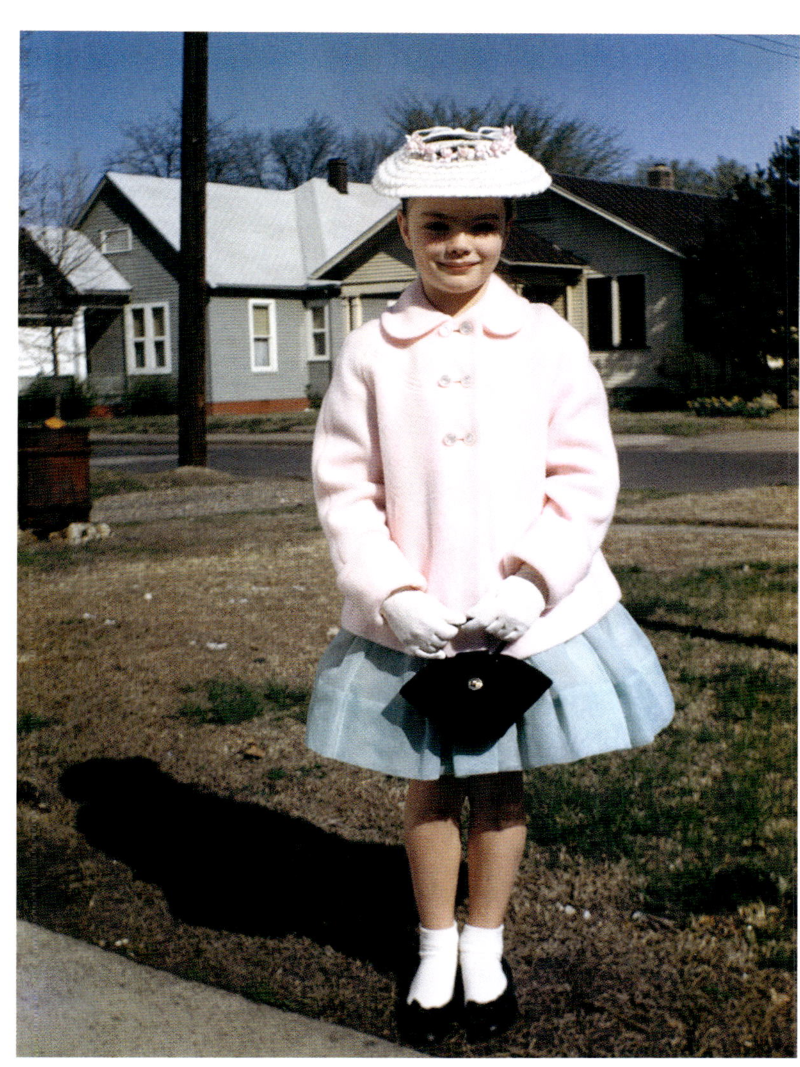

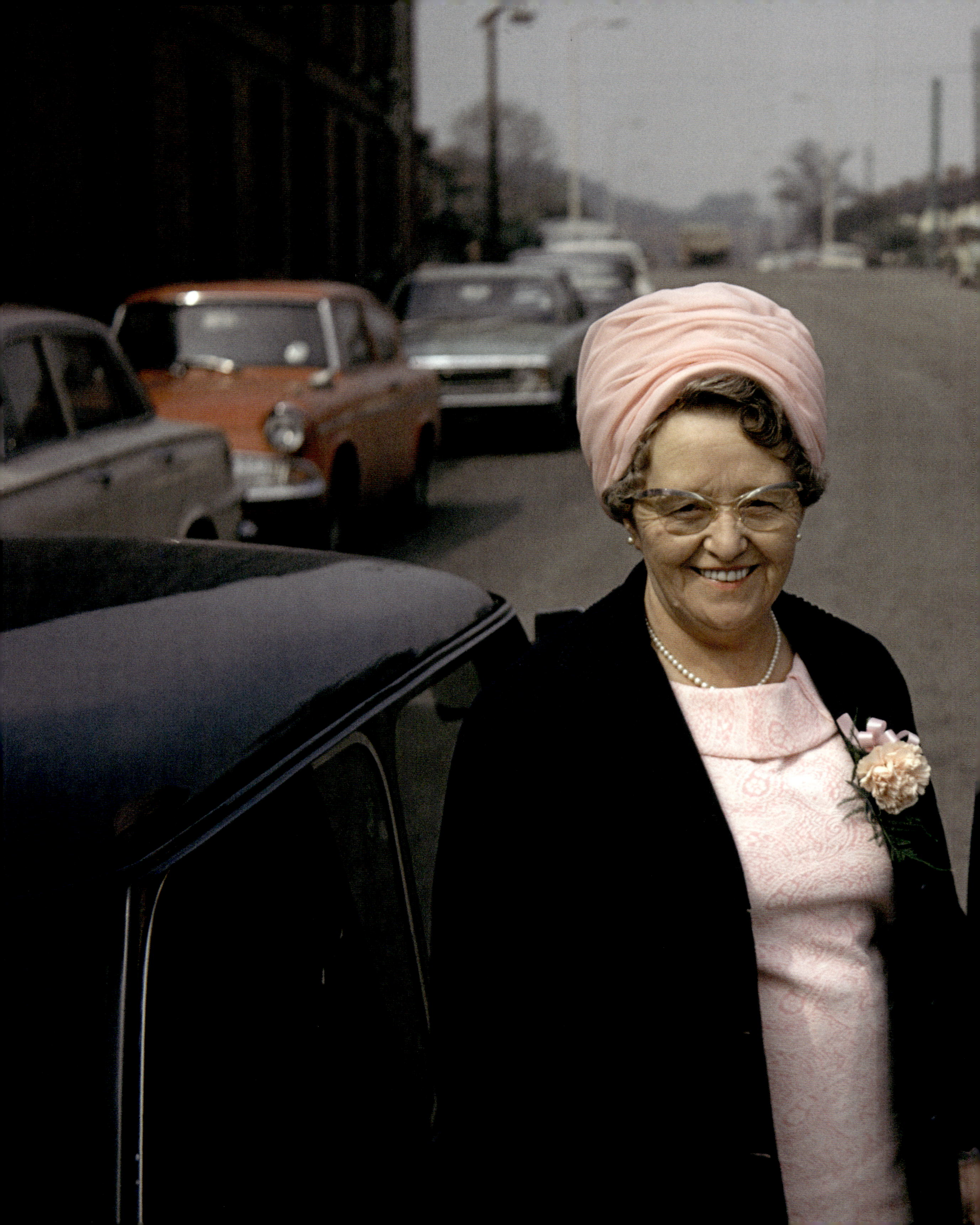

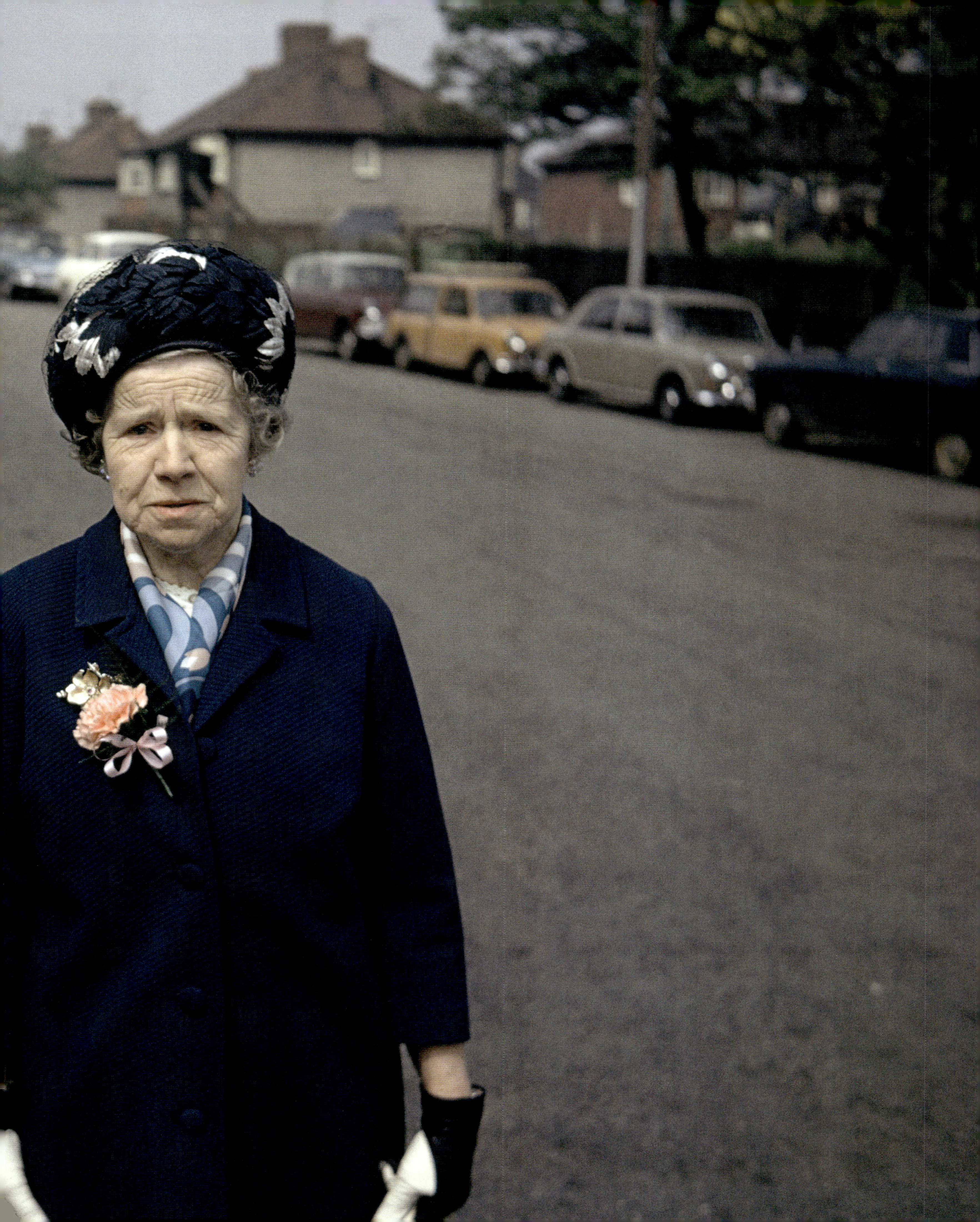

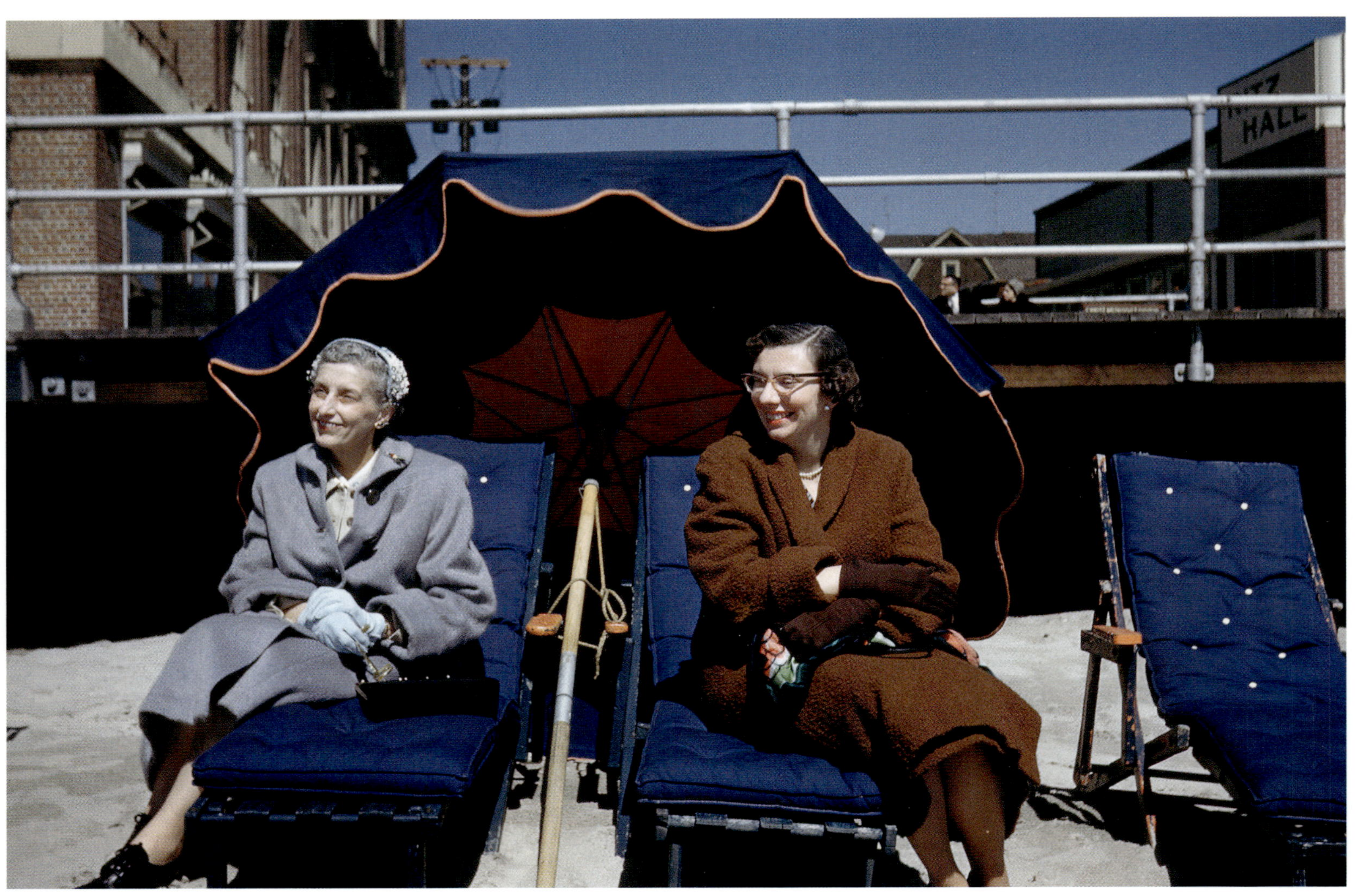
HALL

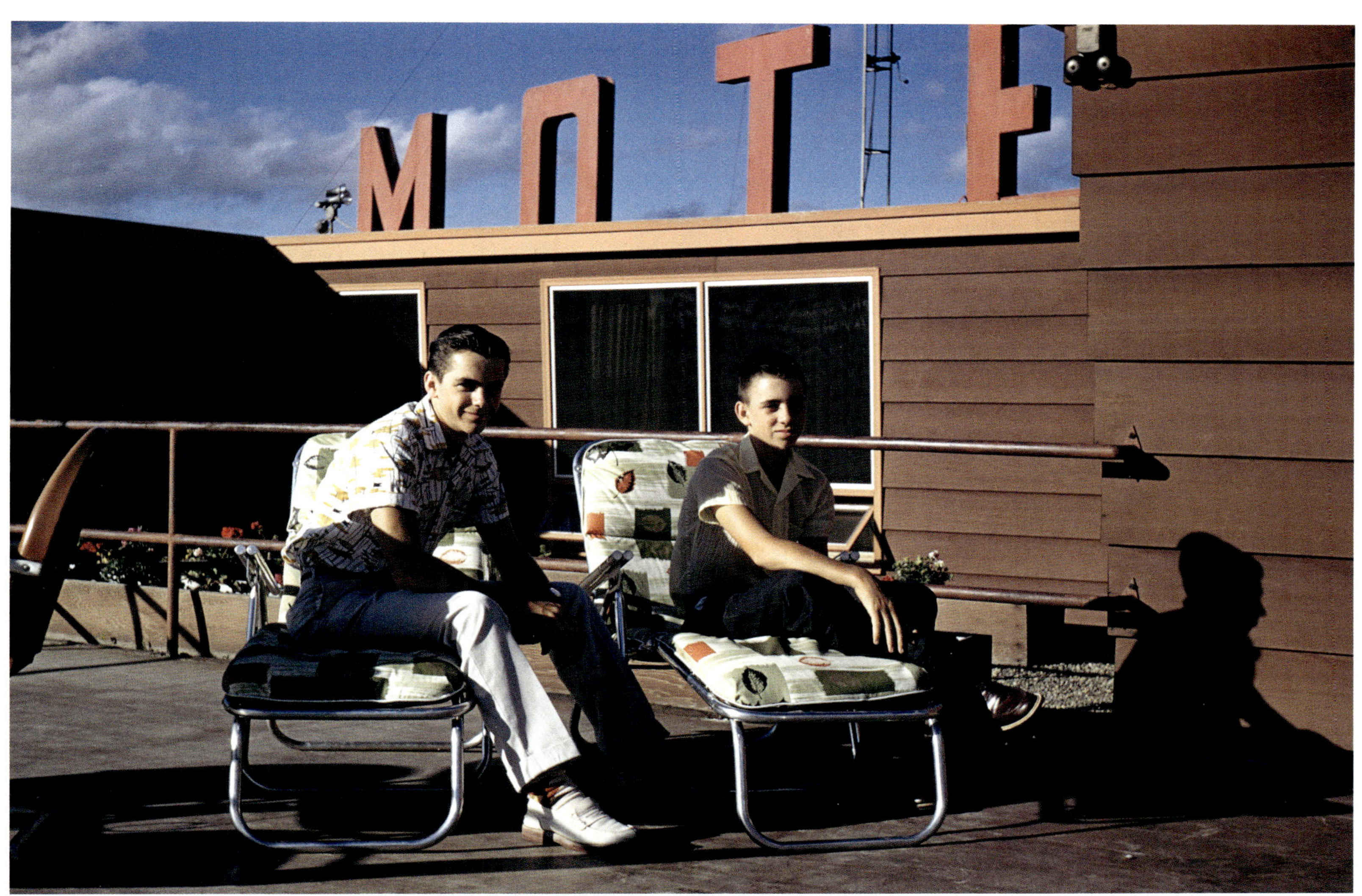

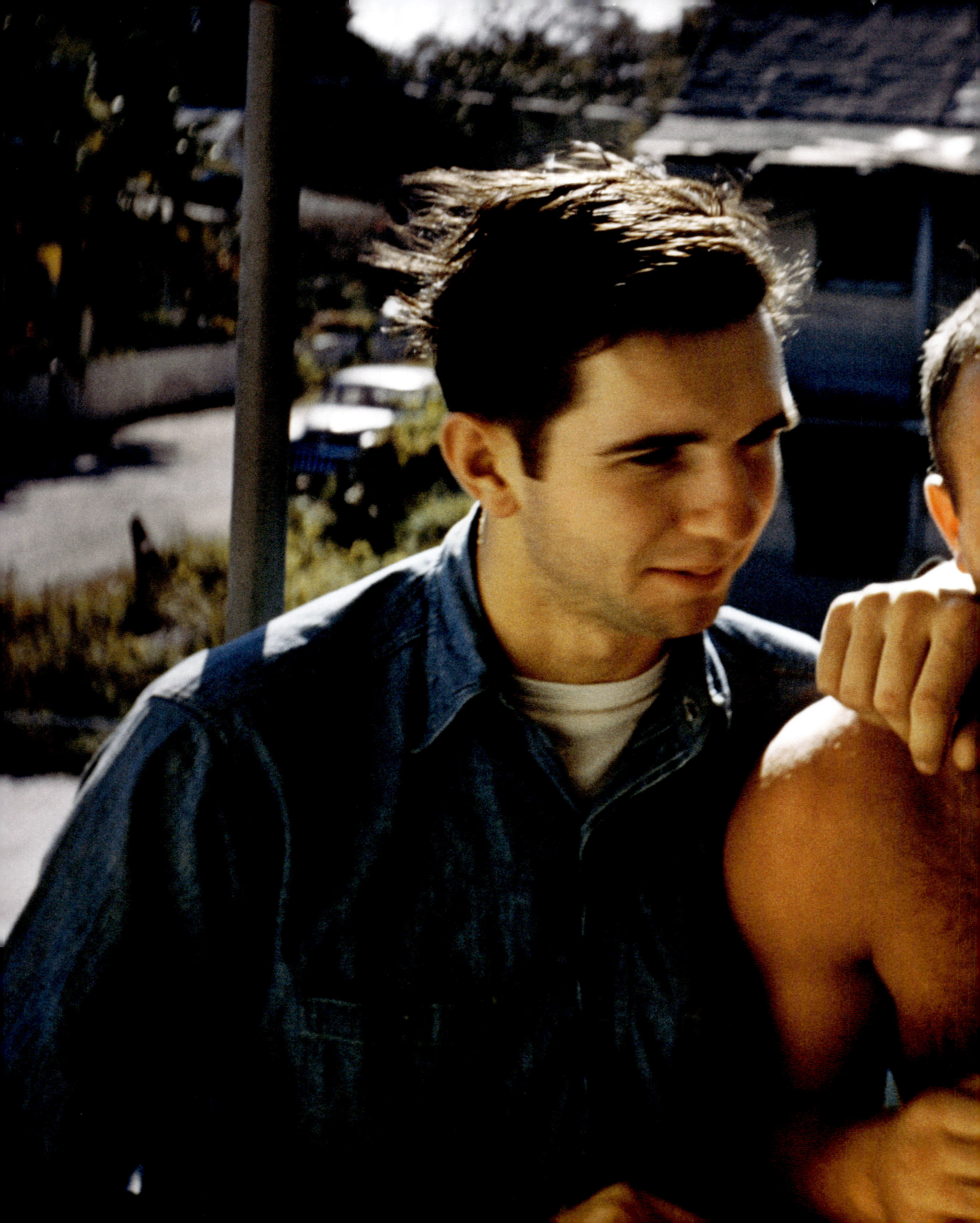

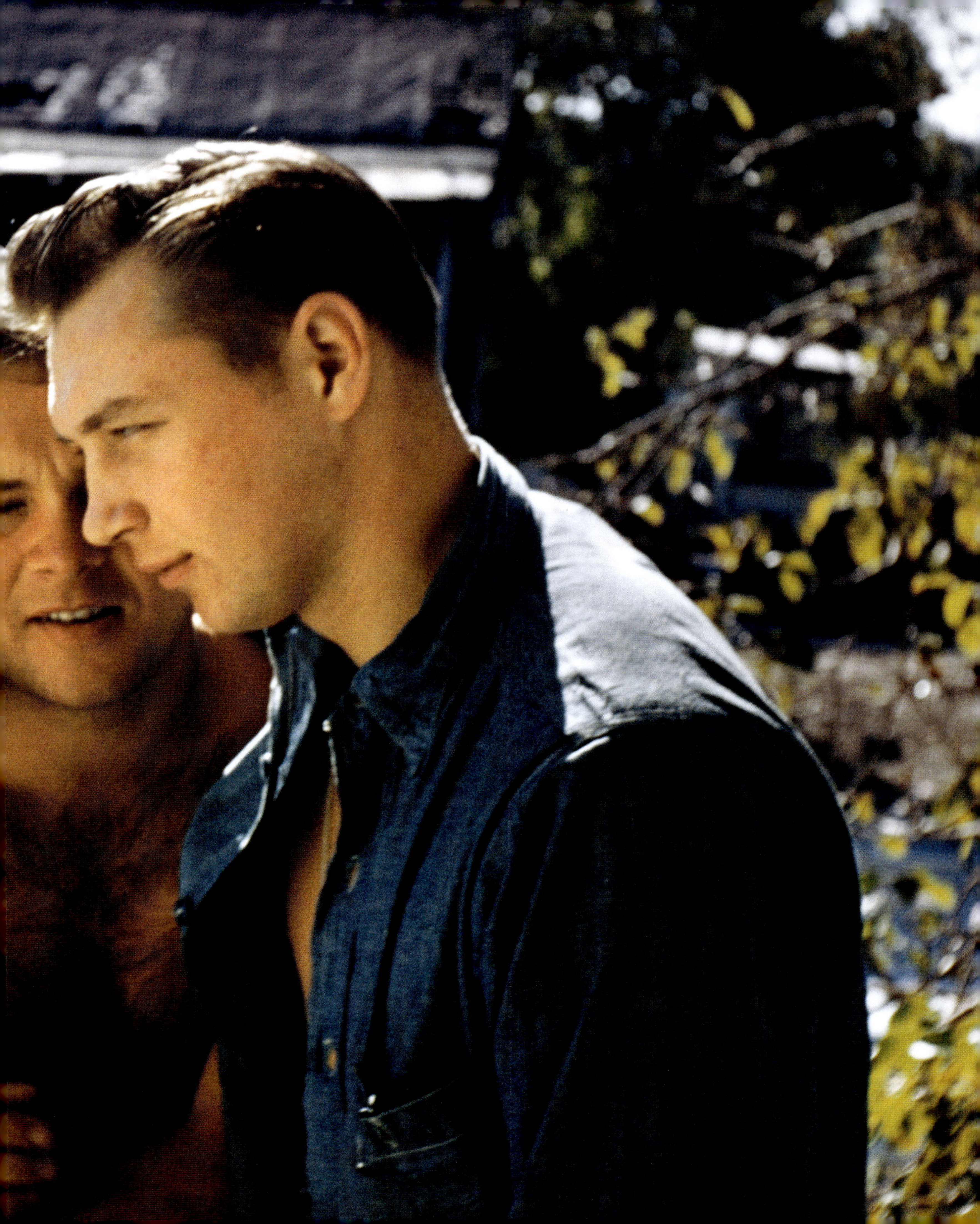

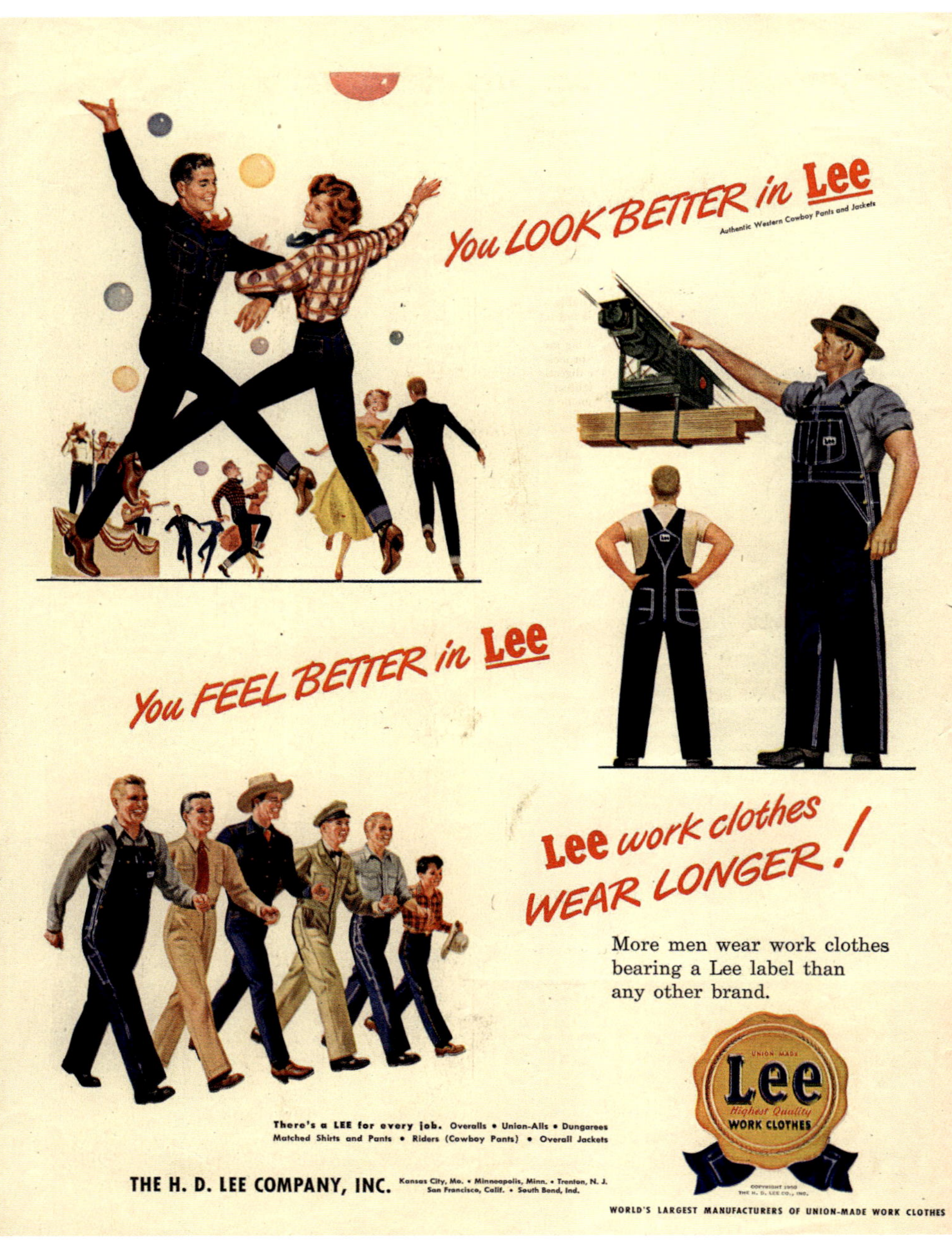
You LOOK BETTER in Lee
Authentic Western Cowboy Pants and Jackets
You FEEL BETTER in Lee
Lee work clothes WEAR LONGER!
More men wear work clothes bearing a Lee label than any other brand.
There's a LEE for every job. Overalls • Union-Alls • Dungarees
Matched Shirts and Pants • Riders (Cowboy Pants) • Overall Jackets
THE H. D. LEE COMPANY, INC. Kansas City, Mo. • Minneapolis, Minn. • Trenton, N. J.
San Francisco, Calif. • South Bend, Ind.
UNION MADE
Lee
Highest Quality
WORK CLOTHES
COPYRIGHT 1950
THE H. D. LEE CO., INC.
WORLD'S LARGEST MANUFACTURERS OF UNION-MADE WORK CLOTHES

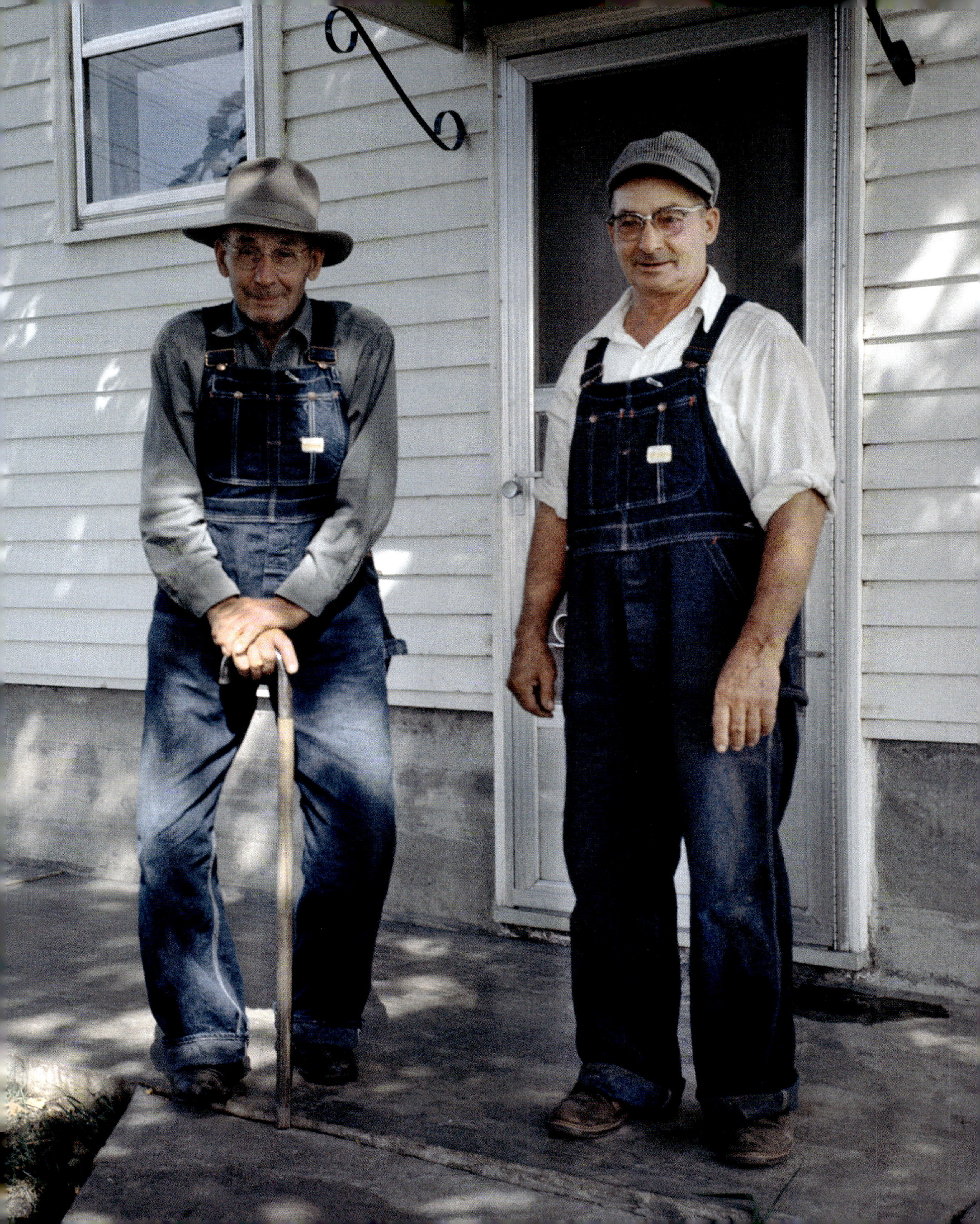

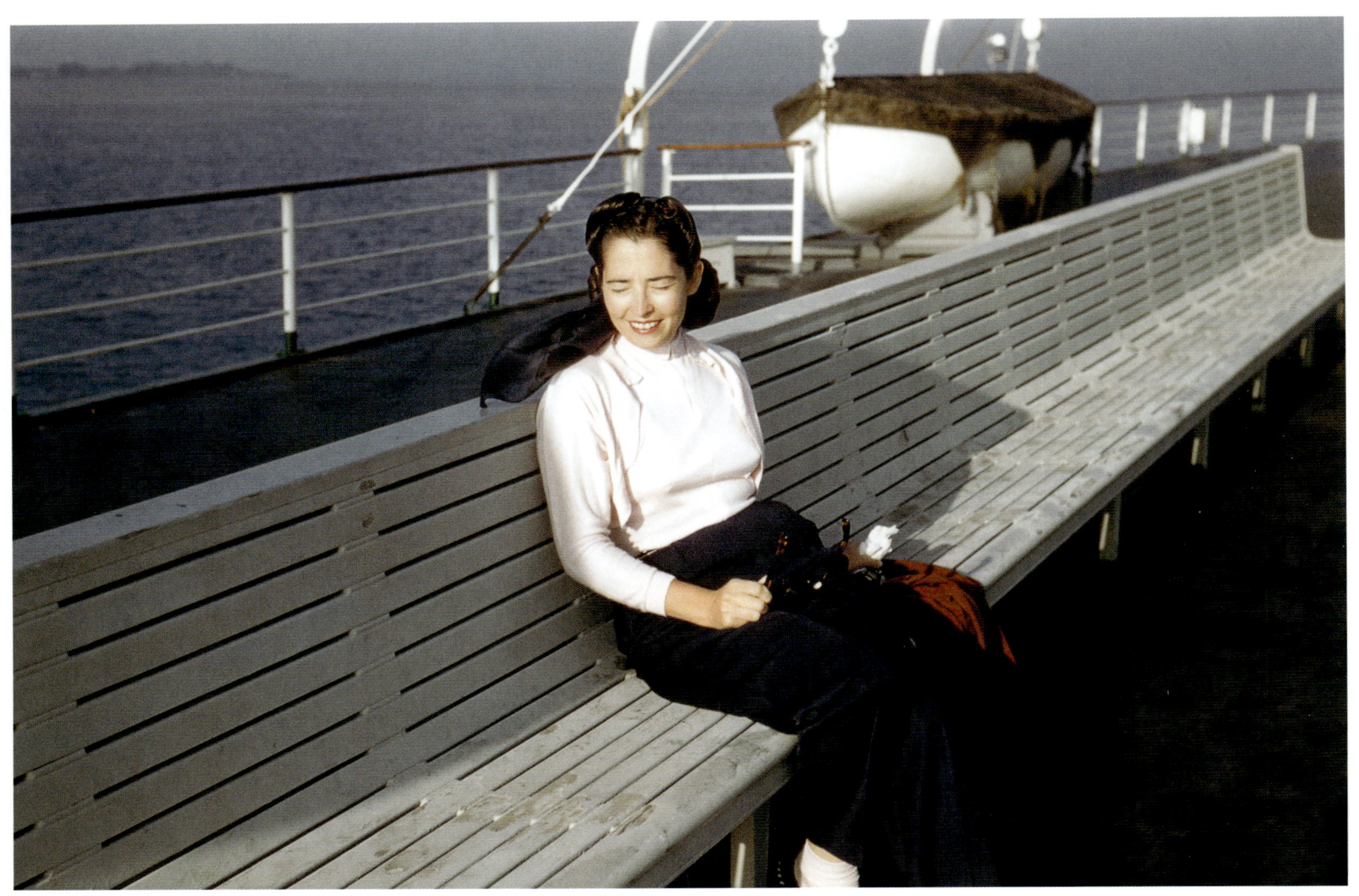

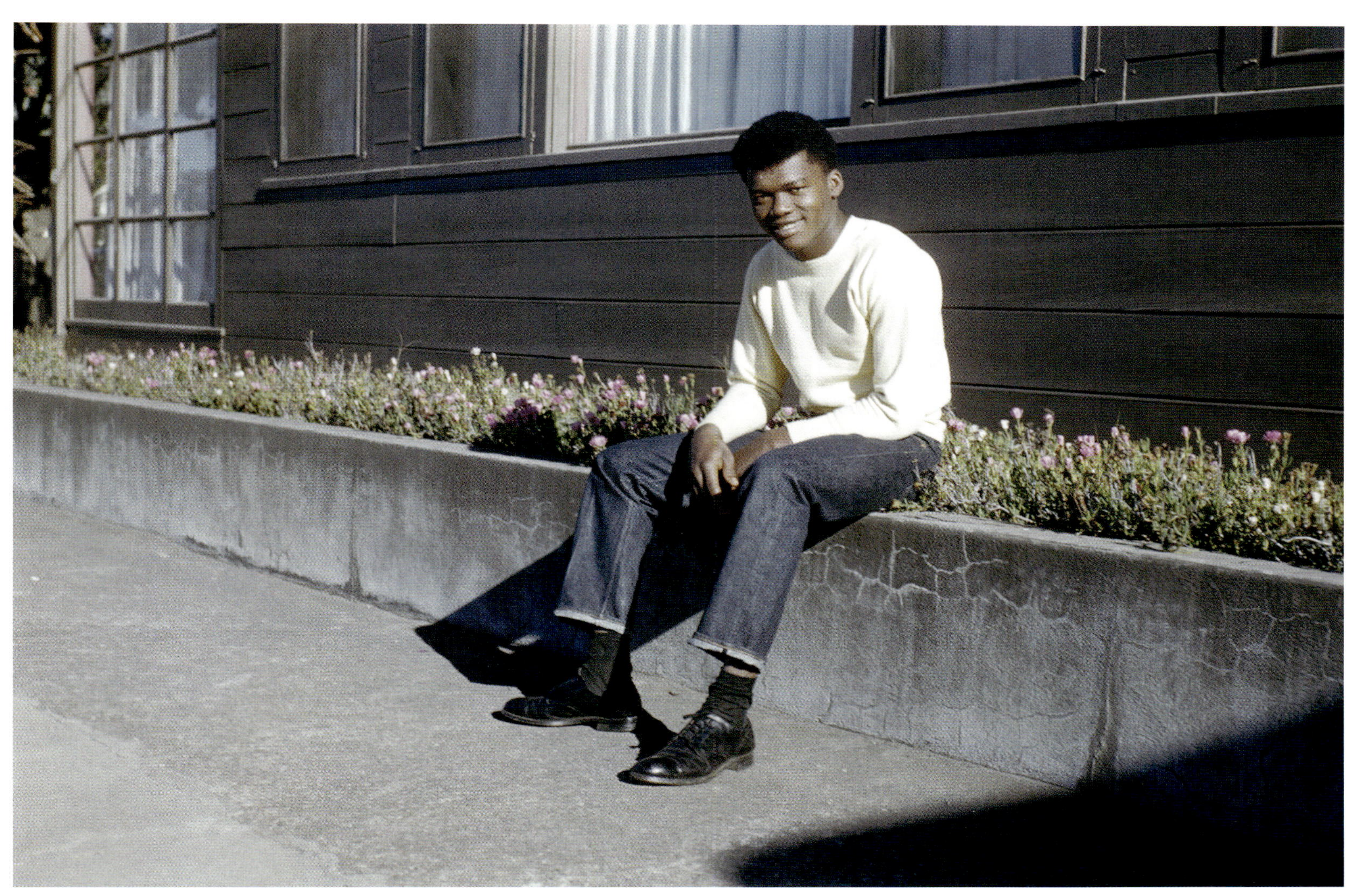

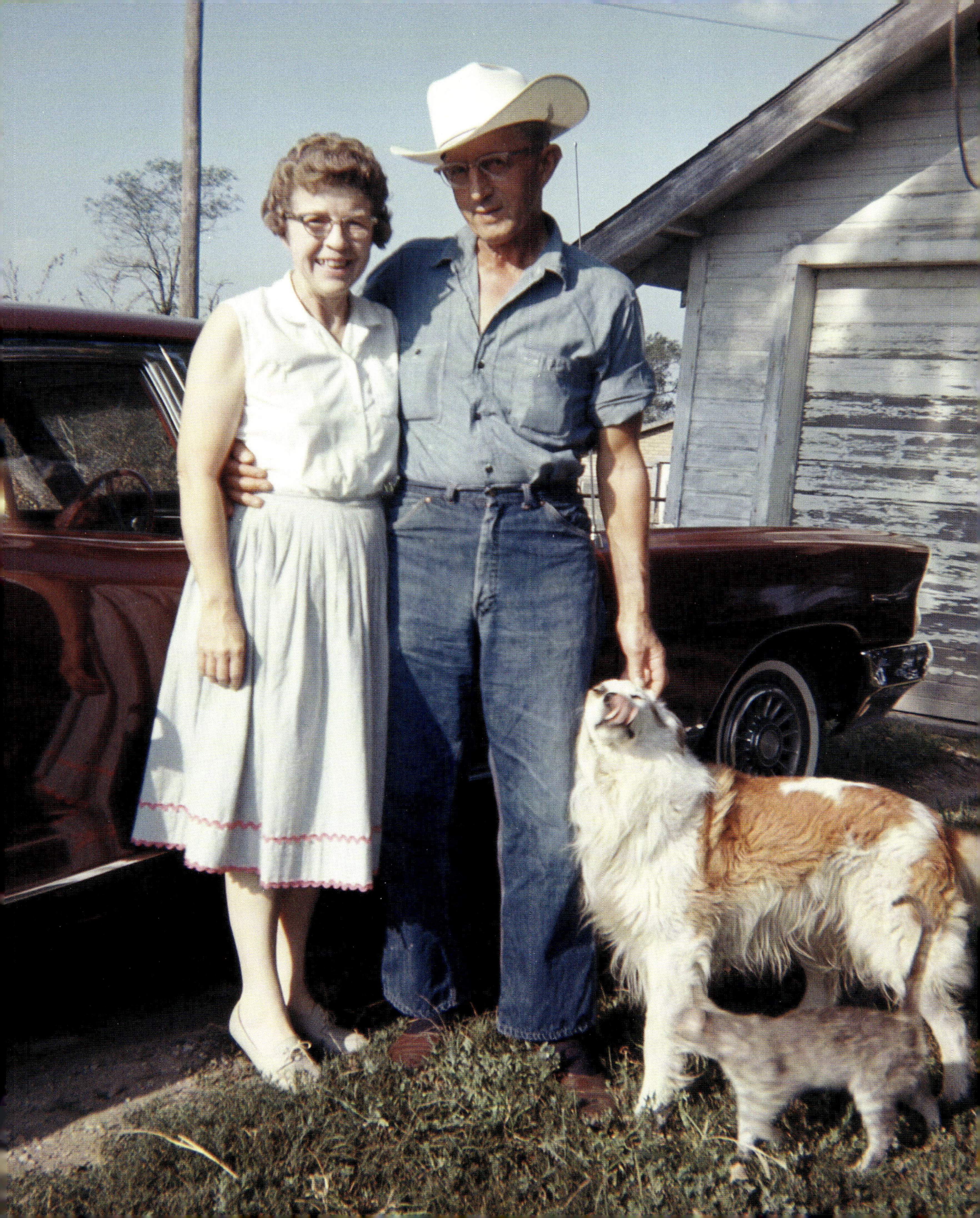

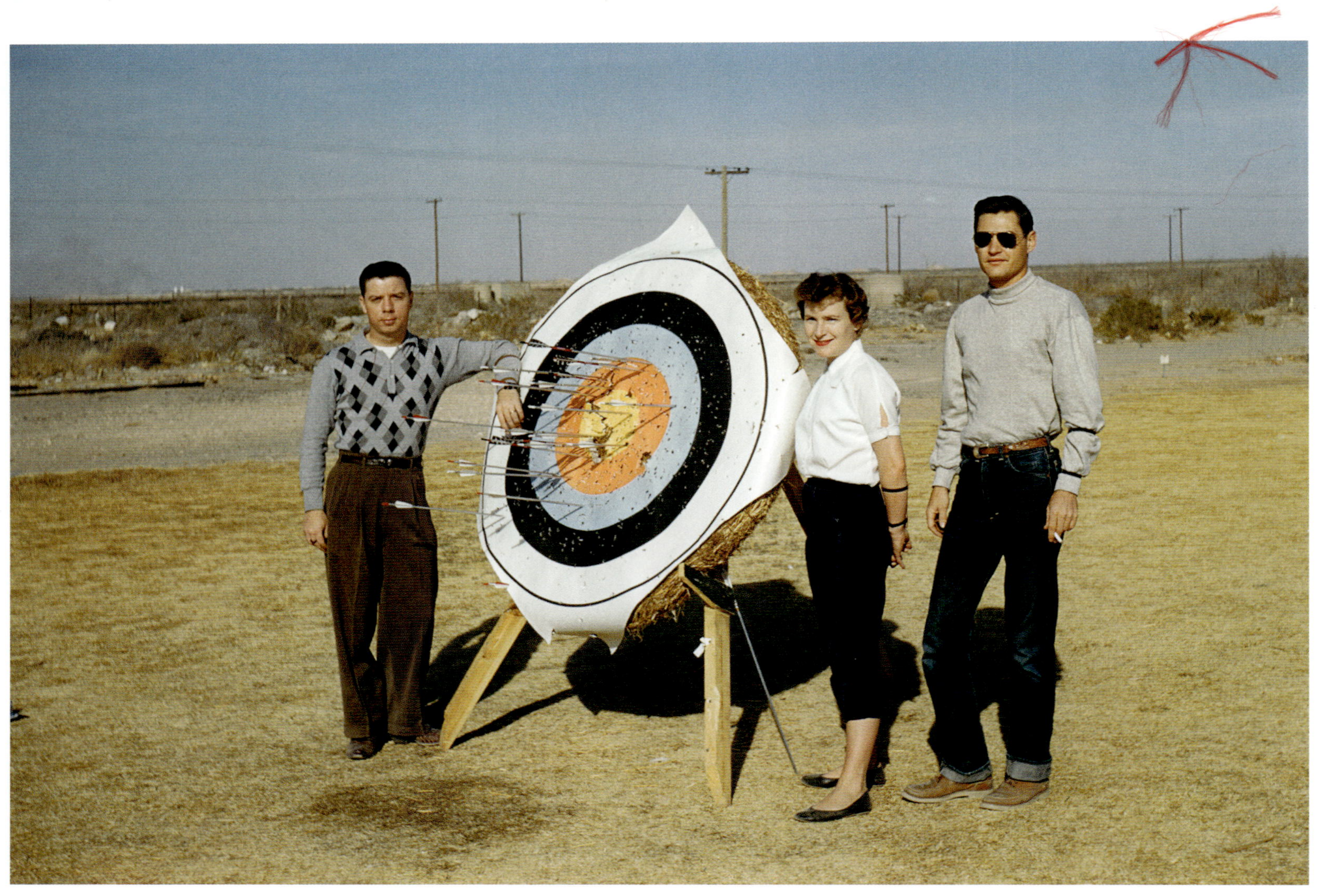

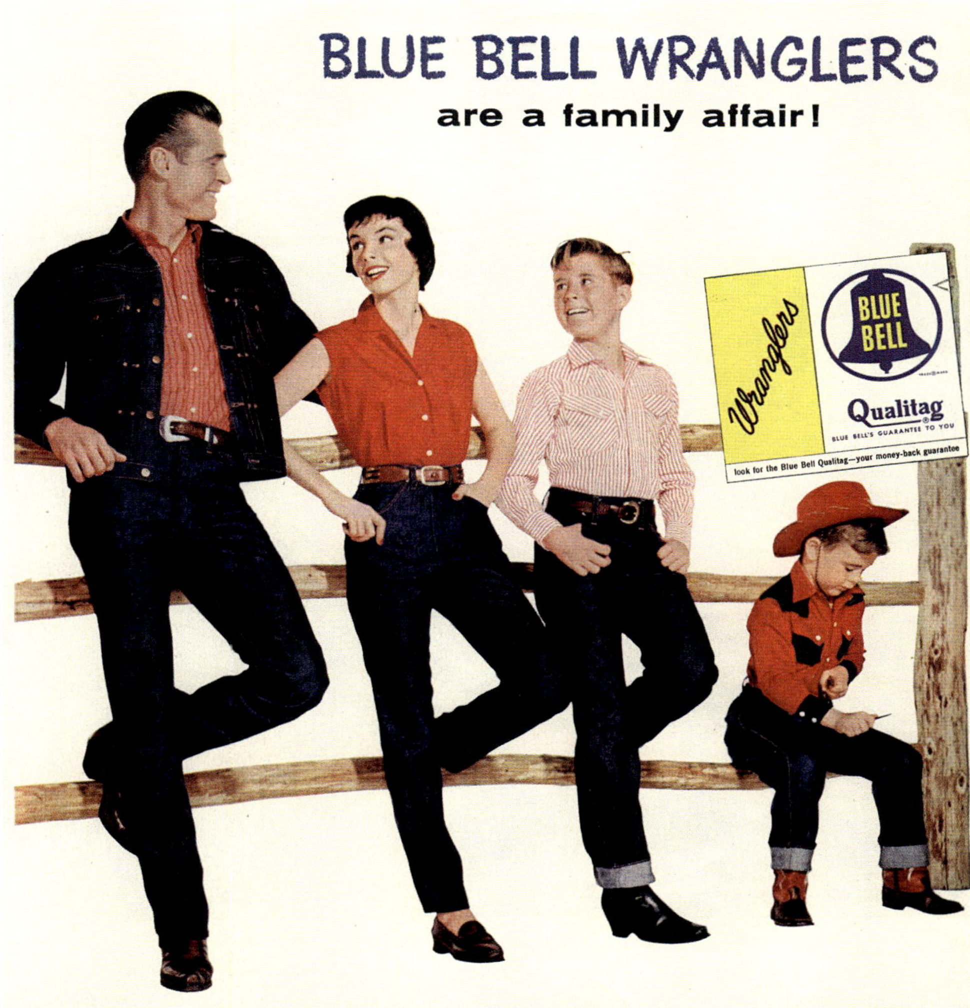

authentic Western wear for men

Blue Bell Wrangler jeans, with slim tapered legs, zipper closure, no-scratch rivets, 4 roomy pockets. Sanforized, extra-heavy weight, coarse-weave denim, sizes 31-42, $3.69

Sturdy Wrangler jacket, with comfort-cut action back, Sanforized. Men's sizes 30-50, $4.29; boys' sizes 2-12, $2.59; 14-16, $2.98

trim 'n slim for women and girls

Figure-flattering Wrangler jeans, true Western styling, Sanforized. Front or side zipper. Misses' sizes 10-20, in tall, medium, short lengths, $2.98; girls' sizes 7-14, $2.79

Pert sleeveless Jeanie blouse. Cheerful solids, stripes and plaids in fashion-right colors . . . Sanforized. Sizes 30-40, $1.98

Western comfort for growing boys

Wrangler jeans of tough, Sanforized, extra-heavy, coarse-weave denim, with zipper closure, in the brand champion cowboys choose. Sizes 1-6, $1.98; 4-12, $2.79; 13-16, $3.39

Wrangler shirts for Junior and Dad, too! Close-fitting, comfortable Western cut. Checks, plaids, stripes, solids, all Sanforized. Men's sizes 14-17, $3.98 to $4.98; boys' 2-16, $2.98 to $3.69. (Gals like them, too!)

long-wearing for little buckaroos

Blue Bell's brand-new Wranglers, with reinforced knees that will actually outwear the dungarees. In the heaviest denim made . . . Sanforized . . . and Western as the Rockies! Sizes 4-12, $2.98

Maverick shirts in two-tone combinations—red and black, navy and gold, maroon and grey. Novelty snaps, fast colors and Sanforized. Sizes 2-12, about $2.69

Long-wearing, low-priced Blue Bell casual clothes for everyone in your family

At your favorite store—or write Blue Bell, Inc., Empire State Building, New York 1, N. Y., for name of your nearest dealer.

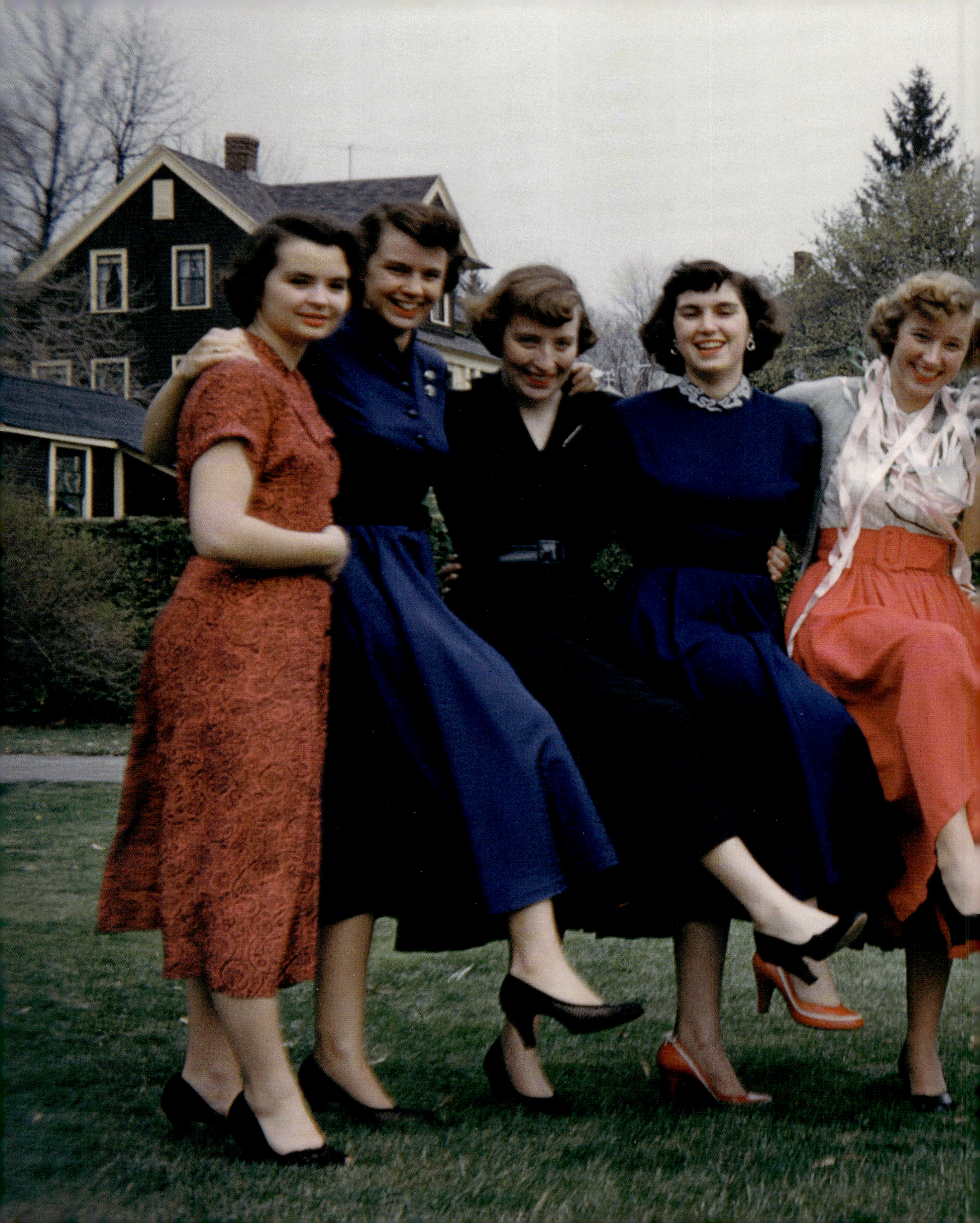

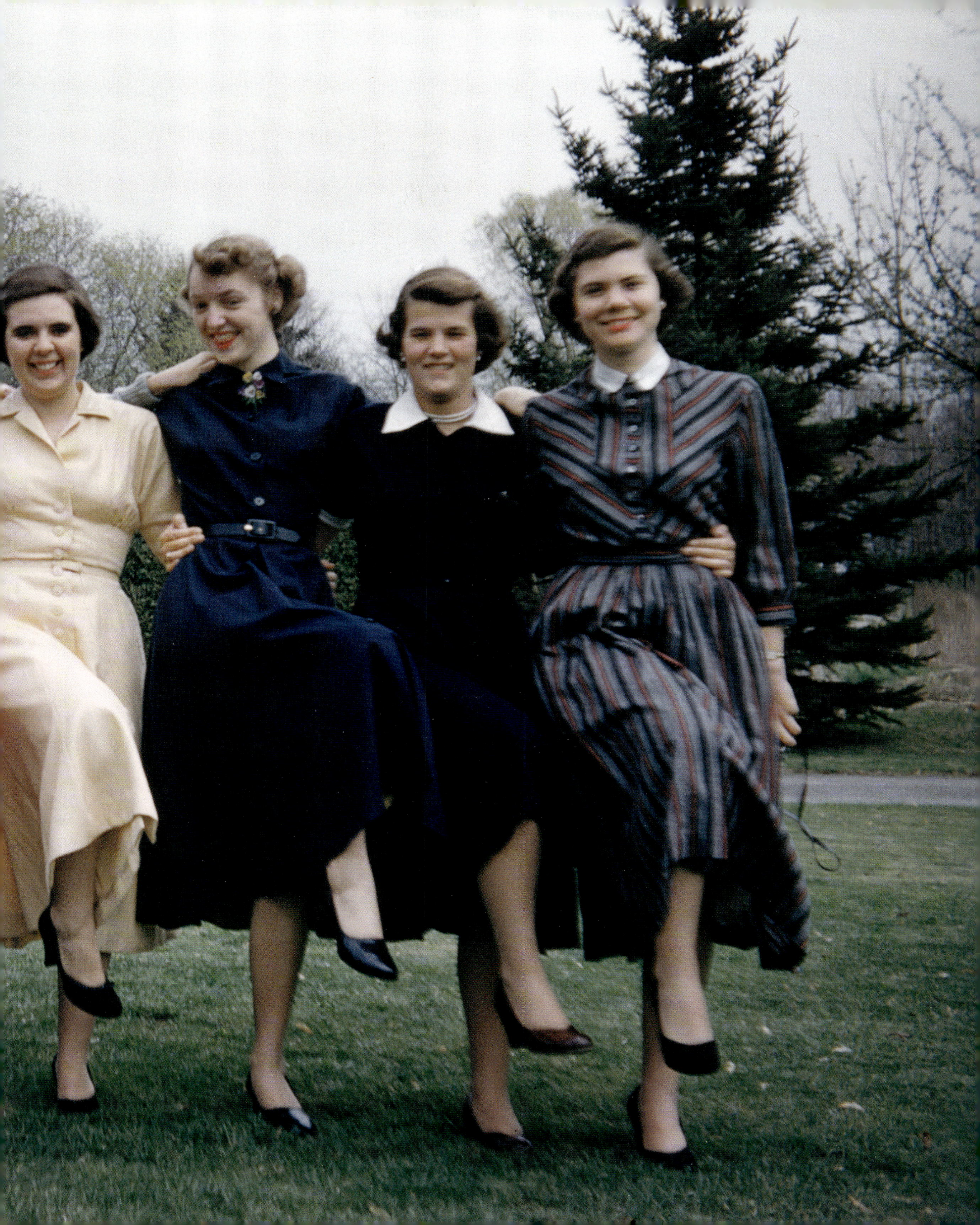

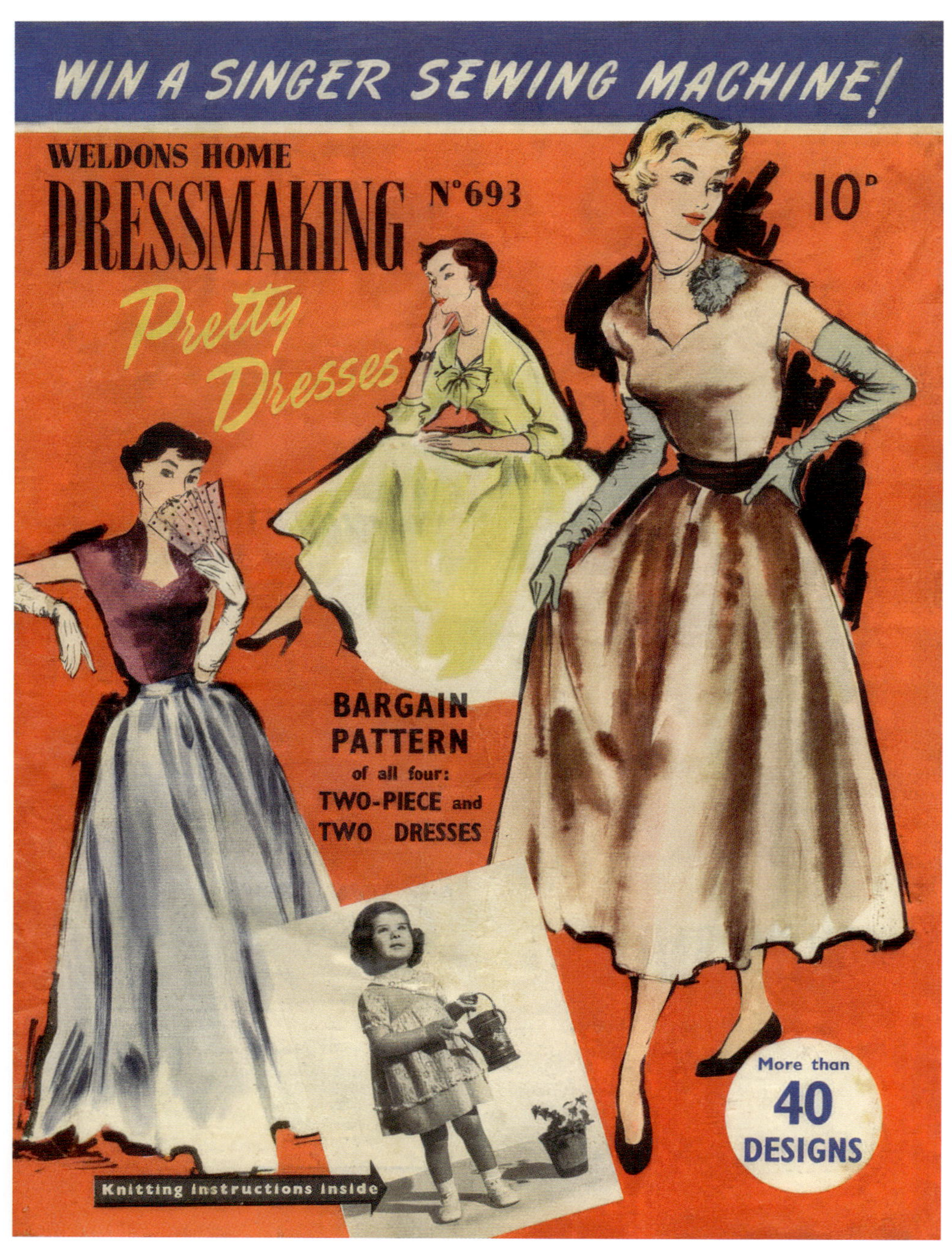
WIN A SINGER SEWING MACHINE!
WELDONS HOME
DRESSMAKING
N°693
10D
Pretty Dresses
BARGAIN PATTERN
of all four:
TWO-PIECE and
TWO DRESSES
More than
40
DESIGNS
Knitting instructions inside

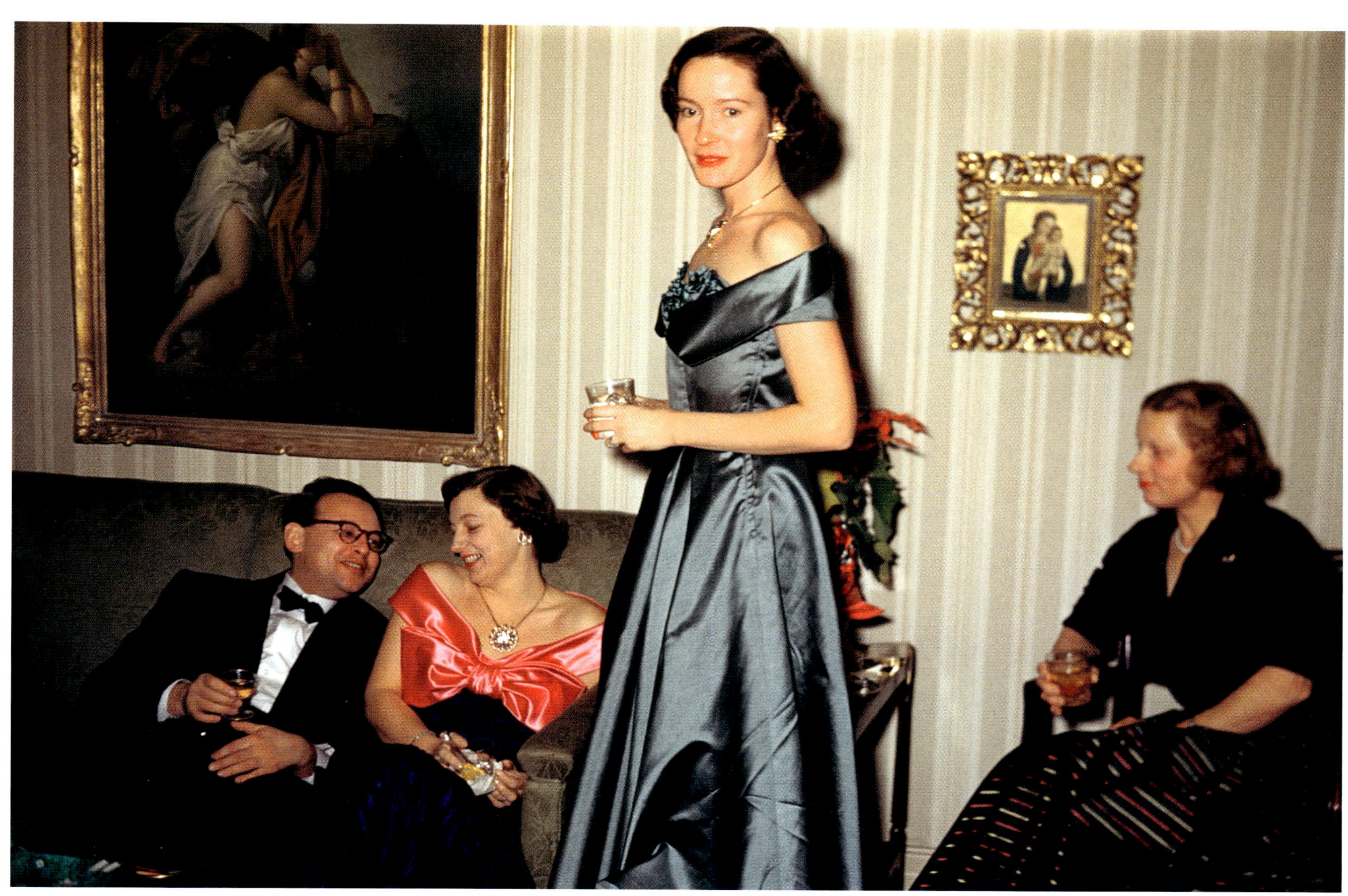

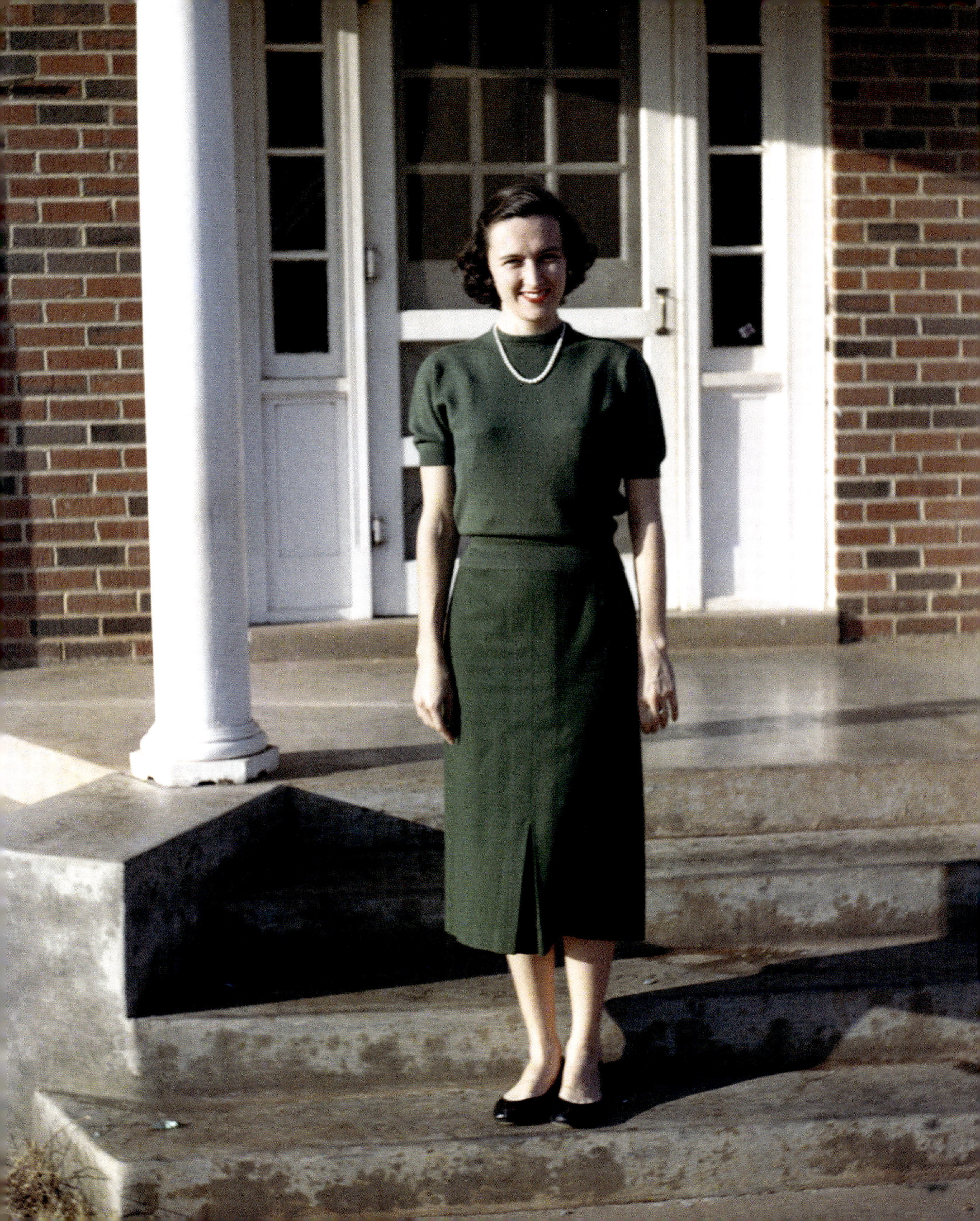

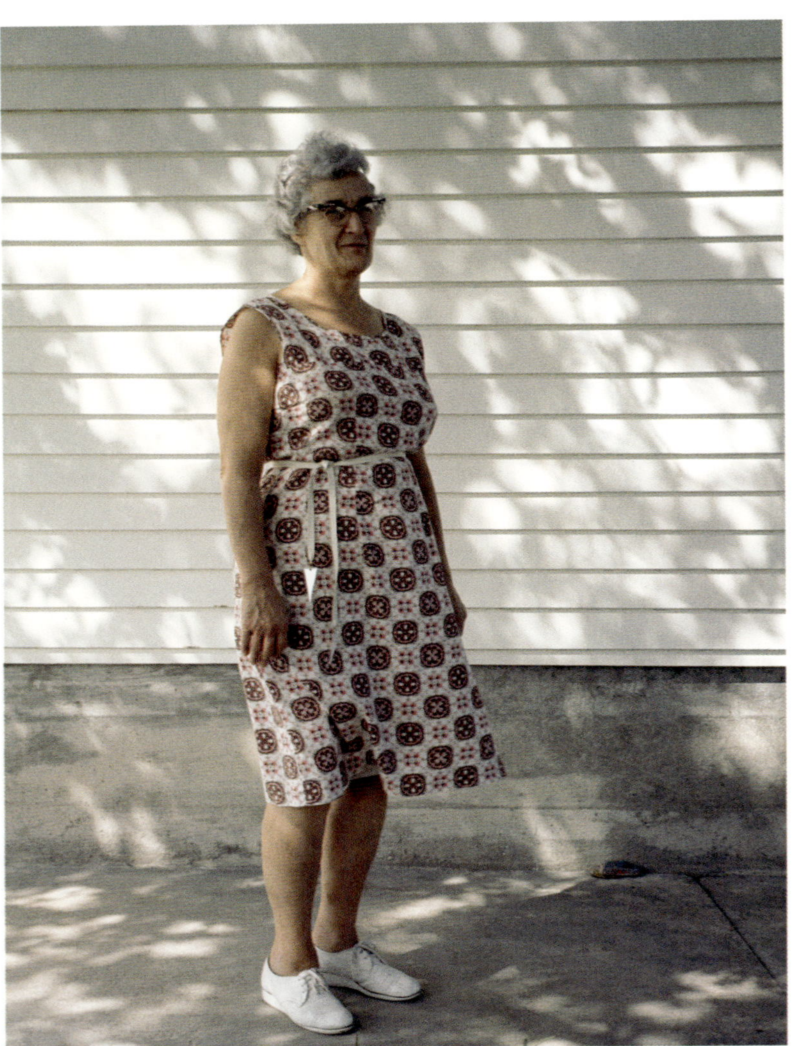

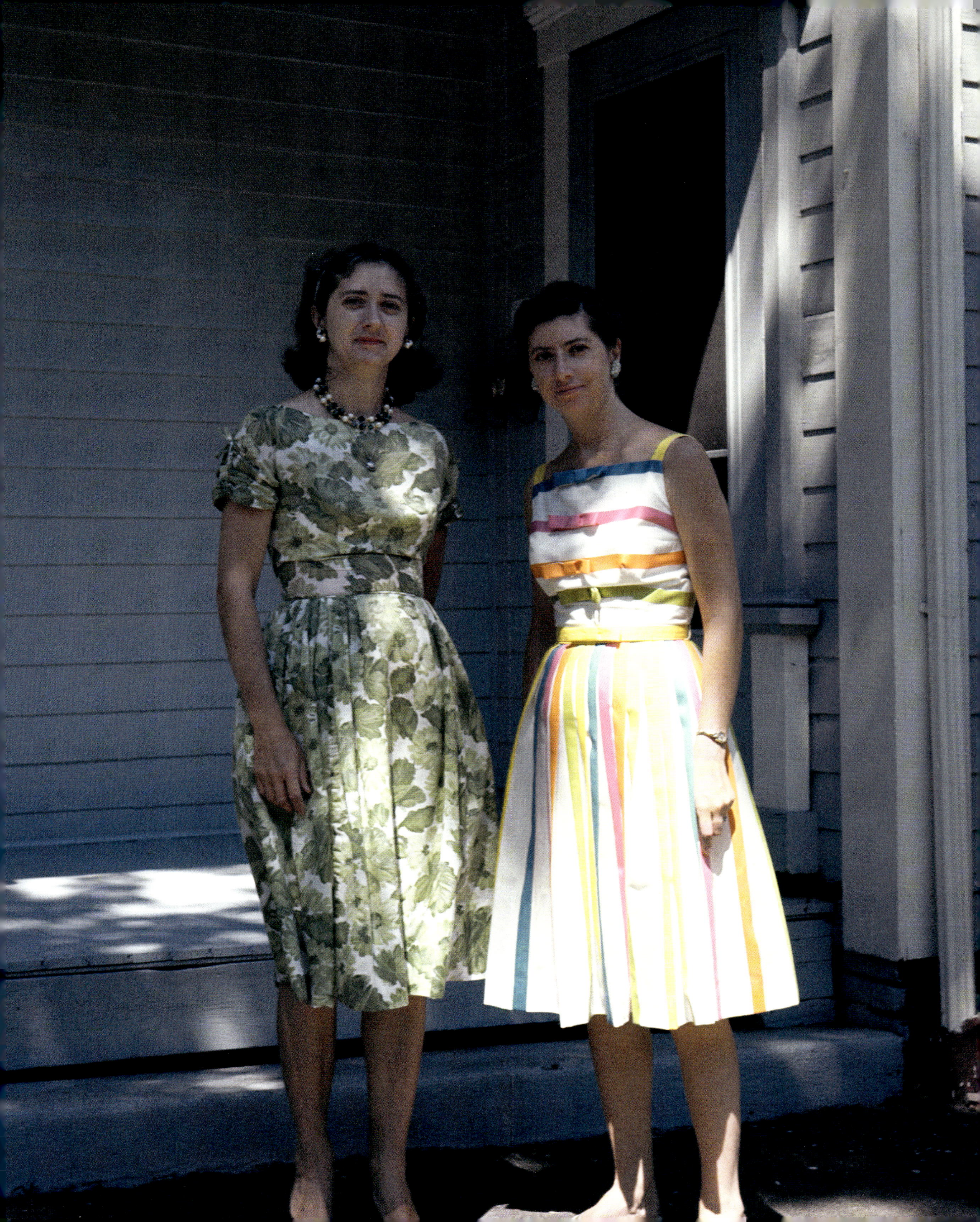

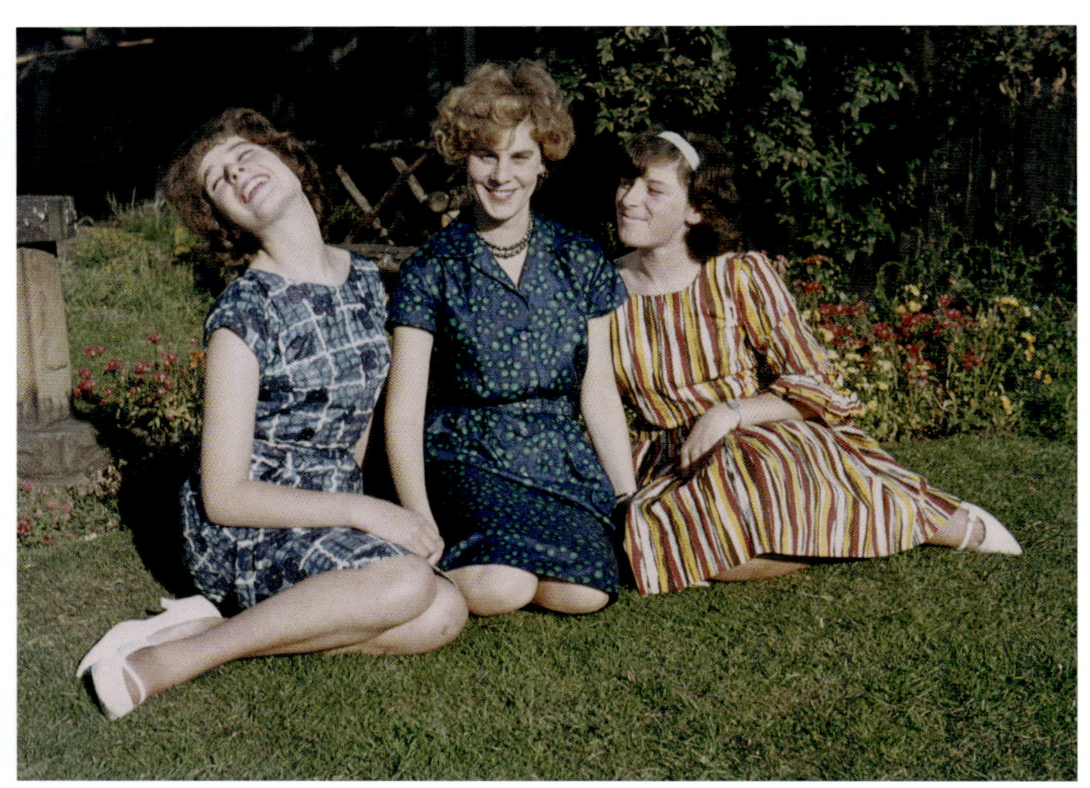

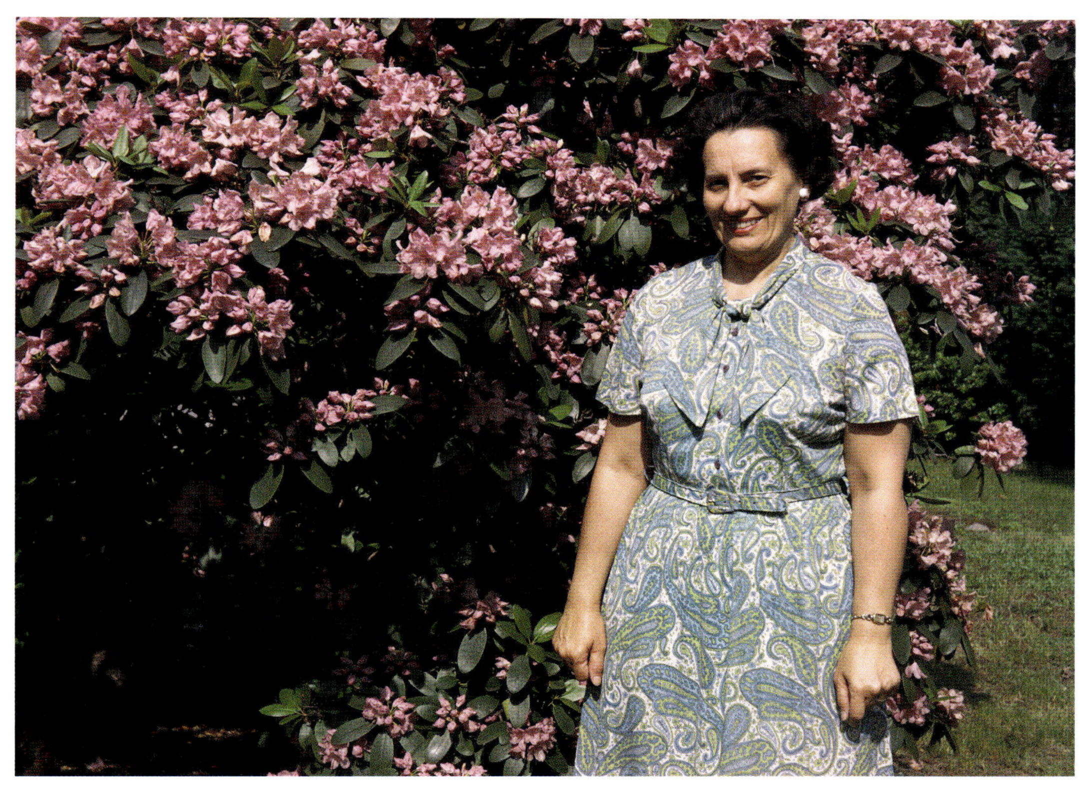

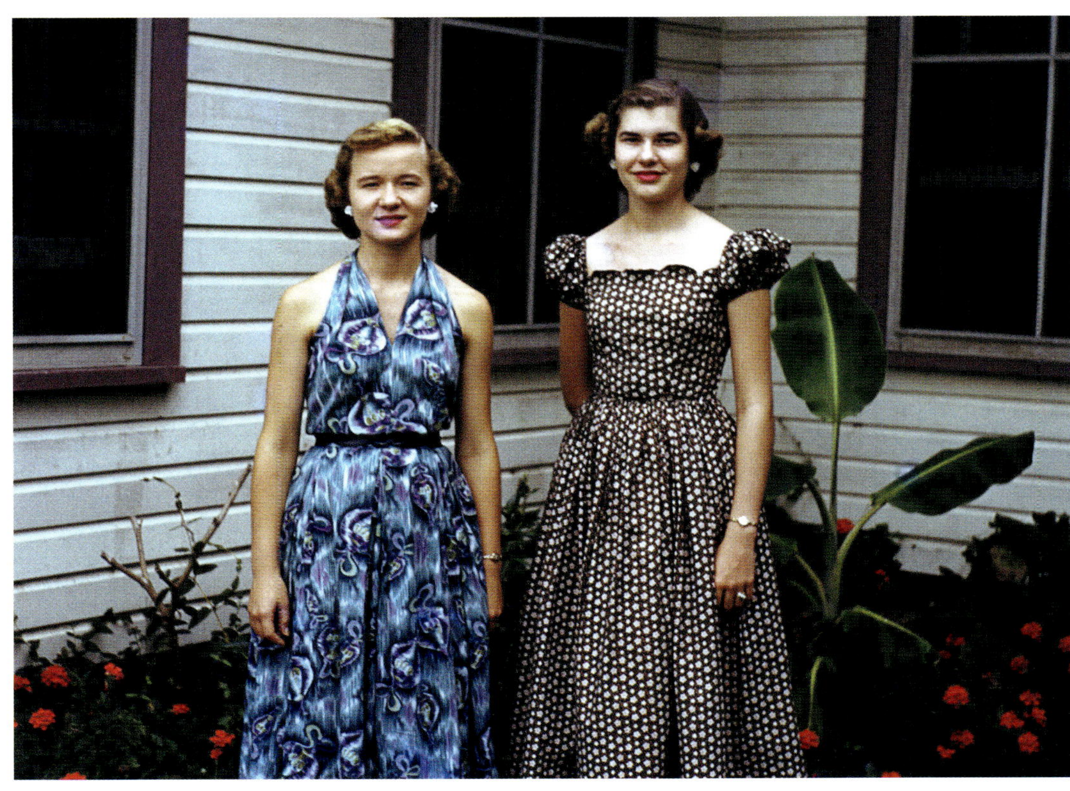

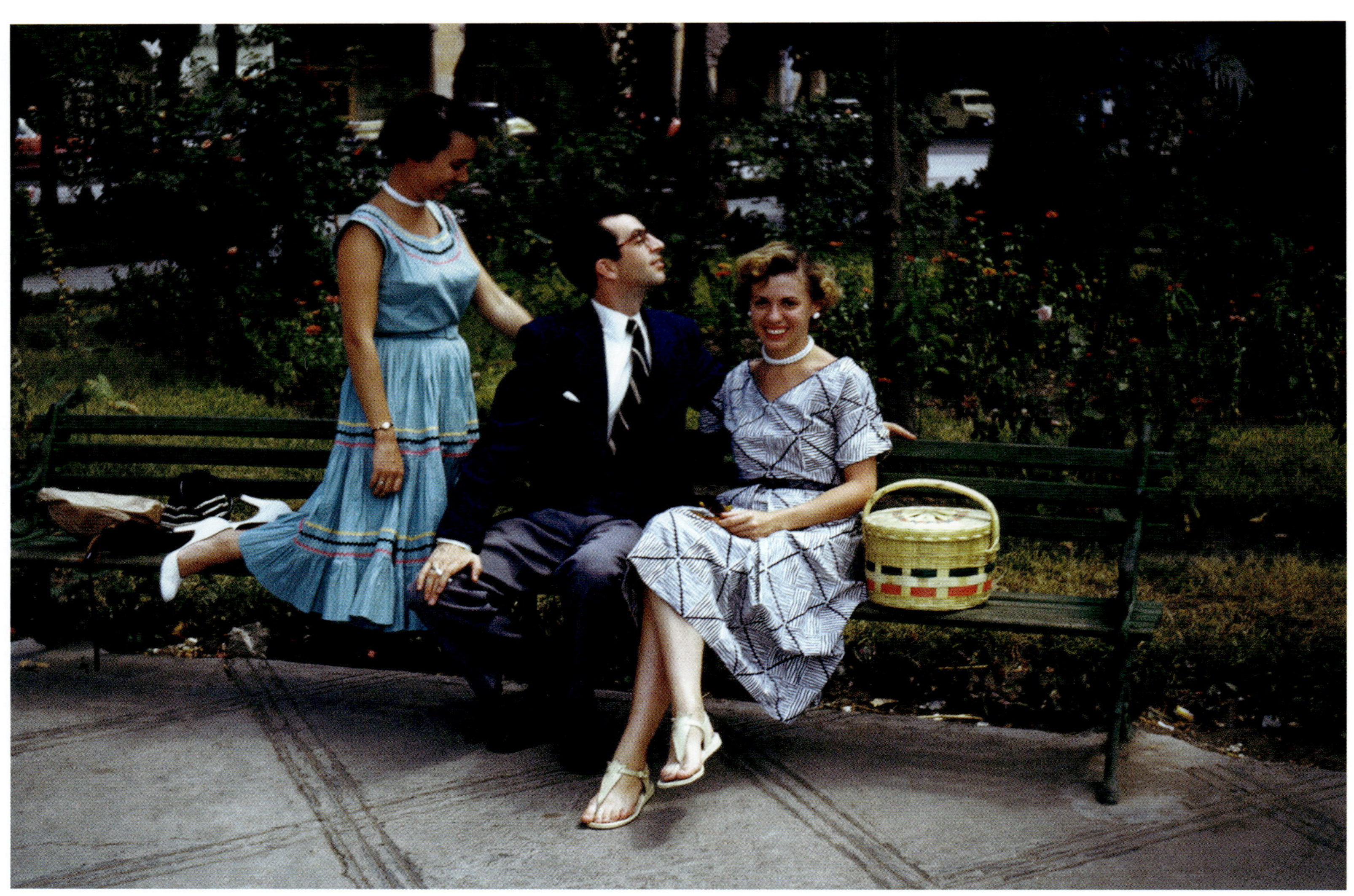

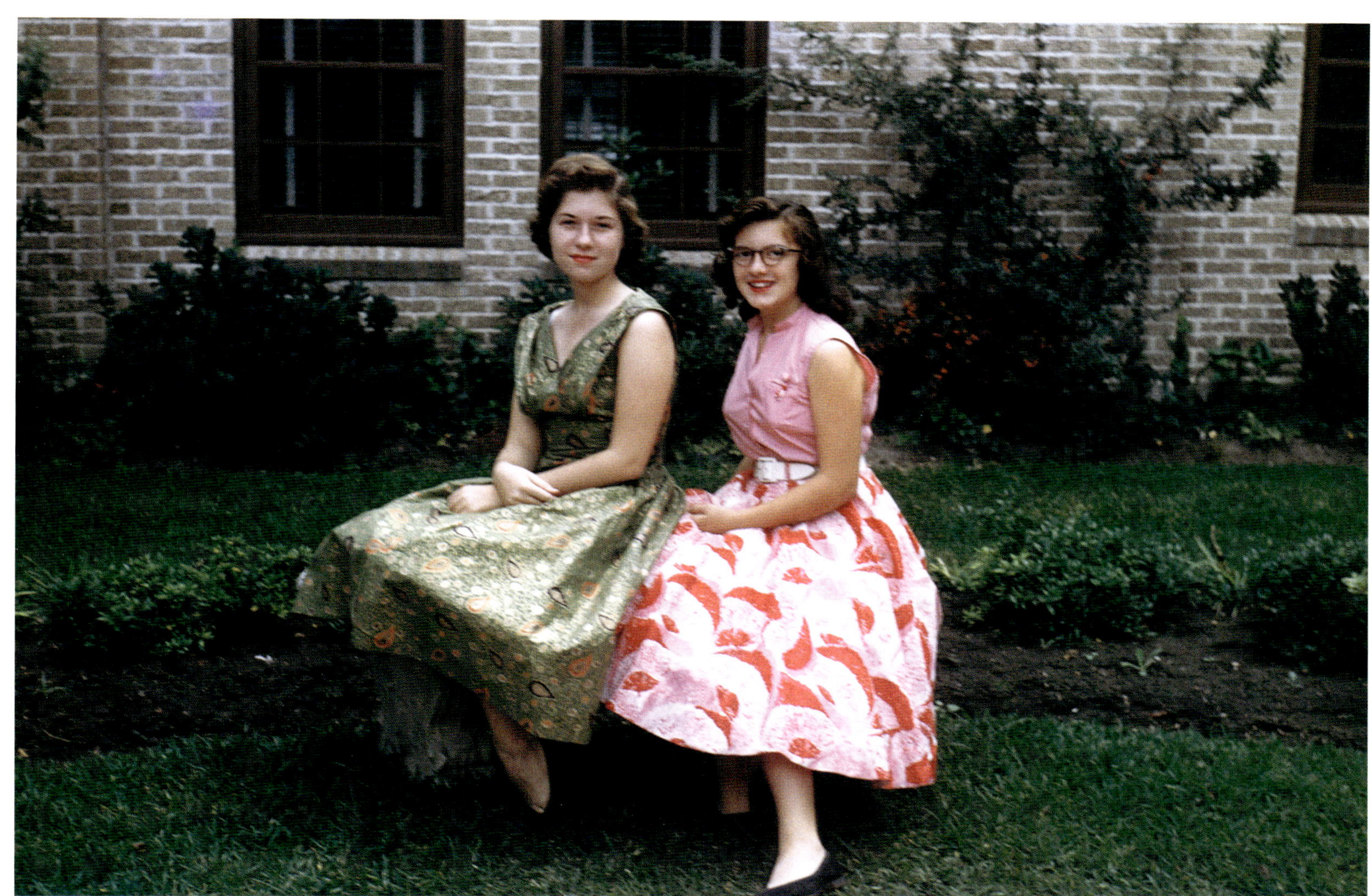

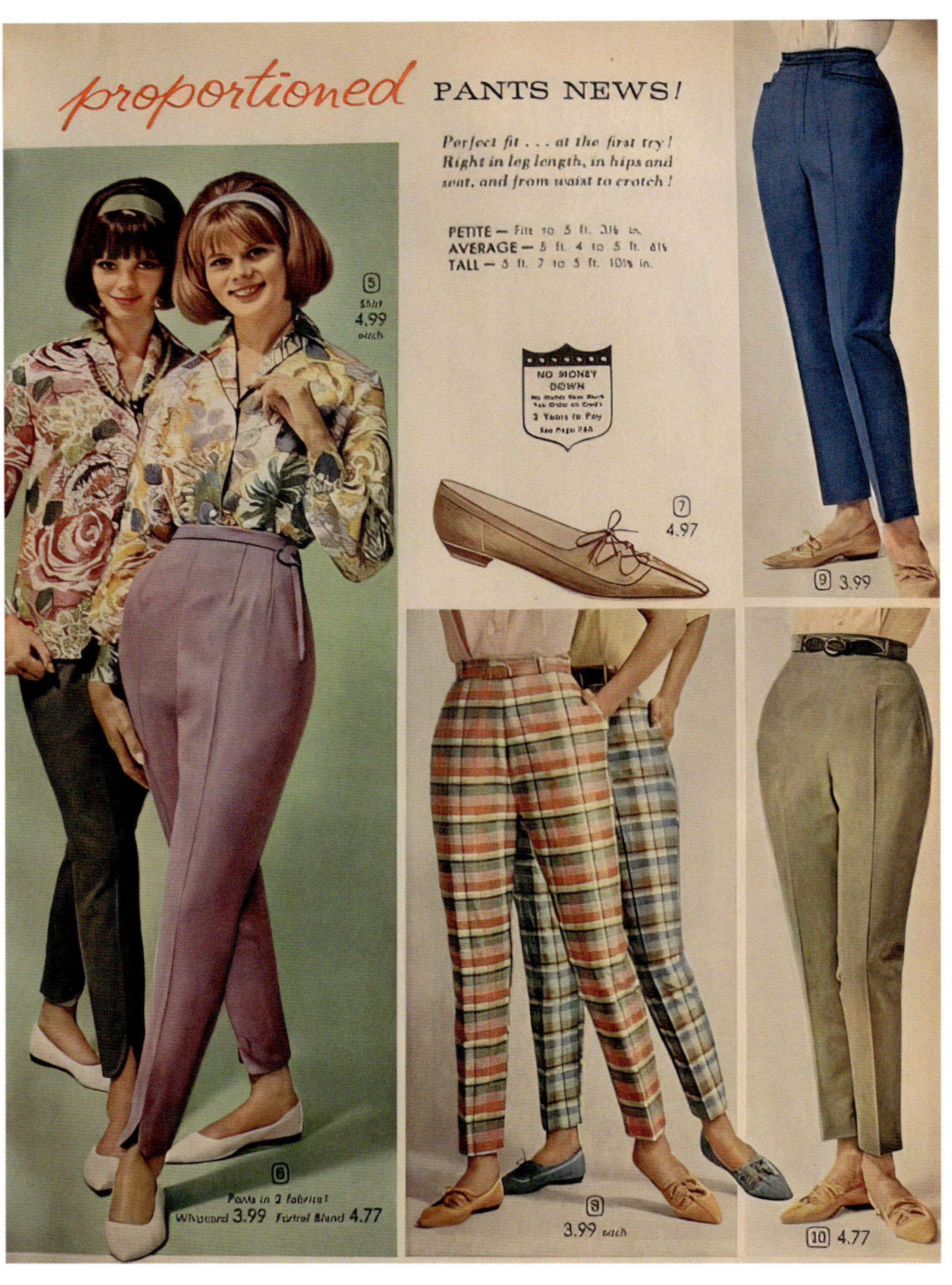
proportioned PANTS NEWS!
Perfect fit . . . at the first try! Right in leg length, in hips and seat, and from waist to crotch!
PETITE — Fits to 5 ft. 3½ in.
AVERAGE — 5 ft. 4 to 5 ft. 6½
TALL — 5 ft. 7 to 5 ft. 10½ in.
5 Shirt 4.99
7 4.97
9 3.99
6 3.99 4.77
8 3.99
10 4.77

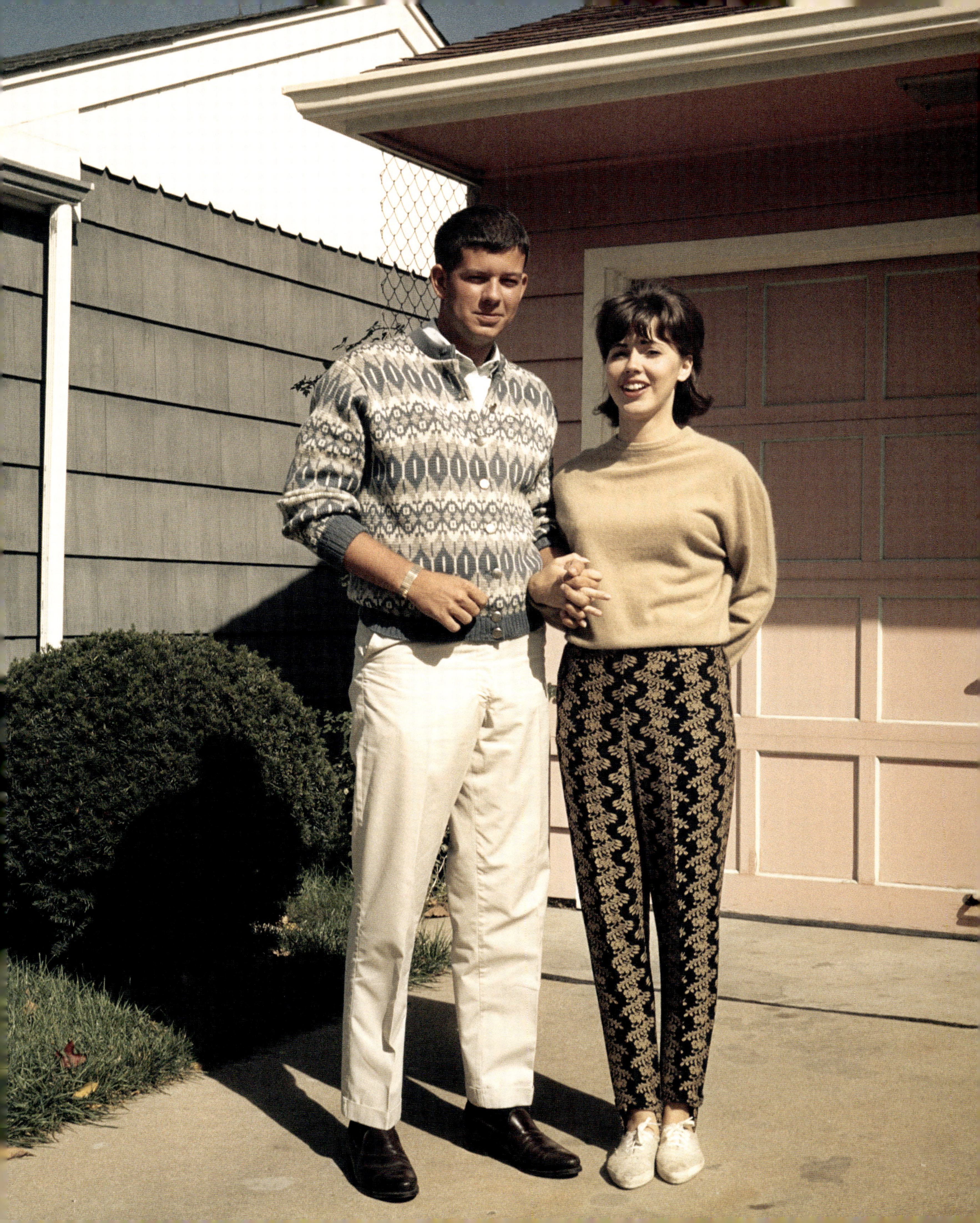

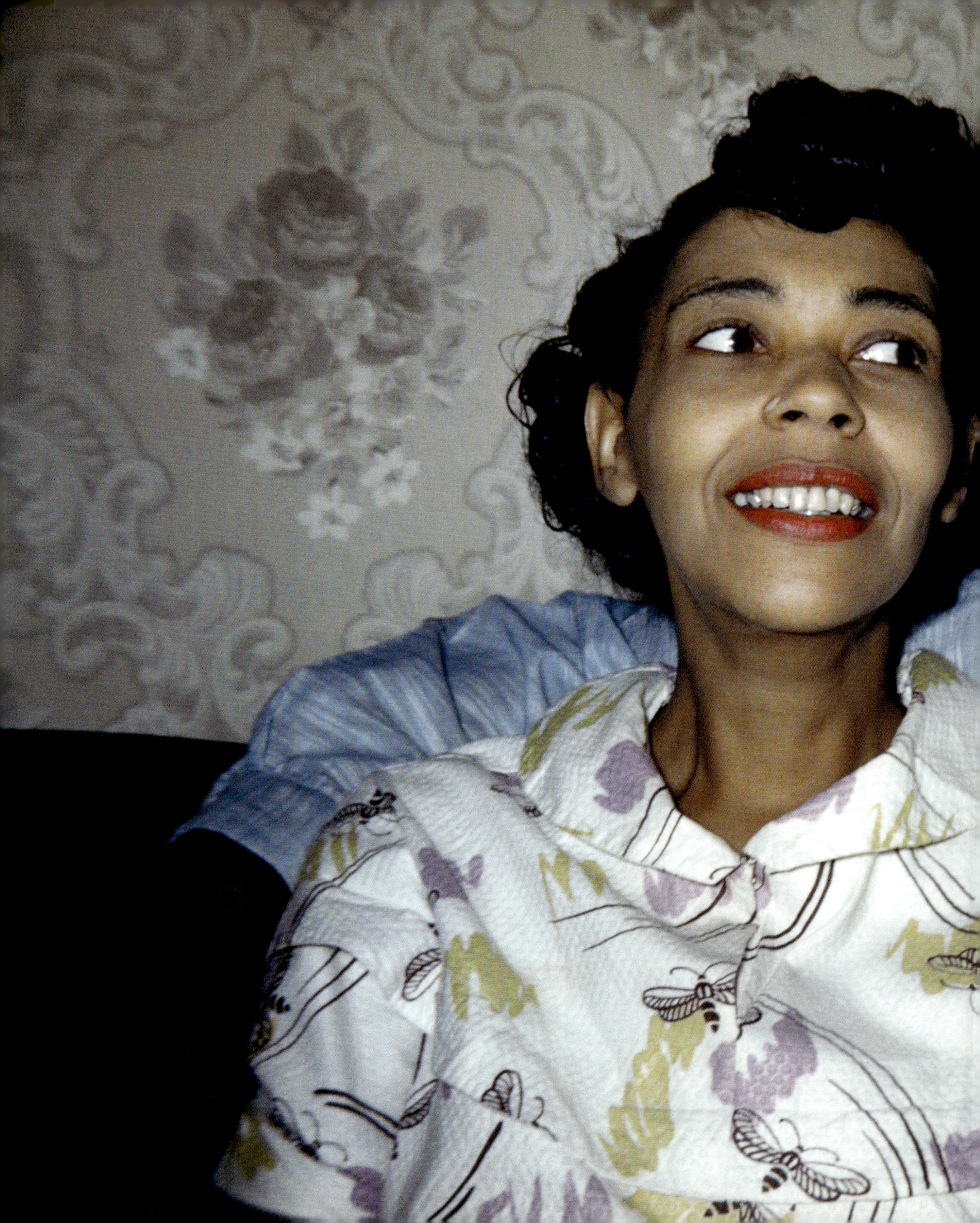

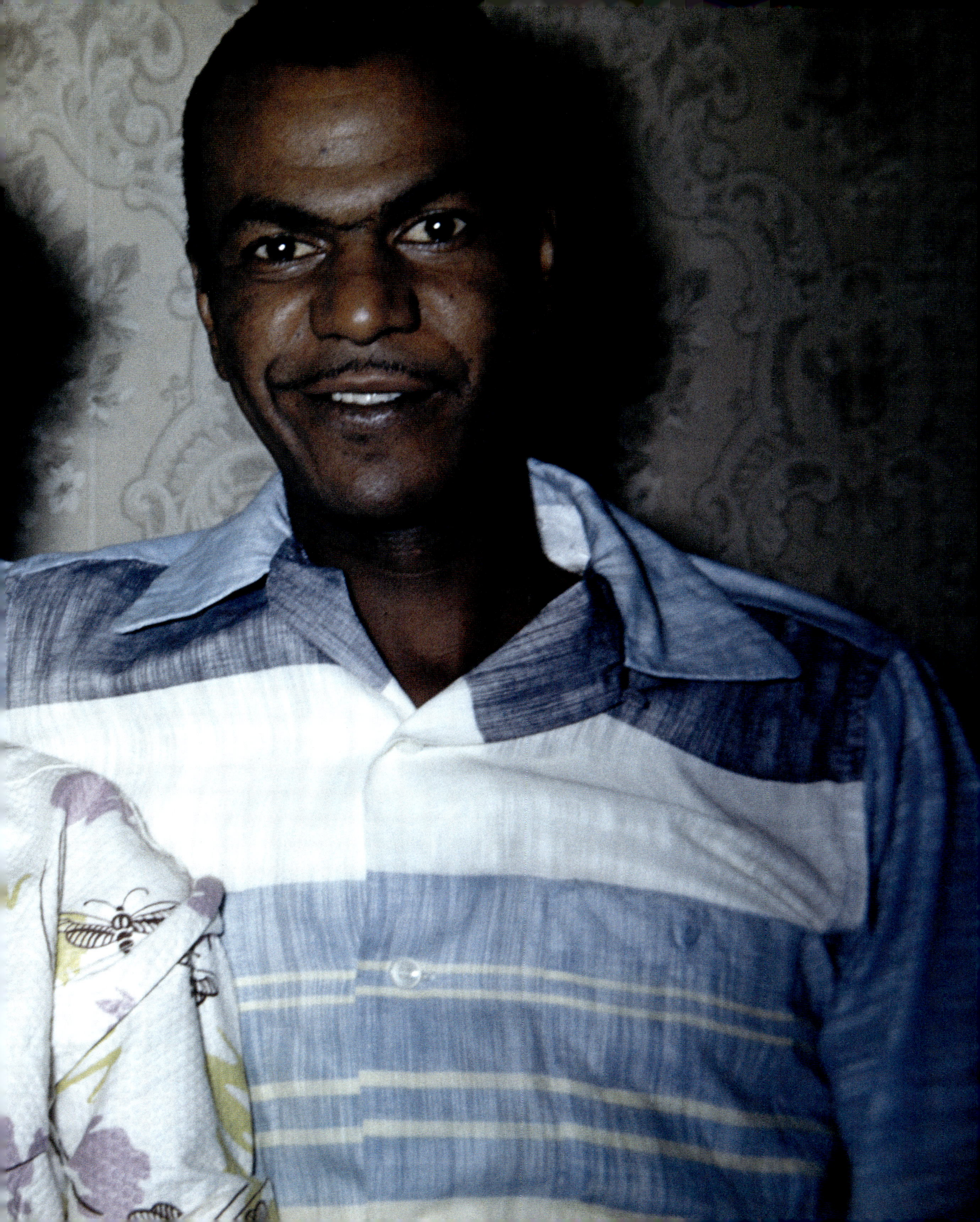

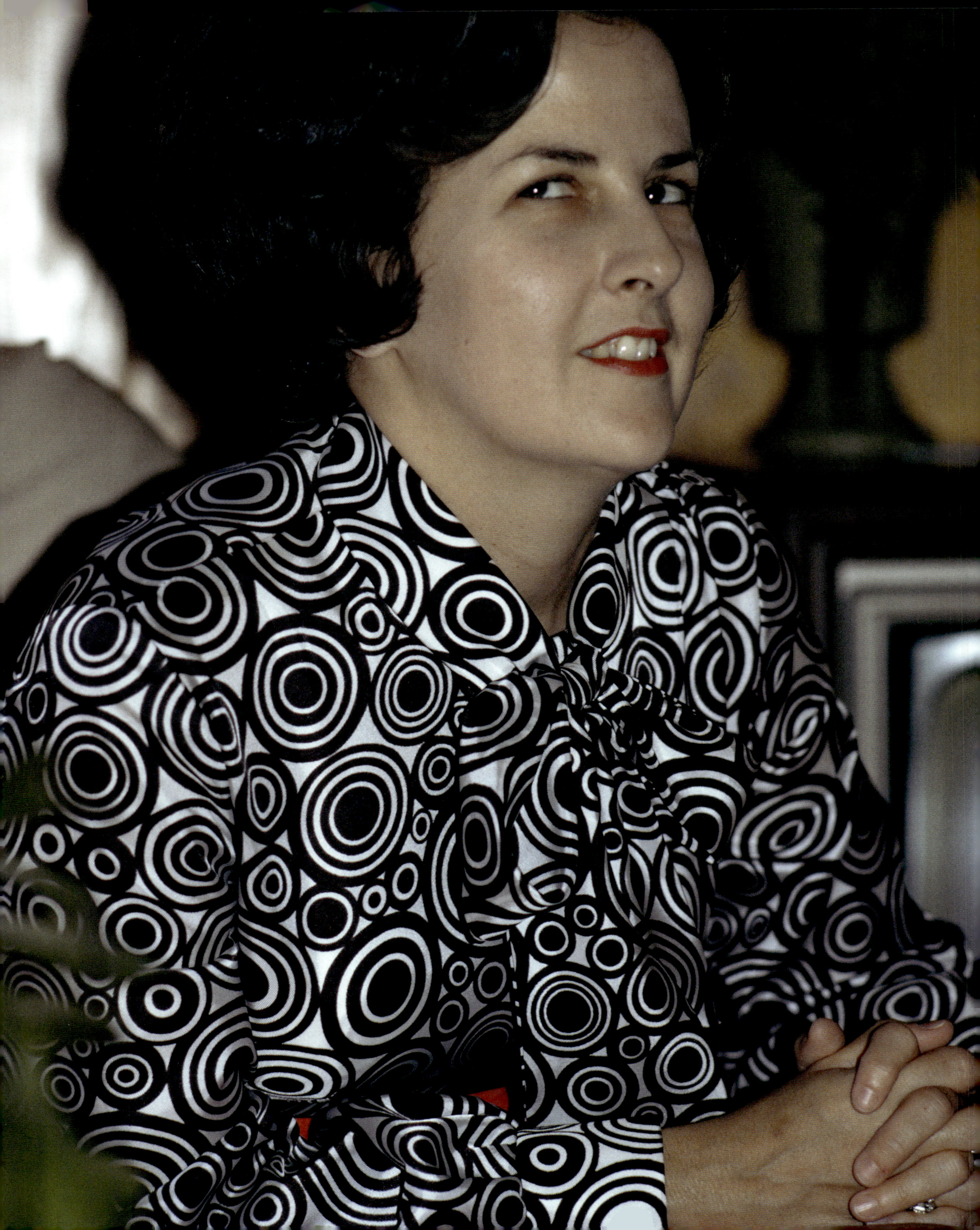

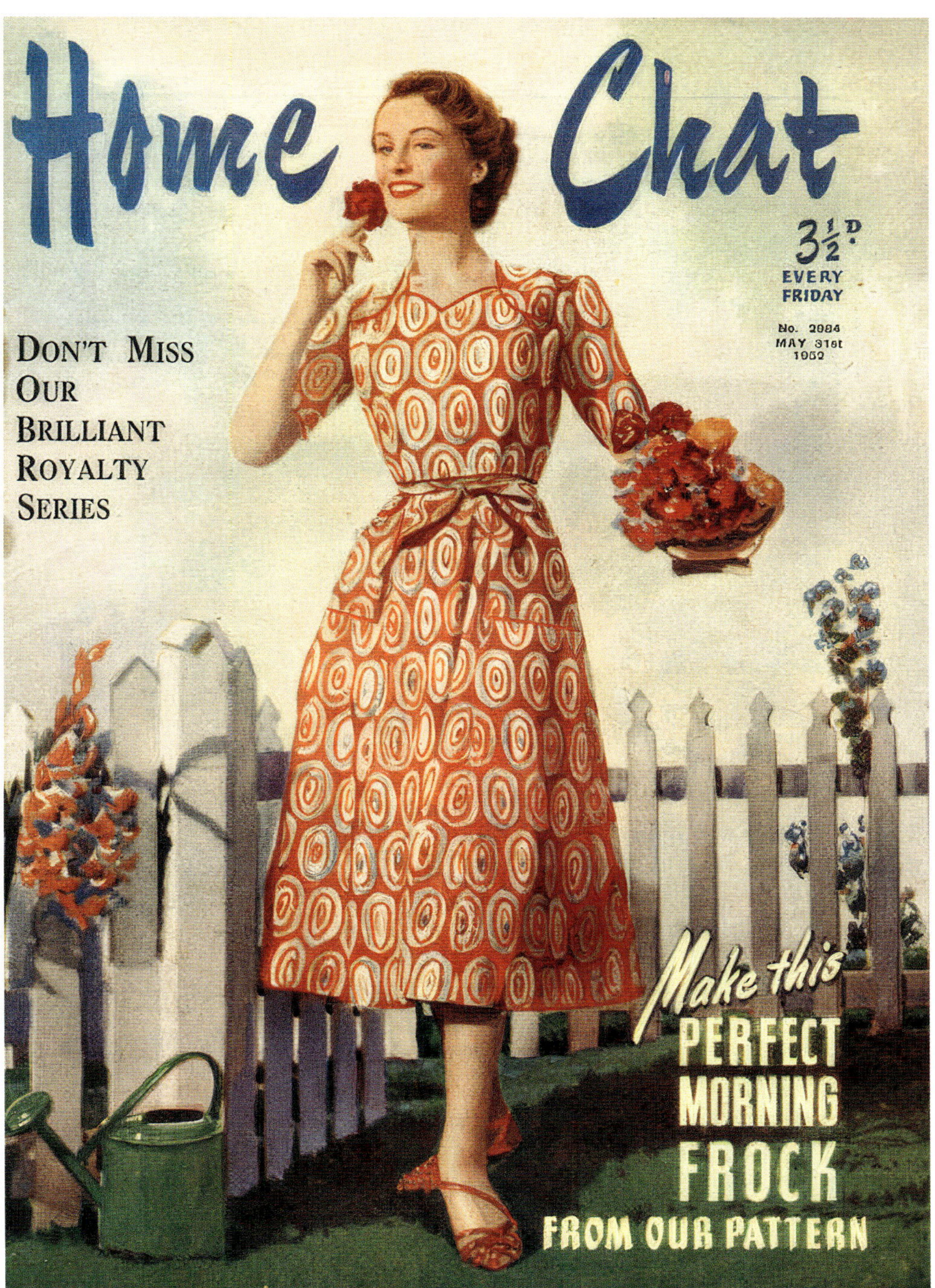
Home Chat
3½D.
EVERY FRIDAY
No. 2084
MAY 31st
1952
DON'T MISS OUR BRILLIANT ROYALTY SERIES
Make this PERFECT MORNING FROCK
FROM OUR PATTERN

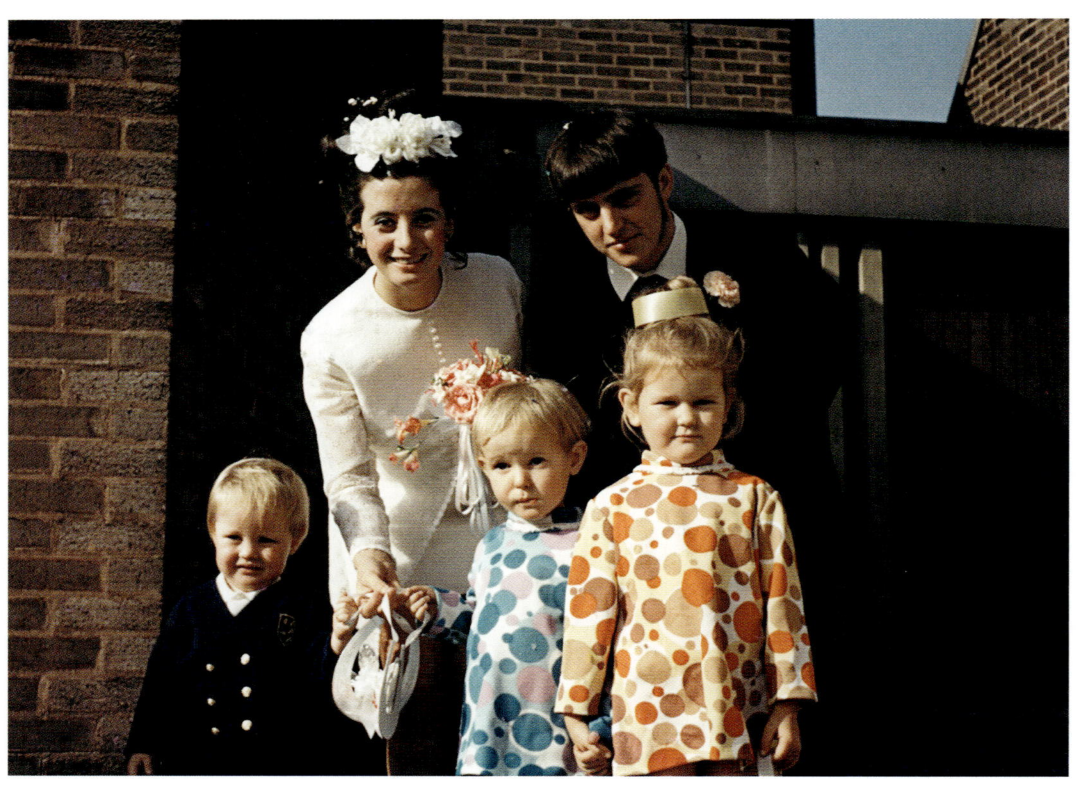

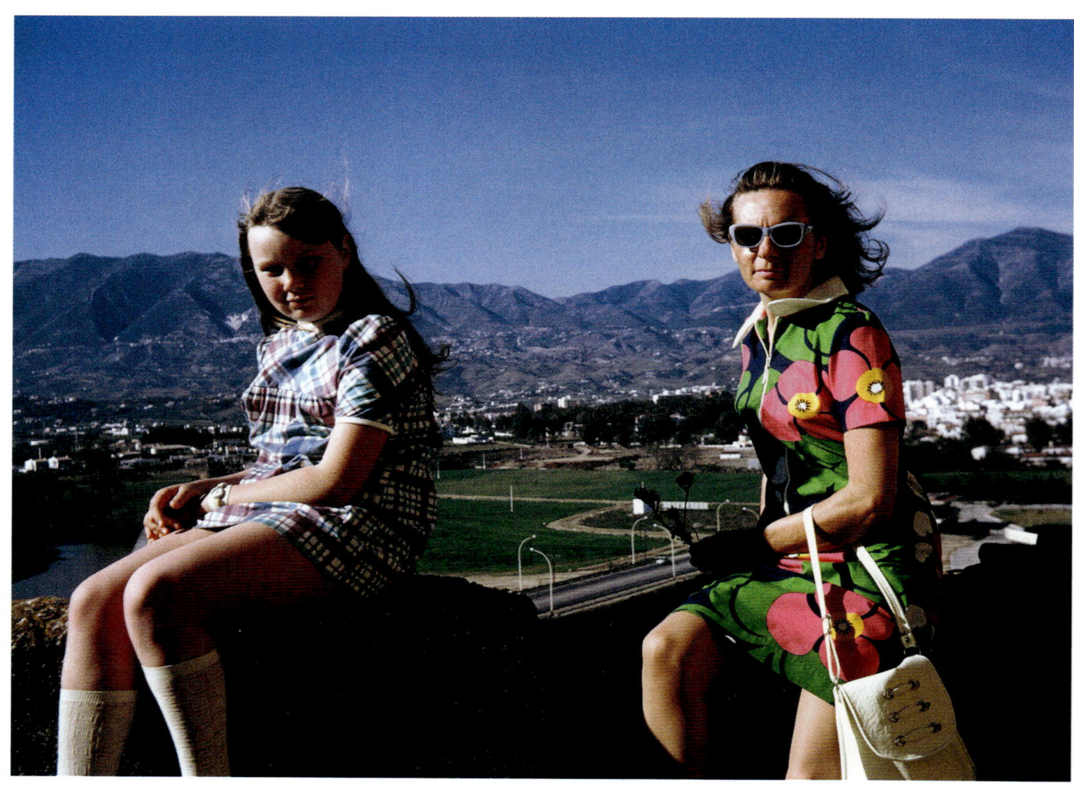

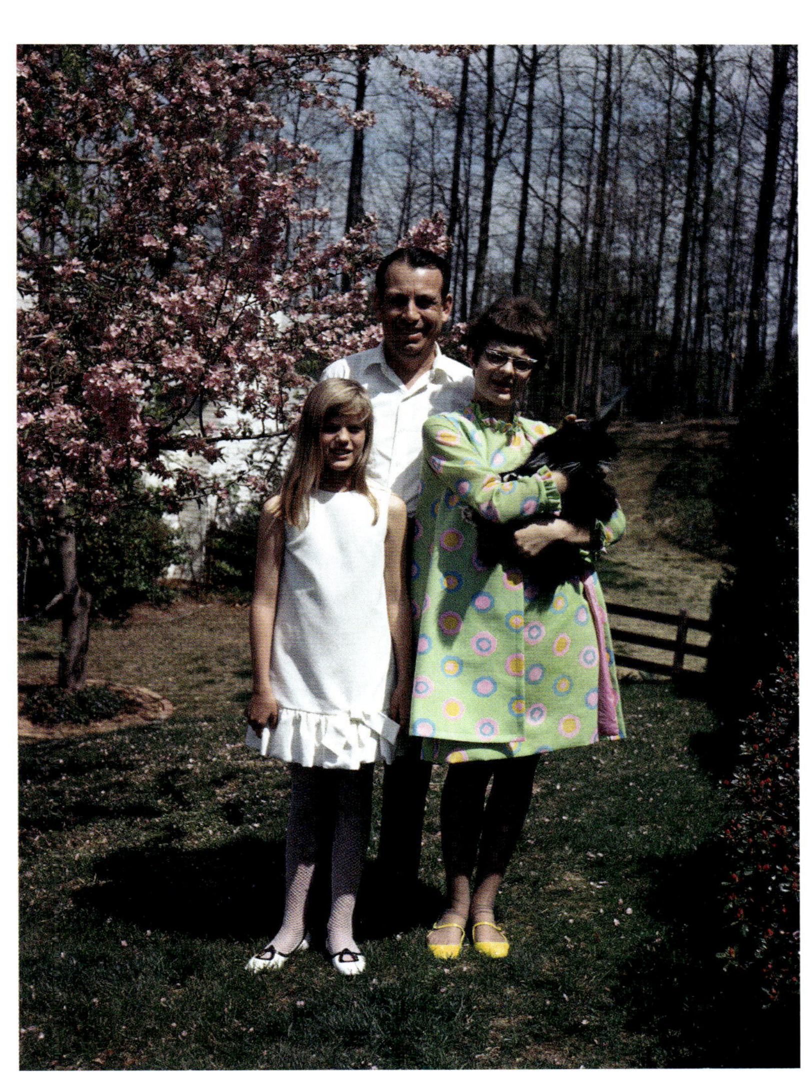

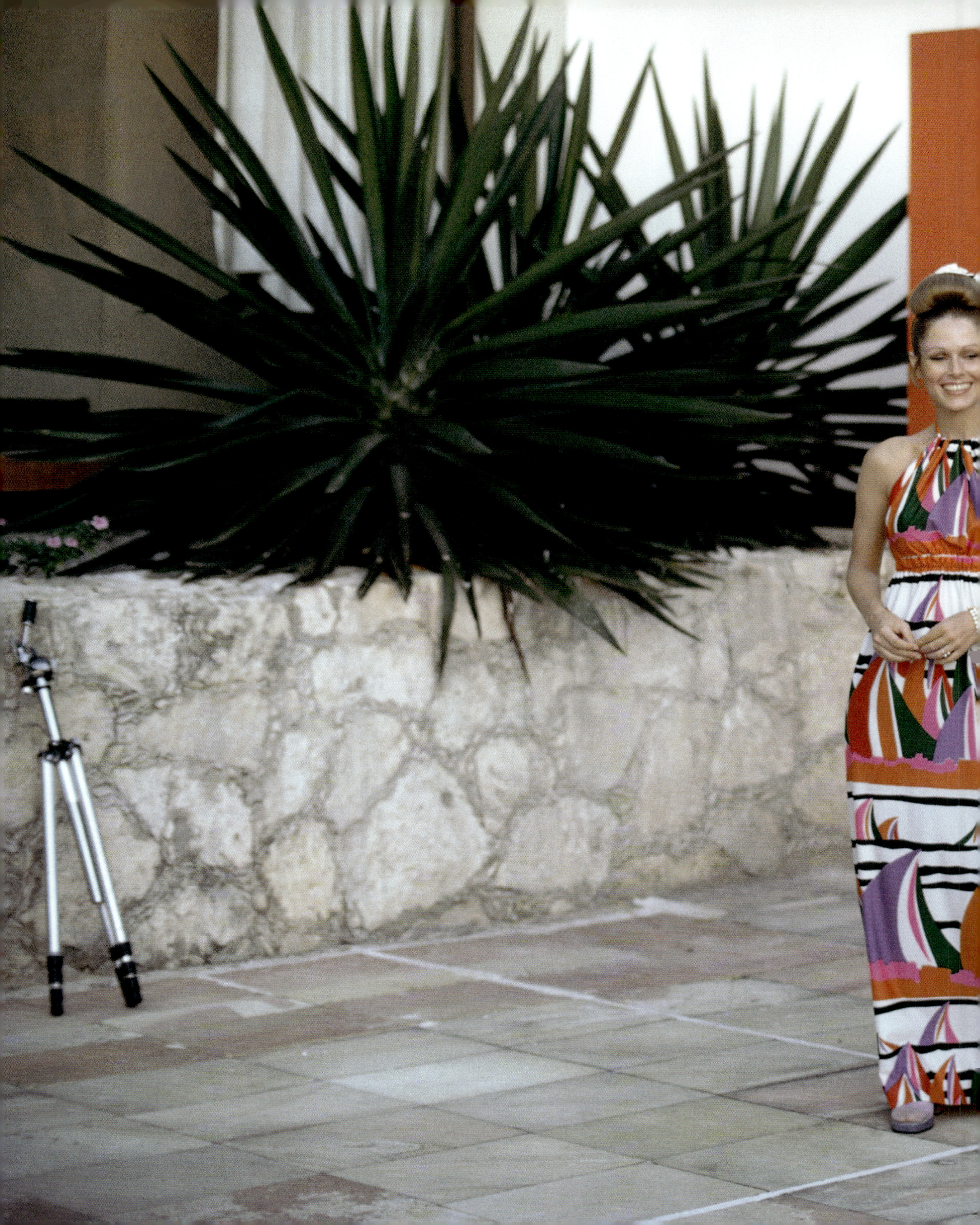

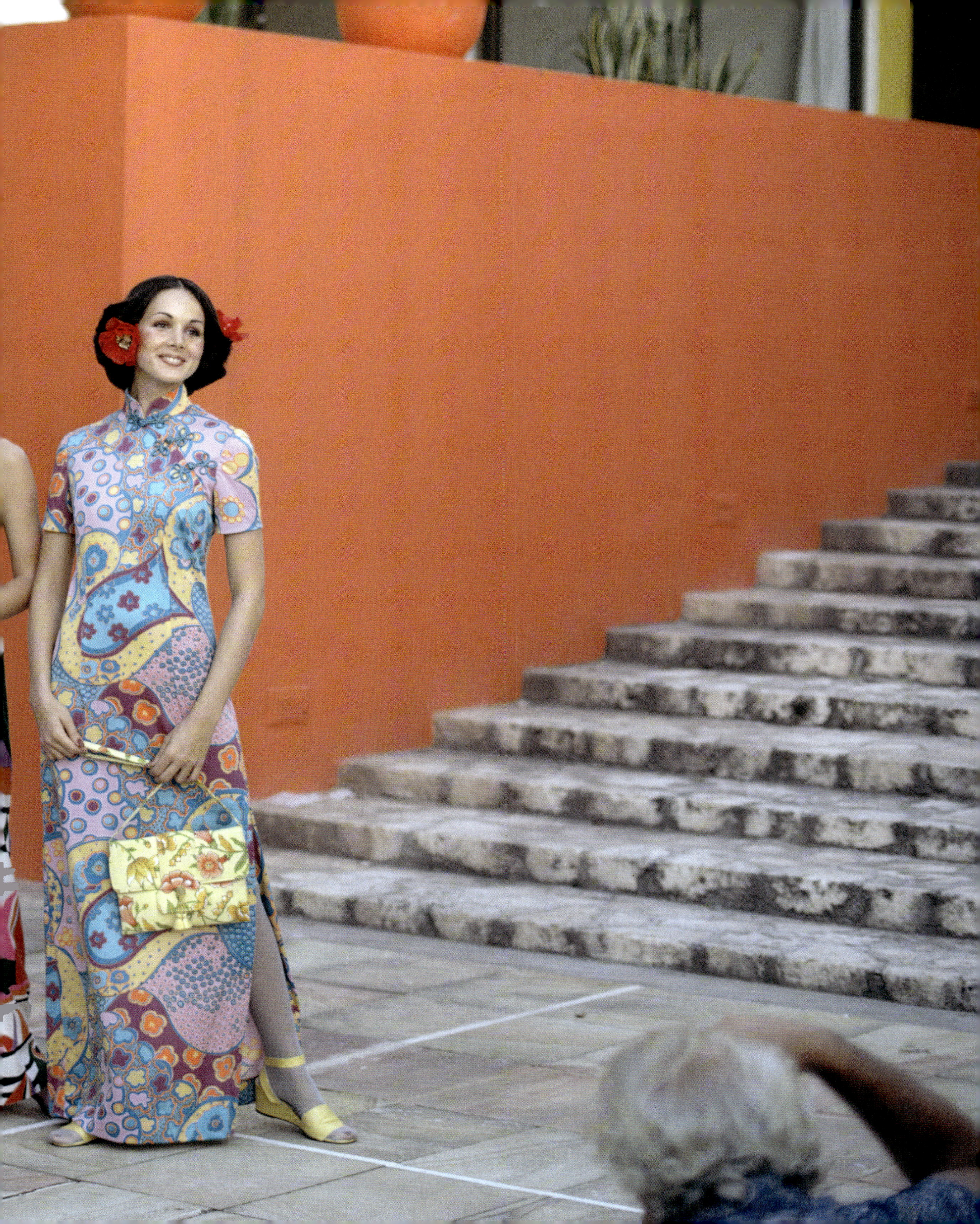

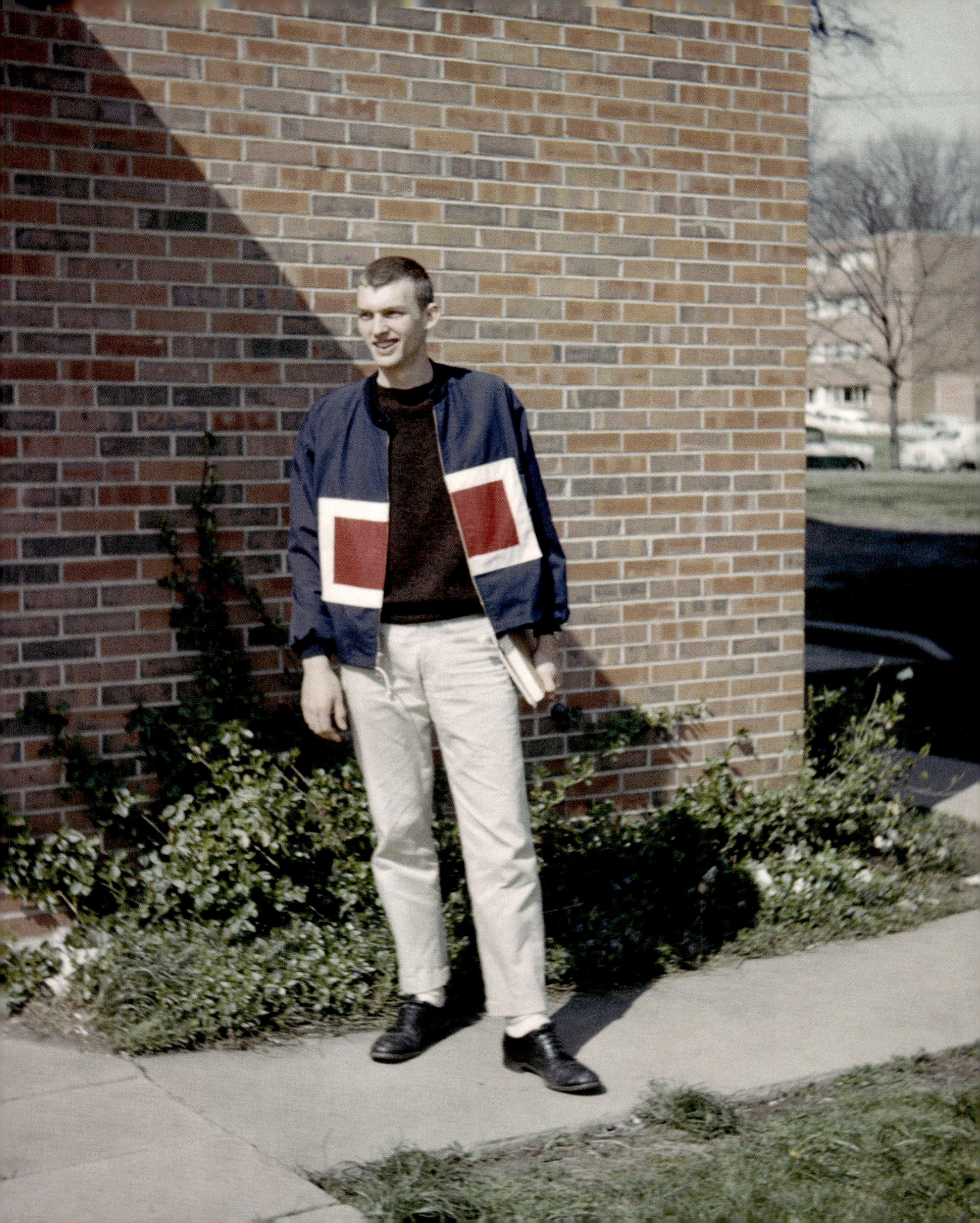

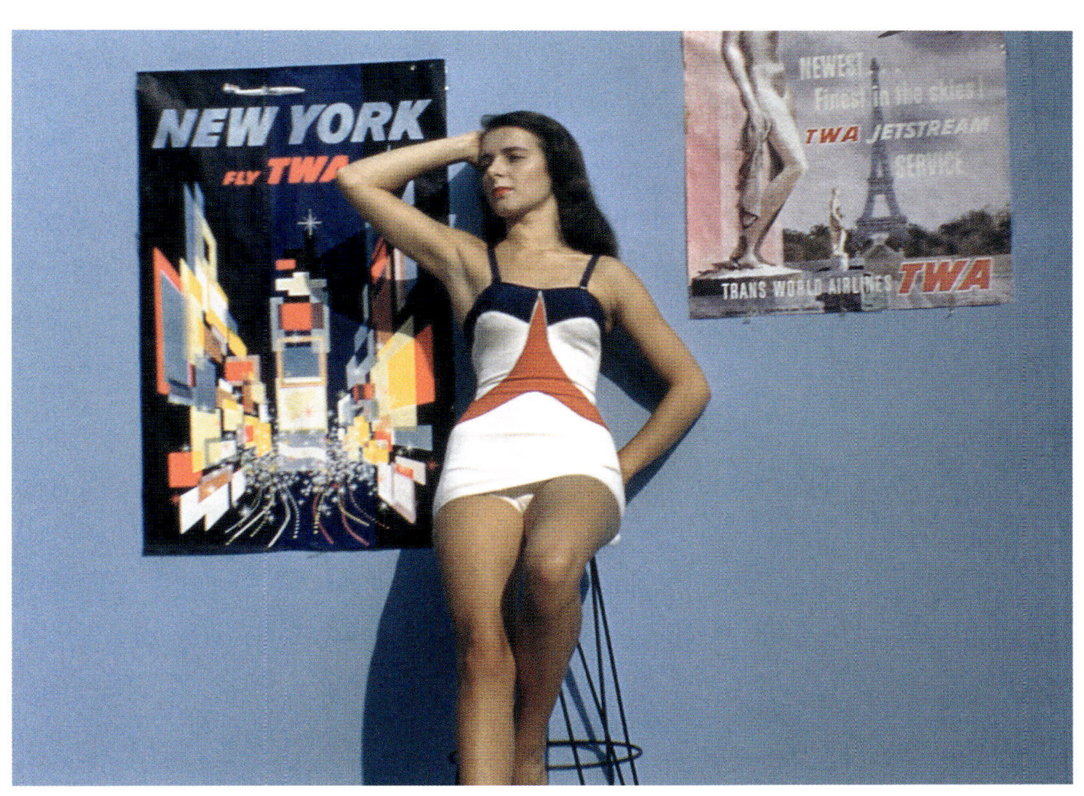
NEW YORK
FLY TWA
NEWEST
Finest in the skies!
TWA JETSTREAM
SERVICE
TRANS WORLD AIRLINES TWA

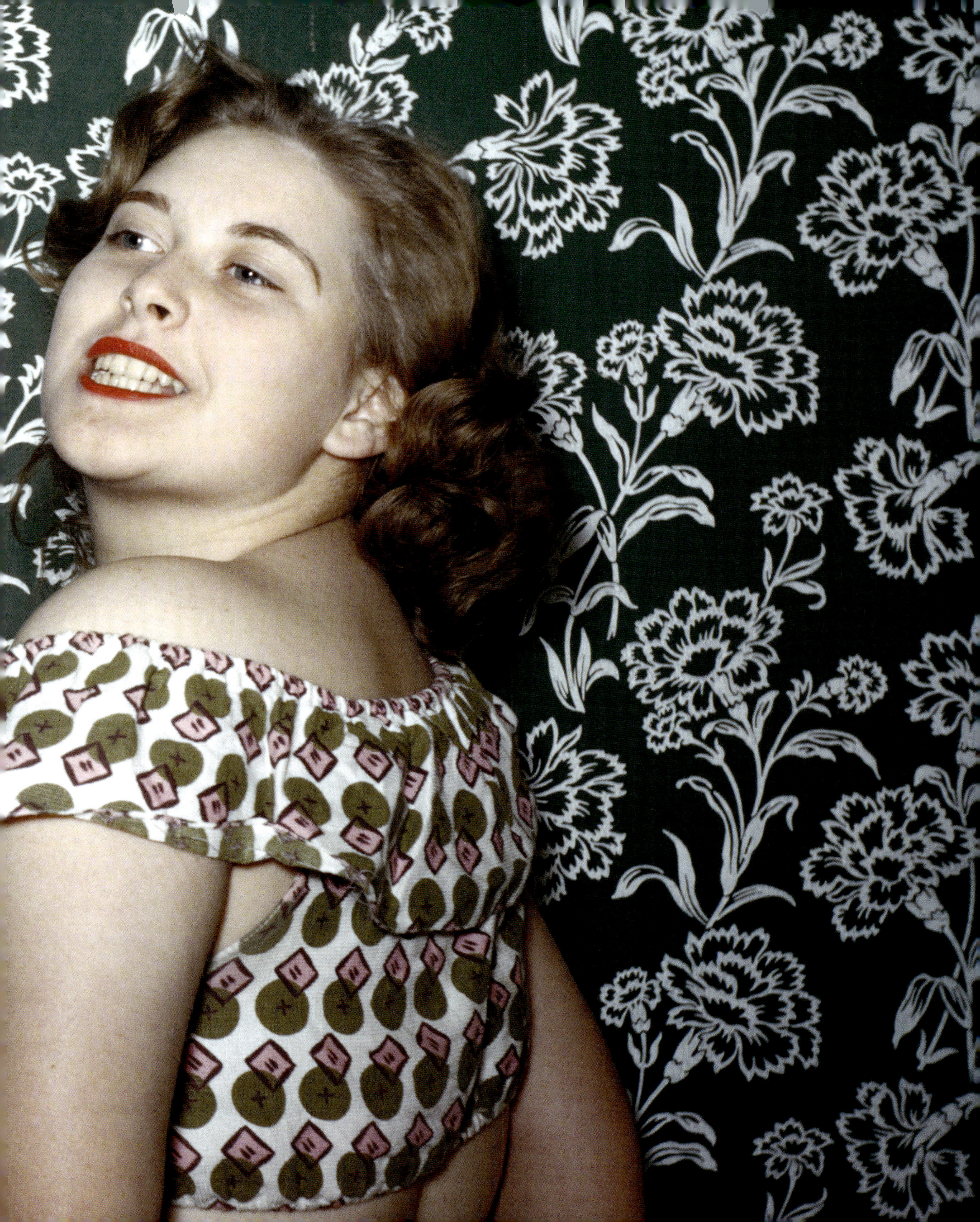

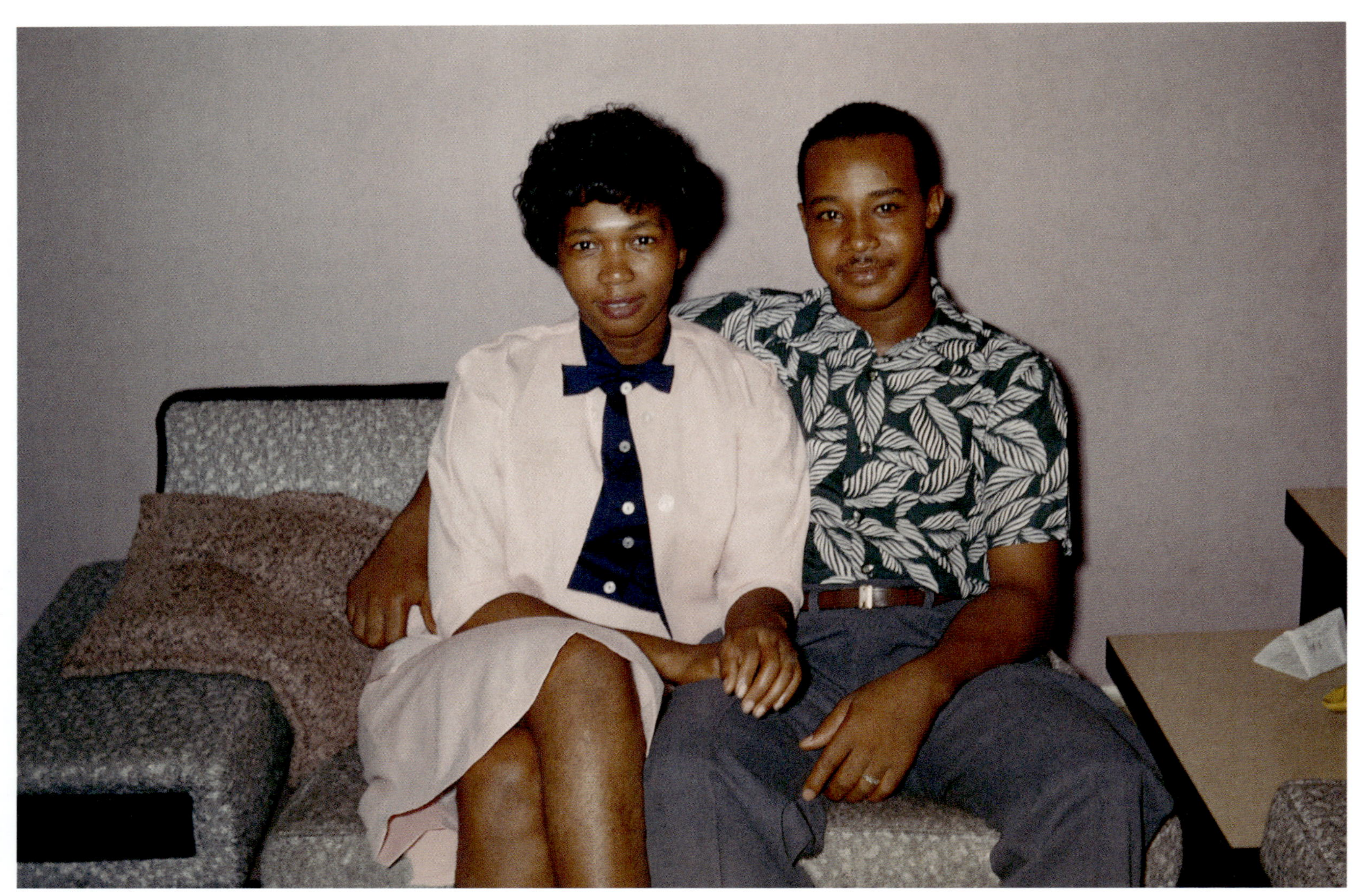

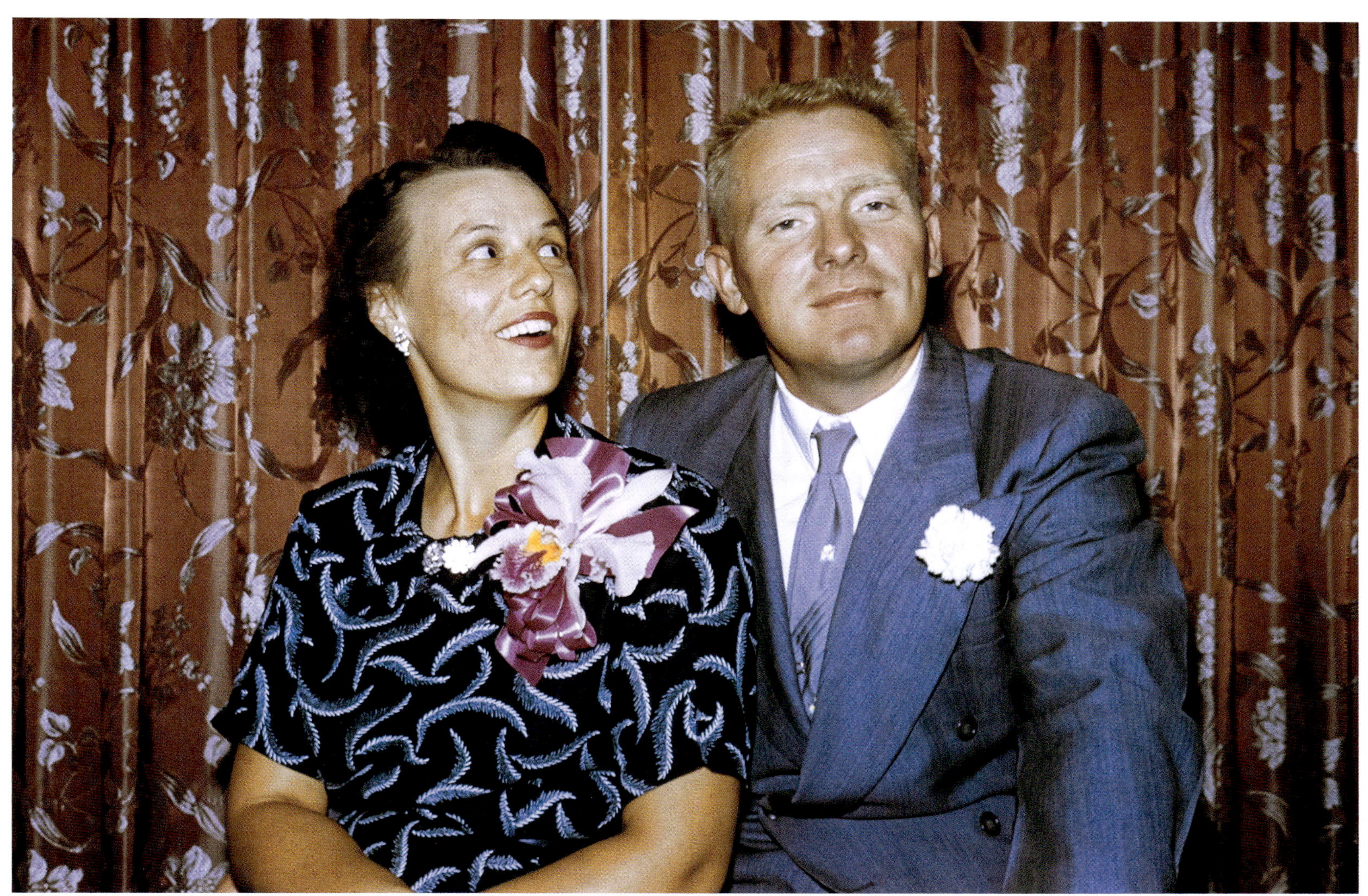

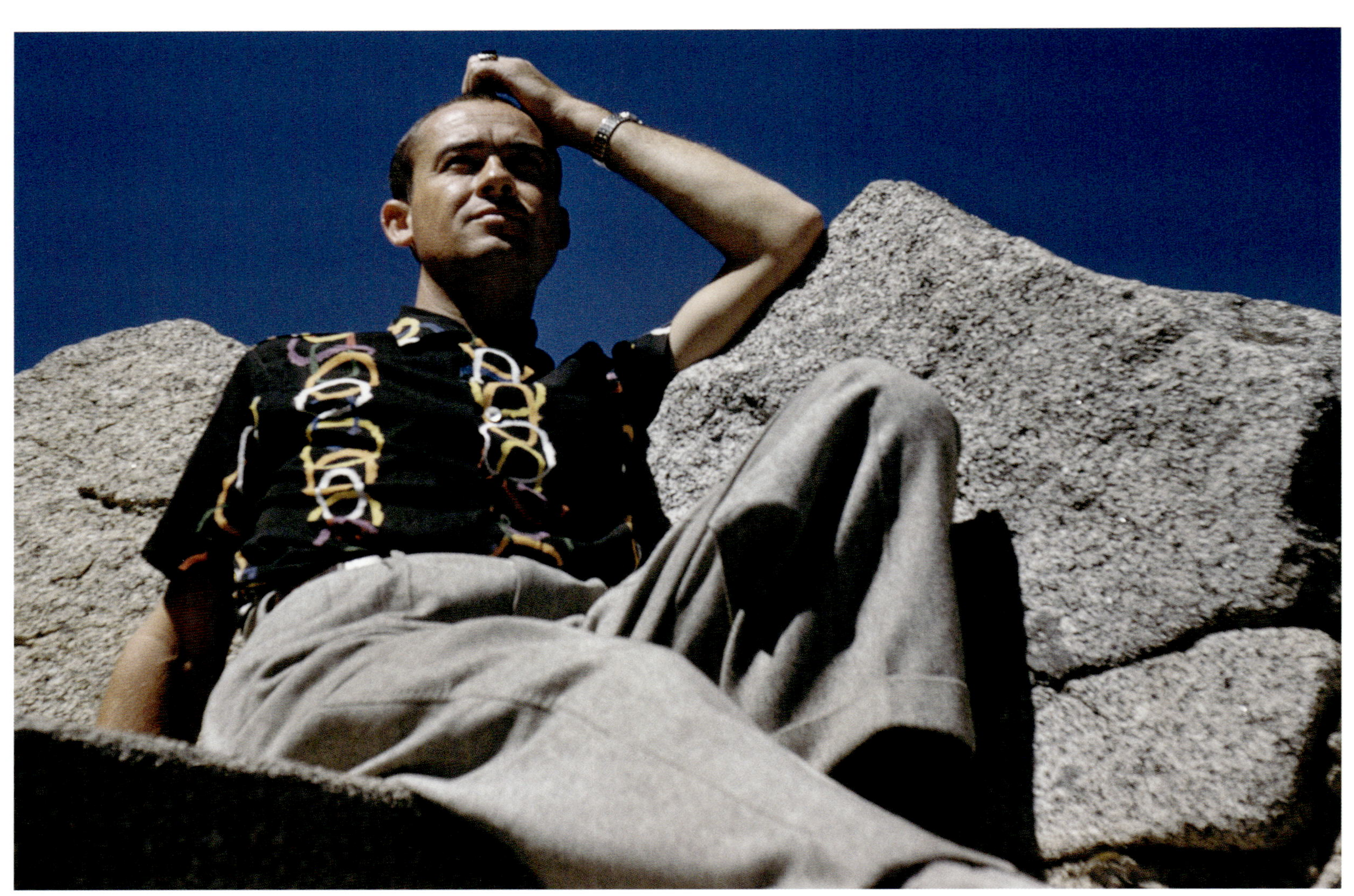

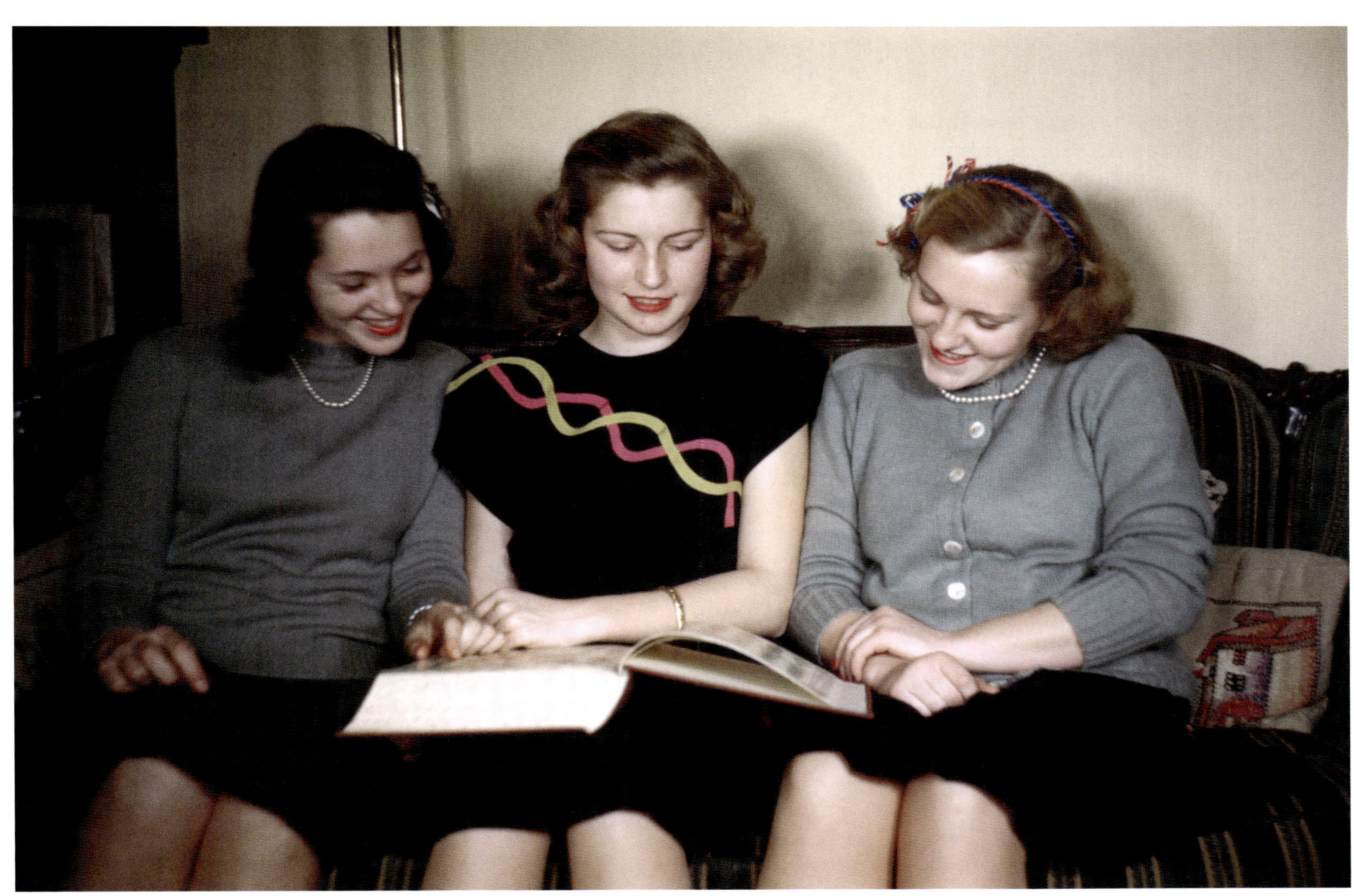

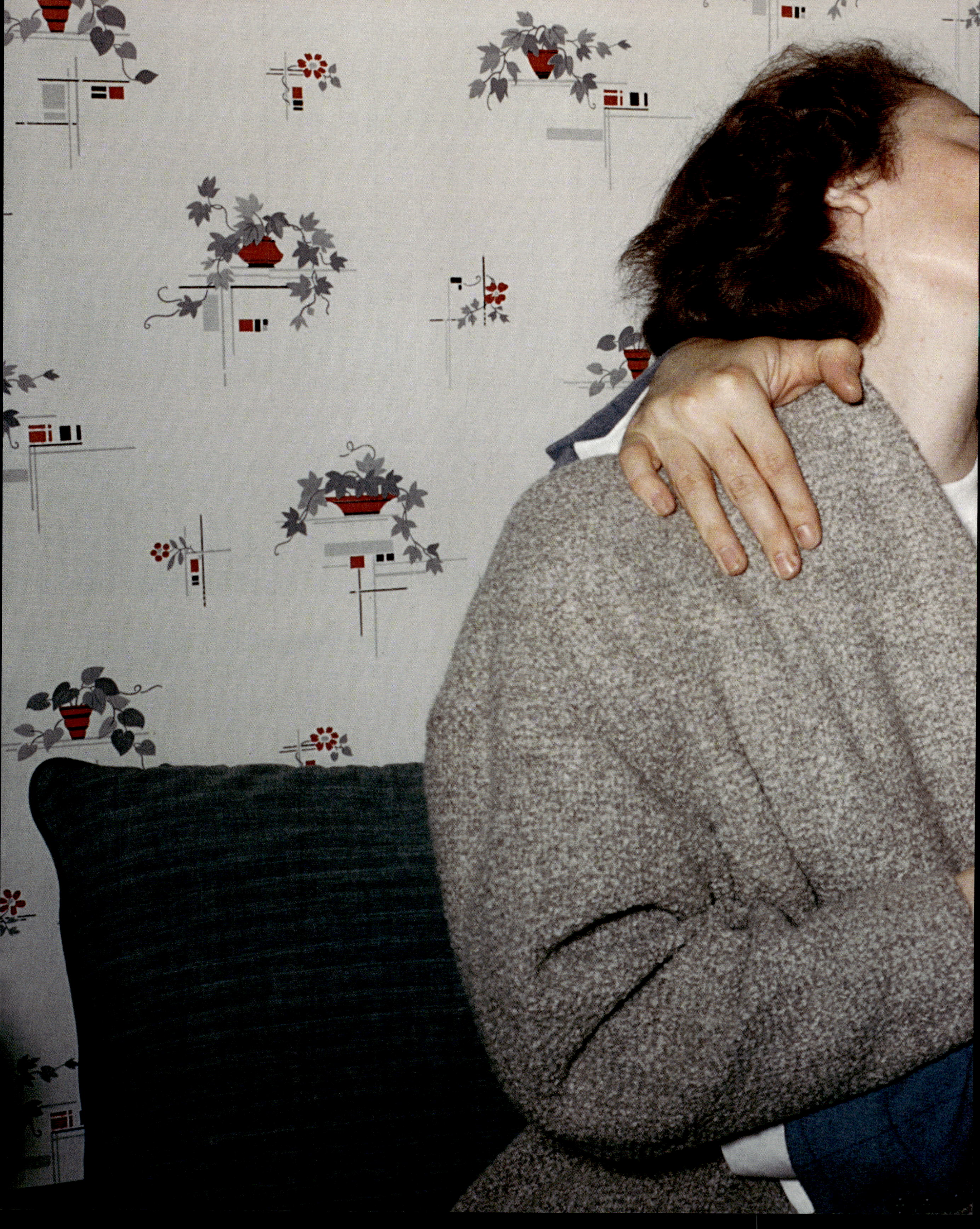

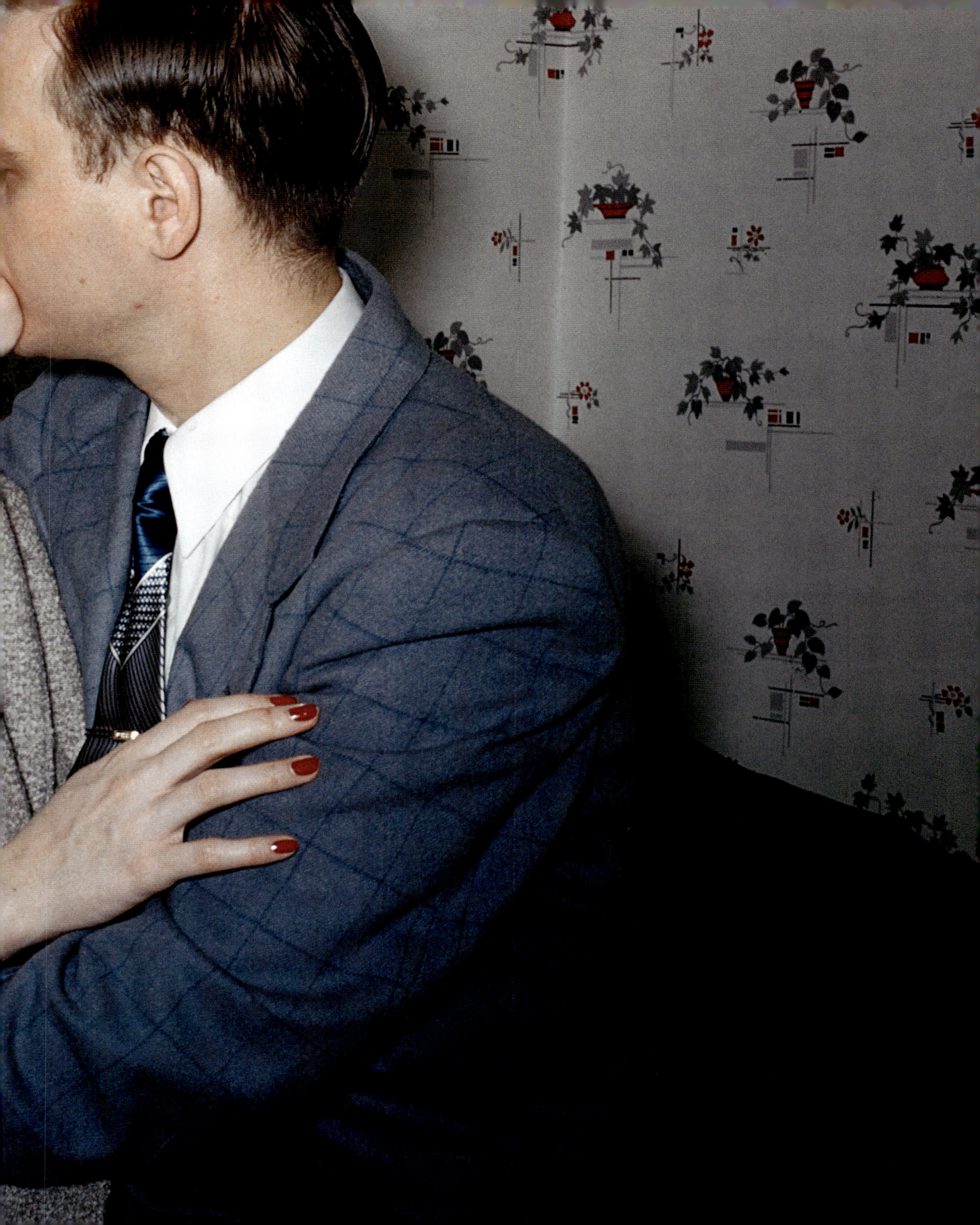

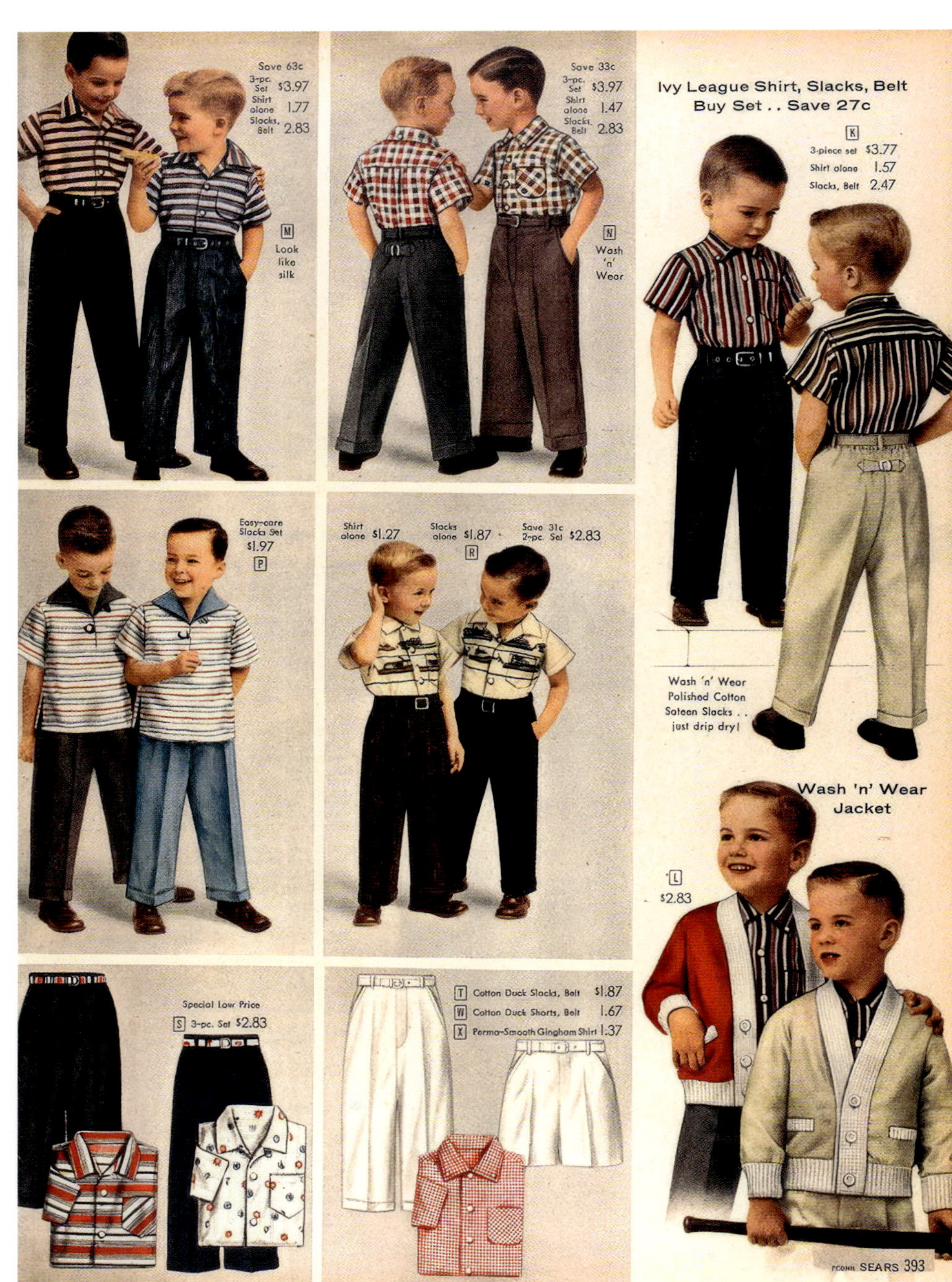
Save 63c
3-pc. Set $3.97
Shirt alone 1.77
Slacks, Belt 2.83
M
Look like silk
Save 33c
3-pc. Set $3.97
Shirt alone 1.47
Slacks, Belt 2.83
N
Wash 'n' Wear
Ivy League Shirt, Slacks, Belt
Buy Set . . Save 27c
K
3-piece set $3.77
Shirt alone 1.57
Slacks, Belt 2.47
Easy-care Slacks Set
$1.97
P
Shirt alone $1.27
Slacks alone $1.87
R
Save 31c 2-pc. Set $2.83
Wash 'n' Wear
Polished Cotton
Sateen Slacks . .
just drip dry!
Wash 'n' Wear
Jacket
L
$2.83
Special Low Price
S 3-pc. Set $2.83
T Cotton Duck Slacks, Belt $1.87
W Cotton Duck Shorts, Belt 1.67
X Perma-Smooth Gingham Shirt 1.37
SEARS 393

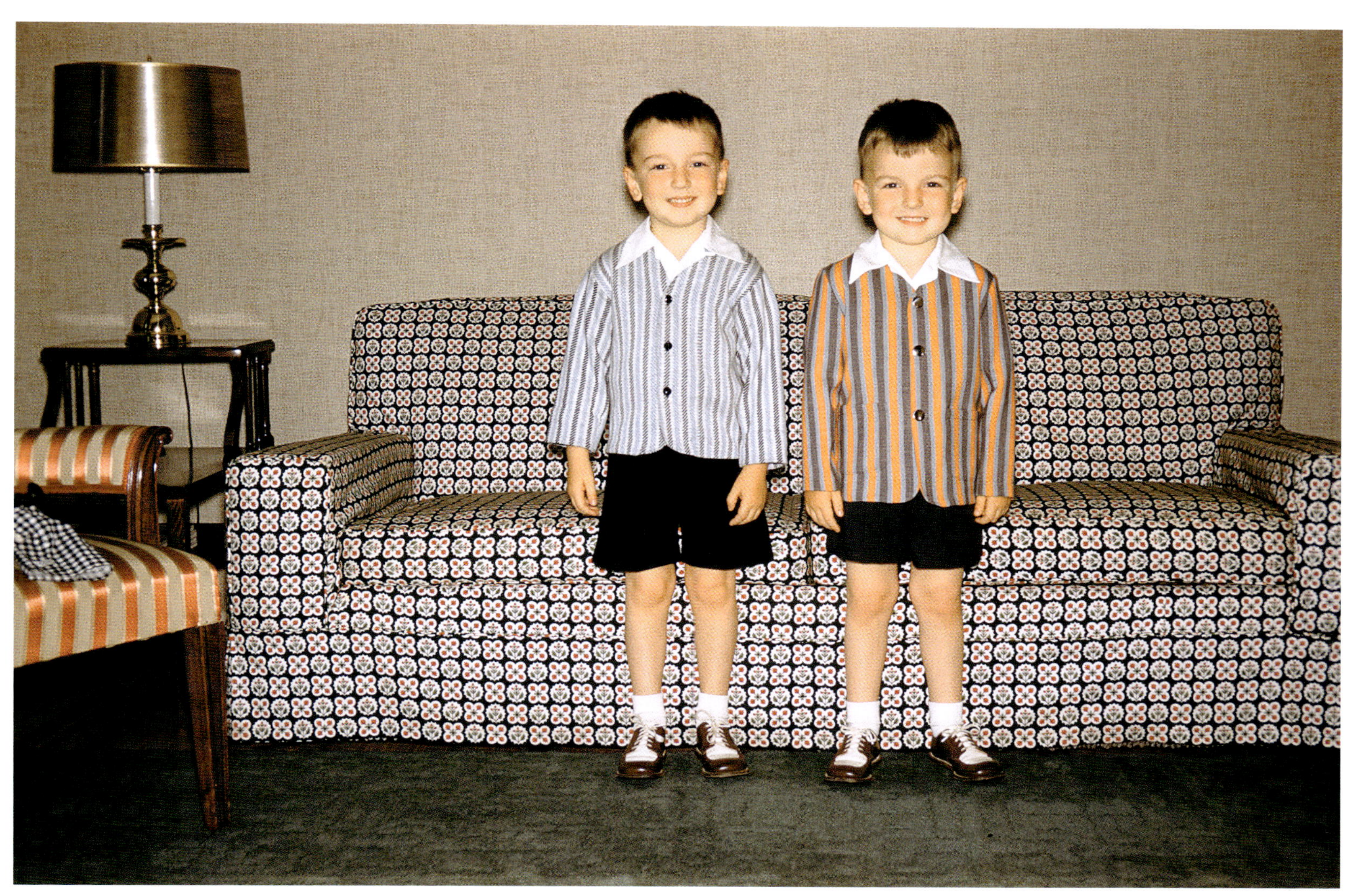

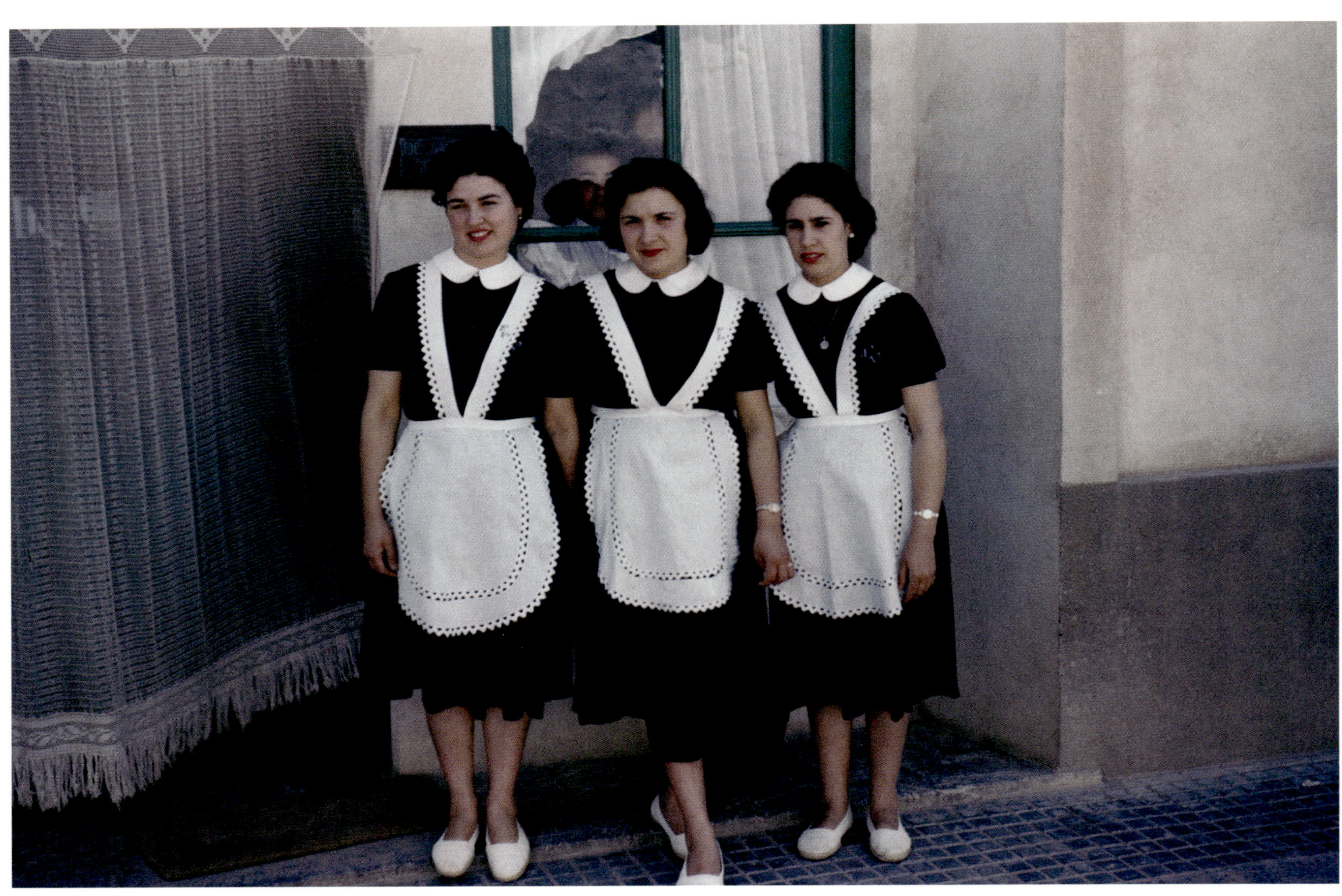

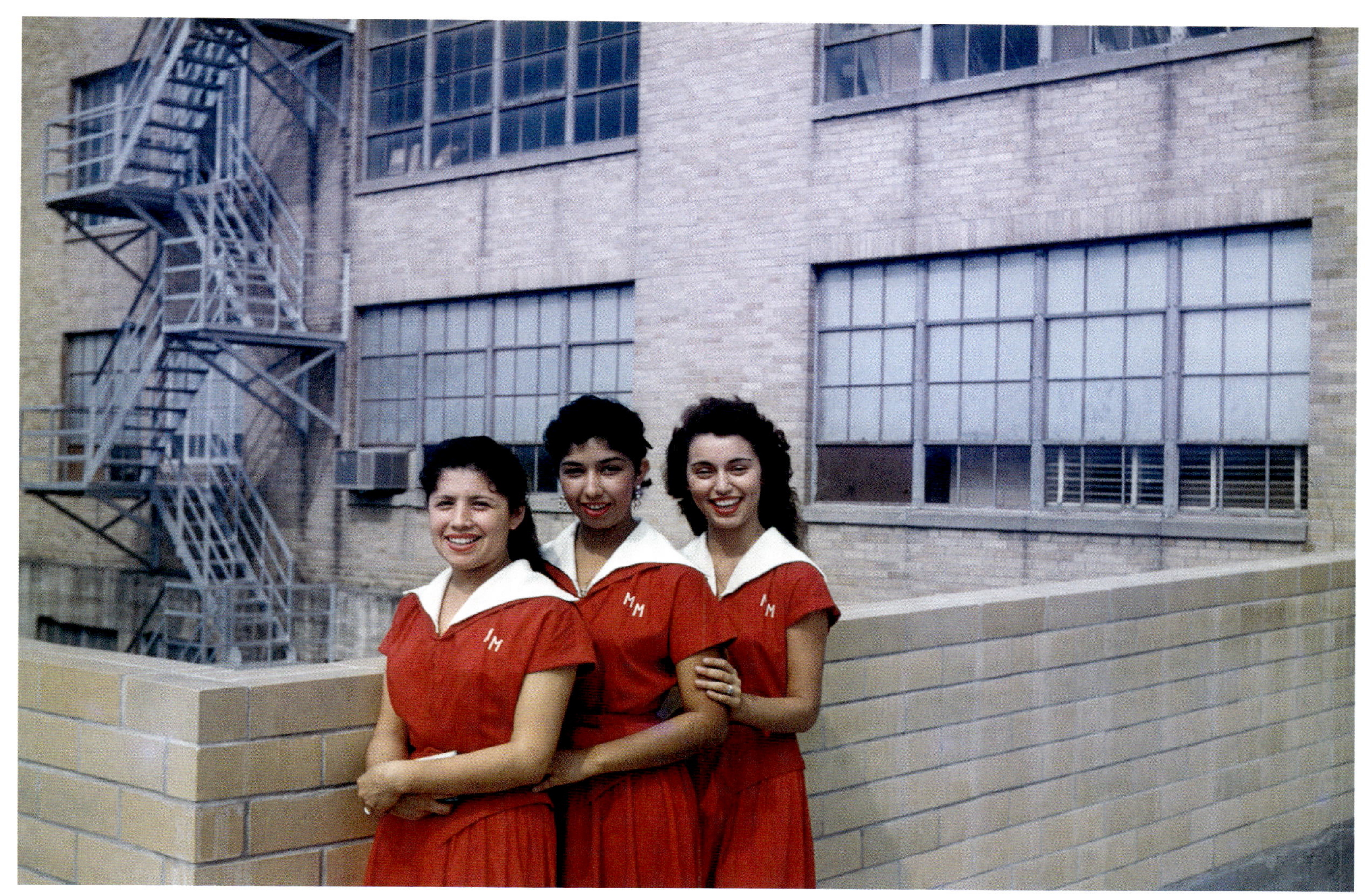

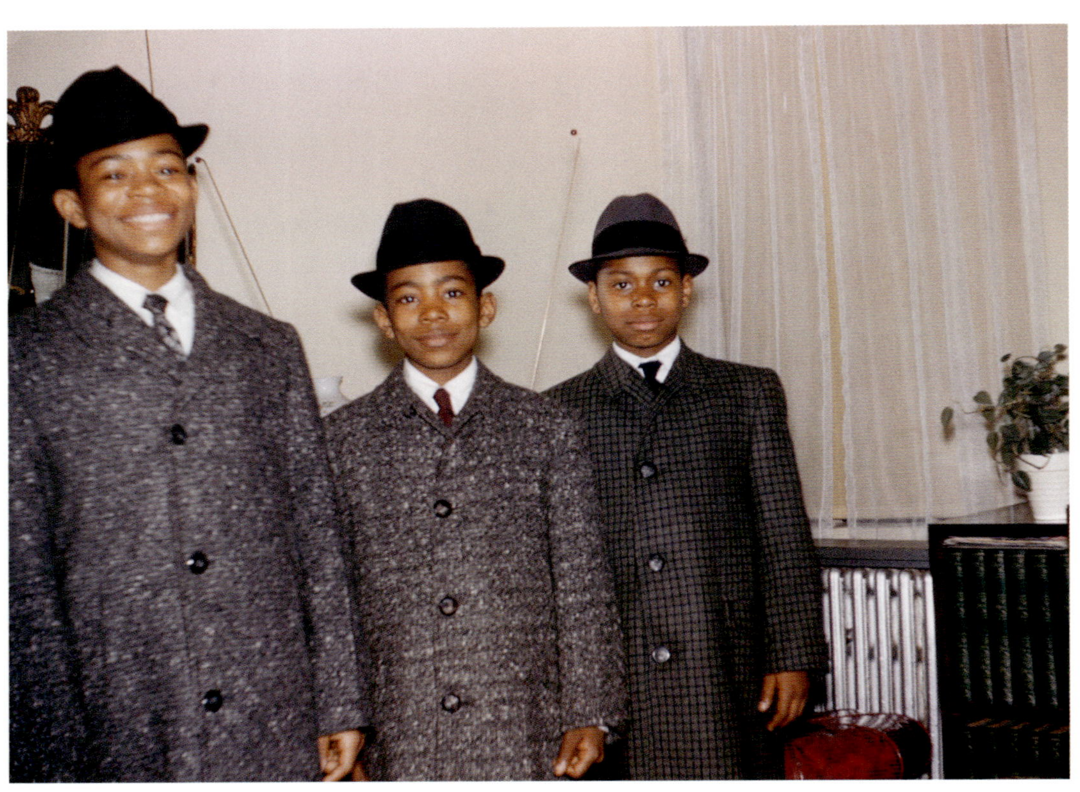

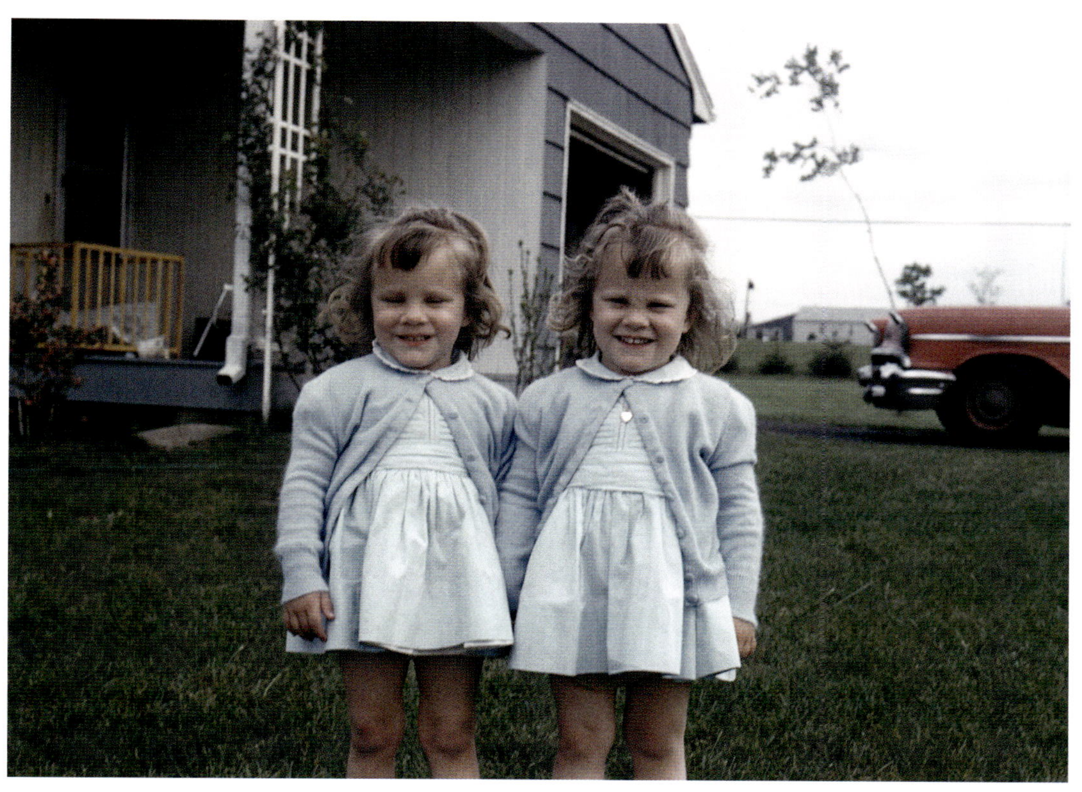

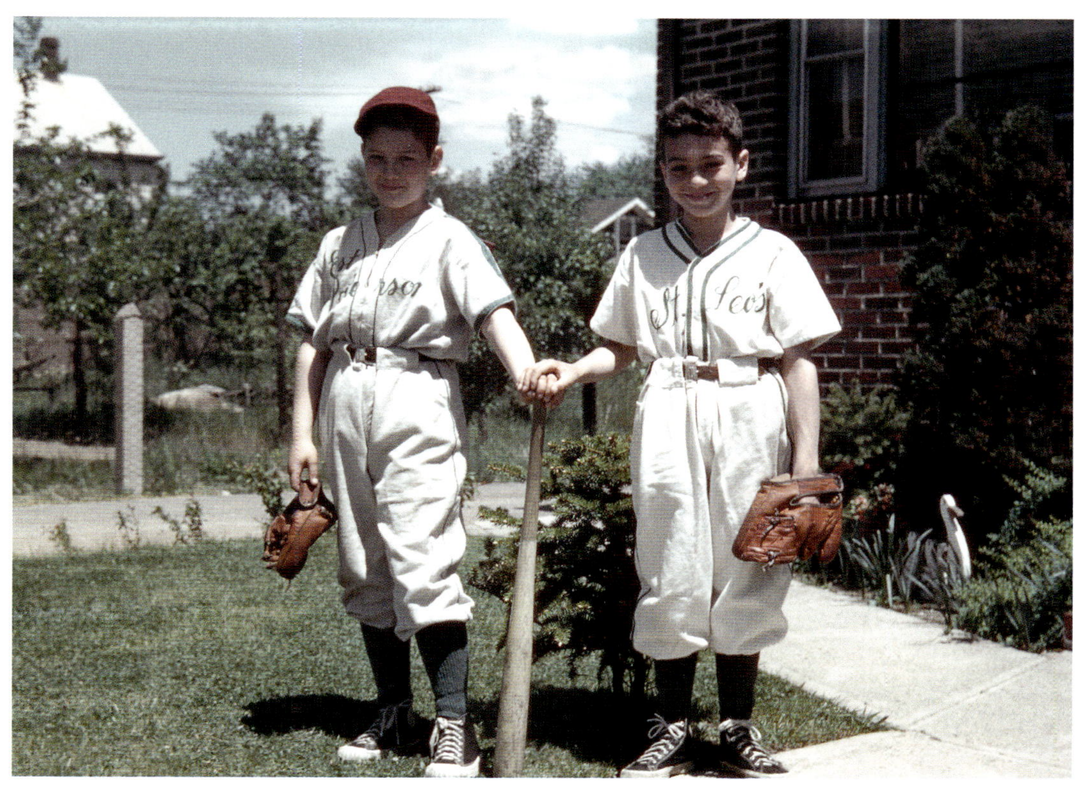

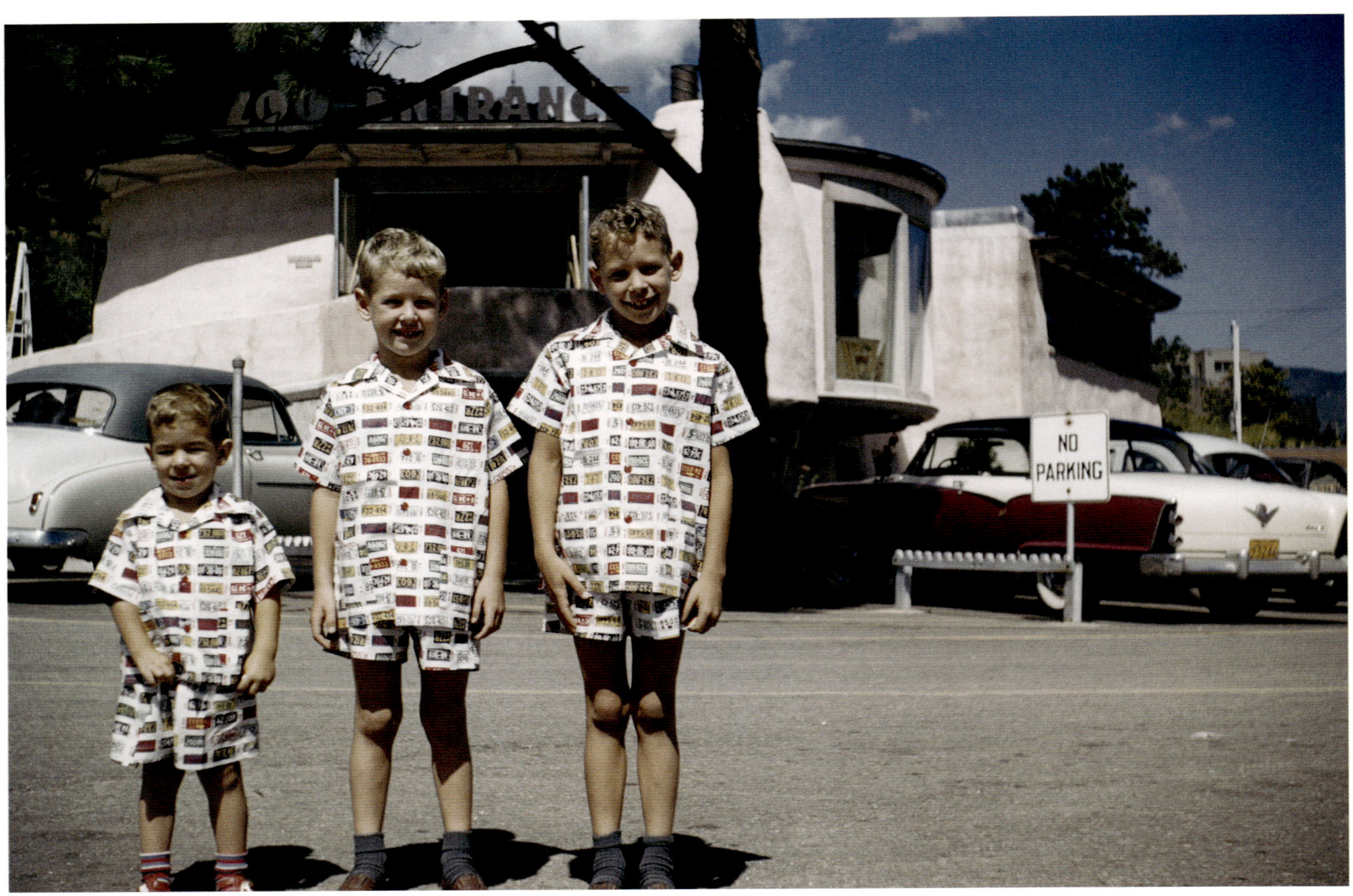
ZOO ENTRANCE
NO
PARKING

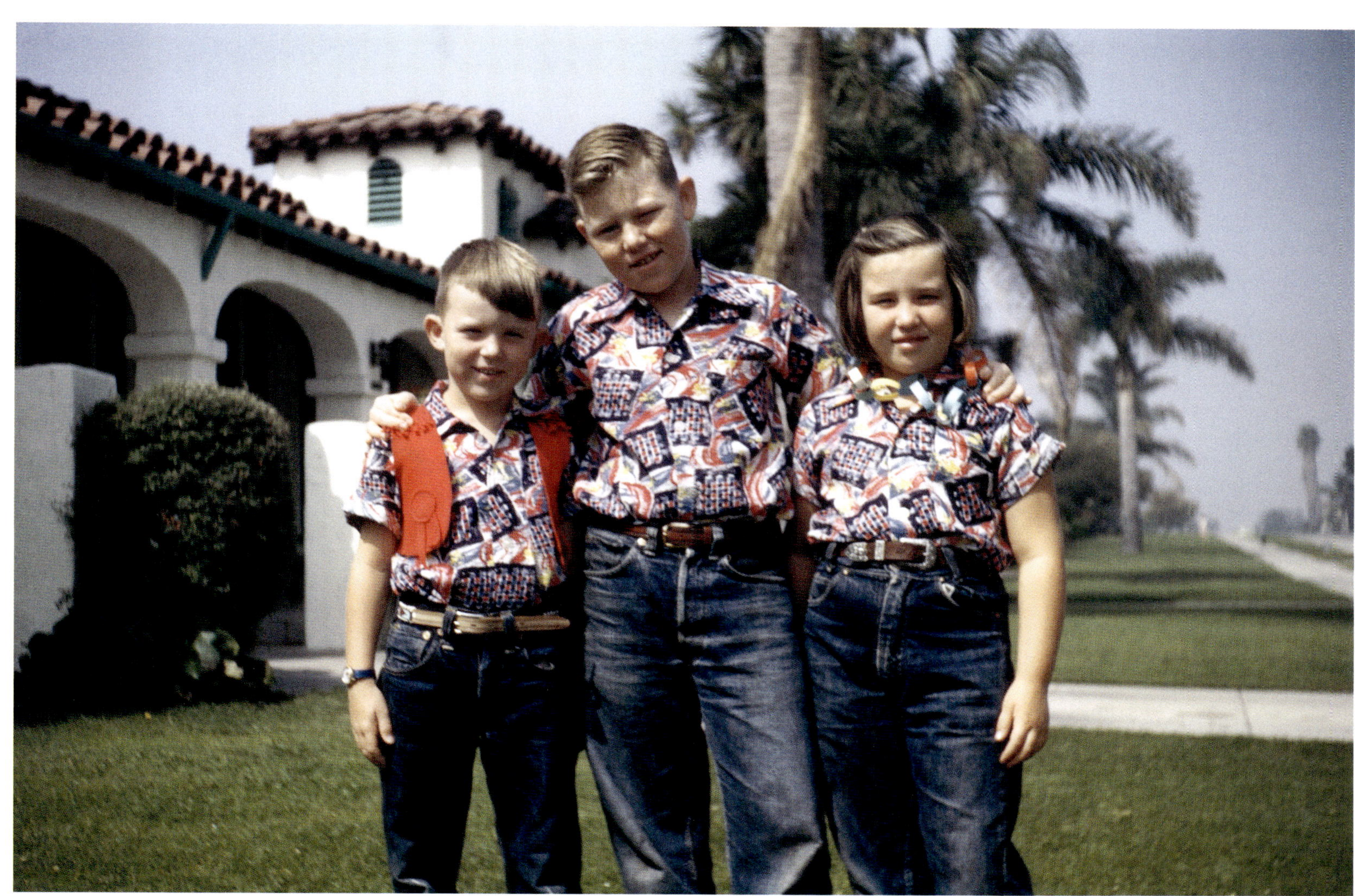

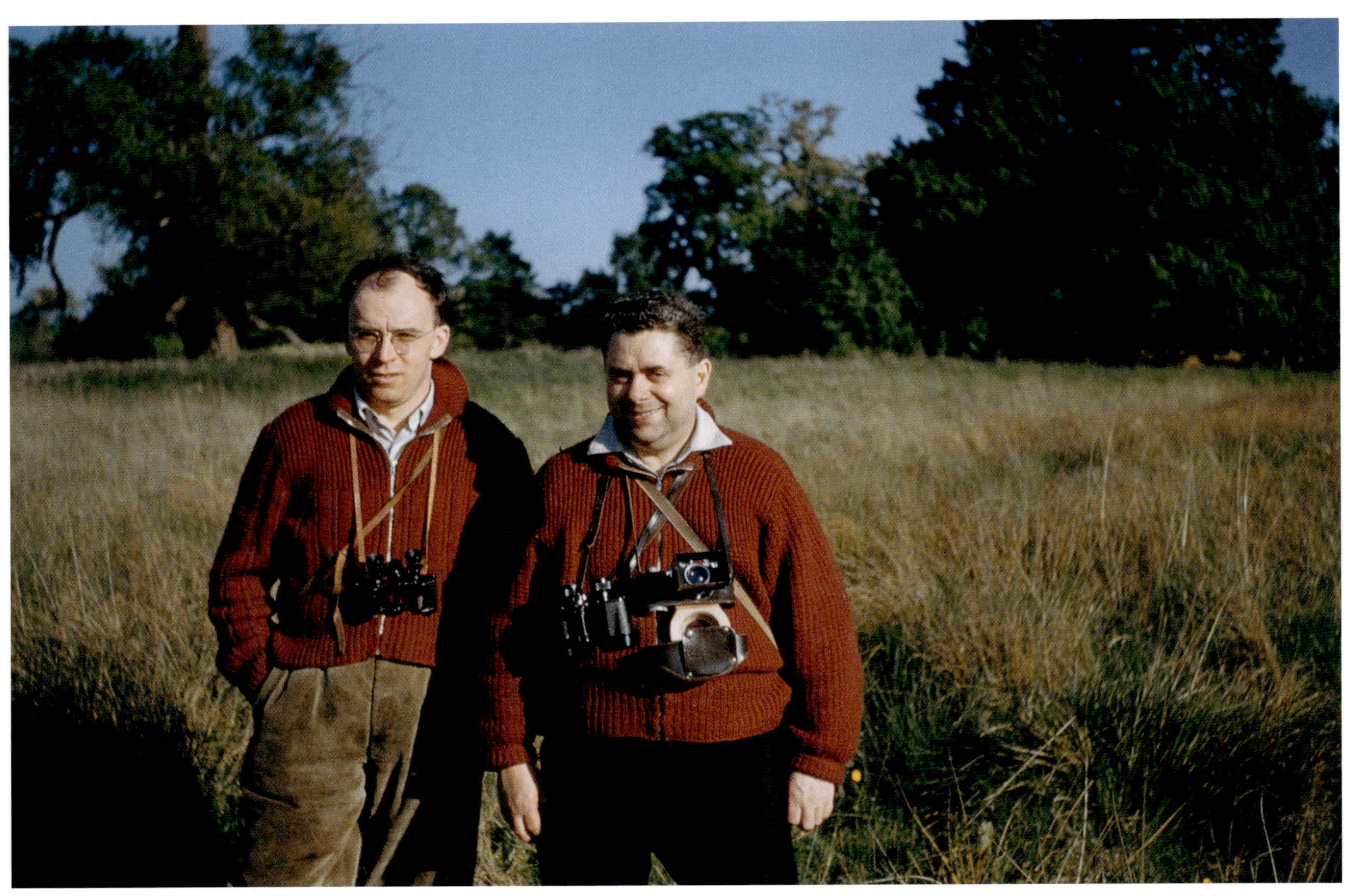

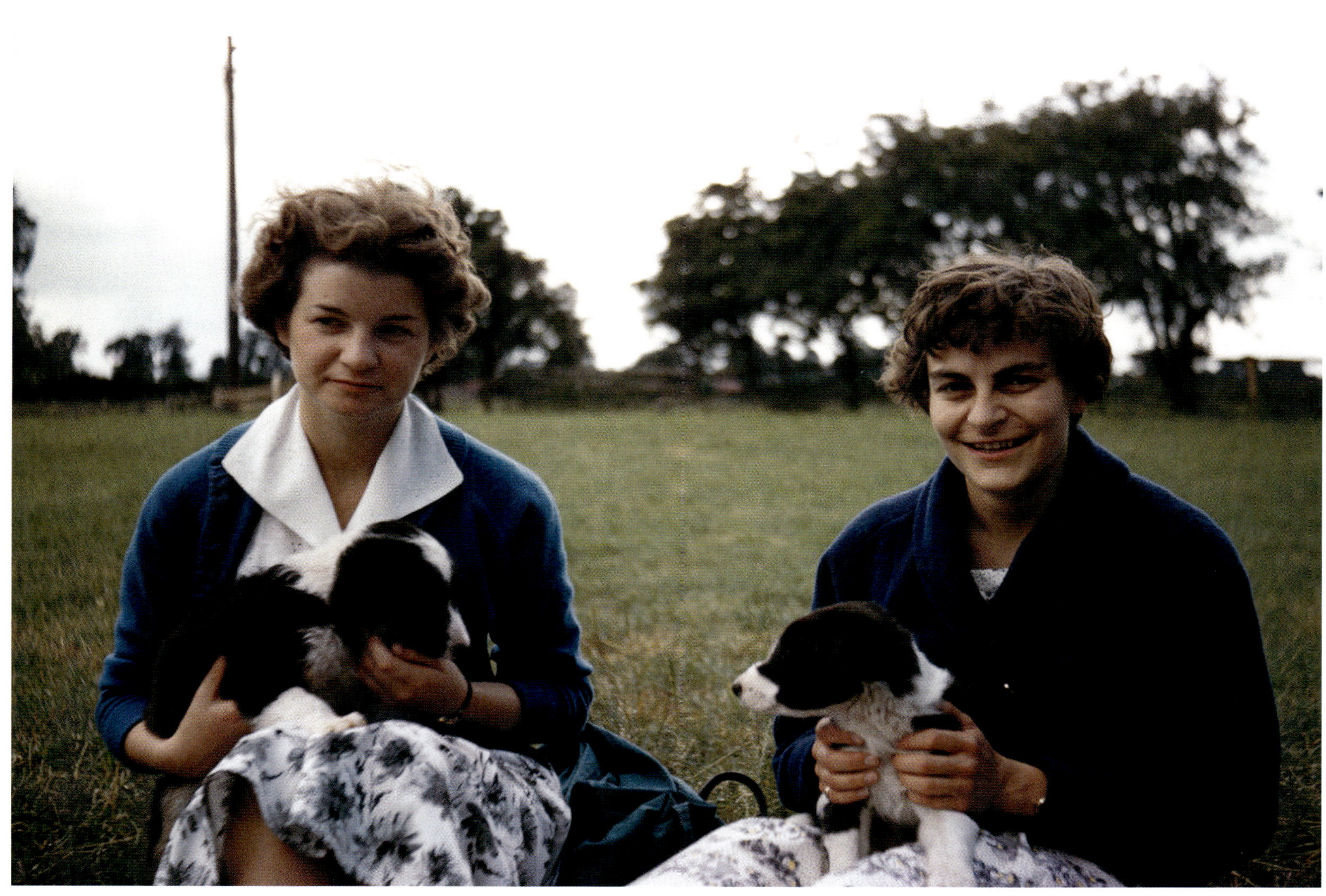

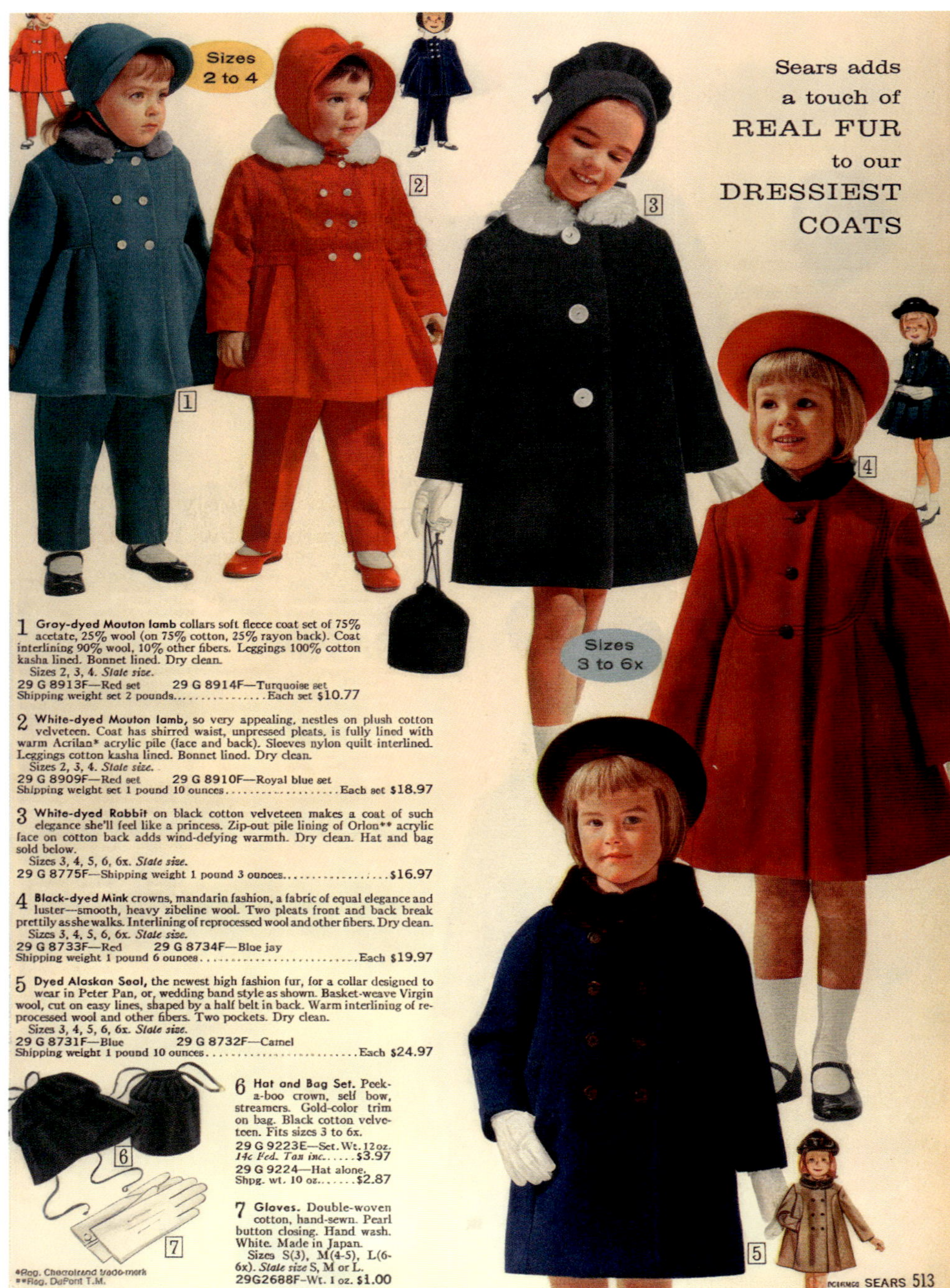

Sizes 2 to 4

Sears adds a touch of REAL FUR to our DRESSIEST COATS

Sizes 3 to 6x

1 **Gray-dyed Mouton lamb** collars soft fleece coat set of 75% acetate, 25% wool (on 75% cotton, 25% rayon back). Coat interlining 90% wool, 10% other fibers. Leggings 100% cotton kasha lined. Bonnet lined. Dry clean.
Sizes 2, 3, 4. *State size.*
29 G 8913F—Red set 29 G 8914F—Turquoise set
Shipping weight set 2 pounds................Each set $10.77

2 **White-dyed Mouton lamb,** so very appealing, nestles on plush cotton velveteen. Coat has shirred waist, unpressed pleats, is fully lined with warm Acrilan* acrylic pile (face and back). Sleeves nylon quilt interlined. Leggings cotton kasha lined. Bonnet lined. Dry clean.
Sizes 2, 3, 4. *State size.*
29 G 8909F—Red set 29 G 8910F—Royal blue set
Shipping weight set 1 pound 10 ounces....................Each set $18.97

3 **White-dyed Rabbit** on black cotton velveteen makes a coat of such elegance she'll feel like a princess. Zip-out pile lining of Orlon** acrylic face on cotton back adds wind-defying warmth. Dry clean. Hat and bag sold below.
Sizes 3, 4, 5, 6, 6x. *State size.*
29 G 8775F—Shipping weight 1 pound 3 ounces..................$16.97

4 **Black-dyed Mink** crowns, mandarin fashion, a fabric of equal elegance and luster—smooth, heavy zibeline wool. Two pleats front and back break prettily as she walks. Interlining of reprocessed wool and other fibers. Dry clean.
Sizes 3, 4, 5, 6, 6x. *State size.*
29 G 8733F—Red 29 G 8734F—Blue jay
Shipping weight 1 pound 6 ounces..........................Each $19.97

5 **Dyed Alaskan Seal,** the newest high fashion fur, for a collar designed to wear in Peter Pan, or, wedding band style as shown. Basket-weave Virgin wool, cut on easy lines, shaped by a half belt in back. Warm interlining of reprocessed wool and other fibers. Two pockets. Dry clean.
Sizes 3, 4, 5, 6, 6x. *State size.*
29 G 8731F—Blue 29 G 8732F—Camel
Shipping weight 1 pound 10 ounces..........................Each $24.97

6 **Hat and Bag Set.** Peek-a-boo crown, self bow, streamers. Gold-color trim on bag. Black cotton velveteen. Fits sizes 3 to 6x.
29 G 9223E—Set. Wt. 12 oz. *14c Fed. Tax inc.*.....$3.97
29 G 9224—Hat alone. Shpg. wt. 10 oz.......$2.87

7 **Gloves.** Double-woven cotton, hand-sewn. Pearl button closing. Hand wash. White. Made in Japan.
Sizes S(3), M(4-5), L(6-6x). *State size* S, M or L.
29G2688F–Wt. 1 oz. $1.00

*Reg. Chemstrand trade-mark
**Reg. DuPont T.M.

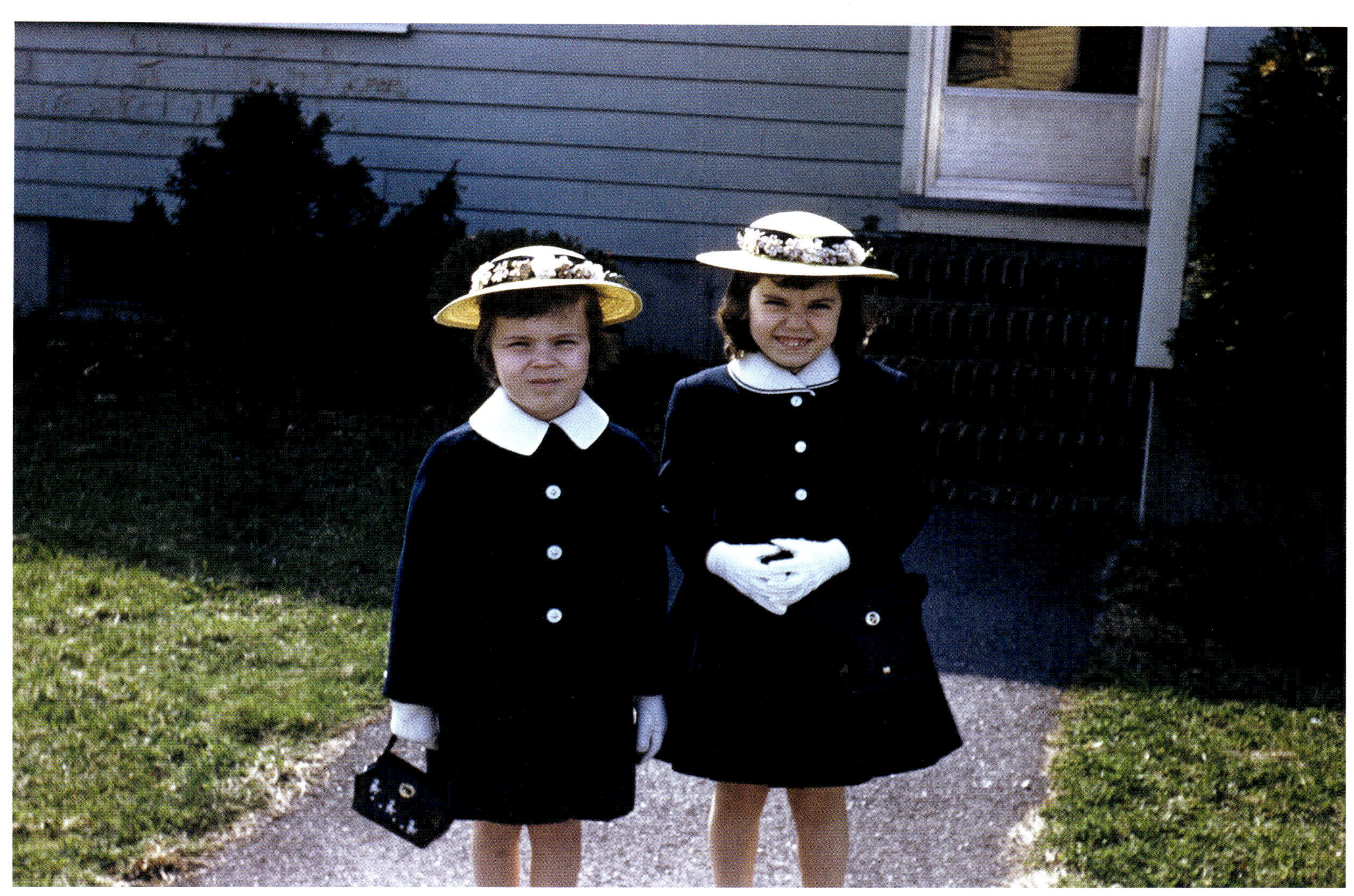

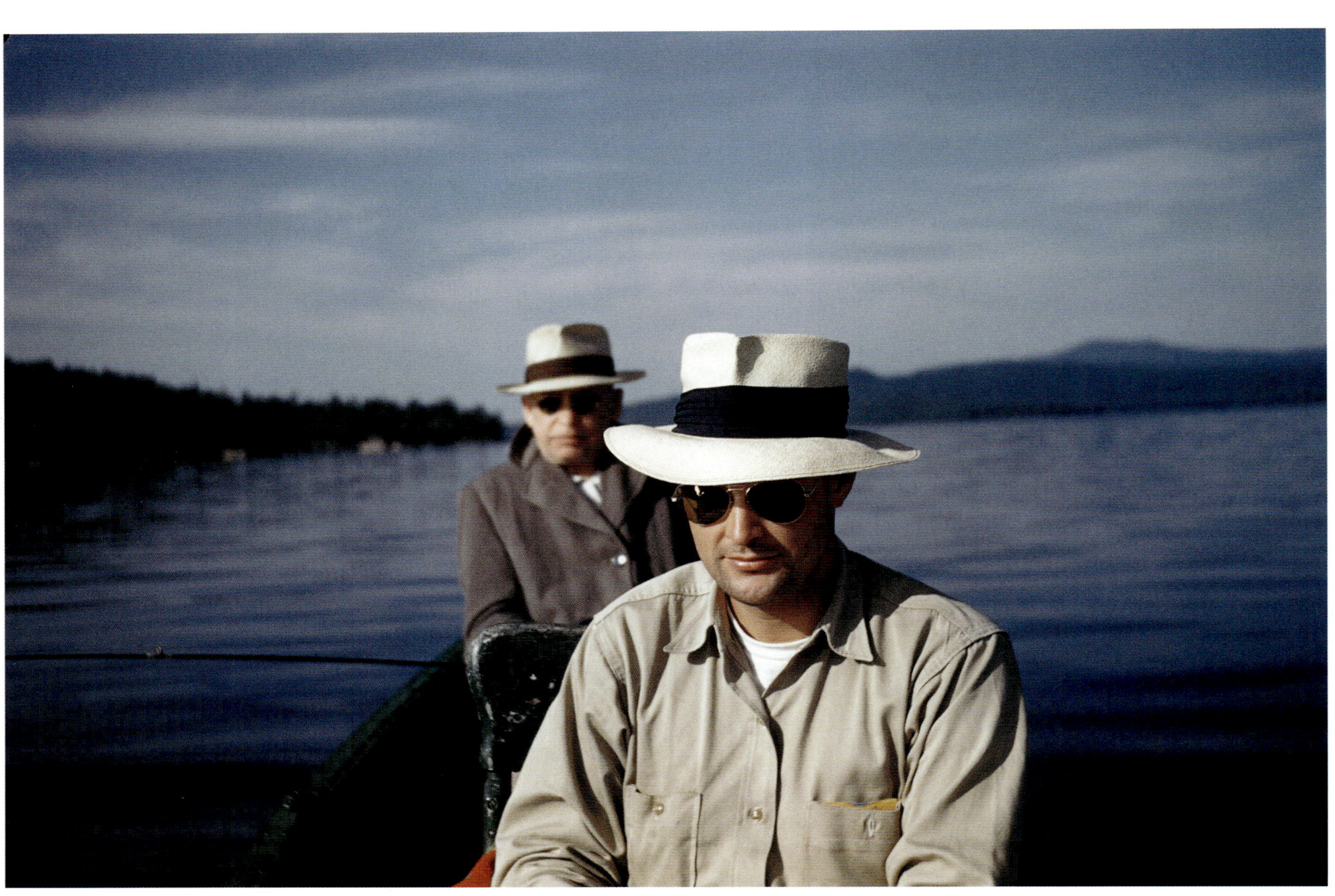

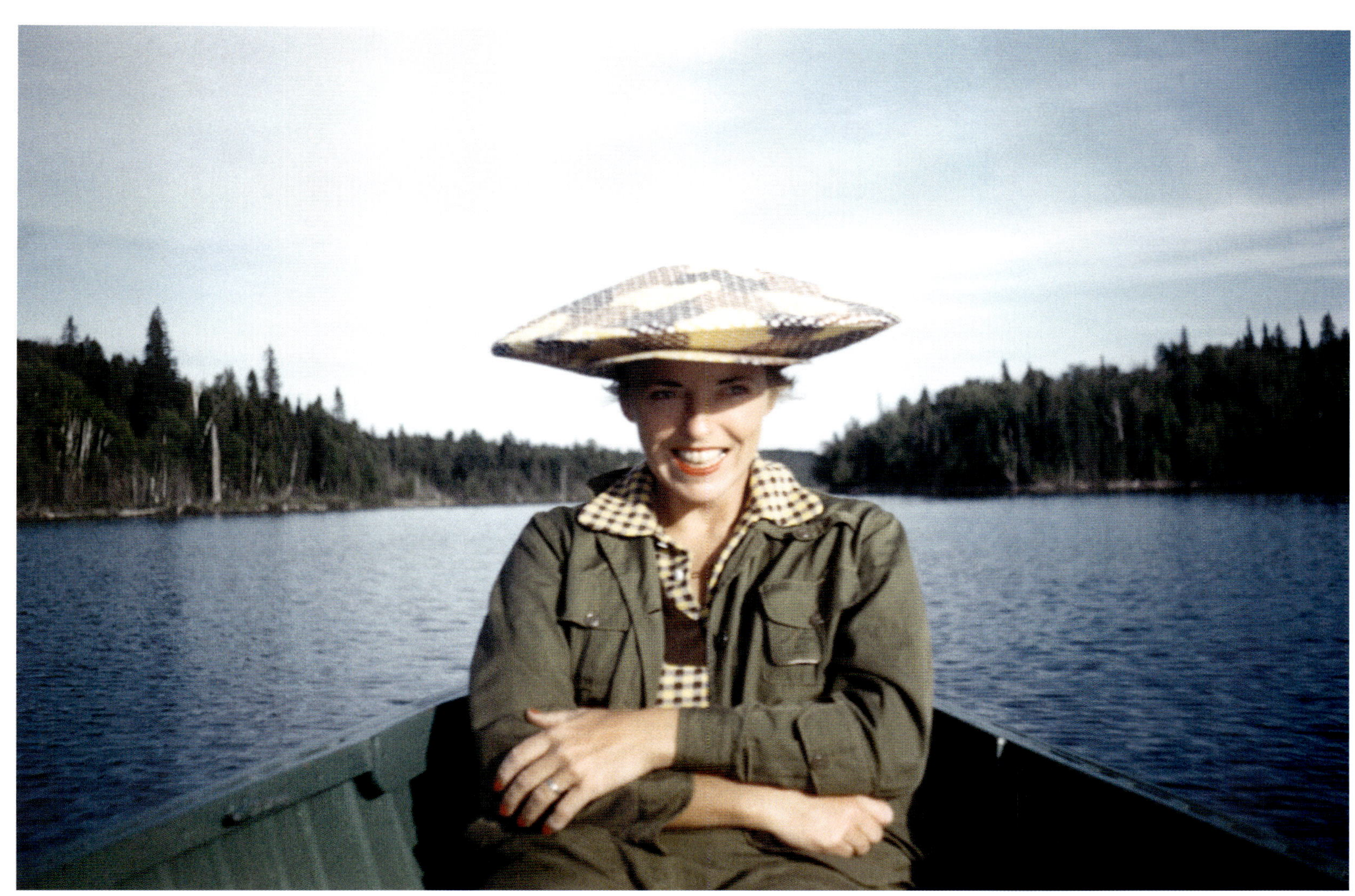

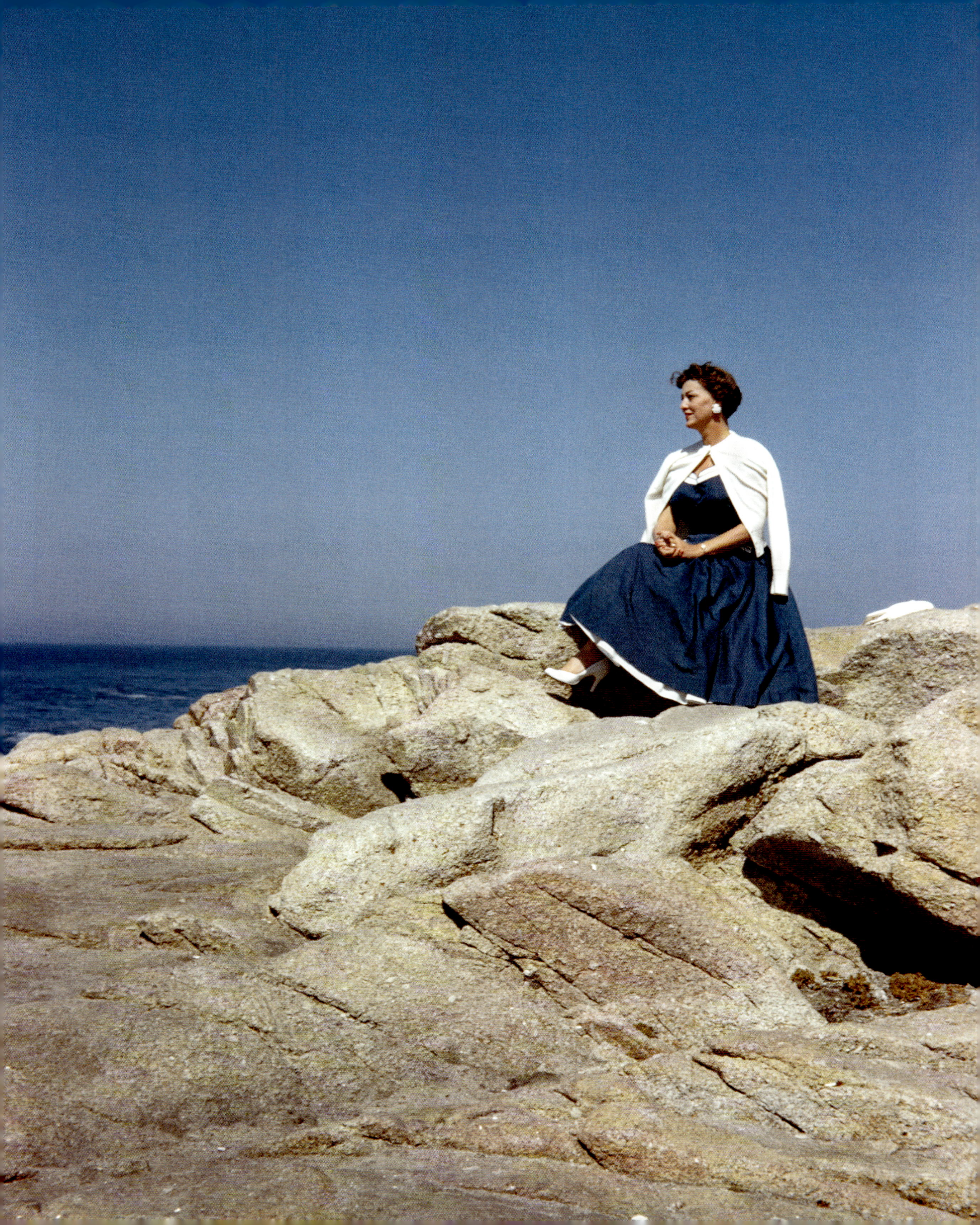

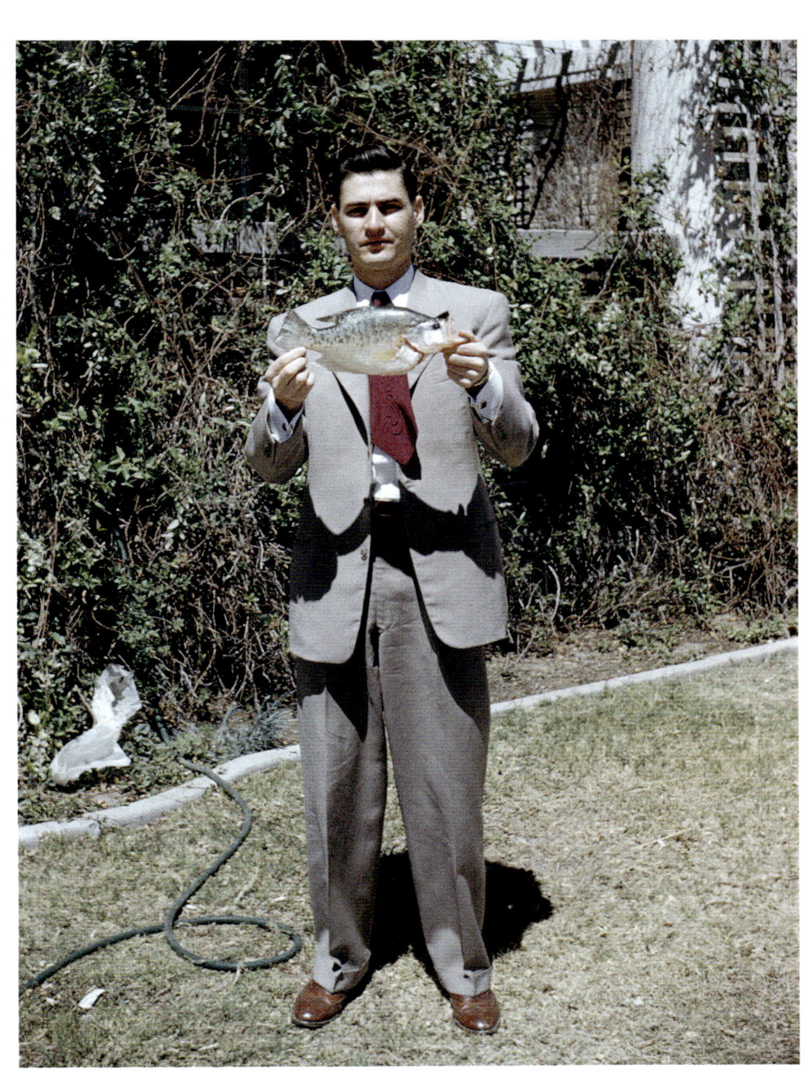

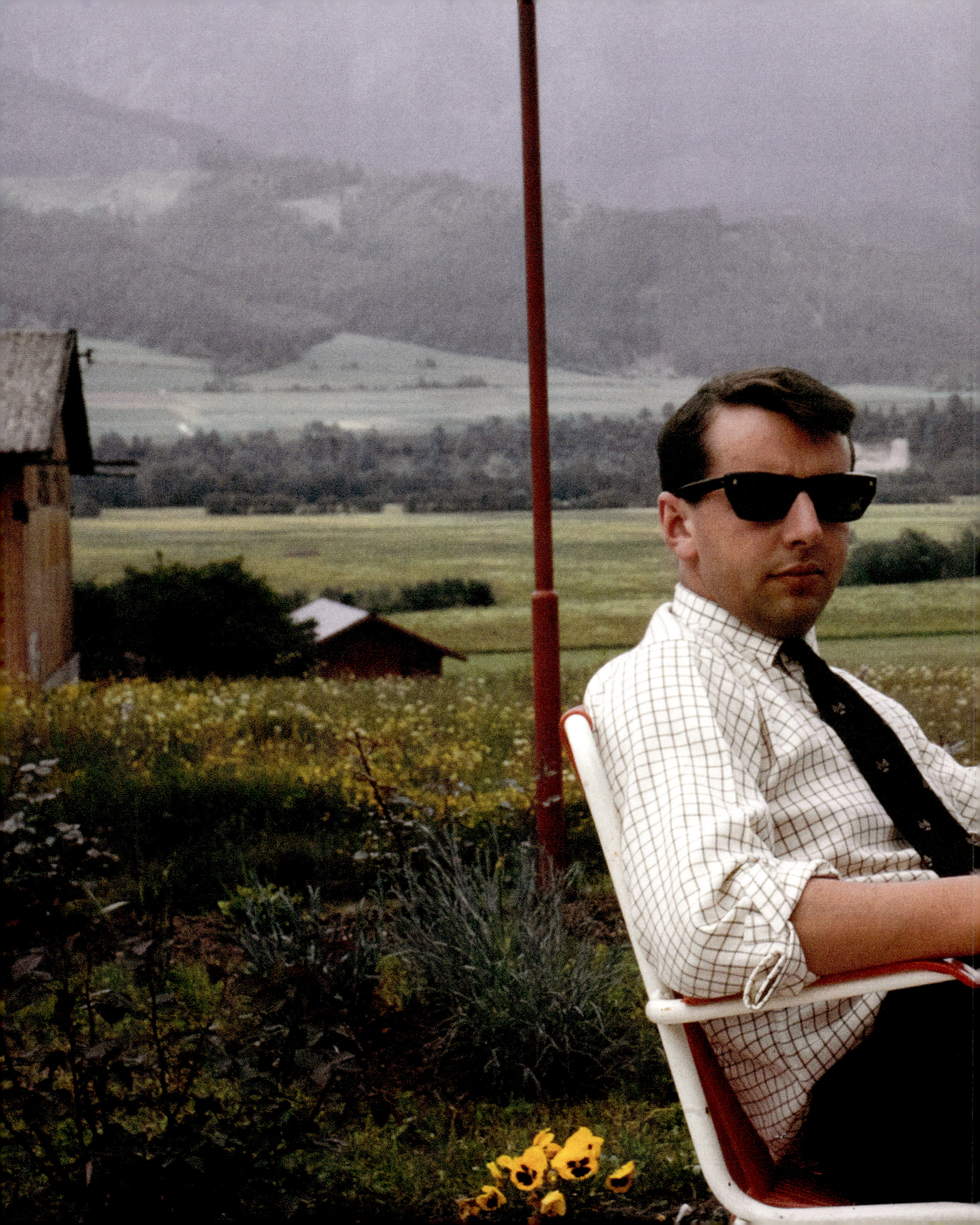

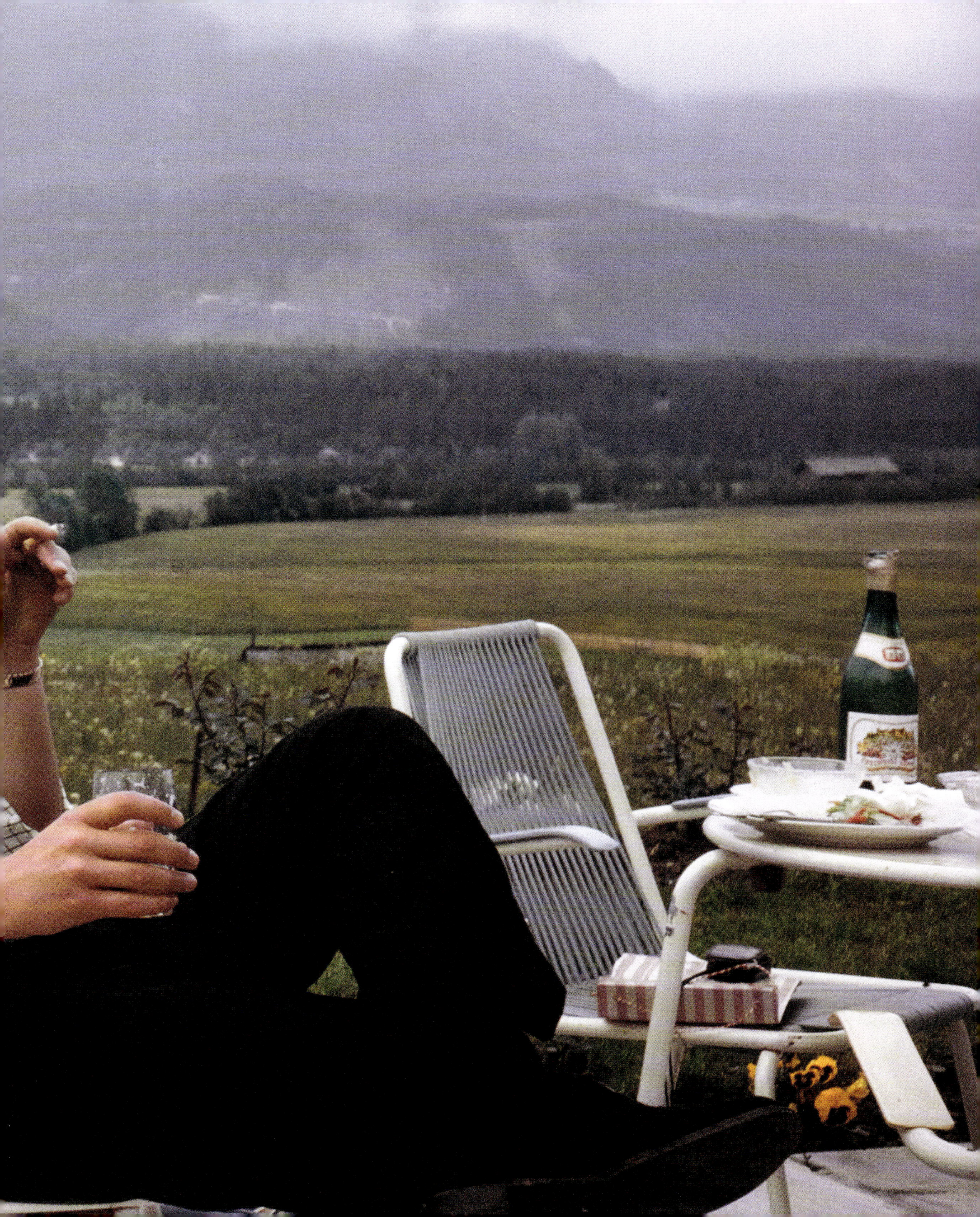

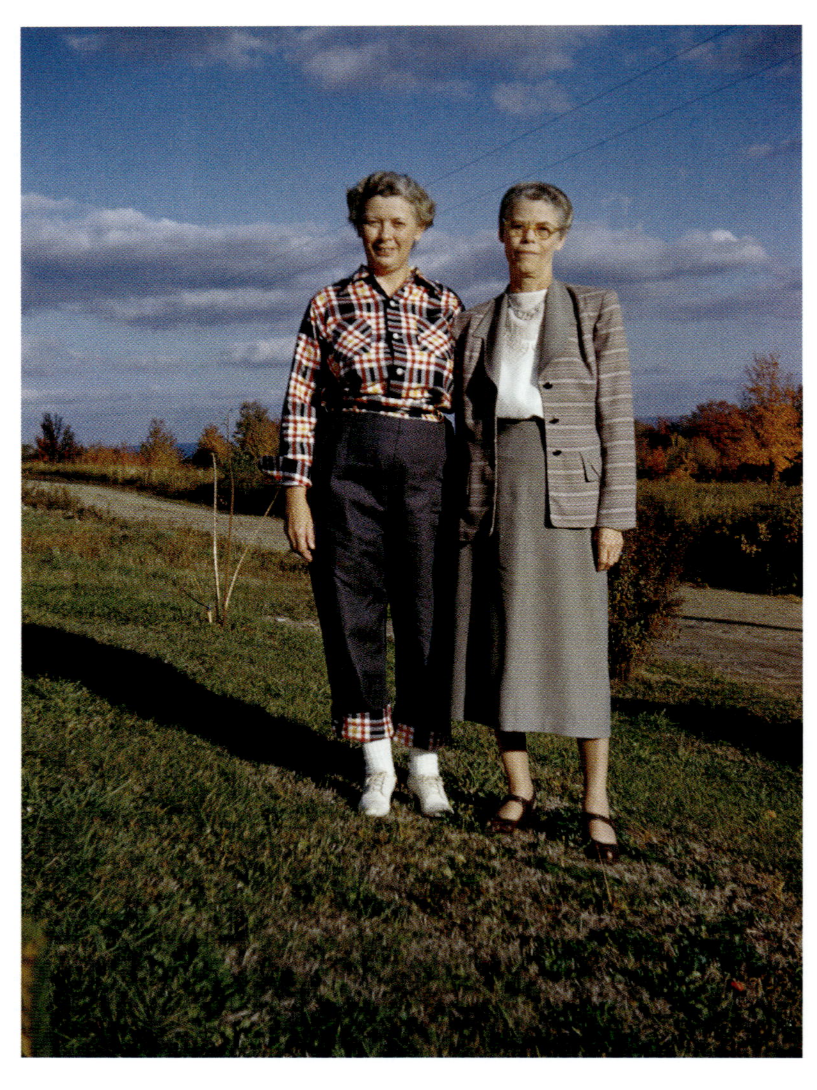

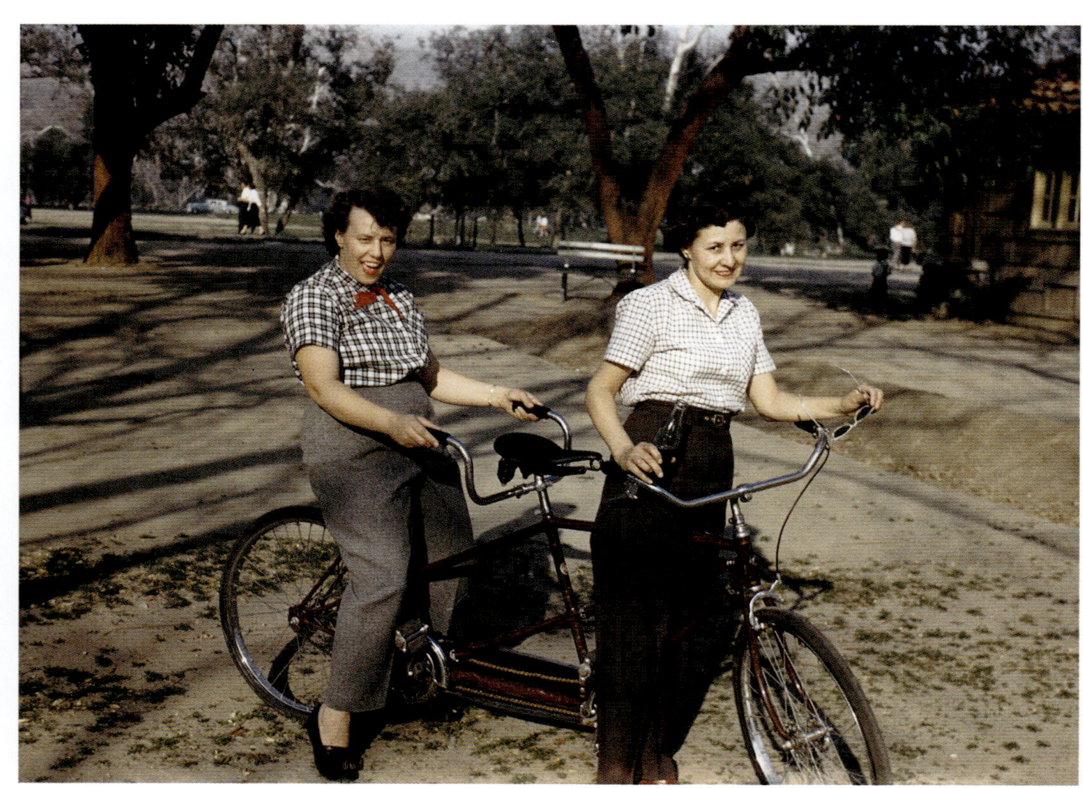

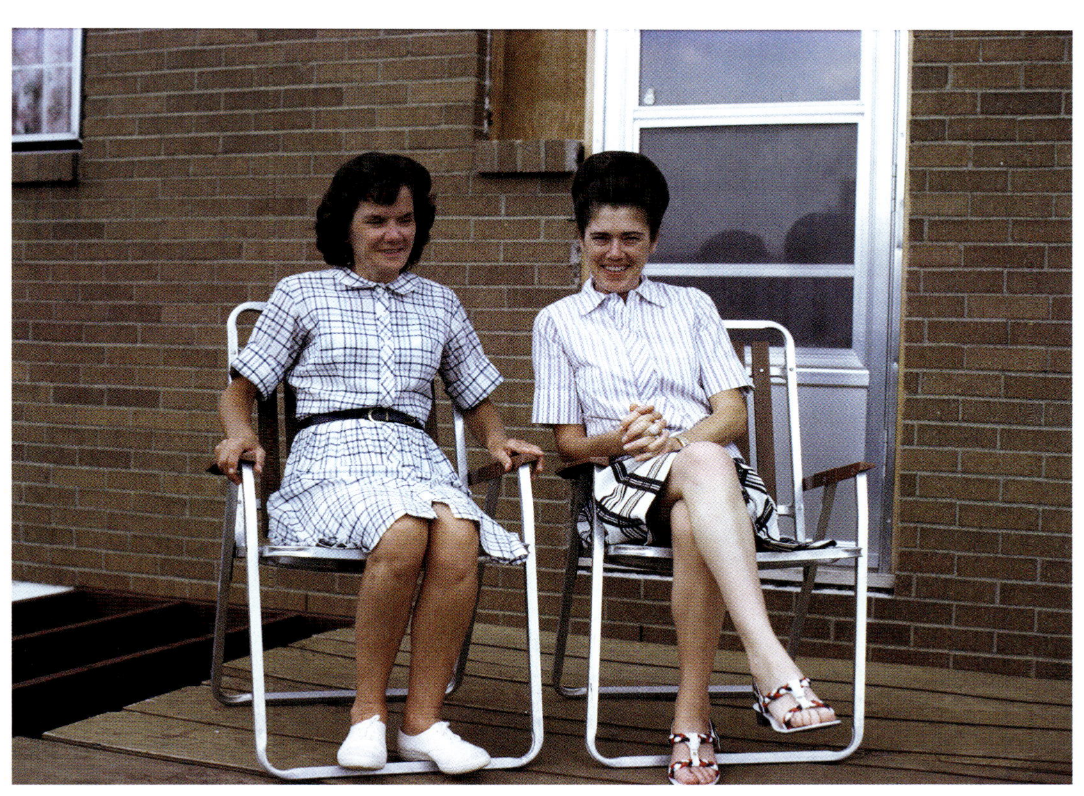

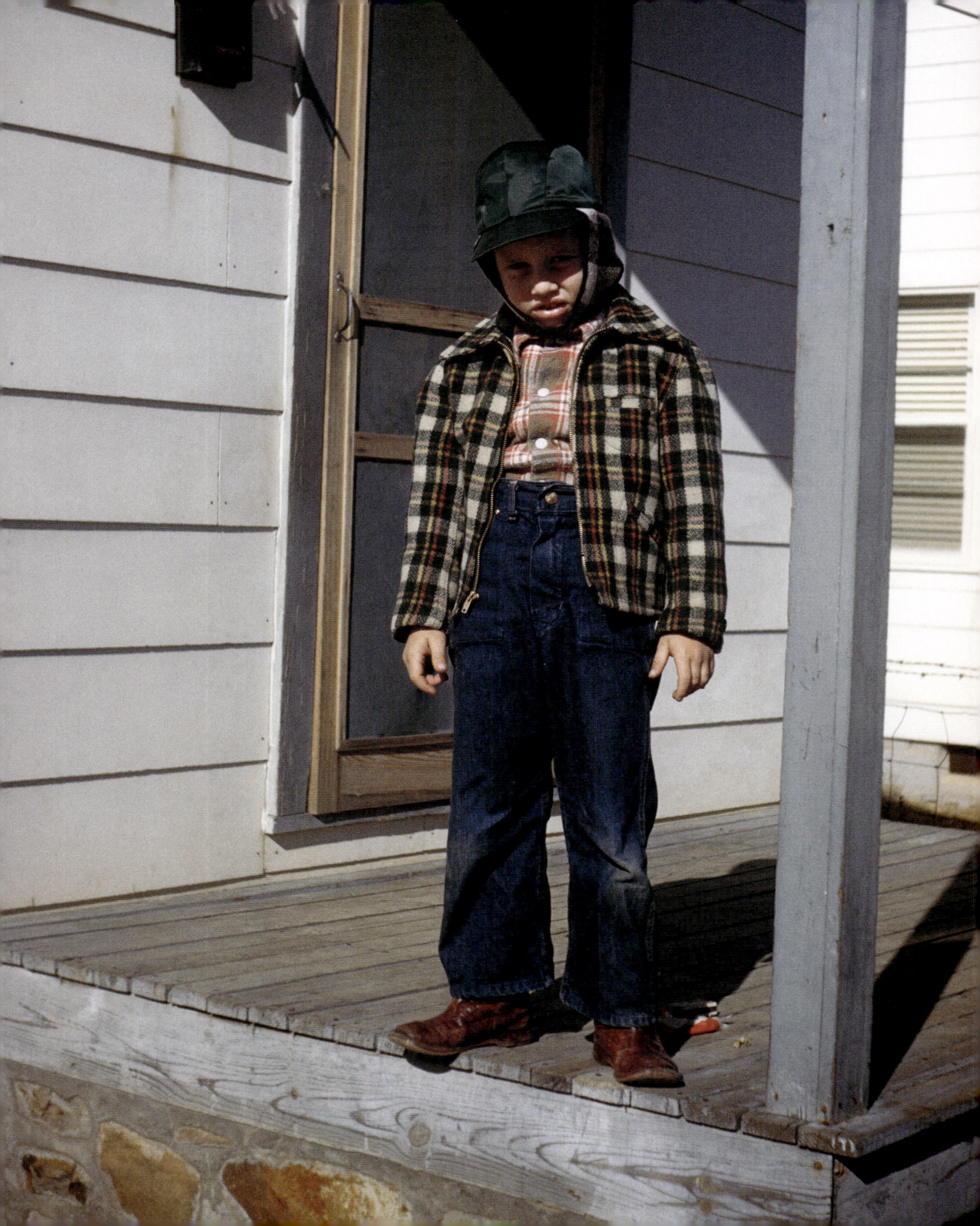

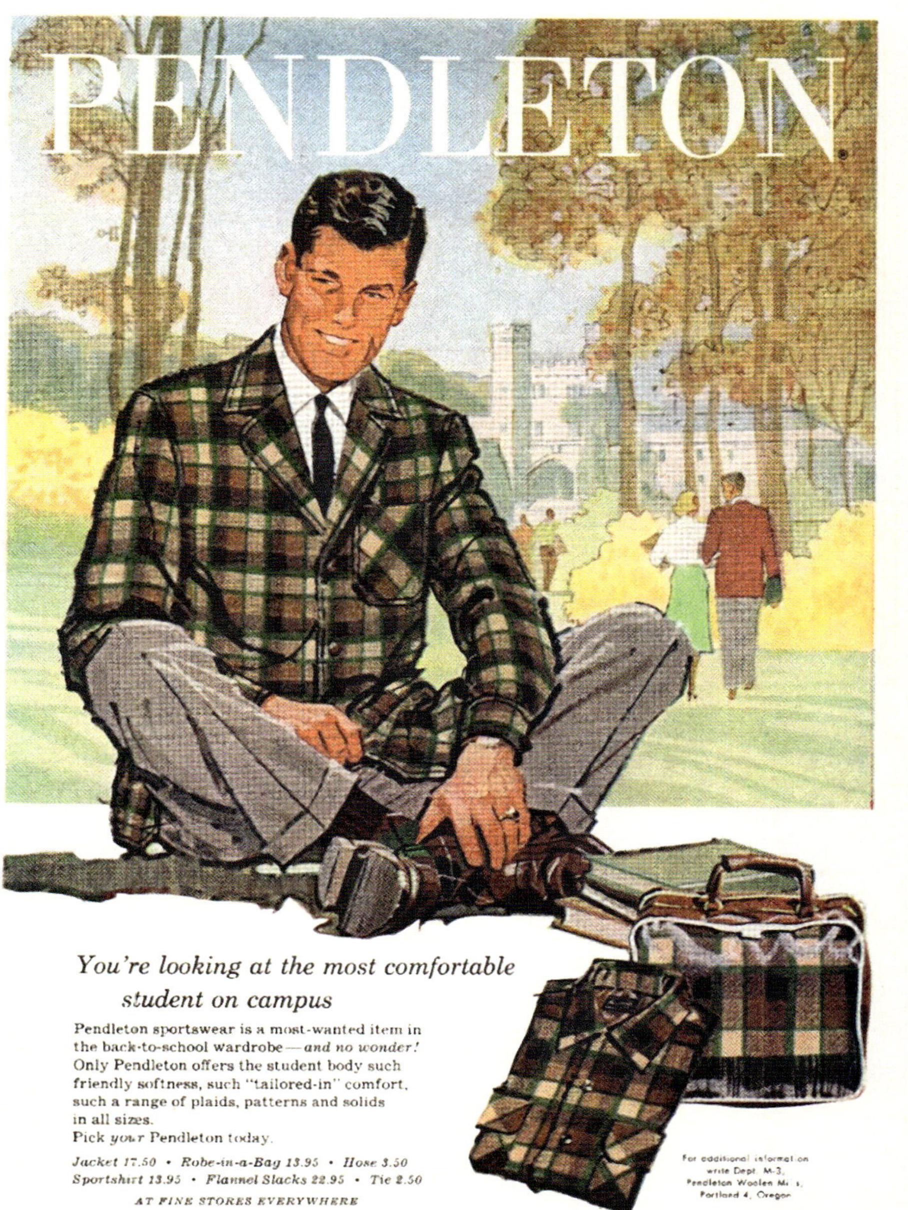
PENDLETON
You're looking at the most comfortable student on campus
Pendleton sportswear is a most-wanted item in the back-to-school wardrobe—and no wonder! Only Pendleton offers the student body such friendly softness, such "tailored-in" comfort, such a range of plaids, patterns and solids in all sizes.
Pick your Pendleton today.
Jacket 17.50 • Robe-in-a-Bag 13.95 • Hose 3.50
Sportshirt 13.95 • Flannel Slacks 22.95 • Tie 2.50
AT FINE STORES EVERYWHERE
For additional information write Dept. M-3, Pendleton Woolen Mills, Portland 4, Oregon
There is only one Pendleton . . . always virgin wool

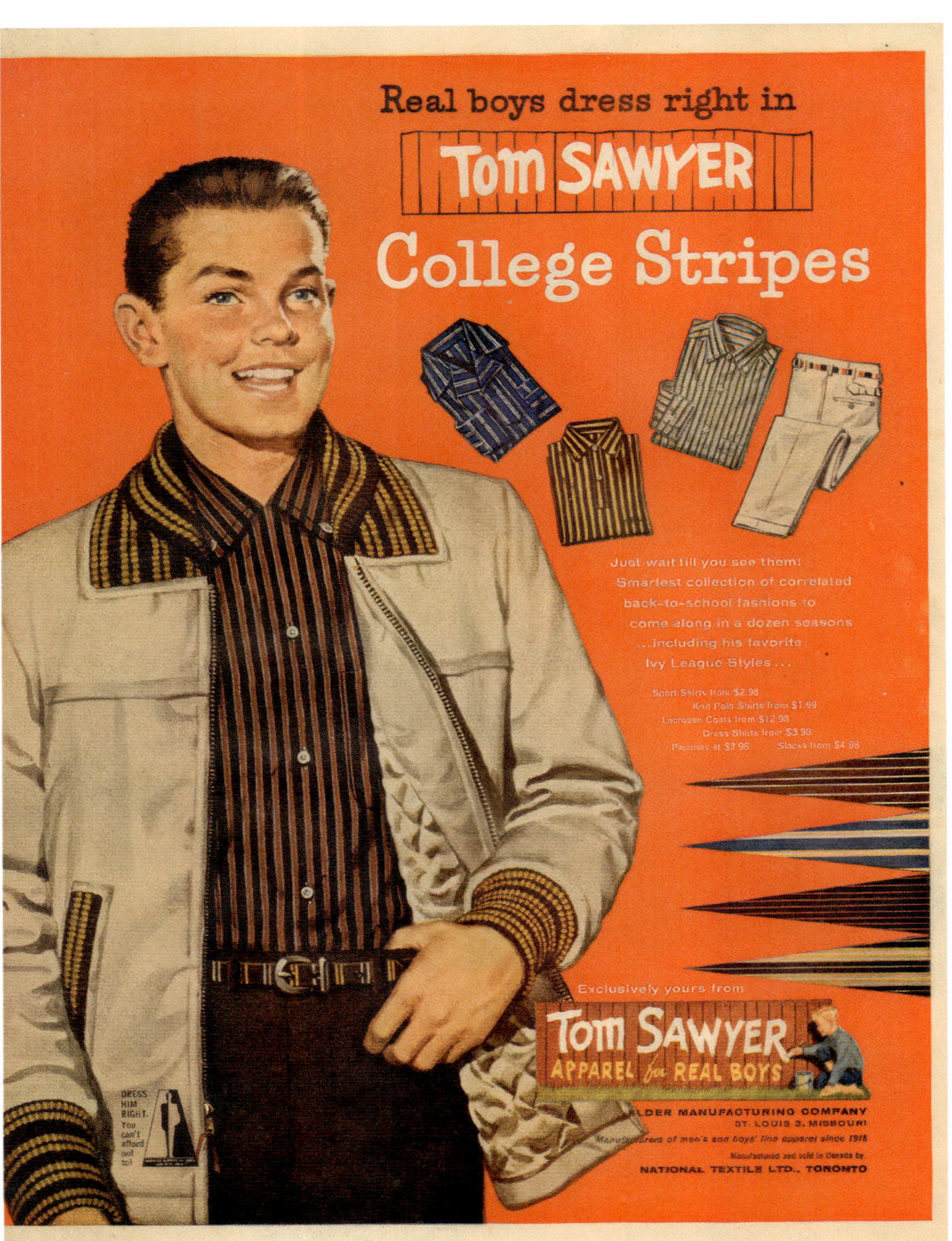
Real boys dress right in
Tom SAWYER
College Stripes
Just wait till you see them!
Smartest collection of correlated
back-to-school fashions to
come along in a dozen seasons
...including his favorite
Ivy League Styles...
Sport Shirts from $2.98
Knit Polo Shirts from $1.69
Lacrosse Coats from $12.98
Dress Shirts from $3.98
Pajamas at $3.96
Slacks from $4.98
Exclusively yours from
Tom SAWYER
APPAREL for REAL BOYS
LDER MANUFACTURING COMPANY
ST. LOUIS 3, MISSOURI
of men's and boys' fine apparel since 1918
Manufactured and sold in Canada by
NATIONAL TEXTILE LTD., TORONTO
DRESS HIM RIGHT. You can't afford not to!

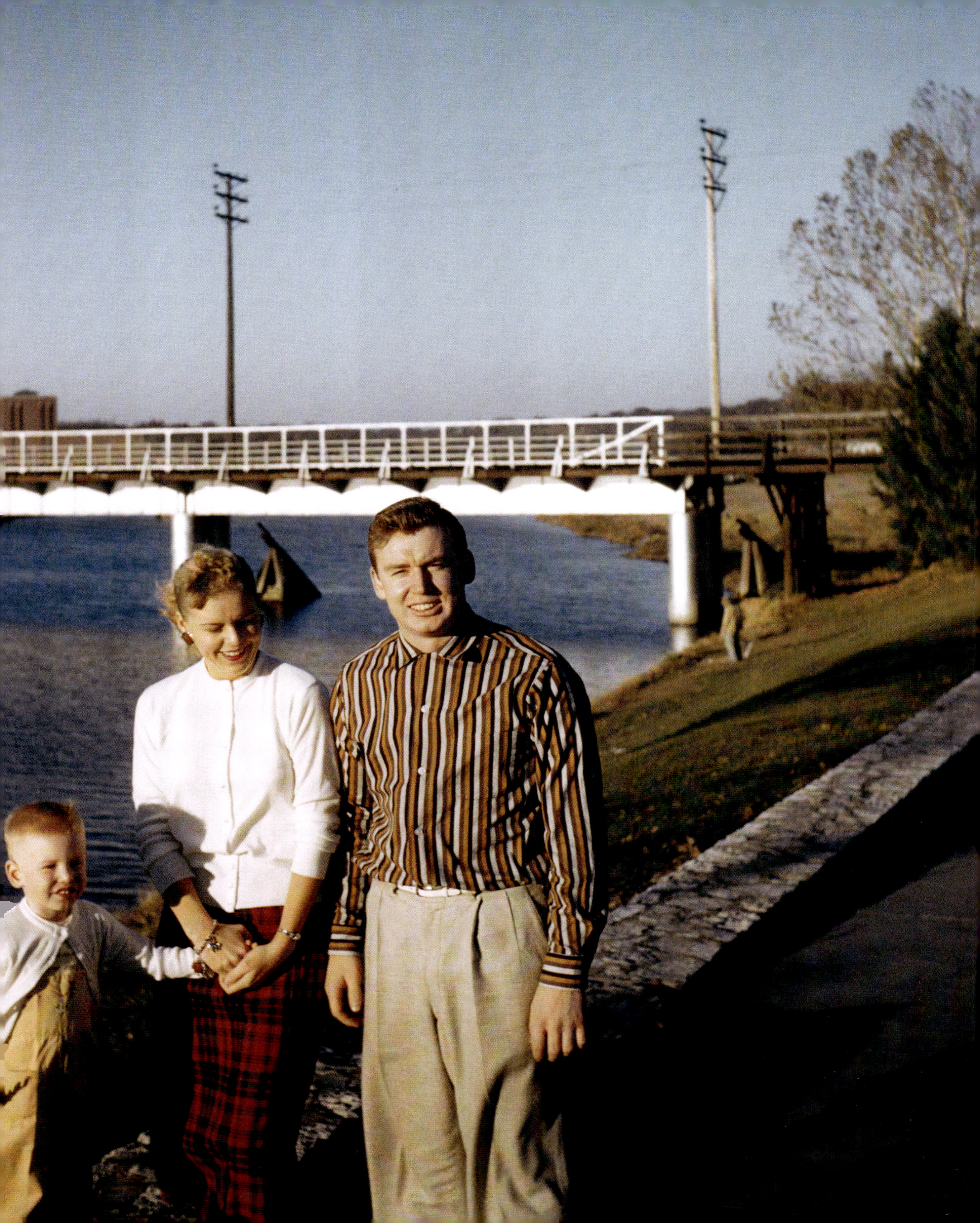

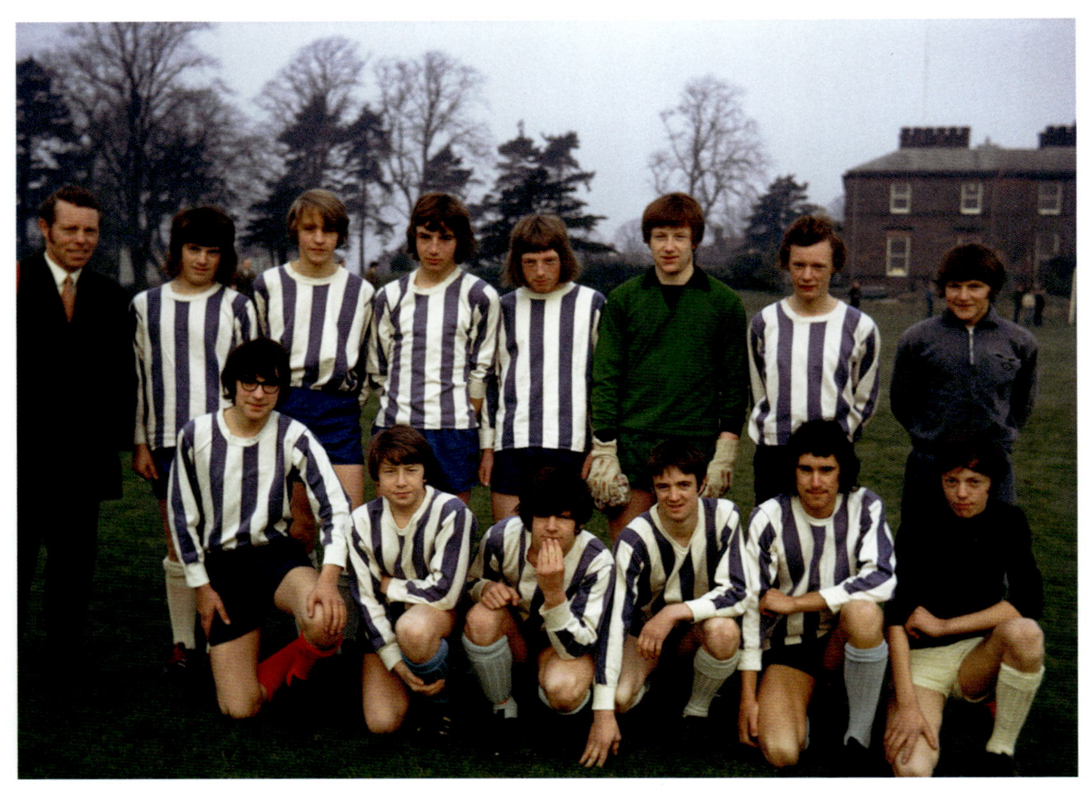

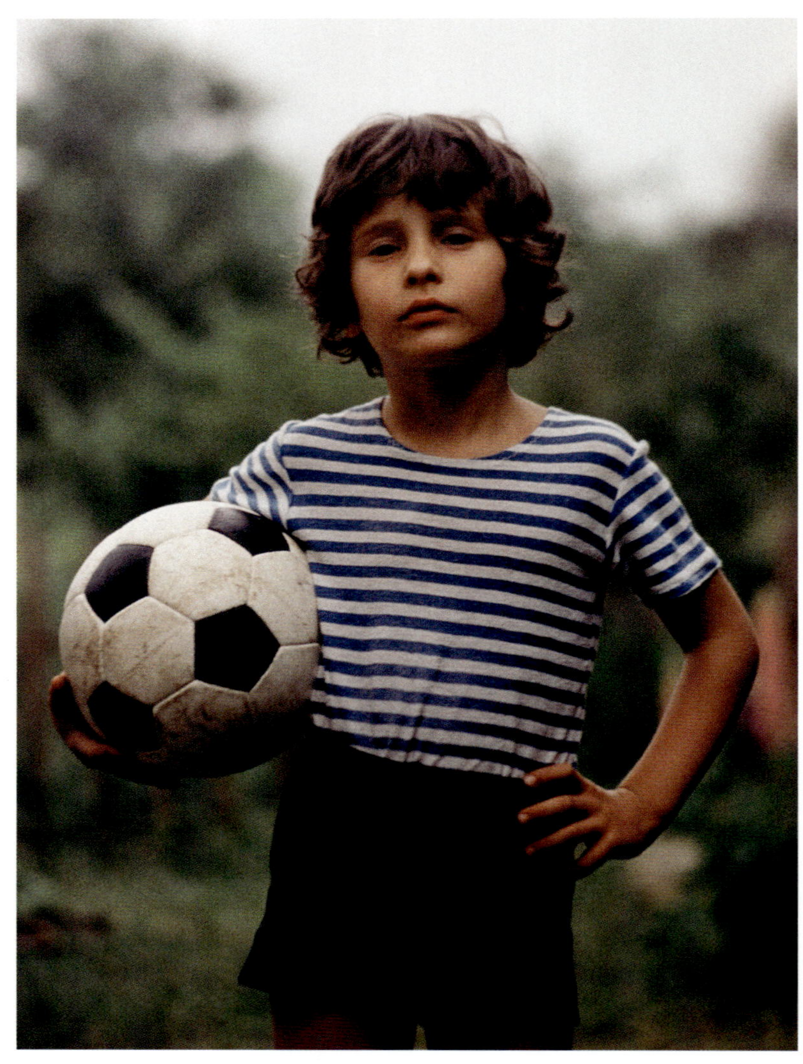

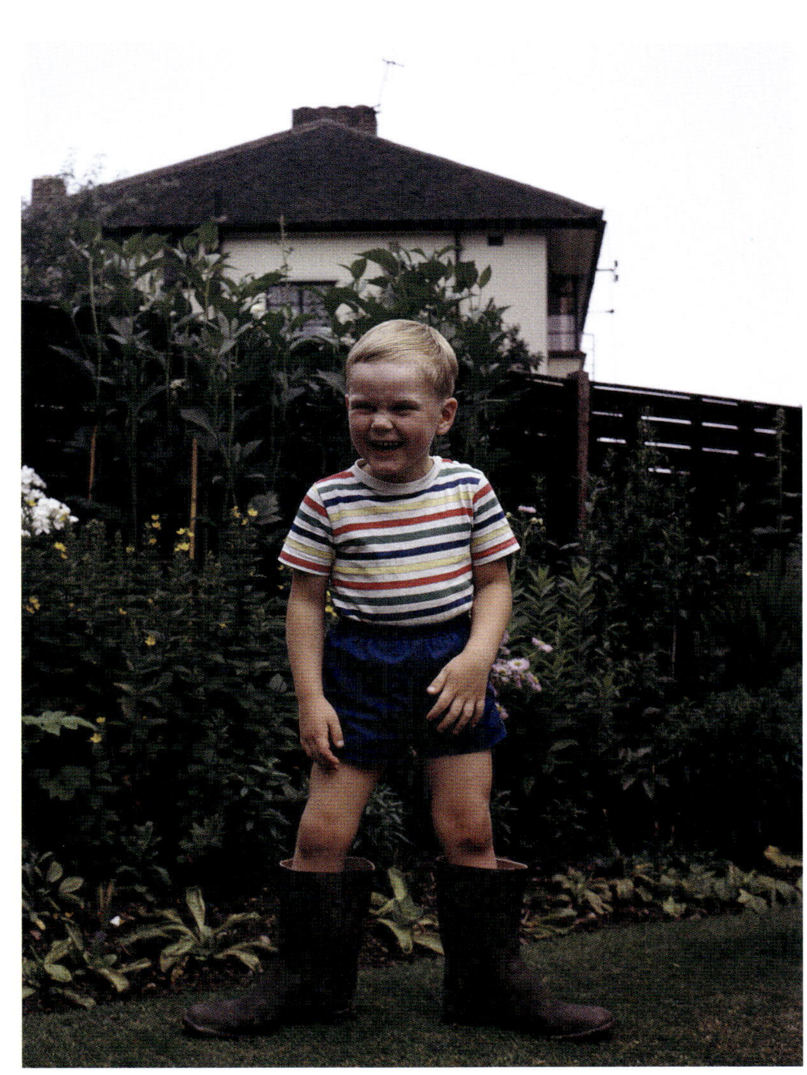

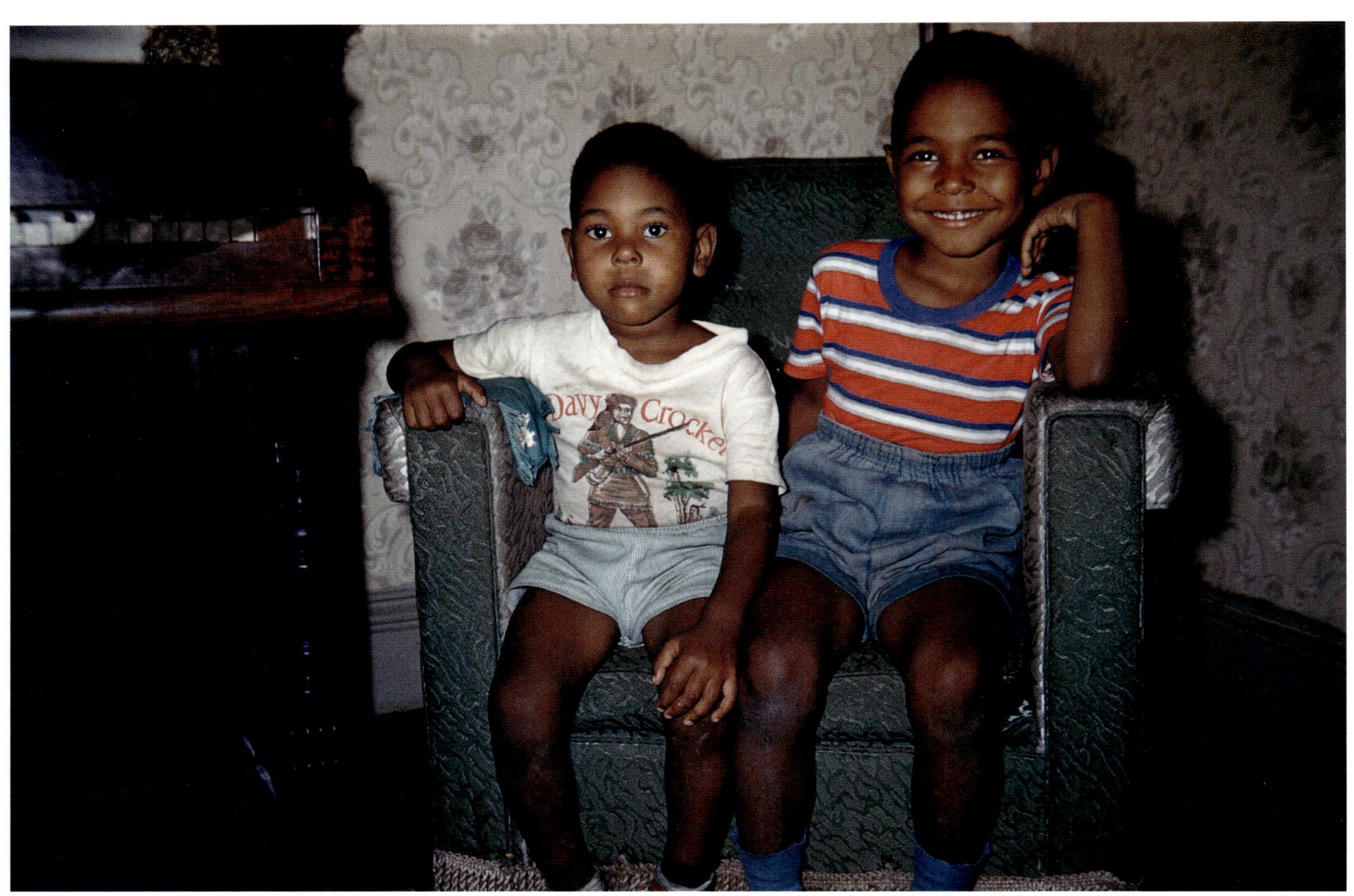
Davy Crocke

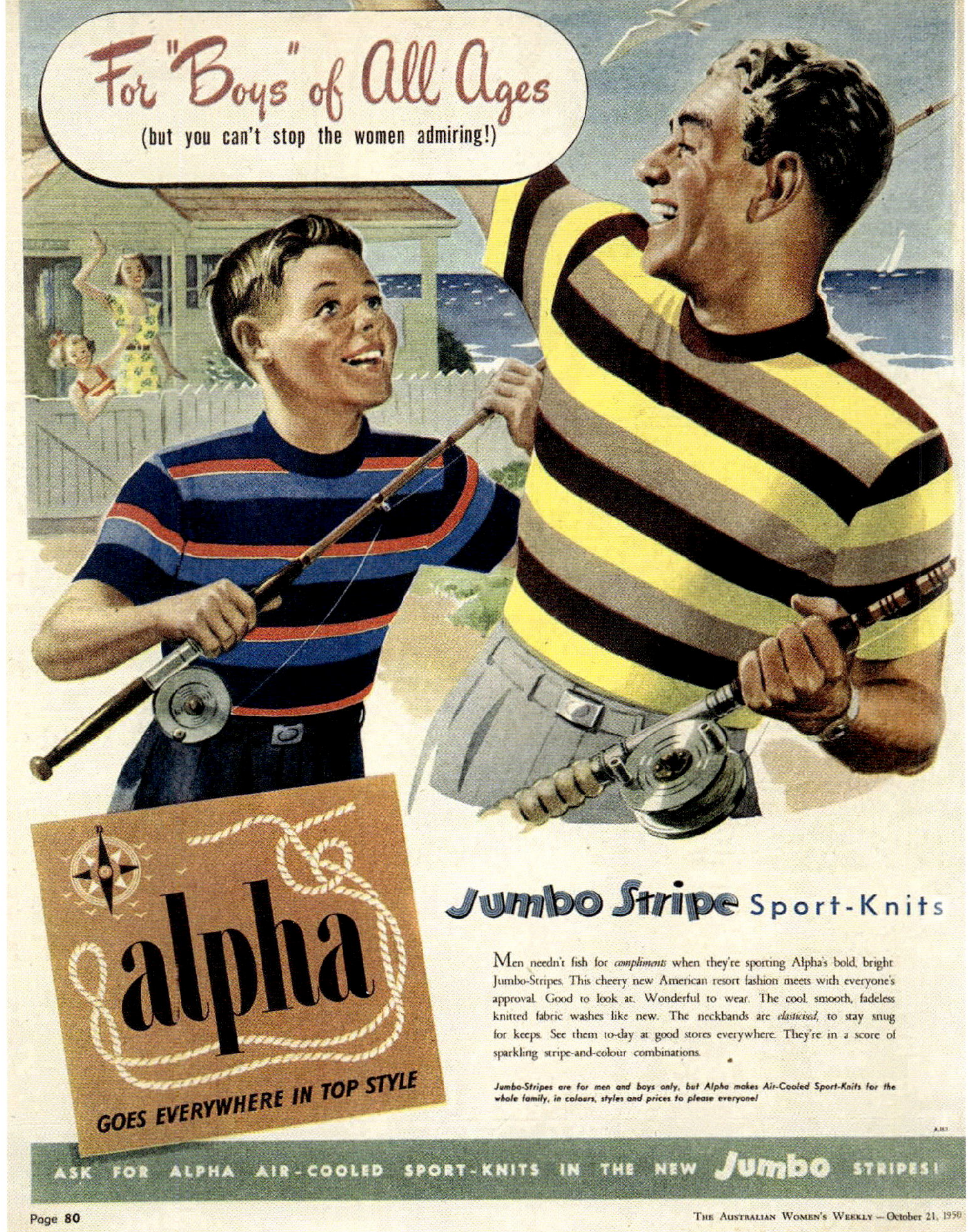

For "Boys" of All Ages
(but you can't stop the women admiring!)
alpha
GOES EVERYWHERE IN TOP STYLE
Jumbo Stripe Sport-Knits
Men needn't fish for *compliments* when they're sporting Alpha's bold, bright Jumbo-Stripes. This cheery new American resort fashion meets with everyone's approval. Good to look at. Wonderful to wear. The cool, smooth, fadeless knitted fabric washes like new. The neckbands are *elasticised*, to stay snug for keeps. See them to-day at good stores everywhere. They're in a score of sparkling stripe-and-colour combinations.
Jumbo-Stripes are for men and boys only, but Alpha makes Air-Cooled Sport-Knits for the whole family, in colours, styles and prices to please everyone!
ASK FOR ALPHA AIR-COOLED SPORT-KNITS IN THE NEW Jumbo STRIPES!
Page 80
The Australian Women's Weekly – October 21, 1950

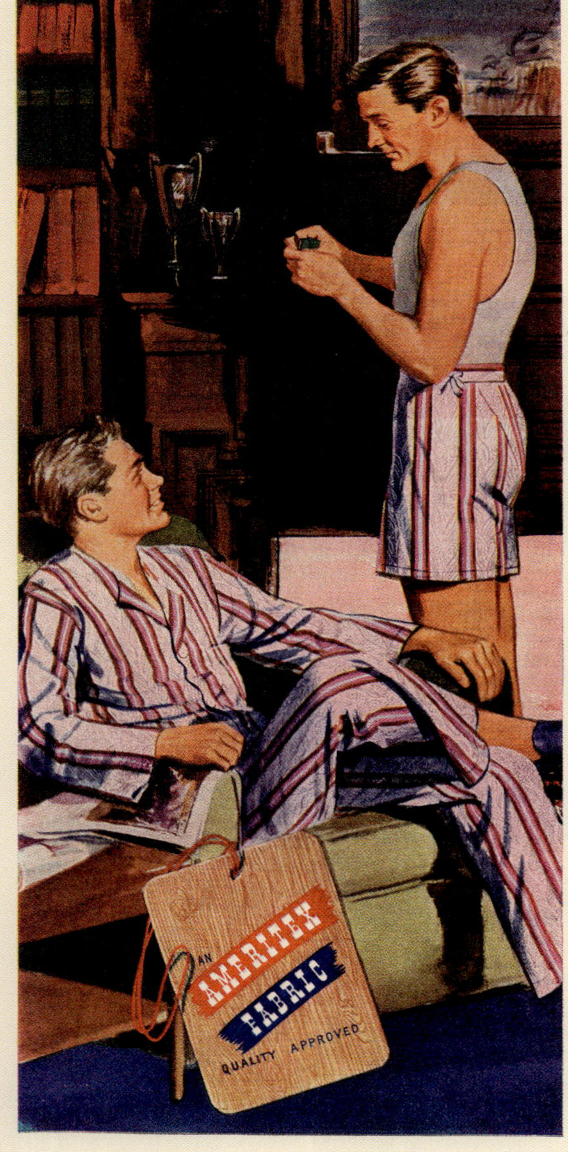

Set your sights on

CITATION STRIPES

SANFORIZED

Faultless Pajamas and Super Shorts

When you can walk casually into a men's furnishings store and buy *Sanforized* pajamas—that's something! And when those Sanforized sleepers happen to be famous Faultless Pajamas—that's something *special!*

Because we feel that the 80th birthday of Wilson Brothers is a special enough occasion, we're marking it with these *matching* Faultless Pajamas and Super Shorts in a new and timely pattern, Citation Stripes. (Choice of maroon, blue, brown, and yes, you're right, *all* Sanforized!)

Both Faultless Pajamas and Super Shorts are roomily cut, quality-built and designed for lots of wear and washings; both are made of a handsome Ameritex fabric. You'll think kindly of the dealer who sold you them, every time you put a pair on.

We at Wilson Brothers have been in this War too, doing our share in producing for the armed forces. So you may not get as many pairs of these Citation Stripes as you'd wish. But we know you will take that in stride. You see, we're getting set to fix you up with all the Wilson Wear you can put on your back, when Uncle Sam gives us the go-ahead.

Invest in Victory—with MORE War Bonds!

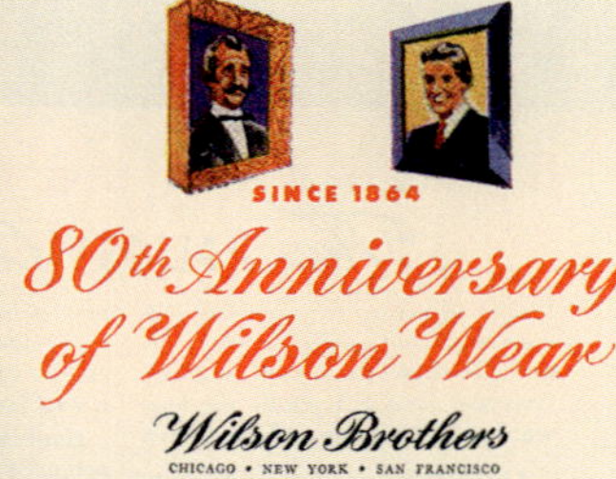

80th Anniversary of Wilson Wear

Wilson Brothers

CHICAGO • NEW YORK • SAN FRANCISCO

Wilson Wear INCLUDES V-SHAPED SHIRTS • FAULTLESS PAJAMAS • SUPER SHORTS • SKIPPER LEISUREWEAR • BUFFER SOCKS • WILCREST TIES • HANDKERCHIEFS

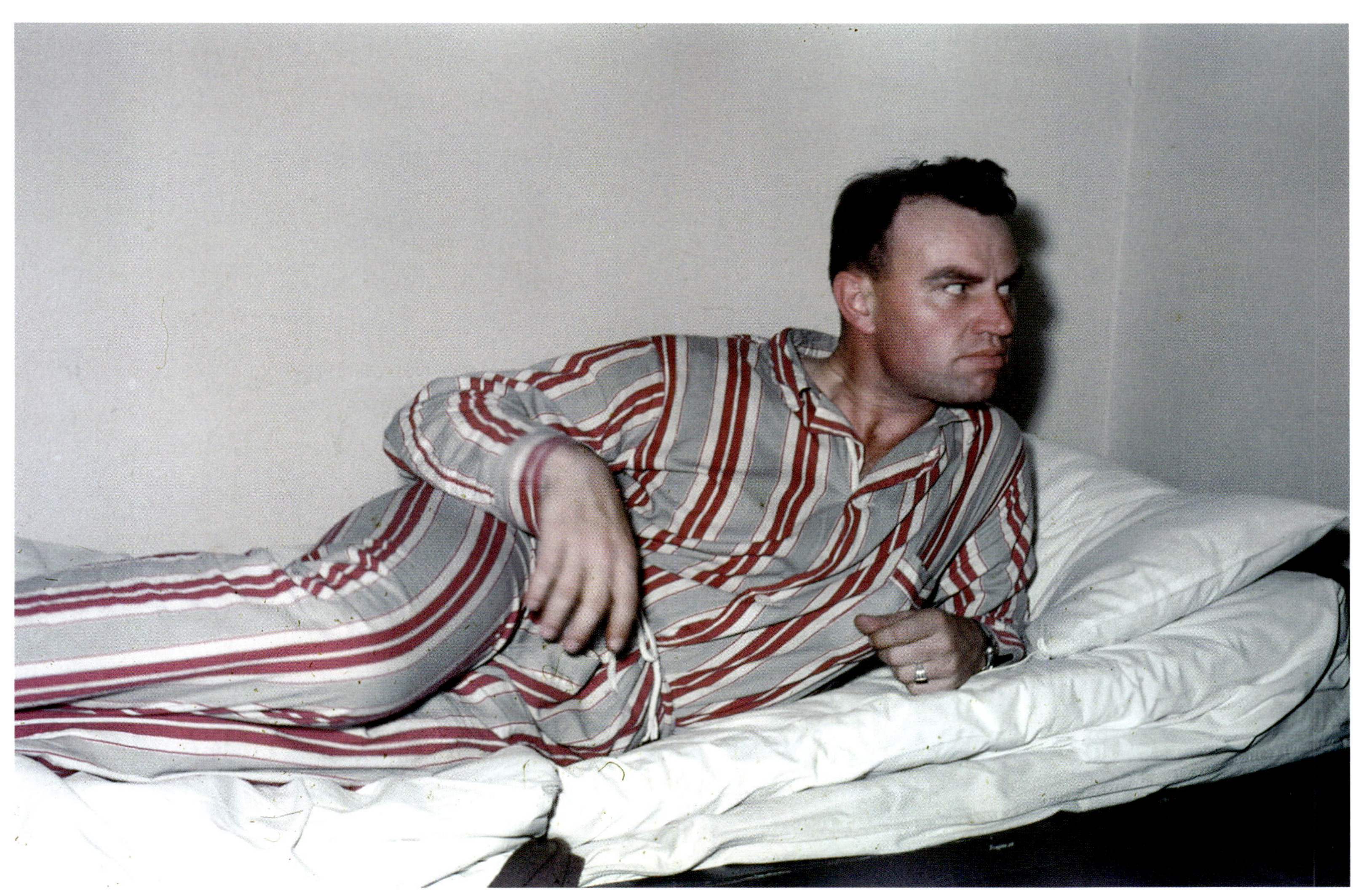

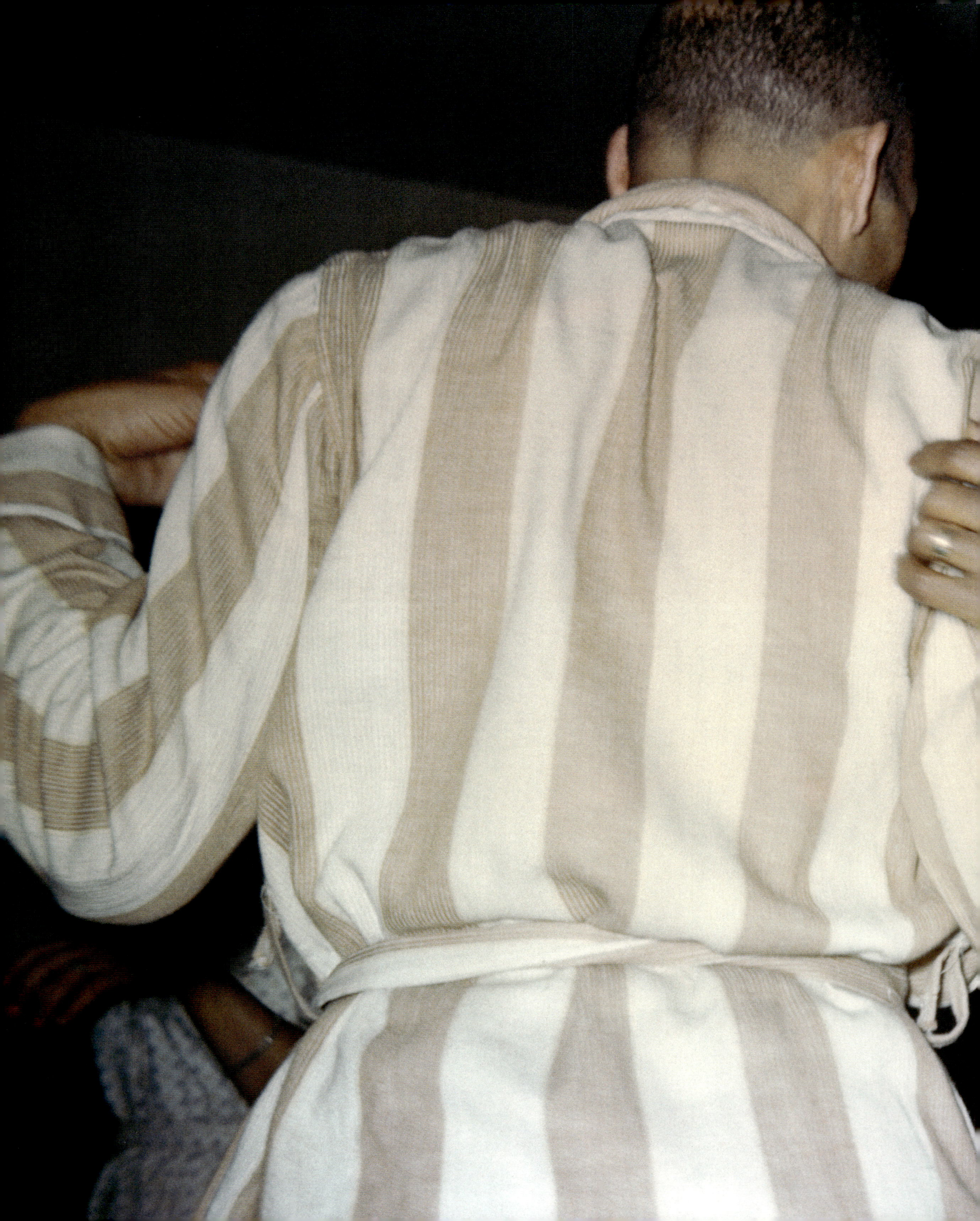

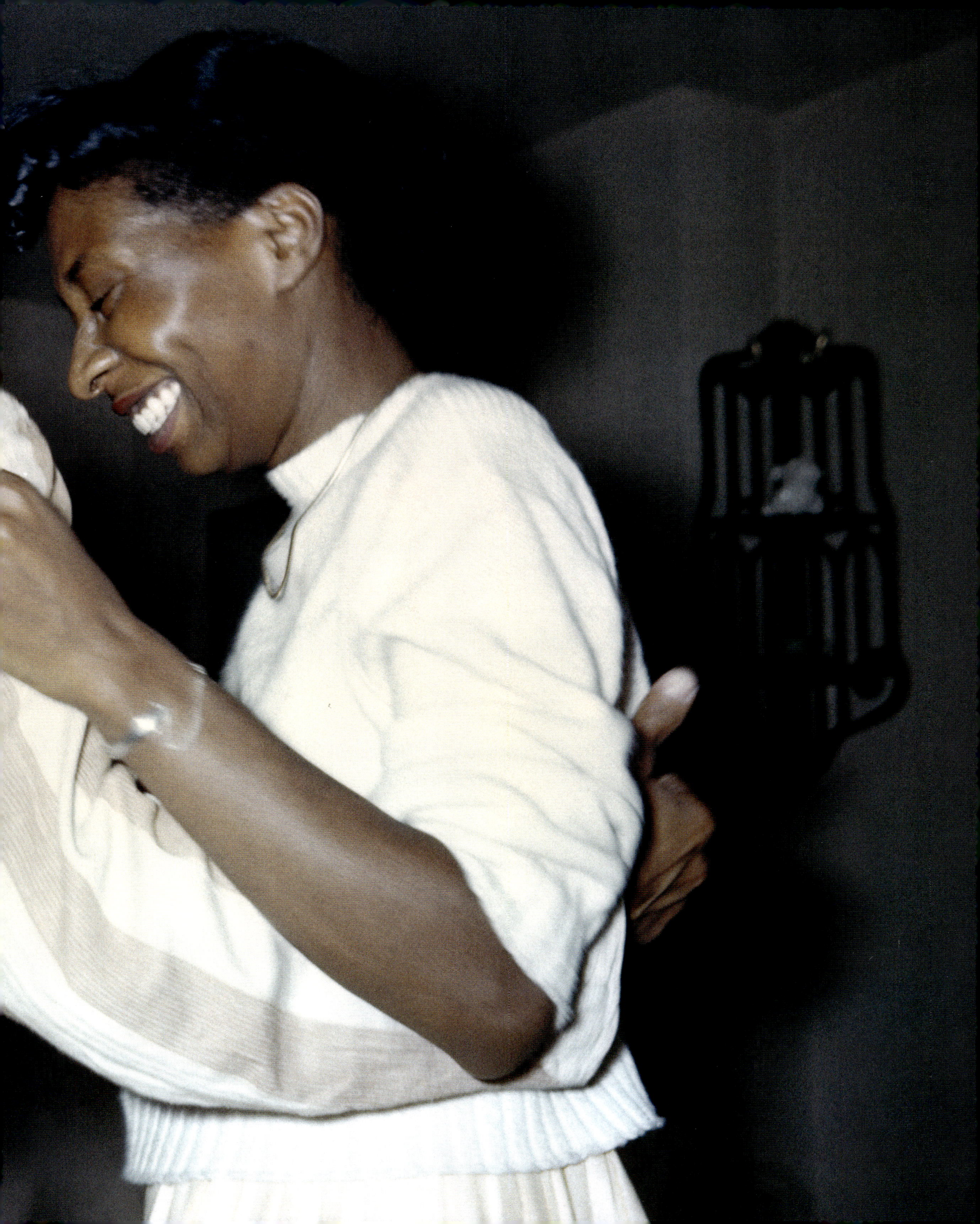

Lee Shulman would like to thank
Curt Holtz, Agnès Dahan, Raphaëlle Picquet,
Déborah Barbe, and all
the impeccably well-dressed people
that feature in this book.

Editorial direction
Curt Holtz

Copyediting
Jonathan Fox

Design and typesetting
Agnès Dahan Studio, Paris
Agnès Dahan and Raphaëlle Picquet

Production
Corinna Pickart

Origination
Reproline Mediateam, Unterföhring

Printing and binding
TBB, a.s., Banská Bystrica

produktsicherheit@penguinrandomhouse.de
(The above information is mandatory
information according to GPSR)

A Library of Congress Control Number
is available. A CIP catalogue record for this
book is available from the British Library.

Paper: Magno Matt

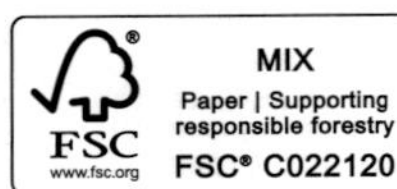

Penguin Random House Verlagsgruppe
FSC® N001967

Printed in the Slovak Republic
ISBN 978-3-7913-9355-1
www.prestel.com